LIONHEARTS

LIONHEARTS

HEROES OF ISRAEL

Edited by
MICHAEL BAR-ZOHAR

WARNER BOOKS

A Time Warner Company

Warner Books, Inc., 1271 Avenue of the Americas,
New York, NY 10020
Visit our Web site at http://warnerbooks.com

This book was originally published 1997, in a slightly different format, in Israel

Photo credits: Israel Army Archives, Jewish Agency Archives, Lavon Institute
Archives, Jabotinsky Archives, Keren Hayesod, Bamahane Archives, The Air
Force Journal Archives, The Gush Etzion History Archives, Maariv Archives, IDF
Spokesman Bureau, The Center for the Babylon Jews Heritage, Diaspora house,
Shturman house, Eli Dassa, Mordechai Naor, Joseph Nahmias, Muki Betzer,
Moshe Shai, Mike Eldar, Ilan Bruner, Eli Landau, Meir Knafu, Hen Mark,
"Operation Susana"—Yediot Aharonot, the Heroes' families.
Drawings by Dani Kerman.

 A Time Warner Company

Printed in the United States of America
First Warner Books Printing: May 1998
10   9   8   7   6   5   4   3   2   1

ISBN: 0-446-52358-5
LC:98-84483

Book design by H. Roberts

To the heroes of Israel, to the fighters for peace.

We express our special thanks to Dr. Amos Carmel and to Mrs. Nili Lurie-Ovnat for their contributions to the book.

We are also grateful to the families of the heroes for their help.

CONTENTS

INTRODUCTION

by Michael Bar-Zohar

"They were swifter than eagles, stronger than lions."

(Samuel II 1:23)

In 1894, a little-known Jewish journalist from Vienna named Theodore Herzl came to France to report on the Dreyfus trial. Alfred Dreyfus, a Jewish captain in the French army, had been unjustly accused of spying for Germany. Herzl was shocked by the virulent anti-Semitism that characterized the trial, and by the shouts of "Death to the Jews!" of the crowd massed outside the court. Back home, feeling "the wings of history flap above his head," he feverishly wrote a book titled *The Jewish State.*

In his book, which was published in 1896, Herzl maintained that the only solution to the Jewish question was the establishment of a Jewish state in Palestine. Palestine, and especially Jerusalem, were known in the Jewish diaspora under the name Zion. In 1897, Herzl translated his idea into action. He convened the First Zionist Congress in the Swiss city of Basel. "In Basel, I created the Jewish State," Herzl wrote in his diary, prophetically adding, "Were I to say this aloud, I would be greeted by universal laughter, but perhaps five years hence, in any case, certainly in fifty years, everyone will agree."

Fifty years later, on November 29, 1947, the General Assembly of the United Nations voted to create a Jewish state in Palestine. On May 14, 1948, David Ben-Gurion, the fiery leader of the Yishuv (literally, Settlement; the Jewish community in Palestine) proclaimed the independence of the State of Israel. Israel came into being in the midst of a bloody war, waged against it by all its Arab neighbors, who had sworn to smother the Jewish State before it was even born. But Israel won the War of Independence, at the cost of the lives of six thousand of its young men and women, who then represented one percent of its total Jewish population.

A long, dramatic struggle that lasted half a century preceded the creation of the Jewish State: years of legal and illegal immigration, settling and cultivating the land, training self-defense units, creating an economic infrastructure, establishing a just society. But at the end it was the long, bitter war that determined the fate of the young Israeli nation. Israel achieved its independence thanks to the determination and courage of its sons and daughters, who did not hesitate to risk their lives for the sake of Jewish independence.

By their bravery the fighters of the War of Independence were carrying on the glorious tradition of volunteering and self-sacrifice that the first modern-day settlers of Eretz Israel (The Land of Israel) had started, and which is still continuing to this day. "In every generation a hero arises, and redeems the nation"—says the Chanuka song. In every generation, in every confrontation, in every battlefield that marks our history, heroes have arisen among us who have had the courage to take the lead. In the distant past, they were Nachshon Ben-Aminadav and Yehoshua Ben-Nun, Gideon and Samson, Devorah and Jephthah, King David's brave soldiers, the Maccabees, Bar-Kochba, and other legendary figures. And in modern times, they were youth from all sectors of society—from the right and the left, secular and religious, men and women—exemplary figures who asked nothing for themselves, neither honor, nor glory, compensation, nor gratitude.

These heroes and heroines had a lot in common: a pure soul and a burning dream, extreme modesty, a humane approach to both their friends and enemies, a deep love of their land and a total identification with their nation. "It is worth dying for Eretz Israel," said Trumpeldor. "I strove for my people," wrote Sarah Aharonson. "Blessed is the match that was burned," wrote Hannah Senesh in a poem. Zvi Brenner said, "I didn't think twice," and Dov Cohen felt that "on a day of service I feel like a copper rod." Avida Shor expressed the moral values of a whole generation faced with the horrors of war when he said, "I am not prepared to kill women and children." And Nir Poraz, a hero and the son of a hero, unknowingly expressed a Zionist testament before his soldiers: "One must give," he said, "give, without asking for anything in return." And like them there were so many others, some of them shy and quiet, some of them very much like the typical Israeli youth, some of them charismatic personalities and leaders from birth.

This book is dedicated to these heroes, and to the hundreds, perhaps thousands, of others like them. A special committee was established by the Defense Ministry of Israel to choose the men and women worthy to be named our Lionhearts. It was not easy to choose the figures presented here as examples and role models. Any choice is arbitrary, and our choices too are liable not to satisfy everyone. Some of the heroes described in this book are unanimously respected for their character and their valor. The recipients of the Medal of Valor, officially awarded by the nation, appear in the book as well. As for the recipients of other medals awarded following Israel's various wars, we chose to mention and describe those who received the highest medals in each war. Still others are men and women who have not received recognition in the past, and whom we found worthy of being considered heroes of Israel.

We chose deliberately not to write about political figures, except for a few cases in which they were awarded the highest medals before turning to politics. But we asked many of the leading political, military, literary, and artistic figures in Israel to participate in the writing of this book. Four Israeli presidents, three prime ministers, ten Cabinet ministers, Knesset members, generals, writers, journalists, and academics have joined together to write the saga of our Lionhearts.

Lionhearts is dedicated to the fighters who fell in battle or on Israel's secret fronts, and to those who are still alive today. But it is also dedicated to the spirit of the fighters, to the qualities of volunteering, self-sacrifice for one's fellow man, utmost courage and nobility, without which a nation cannot exist. In these present days, characterized by the pursuit of material wealth, the preference of private interests over public ones, and the undermining of the values upon which Israel's society was based, we should remember that terms like "patriotism," "sacrifice," and "courage" are not just empty slogans but the expression of noble qualities and feelings of which one should be proud. A hero is not measured by the size of his bank account, or by his fame or his personal success, but by his willingness to take risks for his nation and even sacrifice his life for it.

We must, however, remember that the gallantry and sacrifice of Israel's heroes is a testament for the future. A testament of those who shed their blood in the killing fields so that these same fields might change into fields of peace. A testament that envisions the nation of Israel living in its land in security and at peace with its neighbors. Let us hope that someday these stories of valor and sacrifice will no longer be part of our daily life, but will turn into a faraway memory, a thrilling legend from distant days, a reminiscence of the courageous struggle for survival that produced a reality of hope and peace.

PART I

THE
TRAILBLAZERS

1897–1939

The first to arrive in Palestine in the nineteenth century, even before the official birth of Zionism, were the members of the Bilu organization. Coming from Eastern Europe, they settled in the first Jewish colonies throughout the country, many of which were financed by Baron de Rothschild. During the 1880s the Biluim established Rishon LeZion and Zichron Yaacov, Petach Tikva and Gedera, and other agricultural settlements. The Biluim were the main driving force of the First Aliya, the initial wave of immigration to Palestine.

But Palestine in those days was an inhospitable land. It was one of the most neglected, arid, and backward possessions of the crumbling Ottoman Empire. Barren hills and torrid deserts, swamps infested with malaria, hostile Arab villagers, and fierce Bedouin tribes awaited the first Jewish pioneers, mostly city youths, unaccustomed to physical labor and untrained in the use of weapons.

Yet in spite of the corrupt Turkish administration and the hostile Arabs, the Second Aliya (1904–14), led by young Zionists imbued with Socialist views, virtually carried out a revolution in Eretz Israel. The young men and women created a new way of life with tremendous zeal. They succeeded to "conquer the labor," and become daily agricultural workers beside the local Arabs. They managed to "conquer the guard" and become the guards and the watchmen of the Jewish settlements instead of the hired Arab and Circassian guards. They invented the kibbutz and the moshav—communal and cooperative settlements—established the Bar-Giora and Hashomer self-defense groups, revived the use of Hebrew, and tried to befriend the Arab population.

When in 1914 World War I broke out, the Jewish community was divided. Some claimed they should side with the Turks and the Germans; several young men even joined the Turkish army as soldiers and officers. Others escaped or were exiled to Egypt, Europe, or America, where they joined the Western allies. In 1917 Great Britain published the Balfour Declaration, recognizing the right of the Jews to establish "a national home" in Palestine. Jewish soldiers enrolled in the Jewish Legion and marched into Palestine with the liberating British army.

When the war ended, Palestine became a British mandate, and the Third Aliya began. The Palestinian Arab population, though, was deeply alarmed by the influx of mostly European Jews, whom it saw as aliens, coming to take its lands. In 1920–21, 1929–30, and 1935–36, the Arabs revolted and carried out bloody assaults against the Jews. The British policy fluctuated. For the next twenty years it zigzagged between supporting Jewish immigration (in 1935 alone, sixty-five thousand Jewish immigrants came to Palestine) and banning it totally, between allowing an expansion of Jewish settlements and freezing them, between arming—and disarming—the budding Jewish military forces.

The Jewish community itself, and its supporters abroad, were torn between left-wing and right-wing Zionist parties. The left-wing Socialists believed in a step-by-step approach, based on gradual acquisition of lands, on immigration, on establishing a powerful defense organization, the Hagana, on building a strong infrastructure for the future, like the Histadrut, the General Federation of Hebrew Workers, that was to become one of the most powerful and diversified labor unions in the world. This idea, also known as "one more goat, one more plot," was supported by the charismatic president of the Zionist movement, Dr. Chaim Weizmann. The emerging Palestinian leader of the Labor movement, even though he was not Weizmann's favorite, was David Ben-Gurion.

The right-wing movements crystallized around the powerful figure of Zeev Jabotinsky, who believed in a more abrupt and fast takeover of Palestine by the Jews by means of a petition that would stir a huge wave of immigration to Palestine, and by pressuring the British to establish a Jewish state. Jabotinsky's ideas also stressed the importance of a Jewish military force. Ben-Gurion and Jabotinsky clashed in the 1933 elections for the Zionist congress. The Labor movement won, and Ben-Gurion became the chairman of the Zionist Executive, and of the Jewish Agency for Palestine. Jabotinsky split from the Zionist movement, establishing his own Revisionist movement. The rift between Labor Zionists and Revisionists, between Jabotinsky and Ben-Gurion, has dominated the Zionist and Israeli political scene until this very day—through the rivalry between Ben-Gurion and Begin, Peres and Shamir, Rabin and Shamir, Barak and Netanyahu.

In 1939, influenced by growing unrest in the Arab world and the rising winds of war, Great Britain backed away from her commitment to the Jewish people and published a White Paper that included draconian measures against the Palestinian Jewish community. It put a limit on immigration, froze the creation of Jewish settlements, and condemned the Jews to remain an eternal minority in Palestine. Ben-Gurion led the Yishuv in a violent struggle against the British. But when World War II broke out, Ben-Gurion declared, "We must help the British in their war [against Hitler] as though there were no White Paper, and we must resist the White Paper as though there were no war!"

To Die for One's Country

Joseph Trumpeldor

by Nakdimon Rogel

"It is good to die for our country." This phrase is engraved on the pediment of a statue of a roaring lion, which stands in Kibbutz Tel Hai, in the Upper Galilee.

It is attributed to the legendary hero Joseph Trumpeldor, and has become the symbol of heroism and devotion for many generations of Israelis. Scores of thousands of young Israelis have been raised to emulate the patriotism and self-sacrifice of the great hero, who whispered these words on March 1, 1920, when he was dying, slain by Arab marauders. Trumpeldor had been decorated for heroism in the Russo-Japanese War, had fought in the First World War, and volunteered for the defense of Tel Hai, where he had lost his life. A worldwide Jewish youth organization, Betar, was named after Trumpeldor, as well as countless streets, neighborhoods, institutions, museums, and research institutes.

Did he really say these words? And what kind of man was he?

"There was a hero once upon a time/ a man of mystery, with only one arm." That was the poet A. Broides's description of Joseph Trumpeldor. During his stormy life, Trumpeldor had indeed the aura of an enigma. Today the enigma has been solved. For our generation Trumpeldor actually is a very open man, not a man of mystery at all. His letters and diaries expose the dreams and the convictions of the most famous fighter who fell at the battle for Tel Hai on the 11th of Adar, 5680 (March 1, 1920).

"Trumpeldor's whole life prepared him to become the legendary hero he was at his death. He was a proud man, always striving for perfection, moved by a sense of mission and responsibility, determined to complete the tasks he undertook; his personal courage was balanced by a remarkable self-control that restrained the desire for revenge burning inside him. These were the qualities that made him worthy of the title This National Hero, which was awarded to him on the front page of the newspaper *Haaretz* on March 5, 1920, where his death in battle was announced.

The Russian-born Trumpeldor inherited his willpower and his iron character from his father, Wolf, who was kidnapped in his childhood to serve in the Tzar's army. It was a common custom in nineteenth-century Russia to kidnap Jewish boys and force them to serve in the army for twenty-five years. Trumpeldor's father served as a field medic for a quarter of a century, while still maintaining his Jewish identity despite endless pressure from a hostile environment. The religious devotion of the father became national awareness in the son, who was born in 1880 in Pyatigorsk, in the Caucasus. Young Joseph was also influenced by the socialist-utopian views that were widespread at the time, with a touch of anarchism. At the age of fourteen, Joseph became a vegetarian, and from then on spent many hours developing his physical strength. As an adult, he neither smoked nor drank. From an early age he encountered anti-Semitism, which prevented him from studying at the Pyatigorsk Technological School. Instead he went into dentistry. After the First Zionist Congress in 1897, he became an ardent Zionist.

The Tolstoyan, antimilitarist Trumpeldor did not evade military service in the Tzar's army as did many other Jewish youths at the time. He did not want to be considered a draft dodger and a coward and thus justify the anti-Semitic attacks against the Jews. The need to prove that his people were able to volunteer, to take risks, and to display courage, was a need that would remain with Trumpeldor all his life. In the Russo-Japanese War, which erupted in 1904, after volunteering to serve in a special fighting unit, he was wounded and lost his left arm. Despite his disability, he requested to return to the battlefield, and his request was granted. He was taken prisoner and spent a year in a Japanese POW camp, taking care of his Jewish comrades in arms and discussing with them his dream to immigrate to Eretz Israel. His faith in the Jewish soldier would be strengthened in the battlefields of his life, Gallipoli and Tel Hai. He wrote in his diary, "If the Gogols and Dostoyevskys and other Russian writers could have seen that handful of brave, daring [Jewish] boys, they would surely have presented their Jewish characters in a completely different way."

About Trumpeldor himself, a close friend wrote, "He does not mind danger. In fact, he loves the experience of daring. He is not awed by death. He believes in fate." Trumpeldor added, "Danger is an old friend; as for death—it does not hold any attraction for me, but it wouldn't dare pretending that I am afraid of it."

When he returned from the Japanese prison camp, he was awarded medals of honor, and promoted to the rank of officer. His friends and relatives regarded him with awe and respect. A Jewish military hero was not a common phenomenon these days. But Trumpeldor was not dazed by medals and uniforms. He aspired to a civilian life. After his discharge he went off to study at the University of Petrograd. He wanted to study agriculture but was accepted by the law school. In 1911 he received a third-grade diploma, after failing the exam on Russian Orthodox church law. He did not give up. He didn't want it to be said that a Jew scorned church law and so failed his tests; therefore, he passed the exam a year later, and got a first-grade diploma.

Trumpeldor's Zionist convictions made him aware of a dual need: to establish a national home for the Jews in Eretz Israel, and to place the ruling power in the hands of the workers. While still imprisoned in Japan he came up with the idea of establishing a kibbutz (communal village) of young Jews in Palestine, and in 1912 he began to realize his dream.

With six friends he immigrated to Palestine, which was then a part of the Turkish Ottoman Empire. The group went to the farming community of Migdal, in the Galilee, in order to learn agricultural work and later join a new settlement. Trumpeldor was adamant that the land should be bought with a loan to be repaid later, not with money "sponged" from public funds. In a short time the group broke up, apparently because of Trumpeldor, who was not willing to compromise his principles in any way and would not allow others to do so either.

After a visit abroad, Trumpeldor moved to Jaffa in order to improve his basic Hebrew, but when he heard that three Jewish guards had been murdered in Degania, Kinneret, and Sejera, three Jewish settlements in the northern part of the country, he went to work in Kibbutz Degania as a laborer. There he demonstrated his great physical strength and his willpower to overcome his disability. There was no doubt in anybody's mind that the one-armed giant was an excellent farm laborer.

When World War I broke out, Trumpeldor, who refused to apply for Ottoman citizenship, was deported from Palestine to Egypt. In Alexandria he met Vladimir (Zeev) Jabotinsky, a young, fiery Zionist leader who dreamed of establishing a Jewish fighting unit that would eventually be sent to Palestine. However, the English were only willing to set up a service unit of Jewish mule drivers. Many of those who had enlisted to serve in a Jewish fighting battalion, with Jabotinsky at their head, withdrew. Not Trumpeldor, though. He declared, "Every front is a front of Zion."

He joined the battalion, which was called the Zion Mule Corps, was appointed deputy commander with the local rank of captain, and left with the corps for the Gallipoli front. He fought there with great bravery, completely disregarding any danger to his personal safety and to the safety of his soldiers. To a father who lost his son in Gallipoli he wrote, "I honor you for your ability to educate your son to be a good man, a good Jew, and also a good soldier. . . . You should know that your son fell as a hero for the Jewish people and the Jewish state." But the Allies suffered a shameful defeat in Gallipoli, and the problematic Mule Corps was sent back to Egypt. In May 1916 it was disbanded.

A few months later Trumpeldor left for London in order to work with Jabotinsky toward establishing a Jewish fighting unit. It took a long time, and when the British refused to draft him into the British army, he lost patience. He went to Russia after the revolution of February 1917. Before he left he wrote to one of his friends: "You should know that I would die happily in the knowledge that I fell for an independent Jewish state."

During the great confusion of the October Revolution and the civil war, Trumpeldor put aside his plan to create a Jewish military force that would reach Palestine through Kazakhstan and Persia. Instead he concentrated on organizing the Jewish defense against the Russian rioters who had slaughtered tens of thousands of Jews. From March 1918 on, Trumpeldor became totally involved in the establishment of the Hehalutz (The Pioneer) Zionist organization and in transforming it into the main human resource for immigrants to Palestine. In the eyes of the Hehalutz youth he was considered a father, a commanding officer, and the final arbiter. Hehalutz was recognized as a legal organization only in the Crimean Peninsula on the shores of the Black Sea, and thousands of young Jews rushed there with the hope of quickly setting sail for Palestine. Some of them infiltrated in all sorts of ways into Turkey, with the hope that they could continue to Palestine, which was under military rule and whose borders were closed. When Trumpeldor reached the Crimea, he began immediately to organize the life of "the boys," to deal with their livelihood training, mutual aid, and cultural activities.

In November 1918 the world war ended. Great Britain was the new ruler of Palestine. The Jewish people were hopeful that the British would help the immigration to Eretz Israel. After all, they had published the Balfour Declaration in November 1917, recognizing the right of the Jewish people to establish a national home in Palestine.

In October 1919 Trumpeldor came to Palestine, to prepare the groundwork for the rapid immigration and absorption of "the boys" from Turkey and southern Russia. When he reached Palestine, Trumpeldor wrote a "manifesto" to the workers of Eretz Israel. There were so few of them, and yet there were already two Zionist workers' parties, bitterly at odds with each other. Trumpeldor called upon them to join together into one workers' union with common institutions that would deal with immigrants and their absorption. The "manifesto" was published in the workers' newspapers in the second half of December. The response was minimal. But the Trumpeldor Manifesto turned out to be a prophecy. A year later, after Trumpeldor's death, his dream would come true, and the workers' parties would establish a unique, powerful workers' union, the Histadrut, which still is the main labor union in Israel, almost eighty years later.

In 1919, Trumpeldor also hoped to meet with Arthur Ruppin, the head of the Eretz Israel Office, and obtain his assistance in acquiring land and financing for the settlement of the Hehalutz people. But Ruppin, a German subject, was still prevented from returning to Palestine; Trumpeldor was forced to sit and wait idly, since he could not go back to his people empty-handed. By chance, he was approached by Israel Shochat, the leader of Hashomer (The Watchman). Hashomer was a small, select organization of armed Jews who had decided to undertake the guarding and protection of the Jewish settlements throughout the country. Shochat asked Trumpeldor to go to the Upper Galilee in his stead for a few days to check up on the security situation of a handful of isolated Jewish settlements there and report back to him. Trumpeldor—who could never have done otherwise—accepted the offer.

Bloody incidents had erupted at the fringe of the Upper Galilee, as a result of the partition of the Middle East between the British and the French after the war. That partition had left many Arabs with the feeling that they had been cheated and used. Four Jewish settlements— Kfar Giladi, Tel Hai, Metulla, and Hamara—were located in a strip of land that now became a territory disputed between the French and the Arabs. It was a no-man's-land, infested by bands of Arab rebels. The isolated Jewish outposts became a target for the attacks of the Arab nationalists.

Tel Hai at the time looked like a small fort—it was composed of a main house, some outbuildings, and a courtyard surrounded by a wall. Trumpeldor's stay in Tel Hai, whether as a commanding officer or as the head of the Defense Committee, was a constant test. How could he command a group of volunteers who declared, "We are not military men. We have never submitted to discipline nor do we intend to"? David Cnaani, who served as Trumpeldor's translator and secretary, reported, "As a military man he found it hard to put up with the lack of order and discipline when he first arrived up north. He began to train them in military exercises and usually in the end he would say: 'Anyway, never mind. We have good boys.'"

He understood well the limitations of a voluntary framework, and did not give orders or try to enforce discipline, as he did in Gallipoli; but instead he explained and convinced with endless patience. Shaul Avigur, a future leader of the Hagana underground, was a Tel Hai volunteer. He remembered later, in awe, how Trumpeldor used to cock his gun with one hand, after placing it between his knees.

During the days he spent in the Upper Galilee, Trumpeldor was torn between his desire to stay with the defenders of the embattled settlements and his commitment to his friends in Turkey and Russia for whom he had come to Palestine.

He wrote to his friend Isaac Kanev (Kanivski) on January 19: "You have probably already heard that I am stuck here. I hope that the situation will calm down a bit and they will find a replacement for me." He was worried about the fate of the settlements. He estimated that a minimum of two hundred people was needed for the defense of the Upper Galilee: a hundred for Metulla, fifty each for Tel Hai and Kfar Giladi. On the eve of the 11th of Adar (March 1), with "maximum manpower," after the arrival of reinforcements on February 28, Trumpeldor had under his command just a few more than a hundred men and women, most of whom were untrained. Despite the lack of manpower, weapons, ammunition, and food, Trumpeldor retook the small village of Metulla, overlooking the green hills of Lebanon. Its residents had left, as had the French troops, under the assumption that eventually the regular Arab army would intervene and it would be necessary to retreat from Tel Hai and from Kfar Giladi. The only open channel of escape would then be northward, through Metulla.

Trumpeldor was in Kfar Giladi on the morning of the 11th of Adar. That morning Arab irregulars, led by Kamal al-Hussein, surrounded Tel Hai and requested permission to search the outpost on the pretext that they had seen French soldiers in the area. Pinchas Schneerson from Kfar Giladi, a member of Hashomer who happened to be in Tel Hai that morning, took command. When Trumpeldor was summoned to Tel Hai from the nearby Kfar Giladi, he found Kamal al-Hussein and his group already in the courtyard. They headed for the house. Trumpeldor accompanied them on their way to the upstairs room, when he heard calls coming from the rooms: "The Arabs want to take our guns." He told his translator to go up with Kamal and his group. Then he heard the shouts of Devorah Drachler, who was in the upstairs rooms, the most secure spot in the settlement: "Trumpeldor, they are taking my revolver." Immediately the sound of a shot was heard. Trumpeldor gave the order to open fire, and he himself rushed back to the courtyard, which was exposed to Arab fire.

Perhaps he wanted to close the wooden gate in the southern wall. But the gate itself had been destroyed. It was defended by Yaacov (Jack) Toker, a soldier who had been released from the American battalion of the Jewish Legion. He was posted on an elevated area, on a kind of scaffolding. Trumpeldor was shot and wounded in his hand and then in his stomach. He remained lying where he fell until some of his friends managed to drag him inside. Toker fired at the Arabs who shot Trumpeldor, and hit one or two of them. Immediately shot himself, he fell from the scaffolding and lay in the courtyard.

Why did Trumpeldor run out into the courtyard, which was exposed to Arab fire? The real answer went with him to the grave. It is clear, in any case, that as on the Japanese front and as in Gallipoli, he ignored the danger he was facing.

Throughout the battle Trumpeldor bore his pain bravely. He instructed one of his men to stuff his intestines, which were spilling out of his belly, back into the hollow of his stomach and dress the wound with a towel. He gave over the command to Shneerson and did not interfere with the rest of the battle. Only toward evening, when the last Arab had retreated, did he urge Schneerson to call for a doctor, Dr. Gershon (George) Gary. Gary later said, "I checked Trumpeldor first. He was in a very weakened condition, pale, but conscious and with his wits about him. He asked to have his wound redressed. He had two large wounds in the upper part of his stomach and one on his right hand. I dressed his wounds and calmed him down. When I asked how he was feeling he answered, 'Never mind. It is worth dying for our country.' He very much wanted to be moved from there."

Avraham Harzfeld, who was with the doctor, wrote that same night to his friends in the Central Committee of the Agricultural Workers' Histadrut, "I approached him and he greeted me. When I asked him how he was he answered, 'Never mind,' without even a sigh, 'It is worth dying for Eretz Israel.'" When they transferred him to Kfar Giladi on an improvised stretcher, Trumpeldor did not say a word. Only once did he complain about a severe headache. The stretcher-bearers dipped a rag in a pool of water and put it on his forehead. On the way he died. He was not even forty at his death.

The poet Joseph Chaim Brenner slightly modified Trumpeldor's last words. In his article "Tel Hai," he quoted the hero as saying, "It is good to die for our country." He ignored the "Never mind," which was a common expression of Trumpeldor's throughout his whole life. He presented Trumpeldor, "the mighty and the chosen one," as "the symbol of pure heroism" and asked, "From now on will every weakling among us say: 'I am a hero! And I will be a hero!' . . . Did we hear the echo of the quiet, majestic cry of the armless hero—'It is good to die for our country'? Good! Happy is he who dies with this spirit on the land of Tel Hai."

In a 1916 letter to the great Zionist writer Achad Haam, Trumpeldor had written: "In my outlook I am not a military man and I am willing to take up arms only when I see no other option." An echo of these thoughts was found after Trumpeldor's death, in the words of A. D. Gordon, one of the ideologues of Labor Zionism. Gordon, the uncompromising antimilitarist, wrote about Trumpeldor: "Despite the fact that he was a true military hero, he was not really a military man, and that is his true human value."

Nakdimon Rogel, the author of a biography of Trumpeldor, is a former director general of the Israeli Broadcasting Authority.

THE FIRST ONE

THE LEGEND OF SANDER HADAD

by Mordechai Naor

"Sander was tall," wrote his friend, the writer Moshe Smilanski; "he had a strong back, and was quick on his feet. The Arabs called him Hawajah Skander (Comrade Skander, which was considered a title of respect). It was a marvelous sight to watch him riding in battle on his noble mare, which was erect and fast as an arrow. He would fall upon the masses of marauders like a storm, flailing right and left. He did not like firearms. From his youth he was not accustomed to using them, and he relied only on his tremendous hands. His arms were made of iron. He needed to do no more than strike his enemies on the head once; and those who would challenge him would fall like hay under the scythe from the mere swing of his hand."

Alexander Krinkin, who was known to all as Sander Hadad, was born in 1859 in the town of Krinkin, near Bialystok in Poland, which at the time was part of Tzarist Russia. He got his family name from his town, but his nickname he got from his occupation, which he inherited from his father, a proud and strong Jew who made his living as a blacksmith. From his early childhood, Sander used to watch his father pounding iron, and he wanted to follow in his footsteps. He often did actually work as a blacksmith, as well as at other trades.

He apparently made *aliya* to Jerusalem in 1872 when he was thirteen, bar mitzva age. It is not known whether he came by himself or with other family members. There he hired himself out as a local blacksmith, and in a short time became known far and wide as one of the best blacksmiths in the city. In Jerusalem he was called Sander Hadad, which means in Arabic "man of iron, the blacksmith." He soon became known by this nickname more than by his original name.

After spending a few years in Jerusalem, Sander Hadad began to wander all over the Middle East. Among other places, he visited Istanbul, the capital of the Turkish Ottoman Empire, and after a while he also reached the island of Cyprus, in the Mediterranean. During his trips people were impressed with his unusual strength, and hired him as a guard. That way he acquired knowledge and experience in this field, which would serve him well in Palestine.

His courage and cunning were legendary. One of the legends about him had to do with a high-ranking Russian officer who had been taken prisoner by the Turks during one of the many wars between Russia and the Ottoman Empire. Sander, still a young man at that time, was the assistant to the supplies contractor on the same front. When he heard that the Russians failed in all their efforts to free the officer, he volunteered for the mission. At first the offer was considered absurd. But since the Russians had nothing to lose, they asked Sander what he intended to do. "Give me two soldiers," he replied, "and the rest you will see for yourselves." Once he was given the soldiers, he disappeared with them for a few days. He got hold of Turkish uniforms and managed to cross the enemy lines. When he came back he brought the Russian officer with him. How did he manage to do it? No one knows.

He returned to Palestine from his wanderings around the time that the modern Zionist enterprise began, during the last quarter of the nineteenth century. The truth is that without Sander Hadad and young people of his kind, it would have been very difficult—perhaps even impossible—to launch this enterprise. Not only did the early settlers experience great difficulties in their relationships with their Arab and Bedouin neighbors, but they were also treated with absolute contempt. Jews were considered weaklings and cowards. The European Jew, and the Jew in general, was, according to Ottoman law, at best "son of a protected minority," and at worst a *walid al-mita* (son of death). That meant that the Jews were a defenseless people, with whom the locals could do whatever they wanted—hurt them, and even kill them. It was told of Zalman David Levontin, the man who founded the city of Rishon LeZion, that a guide who showed him the area, warned him, "Look west! There, on the sand dunes, the cruel Bedouins will lay in wait, and when you build your homes and settle here, scores of men will come on horseback in the dead of night, and rob and kill you." Levontin answered, "Do you really believe we would take that without fighting back?"

But the man who turned these words into reality was Sander Hadad. Already in Poland, and later in Jerusalem, Cyprus, and other places, Hadad was the model of the "new Jew"—tough and strong. His muscles—like the materials he worked with—were cast of iron. Any neighbor who dared to mess with him soon felt the power of his fist. The founders of the new village of Petach Tikva, who came originally from Jerusalem, knew him well. When they decided to build a Jewish settlement in the marshes of Mulabbis, not far from the Yarkon River, they asked him to join them.

When did Sander Hadad actually reach Petach Tikva? This is part of the cloud of mystery that envelops the iron man's life. He probably came to the village in 1883 with the second group of pioneers, who first settled in Yahud, near the Arab village of Yehudia, in the area that is Savyon today.

The beginnings were quite pastoral. In the first days of Petach Tikva, Sander Hadad worked as a farmhand for one of the farmers who lived in Yahud. He worked his fields in Petach Tikva. Since the man was sorely lacking in funds, Sander worked for him as sharecropper, which meant that he received part of the agricultural crop as payment.

Soon the stories about his courage spread throughout the land. A man who actually bore witness to one of Hadad's acts of bravery was Mordechai Lovman, one of the founders of Rishon LeZion. In the summer of 1886, when Sander was still sharecropping for the farmer from Petach Tikva, he was carrying a load of fruit and vegetables to Rishon LeZion in his wagon. Lovman took a ride home with him and discovered to his astonishment that Sander Hadad was traveling on winding back roads and not on the regular road. Lovman asked him why. He was being careful, Hadad said, since he had not long before had a run-in with a Bedouin tribe. Sander, it turned out, had been riding his horse one day and encountered two Bedouins, who struck his horse with a club. In the battle of sticks and fists that ensued, Sander stood one against many, but nevertheless beat his enemies mercilessly. During the heat of battle he rode over a pile of watermelons and trampled them. Thus, he explained to his passenger, the Bedouin were out to get him, first to take revenge for their defeat and then because of the watermelons that had been trampled.

No more than a few minutes later the two travelers realized that the Bedouin were approaching. Men on horseback came tearing down from the neighboring hills, and behind them men on foot suddenly appeared waving sticks. They let out blood-curdling war cries and did not hide their intent—to catch Sander Hadad and to lynch him. Sander whipped up his pair of horses, and, according to Lovman, "the horses ran at breakneck speed, excited by the furor. The dust rose, enveloping the wagon and blocking the sun. Through the cloud of dust our pursuers looked like fearful shadows. Their faces were like those of wild animals, their eyes bulging out of their sockets, their white teeth gnashing, foaming at the mouth. They were shouting, raving, swearing—and running like the wind. From all that anger and exertion they tore off their robes and began to run absolutely naked. . . . When they came near us they began throwing their clubs at us, most of which whizzed over our heads like arrows. Some of them landed inside the wagon, but did not hurt us."

Sander Hadad, as was mentioned above, never used firearms. But Lovman had a revolver, and he tried to use it against their attackers. However, as luck would have it, the gun jammed at the critical moment. The Bedouin saw this immediately since they were not far off. They doubled their efforts to overcome their fearful enemy. They now entered the range of Sander's whip and club. He excelled in the use of both of these weapons. Whoever came too close was struck a blow or a lashing that took him out of the battle.

After close to an hour Sander Hadad's wagon stormed into Petach Tikva. The disappointed Bedouin gave up the chase, and, according to Lovman, "battered and wounded they returned to the security of the desert without taking out their revenge on anyone. In the tents of the Arab tribes, the mysterious, awesome legend of the Jewish hero spread, and no longer was the disgraceful name *walid al-mita* [the son of death] used to describe the strange Jews who had come from over the seas to inherit the land of their fathers."

After a while Sander went back to being a blacksmith, and set up the first smithy in Petach Tikva. He made plows, repaired wagons, and mainly shoed horses. In those days, the horse was the main "tool" of the farmer, and if the horse wasn't shoed properly it was worthless. It was said of Sander Hadad that he was "the horses' friend," and there was not a horse in the world—even the wildest—that Sander could not shoe.

It did not take long before the robust young man was recruited for the defense of the settlement and its inhabitants. At first he guarded Petach Tikva on a temporary basis, mainly during the spring, when the Arab shepherds and the Bedouin tended to graze their herds in any green field and not leave behind one blade of grass. Sander Hadad worked day and night to defend the farmers' lands. After a while he was recruited to do this job full time. From then on he was the guard of the settlement—the defender of the residents and their property. This was a revolution in the Palestinian way of life. Until then, most of the guards who defended Jewish villages had been hired Arabs or Circassians. Nobody had seen Jews use force to defend themselves. But Sander Hadad succeeded in his job; he brought back animals that had been stolen and more than once routed threatening neighbors.

The founders of Petach Tikva said that he was "furious and awesome" in battle, while at the same time, in daily life, he was easygoing and pleasant. He was very sociable with both Jews and Arabs. He could often be seen drinking tea, in Arab or Russian fashion, with a group of friends in the local restaurant, joking and telling stories. At other times, he would sit cross-legged in the shadow of a tree in friendly conversation with Bedouin from a nearby encampment, trading stories with them about acts of bravery, about horses, about women. . . .

For ten years Sander Hadad guarded the people and property of Petach Tikva. He did so in a cordial manner whenever it was possible. But when it was necessary he used strong-arm tactics, beating more than a few. He too suffered a few blows. This did not deter him. In general, getting beaten up at that time was considered an integral part of the job, a way of training the body to endure stress and pain.

In one of his encounters with the marauding Bedouin, who were trespassing on the fields of the settlement, furious blows were exchanged. As a result Sander's lungs were affected, and from then on his health gradually deteriorated. This robust man, who was not yet forty, was forced to walk with a cane. He slowly regained his strength, and then the bitter hand of fate intervened. One day in 1899 he was riding in his wagon to what were at the time the southernmost settlements—Gedera and Beer Tuvia. A few kilometers before he reached Beer Tuvia the wagon overturned, and he was badly wounded. If this had happened to him when he was still in good health, he might have recovered, but in his weakened condition he was unable to hold on, and he died a few hours later. The people of Beer Tuvia wanted to bury him on their land, but as soon as the news reached Petach Tikva, a mounted delegation was sent out headed by one of Sander's youngest disciples, the future guard leader Avraham Shapiro. Sander Hadad's body was brought back to Petach Tikva, where he was laid to rest at the young age of forty.

For years there was no headstone on his grave. His wife and son were left penniless, and disappeared without a trace. Only at the end of 1947, close to fifty years after his death, some of the founding families of Petach Tikva, who held his memory dear, decided to correct the situation. On his gravestone, which was made from Jerusalem stone, was carved a hand holding a club. This was a symbol and a testimony to the image of Sander Hadad, as the settlement founders remembered him—a valiant Jewish watchman, who defended himself and his people with courage, but refrained from using lethal weapons against his enemies.

Dr. Mordechai Naor is the head of the Department of Israel Studies at Beit Berl College.

SARAH, THE FLAME OF NILI

SARAH AHARONSON

by Limor Livnat

Thousands of girls born each year in Israel are named "Nili" in memory of a wonderful heroine, Sarah Aharonson, who was a leader of the Nili secret organization during World War I. A pretty and daring young woman, Sarah sacrificed her life in a tragic battle for the liberation of Palestine. Yet, in spite of her heroic life and death, it took years for the Jewish community in Palestine to accept Sarah with love as a part of its heritage. For years the Palestinian Jews failed to understand the vision that guided the activities of Nili. It also took them years to see the historical justification for Nili's daring endeavor.

"Your studies are not the most important thing in life. For me what is most important is character. Your character is what you should develop," said Sarah's mother, Malka Aharonson, to her children. "Do your duty before everything else, and you will always have time for the rest," their father, Ephraim Fishel Aharonson, drilled into them. Thus the moment she understood, as did her brothers, that the Jewish settlements in the land of Israel had no chance of surviving under Turkish rule, Sarah knew what she had to do, and did it, in her opinion, "before everything else."

The First World War changed the way of thinking of the Zionist movement. Until then it was assumed that the future of the Zionist enterprise depended on integration into the Ottoman Empire. The first two Zionist waves of immigration came to Palestine, which was under Turkish Ottoman rule; many of the Zionist leaders tried to integrate newcomers into the Ottoman political structures. Even young David Ben-Gurion, the future father of the State of Israel, studied law in the Ottoman capital, Istanbul. Wearing a Turkish *fez*, he enrolled in Istanbul University, hoping to one day become a member of the Turkish parliament. That way, he thought, he would be able to help the immigration of Jews to Palestine.

All these hopes were shattered when the world war broke out, in August of 1914. The Ottoman Empire aligned itself with the Germans at a time when it had already begun to crumble from within. Its troops adopted a cruel attitude toward the Palestinian Jews. Ben-Gurion and many of his friends were expelled from the country; other eminent Zionists were thrown in jail. Certain leaders in the Jewish community began to gradually rethink their political concepts, as the realization came to them that the war was going to change the whole world order, which could then create a historic opportunity for the Jews of Palestine as well.

Still, these new ideas affected only a tiny minority. Most of the local Jewish leaders did not accept this approach or were afraid of it. They preferred to protect their small, fragile community, preserve what had been achieved, and not clash with the Turks. The decrees of the Turkish rule were harsh, and the Jewish leaders directed most of their efforts toward having them canceled, or at least moderated.

Only a small group of a few dozen men and women, which called itself Nili (the initial letters of the Hebrew verse "Netzach Israel lo yeshaker"—"The strength of Israel will not lie" [Samuel I 15:29]) had a different approach. Its members were sure that for the good of the Jews it was necessary to align themselves with the interests of the British, and work toward their victory in the war and toward their gaining control of the Middle East.

To the skeptics they answered that the Ottoman Empire, which was losing power in any case, would not be able to win the war. The British armies, based in Egypt, were already close to Palestine's borders. The longer the British conquest of Palestine was delayed, they said, the longer the Jews would suffer and the greater the danger to their very existence would be.

They secretly agreed that if the traditional Jewish establishment could not find the courage to take a strong stand against their oppressors, then they would have to act on their own. The members of Nili were the sons and daughters of the founders of the Jewish agricultural villages established during the First Aliya (1882–1903). Most of them had been born in Palestine. They had already established the Gidonim, a short-lived semiclandestine group for sons of farmers. As they represented a different social class, they had managed to clash a number of times on different issues with the members of the Second Aliya (1904–14), first and foremost with the Hashomer watchmen who had been trained in the tradition of the Russian revolutionaries.

Avshalom Feinberg was the founder of Nili. He was a romantic poet and the son of a member of Bilu, one of the first Russian Zionist organizations. He saw himself as a new Jew, the master of his fate.

He got Aharon Aharonson, whom he considered his mentor, involved in Nili as well. Aharonson was a world-famous botanist, the discoverer of the wild emmer wheat in the Galilee. He also had established a renowned agricultural experimentation station in Atlit, on the Mediterranean coast. The two of them brought in Alexander Aharonson, the head of the Gidonim; Naaman Belkind, Avshalom's cousin; and Yosef Lishansky from Metulla, a former member of the Hashomer group. Soon afterward Sarah Aharonson joined them.

When the war started, Sarah was twenty-four. She was born in the family home at Zichron Yaacov, a village built on a cliff overlooking the Mediterranean. She was charming, gifted in languages, and an expert horsewoman. Shortly before the war Sarah had married a wealthy Bulgarian merchant named Chaim Abraham, and in 1915 she was still living with him in

Constantinople. But her marriage was not a happy one. Some historians believe that she had decided to marry Chaim Abraham, whom she didn't love, after finding out that the man she was truly in love with, Avshalom Feinberg, was attracted to her sister, Rivka. In Istanbul Sarah felt lonely and uprooted. She missed her beloved family, and especially her brother Aharon, whom she admired greatly. She also missed the life on the settlement, the wide-open spaces of Carmel, and the beaches along which she used to gallop on her horse, feeling free as the wind. She could not adjust to the boring social life of the Ottoman capital, with its strict, clearly defined rules of conduct. She looked for a way to return home.

In the meantime Avshalom, Aharon, and Alexander had begun to develop a plan of action. They tried, unsuccessfully, to establish contact with the British Command in Egypt. Alexander and his sister Rivka, who was engaged to Avshalom, left for Egypt in July 1915, hoping to meet with British military intelligence. But they were rebuffed and were even warned subtly to leave the country immediately. On the way Rivka managed to send off letters to Sarah hinting at the difficult situation at home.

Rivka's letters, as well as other pieces of information that reached Sarah, painted a grim picture. Gradually Sarah became aware that her loved ones in Palestine were in grave danger. The Ottoman army was treating the Jews cruelly, conscripting some of them as soldiers and others as forced laborers, confiscating their property, imposing all kinds of restrictions and prohibitions. She also heard about the plague of locusts that was spreading in the country, eating up all the best land. She knew that Aharon had been appointed to combat the plague. At the same time, she learned in Constantinople that the Turkish army was in dire straits, and that if the British continued their attacks on the beaches of Gallipoli, they would manage to overpower the Turks.

And suddenly there was silence. No word came from Rivka, no word from Avshalom or Alexander. Aharon hinted that they had left the country, but Sarah knew well that her family would not go off on some pleasure trip at a time like this. She decided to return home.

The Turkish bureaucracy was legendary for its inefficiency; but Sarah, deploying her personal charm, and by making use of all her connections and influence, managed to overcome all the obstacles, and acquire the necessary permits. She finally set out on her journey home, to Palestine.

For four weeks she was jostled in trains crowded with soldiers and riffraff, in farmers' wagons and trucks, on dangerous mountain roads. But much worse than the physical discomfort was the horrible sight of the savage persecution of the Armenian people. A million and a half Armenians were being tortured and butchered, their wives raped and degraded. Sarah witnessed these atrocities during her journey and silently swore to do whatever she could to save her people from such a fate.

Sarah reached her home in Zichron Yaacov in the middle of December 1915, to the joy of her family and loved ones. But Avshalom was not there. He had left for Egypt in another attempt to make contact with the British intelligence. He had been captured on the way and was imprisoned in Beersheva. Aharon managed to convince Jamal Pasha, head of the Turkish military administration, that Avshalom had been sent by him to look into the plague, the source of which was in Egypt. Avshalom was released, and he returned to Zichron Yaacov. There he met Sarah. The two young people were passionately drawn to each other.

Long days and nights of discussions began, during which the idea of Nili was formed. The birth pangs of Nili as a spy ring were hard. The attempts to convince the British in Egypt to accept the help of Jews from Palestine continued for over a year. In the end Aharon himself had to set out on a long journey, through several countries, to Egypt. Only after great efforts, and due to his good name and character, did he manage to get appointed as an advisor to the British Command in Cairo. There he was able to open a few doors for Nili and to become involved in the planning of the campaign to capture Palestine.

After Aharon left, Sarah and Avshalom Feinberg took over coordination of the espionage activities. Yosef Lishansky and Naaman Belkind were in charge of the south. They met with dozens of settlers all over the country, and commandeered them, along with the workers at the experimental station, into a network that collected a great deal of information on the state of the Turkish army and on the concentration of its troops.

The need for a connection with the British was becoming both critical and urgent. But due to the difficulties of keeping in contact with Aharon, the leaders of Nili had begun to lose hope that they would ever carry out their plans. Avshalom couldn't wait any longer. He and Yosef Lishansky decided to risk sneaking through the front lines to the British military camps in El Arish. Sarah begged Avshalom not to go. Deep in her heart she knew he would not return.

Alexander Aharonson described their separation in his book *Sarah, the Flame of Nili*:

> Avshalom now faced his most painful moment—taking leave of Sarah. During the last few months she had been his guiding light and inspiration. During the difficult hours and days, her smile, her glance, her courage, her strength of character had given him the strength to live.

He added:

> Sarah, who was still a married woman, knew that her husband still loved her, and she respected him and felt a responsibility toward him. Avshalom was also not a free man. Far away in America waited the long-suffering Rivka, the girl whom, in the happy years before the war, he had chosen to be his wife. If Rivka had heard about the love between Sarah and Avshalom she would surely have released him, magnanimously, from his commitment. But neither he nor Sarah could accept such a sacrifice. They were not the types to thirst after muddy waters, but rather aspired to lofty heights, from which crystal-clear spring streams descend. . . .

Avshalom took leave of Sarah. What words they exchanged before his departure have remained their secret, a beautiful, sacred secret that will be theirs forever.

Avshalom was killed by Bedouin tribesmen near Dir el-Balah, close to the city of Gaza. Lishansky was wounded but managed to escape and reach Aharon Aharonson in Cairo. He returned to Palestine at the beginning of 1917 on the Royal Navy yacht *Managem*. This yacht, on which Aharon often sailed, was transformed into a spy ship. It became the means by which the Nili spy ring was finally able to establish its long-desired contact with the British intelligence.

Nili's intelligence activities continued for eight months altogether. Sarah was coordinating the activities, riding horseback from beach to mountain, from one location to the next, holding in her expert hands the reins of the spy ring that spread throughout the country. She collected vital military information: the dispatching of reinforcements from Constantinople to the southern front, the number of soldiers, the names of the various units, the kinds of guns, the locations of ammunition stores, and even the secret plans that were discussed in the central command of the Turkish army. She was not afraid of the daily dangers. Her only fear was for the fate of her people.

Nili did not manage to instigate a popular rebellion against the Turks, but it could claim a number of great achievements. It helped the impoverished community overcome the hunger that had descended on the land, by smuggling into Palestine thousands of gold coins from Egypt. It let the world know about the expulsion of the Jews of Jaffa and Tel Aviv by the Turkish authorities. World public opinion reacted with indignation, and the Turks canceled some of the harsher measures. Above all, Nili achieved its main goal—the detailed reports from its members contributed greatly to the British intelligence effort, as the British themselves testified. Aharon supplied British general Allenby, the future liberator of Palestine from the Turks, with information on the best routes to enter the country and on many other matters.

Their enterprise was a success; but their personal fates ended in dark tragedy. Not one of the Nili members besides Aharon lived to see the complete liberation of the country from Turkish rule. Even Aharon did not live much longer, as he was killed in a plane accident in 1919. The series of catastrophes that befell the Nili members began in September 1917. Lishansky, who was being pursued by the Turks, was refused refuge by his fellow Jews, who feared for their lives and their community. Naaman Belkind went into the desert to try to track Avshalom down, and he was captured. His cunning interrogators managed to make him disclose some of Nili's secrets. The trap began to close in upon the spy ring. Finally, on October 20, 1917, the Turks captured Lishansky, after he had failed to find shelter in any Jewish settlement. Hashomer watchmen, believing he would bring a disaster upon the Jewish community if he were captured and interrogated by the Turks, even tried to kill him. Both Belkind and Lishansky were eventually hung in a Damascus prison.

In the meantime, on the first day of the Succot holiday (October 1, 1917), the Turks surrounded Zichron Yaacov. The information that Naaman Belkind had disclosed, as well as a Nili carrier pigeon that had landed in the courtyard of the governor of Caesarea, led them straight to Sarah Aharonson. She knew that her end was near. On the eve of Yom Kippur she had an opportunity to escape on the *Managem* but refused, because she had not managed to arrange for the evacuation of all her friends. She got no other chances. The Turks moved into Zichron Yaacov and arrested Sarah and her whole family, as well as all the Nili members who were in the area.

And then the torture began. The torture that the Turks inflicted upon Sarah, her father, Ephraim Fishel, her brother Zvi, as well as on the other prisoners, was indescribable. Each one of them was forced to watch the torture of their loved ones and each one tried as best they could not to let out any secrets. Only the screams could be heard. Sarah suffered the most. The Turks tortured her for three days; on the fourth day they planned to transfer her to Nazareth, to interrogate her even more cruelly. Sarah knew she would not be able to stand the torture much longer.

She asked the police to allow her to go home so that she could change her dress, which was soaked in blood. She walked barefoot through the streets of the town, her hands tied with rope, her whole body bruised, holding herself erect, her eyes glowing, as if there was no connection between her body and her soul.

When she got home she managed to write a letter to David Sternberg, one of the few people from the settlement who had tried to help her. She was worried about the families of the other prisoners. She heard that the inhabitants of Zichron Yaacov had displayed an open hostility against the Nili members and the Aharonson family. Four women had run in the streets of the village, rejoicing over the torture. She wrote, "These scoundrels don't matter to me. I strove for my people, for the good of my people. If my people is contemptible—so be it!"

She also sent her last order to Lishansky: "He should never turn himself in. It is better that he should kill himself. . . ." After that she took out a small revolver that was hidden in her cupboard, stepped into the bathroom, and shot herself in the mouth. She lay dying for three days, begging only for the lives of her loved ones. Finally, she died.

Something suddenly happened to the people of Zichron Yaacov, as if her death had transformed their lives. Suddenly they all came out of their houses to take part in Sarah's funeral, and to follow her tortured body, wrapped in a makeshift shroud, to its grave. When it was over, the first rain began to fall, as if to clean away the alienation, the hatred, the fear. . . . Each of them knew: Sarah had died for their sake.

Limor Livnat is the Israeli minister of communications.

LAND, MY LAND

ALEXANDER ZEID

by Rafael "Raful" Eitan

When he was killed in the summer of 1938 I was nine years old, but I still remember today the shock that stunned everyone in our home and in the Jezreel Valley. Alive or dead, Alexander Zeid was an integral part of the memories of my childhood and youth.

Among those memories are his visits to us in our moshav (a cooperative village of small, privately owned farms), Tel Adashim, and ours to the farm that he built on the hills of Sheikh Abrek, in the Jezreel Valley. Other memories are of Zeid's sons. There was Giora, whose father taught him from childhood not to be afraid of the stones that the Arabs were throwing. Giora was always involved in all sorts of mysterious activities connected to the Hagana. I later heard that he was involved in mobilizing Arab agents and was actually one of the first members of the intelligence community. Then there was Yiftach, the well-known athlete and unbeatable boxer. I also remember Zeid's memorial—a large pile of stones on top of which was a metal statue of Zeid on horseback, looking out toward the horizon. Below it was written the words ALEXANDER ZEID, WATCHMAN OF ISRAEL.

My memories also included stories about Zeid—the stories that my father, Eliahu Eitan (Kaminetzki), used to tell me. He liked to describe how he had met Zeid in Jerusalem during the first years of the Second Aliya (1904–14) and how Zeid had drafted him to work as a guard. Other stories were told by the old-timers on our moshav who had been with Zeid in different places, and never forgot to mention that he was "one of ours," one of the first residents of Tel Adashim. Besides all of these, there were the stories of the writer Eliezer Smoli, which we read eagerly—first *Frontiersmen of Israel*, in which Zeid "starred" as the watchman Hermoni, then *The Lives of the Founders*, which included adapted entries from Zeid's diary. From these books, and from various other sources, emerges the personality of a very unique individual: a solid, robust man, a dreamer, yet with both feet on the ground, someone ready to do whatever is necessary, to help out in any task without considering the personal price, a man forceful and firm in his opinions, a pillar of the community.

I look at his picture among the first members of the Hashomer watchmen, between Israel Shochat, the founder of the organization, and Israel Giladi, the leader in the field. And I know, with all due respect to these two men, that without the tenacity of Alexander Zeid, without his decisive role in the history of Jewish self-defense in Palestine, the Hashomer organization might never have come into being; nor would it have had such a great influence on the history of our country.

Alexander Zeid was born in the region of Irkutsk in Siberia in 1886. His father, a Jewish intellectual and a member of the early Zionist movement Hovevei Zion (Lovers of Zion), was exiled to Siberia by order of the Tzar for political reasons. His mother was sent there for religious reasons. She came from a family of Subotniks, a sect of Christians who observed the Sabbath on Saturday and thus had aroused the wrath of the church and the establishment. After the young Subotnik girl met Zeid's father she converted to Judaism. In 1899, when Alexander was thirteen years old, the family returned to his father's birthplace, Vilna. In Vilna, Alexander became involved with Zionist and Socialist groups. He was one of the first members of Poalei Zion, a Zionist Socialist movement. In 1903, when the Kishinev pogroms broke out, he anxiously followed their progress, and he joined a self-defense group that was determined to defend the Jews against any attack. In Vilna he also met Michael Halperin, a man of means and yet a romantic dreamer, who had already managed to cause a furor in Palestine among the members of the First Aliya (1882–1903) by supporting the workers' struggle against the Baron de Rothschild's management of Rishon LeZion. But Halperin's real dream was to organize a Jewish military force that would conquer Eretz Israel and establish a Jewish government in the land. The charismatic, eloquent Halperin had come to Russia to win converts to his ideas and to advocate self-defense. Alexander Zeid was deeply influenced by the fascinating Halperin, with his long hair and beard, a man twenty-six years his senior. Mainly because of Halperin's ideas, the eighteen-year-old youth decided to make *aliya* to Palestine. On his way to Eretz Israel he already managed to demonstrate his fighting skills, beating up a Russian army officer who traveled on the same train, because the officer had vilified the Jews.

Zeid described his first impressions upon his arrival in Jaffa: "When I got off the boat," he wrote, "I was arrested by the Turks because I didn't have a passport. I was able to secure my release with the help of a silver watch that my father had left me, and a few rubles. While I was in jail I was extremely depressed and prepared to do anything to avoid being sent back to Russia. I was ready to escape to Jaffa and fight to my last breath if they tried to catch me. I was boiling mad: 'Who are these people to expel me from Eretz Israel, our country?'"

A few days later he went to work in Rishon LeZion. In this settlement, while working in the wine cellars, he met Israel Shochat, a frail boy, a year younger than he. Shochat dreamed about establishing a group of Jewish watchmen to defend the settlements. Shochat belonged to a group of pioneers who strongly believed that Jews should not only work the land of Palestine, but also guard and defend their settlements against their enemies: thieves, marauders, hostile Arab and Bedouin tribes. The very idea of having Jews patrolling their own fields, and using real weapons to defend themselves instead of relying on others, was utterly revolutionary. Shochat and Zeid soon became friends. Shochat, who was very impressed by Zeid's strong physical appearance and by his ardent spirit, told him of his dreams. Zeid listened intently to Shochat's words, then declared formally, as was the custom at the time, "You have understood my deepest convictions and given them the right expression. I am with you in life and in death. Let us begin immediately."

But the beginnings were delayed for a while. In the meantime Zeid set out to discover the land of Israel, and had quite a few opportunities to demonstrate his courage. Palestine was a wild frontier land where the young Jewish immigrants often had to fight for their lives. Zeid described an encounter on one of his trips: "Several Arabs attacked us. One of them jumped us with a sword in his hand. But we had our own weapons ready—a revolver and a dagger. The Arab returned his sword to its sheath." Later he moved to Petach Tikva, where he received a message from Israel Shochat that he had found work as secretary of Shfeya, an agricultural school that had been established for the orphans of the Kishinev pogrom. Shochat and other friends who gathered around him began to examine the possibility of working as guards in the settlements in the Shomron region. The settlers liked the idea; Shochat immediately invited the small group in Petach Tikva, to which Zeid belonged, to come and join them.

Zeid began his career as a guard in a couple of vineyards at Shfeya. "The owner of the vineyard," he wrote, "gave me an old rifle that didn't work, and wet gunpowder. On the first night Arab guards from the nearby vineyards came from time to time, talked to me, and went through my belongings." Zeid got rid of them, but the incidents continued and even got worse. The Arab guards also worked at Shfeya, and didn't like the young Jew who was taking one of their jobs. One morning, when Zeid had fallen asleep, his rifle was stolen. This was a severe blow to Zeid's pride. From then on he went out to guard duty armed only with a dagger. He therefore had to change his tactics, and he began to lie in ambush for the thieves. One night he let them fill up a whole sack with grapes from the vineyard, and then he jumped them and beat them up. They barely escaped with their lives, leaving behind them some clothes, shoes, and an old rifle. The following day they announced that their revenge was yet to come. Zeid demanded a revolver from his employer, and when he did not receive one he decided not to go on guard duty that night. But when he saw a thief in the vineyard he couldn't control himself. He chased after him and fell into an ambush of the Arab guards. He again fought them with all his strength but also incurred several blows. He reached Shochat's room, and there he was taken care of. "I had lost a lot of blood," Zeid said, "and after that I was feverish. My memory was also greatly impaired. In time my memory returned, but not completely."

He didn't give up, however, and was determined to continue working as a guard despite the dangers. For a while, though, he worked in Jerusalem as a stonecutter, and spent a lot of time talking to Yechezkel Chankin, who was considered a hero both in Russia and in Palestine. Among other things, according to Zeid, they talked about "the organization of a group of people with a national goal—to create a Jewish force that would defend us and all that we have built in our country." This was one of the first vague ideas that would lead to the establishment of a Jewish armed underground, and later, of the Israeli army.

The two of them began to recruit other young men with similar ideas. One of them was my father. They exchanged letters with Shochat, who tried to pull strings from his end. During the festival of Succot, in September 1907, a clandestine meeting was held in Jaffa. Eight young men sneaked to the secret conclave. Among them were Zeid, Chenkin, Shochat, and Itzhak Ben-Zvi, a future president of the State of Israel. At this meeting it was decided to establish "a secret order," which was called Bar-Giora, after a legendary hero of the ancient Jewish revolt against Rome. As their slogan they chose the words of Yaacov Cohen's famous poem: "In blood and fire Judah fell, in blood and fire it will rise again." Bar-Giora's declared aim was no more and no less than "the liberation of the people and the homeland and the establishment of a Jewish state." In his memoirs Zeid wrote that "the meeting passed with no friction and no arguments. Everyone expressed faith in the idea." From Ben-Zvi's memoirs we learn that they discussed, among other things, the following items: "Jewish labor," "Jewish defense," and "the establishment of a defensive fighting unit."

As a result of the meeting the members of Bar-Giora began to congregate at the Jewish village of Sejera in the Lower Galilee, where they found suitable conditions for their clandestine activities. Zeid arrived from Jerusalem after a few months, along with my father and "Comrade Gabriel." That was the code name of Tsipora, Zeid's girlfriend, who traveled to Sejera disguised as a man. In Sejera the members of Bar-Giora set up a collective that was the basis for the idea of the kibbutz. They managed to set up guard duty as well (Zeid was among the first guards) and to acquire some rifles of their own. There also they started planning the establishment of a large settlement of guards on the biblical plateau of Horan, better known today as the Golan Heights. In their dreams they visualized it as a kind of settlement of Jewish Cossacks. From Sejera they reached the neighboring Jewish settlement, Mescha, which became known as Kfar Tavor. The members of Bar-Giora took upon themselves to guard and work in this settlement. When they saw that things were going well, they founded the Hashomer organization during the festival of Passover, in April 1909. Hashomer's goal, as defined by its founders, was "to develop in our country an element of Jewish guards that are worthy of this job." Their real long-term goals were those of Bar-Giora.

Hashomer was a legal organization that paraded openly with its own flag and weapons. Its members began to take over the defense of the settlements by means of written contracts. Zeid immediately became a prominent figure in the organization. He was considered one of the best guards and was sent wherever problems arose. He took an active part in defending Jewish farmers who were plowing disputed lands. He guarded in Mescha and Yavniel. He also worked in the town of Hadera, which had to deal simultaneously both with malaria and with harassment by Bedouin and Circassian neighbors.

One morning Zeid was on guard duty in the fields of Hadera with some of his friends, including the legendary hero Chaim Shturman. "The Circassians and their neighbors," he later wrote, "attacked the farmers, and the riders stormed the enemy. I think the whole incident lasted only a very short time. I saw Shturman's mare sway under him—she had been hit in the head with a club—and at the same time I felt my head falling on my chest, and I couldn't lift it. I fainted for a moment. I too had received a strong blow. Nevertheless, I stayed in the saddle and chased after one of the Circassians. The enemy was repelled, and we returned victorious."

After Hadera came Rehovot, where Alexander and Tsipora Zeid were married under a wedding canopy made from a Hashomer flag held up by four rifles. Then they went to Karkur, as well as a few other places, and made an attempt to set up a watchmen's settlement in Tel Adashim. This settlement was attempted after World War I had already broken out. The activities of Hashomer had become more complicated because of the tense situation in Palestine and the suspicions of the Turks. Zeid was one of the most enthusiastic supporters of the idea of a watchmen's settlement. He thought that Hashomer needed a permanent home for families and friends who dropped out of the organization. It could also serve as a base for urgently dispatching reinforcements to endangered settlements.

On the other hand, the place they had chosen for the new settlement, in the heart of the Jezreel Valley, seemed to him too safe, too protected. Along with his friend Israel Giladi, he dreamed of a frontier settlement on the northern border of the country. In October 1916 the two began to realize their dream. Their group went up to guard Metulla—due to a lack of funds they guarded barefoot all winter—and while they were there they began to build the settlement. Giladi wanted to call it Kfar Bar-Giora, but after he died suddenly, the name was changed to Kfar Giladi.

Once again Zeid was called upon to demonstrate his resourcefulness and courage. He built Kfar Giladi, was there during the battle for Tel Hai (see "To Die for One's Country"), and returned again to rebuild it after it had been destroyed. He lived there for a few more years.

In 1926 he began a new chapter in his life. He was appointed as the guard for the lands that the Jewish National Fund had acquired in the western part of the Jezreel Valley. He established a family farm on the hills of Sheikh Abrek. From this farm, which he built with his own hands, he fiercely guarded the national lands. Here he fought many a battle against marauders and rioters, including during the bloody Arab riots that swept Palestine in 1929.

Adventurers from every corner of the land gathered at his farm. They came to help Zeid, to hear his stories, and to learn from him the art of self-defense. At that time Zeid launched a new initiative—establishing the Association of Watchmen in Israel, in cooperation with the Hagana. "We have to aspire to the day when we will be deserving of the name Watchman," wrote Zeid.

He did not live to see that day. When the riots of 1936–39 broke out, he returned to organizing the defense of the Jezreel Valley and helped the new settlements that had sprung up in the area: Beit Shearim, Tivon, and Alonim. One night in July 1938 he went out to a meeting at Kibbutz Alonim, and was shot dead by Arabs in an ambush.

The poet Alexander Penn, one of those who had fallen under Zeid's spell, eulogized him in a poem: "Land, my land, merciful until the day I die / Betrothed to me in blood, which flowed red and then stood still."

General (res.) Rafael Eitan, former chief of staff of the IDF, himself a son of Tel Adashim, is the minister of agriculture and ecology.

THOSE WHO LEAD, FALL FIRST

CHAIM SHTURMAN

by Zeev Ibiansky

On the 11th of Cheshvan, 5696 (September 7, 1936), Police Sergeant Moshe Rosenfeld died on Mount Gilboa while chasing robbers. This killing, by the murderous Arab gang Az A-din el-Kassam, took place during the riots of 1936–39, also known as the Arab Revolt. Chaim Shturman, the man who was responsible for the security and reclamation of the lands in the Beit Shean Valley, rushed to Gilboa, along with several British policemen. They arrived at the entrance of the cave where the murderers had been hiding, and suddenly the police found themselves in a very embarrassing situation. They were afraid to go in. "While they hesitated, not knowing quite how to behave," an eyewitness wrote, "Chaim, in his typically quiet manner, walked up to the cave and disappeared inside. . . ." After a minute he came out; the gang had fled. Chaim carried the weapons that the gang had left behind. "We were amazed," his friend wrote. "I must admit that I was very angry with him. I could not forgive him for risking his life like that." But those who knew Chaim Shturman would not have been surprised. This was the way he had behaved all through his life.

"Those who lead, fall first." These were Chaim Shturman's words when he eulogized his friend Moshe Rosenfeld. Shturman's eulogy described his own philosophy of life and perhaps predicted his fate.

There, at Rosenfeld's grave, he set a model of behavior for a whole generation, which was later expressed in the typical command of the Israeli army officers to their soldiers: "Follow me!"

Chaim was not a man of words, but of action. He was modest, quiet, introverted, yet burning with strong faith and vision. He despised pompous language and empty platitudes. He had both feet on the ground. Brave, reasonable, stubborn, he was always attentive to the needs of those around him. He followed through to the end any goal he set for himself. He was also very human and resourceful, the perfect example of a man of the Second Aliya (1904–14). And above all, he was one who always took the lead.

He was born in 1891 in the village of Tchervona, in the district of Kiev, to Moshe and Menucha Shturman. His father was an educated man and an ardent Zionist, who also believed in action, not in words. In April 1906, on the first evening of Passover, the Shturman family landed on the shores of Jaffa, following their oldest daughter, Chaya, who had immigrated a year before. There were three other sisters—Shifra, Esther, and Sarah. All three of them raised families of their own. The sons were Menachem, Zelig, and Chaim, the oldest, who was fifteen when he reached Eretz Israel.

Chaim began his studies in the Hebrew Gymnasium (Secondary School) in Herzliya, but soon had to drop out. When the family got into serious financial difficulties due to the illness of Chaim's father, he decided, to his father's regret, to go out to work. When his father died in 1908 at the age of forty-seven, the mother and children moved to the village of Sejera in the Galilee, to join the daughters who were already living there. From then on, the stations in the life of the Shturman family, and especially Chaim, were spread all over the country—Yavniel, Hadera, Mescha, Zichron Yaacov, Merhavia, Tel Adashim, Degania, Kinneret, Ein Harod, Nahalal, and so on.

In Sejera, Chaim joined the Hashomer watchmen, becoming one of the organization's youngest members. He quickly found a place in Hashomer, as he was a country boy who had grown up in the fields. Shaul Avigur, one of the fathers of the Hagana, said of him, "He was like a rock, like an oak tree, a part of the land's trees and mountains. Because of his knowledge of the country and its roads, because of his visual memory . . . of the paths and the places where there were no paths, of the mountains, the valleys, the desert, in daytime and at night, he had a sixth sense for finding his way. He was a human compass, with a special feeling for the land, which guided him wherever he went."

In the summer of 1912 Chaim was appointed the guard inspector—chief of security—at the village of Hadera. The Bedouins of the neighboring village, Damayra, attacked one of the watchmen, Zvi Nadav, wounded him, and stole his weapon. Chaim launched a retaliation raid against the village, along with several famous watchmen—Mendel Portugali, Meirke Hazanovitz, Ben-Zion Mashevitz, and Zvi Nadav himself. They taught the marauders a lesson. A short time later Chaim Shturman and Zvi Nisanov were called to help out other guards in Yavniel, one of the oldest villages in the Galilee. On the way they were attacked by Arabs, and Nisanov was wounded. Chaim rushed to help, although Nisanov implored him to escape. Both of them were captured by the Turkish police and were sent to prison. They spent two years (1912–14) in the Acre prison. In a letter from prison, Chaim wrote: "There is one thing that inspires us, that gives us strength, purpose and meaning in life. That is the fact that we are striving to achieve an important goal. . . . We are beginning now to defend our ability of regaining our fallen pride, which has been trampled in the dust. . . . In here we hear the Arabs talking about us, saying that there are some Jews who cannot be debased."

In prison he conceived the idea of setting up a settlement of watchmen that would be both a regular settlement and a headquarters for guard activities. When he was released he began to work on the building of Tel Adashim, in the heart of the Jezreel Valley. There he started a family with Atara Krol, whom he had met and courted before his imprisonment.

In Tel Adashim, Chaim rose to his true stature. He was totally involved in the settlement and in defense activities and subject at all times to persecution and arrest by the Turks. Yet, according to Shaul Avigur, he dealt with "the most momentous, the most vital challenges, quietly and modestly, like a farmer who plows his fields row after row." The world war was in its fourth year. The Turks still ruled over Palestine, but their lines were starting to collapse under the pressure of General Allenby, who led a British army across the Sinai. On November 2, 1917, the British government published the Balfour Declaration, a statement of support for the creation of a Jewish national home in Palestine. The Balfour Declaration, in the form of a letter to Lord Rothschild, was written on November 2, 1917, by Sir Arthur James Balfour in his capacity as British foreign secretary. This document augured a new hope for the Jews in Palestine. Chaim and his friends knew that the fate of the Palestinian Jews would now depend on the actual strength they could muster, in their own right, against any enemy.

He got involved in acquiring and stockpiling weapons. His calmness, his caution, his coolheadedness served him in his task as well. "He was not an officer," wrote Eliahu Golomb, his partner in the defense organization, "nor did he have an official capacity, but at every important moment all eyes turned to him for direction." Golomb described a night trip to the Gaza area where they went to buy weapons. The region was densely populated with Arabs, and patrolled by the Turks. They were the only Jews around. They suddenly heard the pounding of horses' hooves coming toward them. "Chaim ordered us to quietly lie down on the ground and he covered us all with his dark wide *abbaya* [an Arab cloak]. Chaim's calmness infected all of us, and the patrol passed by only a few steps from us without even noticing our presence."

After the British army took Palestine from the Turks, many families began leaving Tel Adashim, and the settlement collapsed. But Chaim remained at his post till the very end, dealing with the orderly transfer of the property to new settlers. Only then did he move with Atara to Kinneret, where their son, Moshe, was born. In 1921 the reclamation of two large blocks of land in the central Jezreel Valley was completed, and Chaim was fascinated by the great challenge. His personality, temperament, authority, and experience made him the natural choice to be the main link in the integration of the people of the Second Aliya (1904–14)—the old-timers—and those of the Third Aliya (1919–23), and in the establishment of the large, open kibbutz at Ein Harod. After all, he was one of the "purest" inheritors of the legendary Hashomer tradition. He now devoted his efforts to help the Labor Battalion, a group of young pioneers, men and women, who joined together to work the land and build new settlements. Chaim's calm authority, his inborn simplicity, and genuine distaste for pretense and empty talk, made him extremely popular with the young, fiery pioneers.

When Kibbutz Ein Harod became a reality, Chaim could finally plunge into the life he had dreamed so much about. Now he had a chance to enjoy his love of the land, to use his rich experience in all kinds of agricultural work, his skill in working with his hands. He naturally became the uncrowned leader of the settlement, a model for others and the main source of authority.

When the Arab riots of 1936 broke out, Chaim felt that this was the battle that would determine the outcome of the whole struggle for Palestine. He knew that there was no time to waste. He also knew that the real power that would make the difference was the settlement and reclamation of the land. He therefore dedicated himself to the purchasing of lands in the Beit Shean Valley and in the settlement efforts of the "tower and stockade." The tower-and-stockade formula was a daring method the Jewish settlers used to beat the British regulations against allowing Jews to create new settlements throughout Palestine. The Jews discovered a loophole in the British regulations against establishing "illegal settlements." If, by the time the British patrol reached a new settlement, it was already surrounded by a wall, with a watchtower inside, they couldn't dismantle it. The Jewish pioneers therefore perfected the tower-and-stockade system: they would surreptitiously bring to the chosen site a prefabricated wooden tower and a wall, broken into small components. During the night, the pioneers would erect the tower and build the fence; the following morning the British would find that they had come too late. A new settlement, complete with a tower and a stockade, had sprouted overnight, and the Jewish flag flew above the tower.

Arab irregulars, roaming through the countryside, would try to prevent by all means, including bloodshed, the creation of new Jewish settlements and the sale of lands to Jews. These were Chaim's two main occupations during these fateful days. The tasks that Chaim undertook involved a lot of difficulties and great personal risk. When people would ask him, "What's going to happen?" he would answer, "If despairing helped, I would despair."

In the meantime he came and went in the neighboring Arab and Bedouin settlements, paying close attention to what they had to say, to their moods, and to their problems. He was one of the few who realized, even in the midst of the bloody turmoil, even when he lost his closest friends, that at the end Jews and Arabs would have to find a way of living together. He strongly believed that even in the most cruel, the bloodiest war, one must keep one's humanity, impose limits and restrictions upon his own acts. "Few people could walk among the Arabs with such complete freedom, without any bravado or arrogance, and yet know how to gain their trust and respect, without the slightest bit of hypocrisy or self-disparagement," wrote Shaul Avigur.

At the beginning of June, 1939, Orde Charles Wingate, or "The Friend," as he was referred to by the Jewish community, arrived in Ein Harod. Wingate was a Christian British officer who deeply believed in the right of the Jews to rebuild their ancient homeland in Palestine. He devoted all his efforts to helping create a strong, aggressive Jewish fighting force. (See "Gideon Goes to War.") In Ein Harod he set up the headquarters of his Special Night Squads, a unit made up largely of Hagana fighters whom he trained in unorthodox but highly successful tactics to counter and prevent Arab attacks. Chaim Shturman supported his activities, but had reservations about excesses and did his best to prevent them.

One evening Wingate's men decided to shell the neighboring Arab village of Kumi from the rooftop of the children's house at Ein Harod, as a revenge for the murder of one of them. Chaim Shturman objected, saying that the people of Kumi had nothing to do with the murder. He could not agree, he said, to involve the people of Ein Harod in this bloodshed. When the British officer insisted, Chaim stood in front of the muzzle of the mortar gun and announced that they would have to shoot him first. "We did not invite you here," he said; "we are responsible for the defense of this place. You will shell, destroy, then leave. Tomorrow you'll be gone. But we have to live here forever with our neighbors." Chaim's resolve overcame the lust for revenge of the officer and his soldiers. A few days later they tracked down the real culprits and took their revenge on them and on those who had given them refuge.

Another incident involved blankets that Shturman took on a winter night to Wingate's Arab prisoners, who were freezing from the cold. (A similar story is told about another Chaim Shturman, his grandson, who helped Syrian prisoners who were suffering from mosquito bites during the Six-Day War.)

Chaim's insistence on humane behavior during the long, bloody conflict did not diminish his courage and his faith in the Zionist dream. Wingate was deeply impressed by this unique man. Their mutual interest turned into deep friendship, which remained unspoken, in fact beyond words.

On the morning of September 15, 1938, a delegation from the settlements in the area went out on a tour of the lands of the Beit Shean Valley. These lands had been purchased after long negotiations between Chaim Shturman and the Arab landowners, and the sharecroppers who claimed right of possession over them. The purpose of the tour was to determine the sites of the next two tower-and-stockade settlements, Kfar Ruppin and Neve Eitan. This day was a very special one for Chaim. It was the seventeenth anniversary of the establishment of his kibbutz, Ein Harod, and a good reason for celebration. Suddenly a terrible explosion was heard. Chaim's car, which was at the head of the convoy, had hit a mine. Three of its passengers were killed on the spot: Aharon Etkin from Kibbutz Geva, the veterinarian David Mossinsohn, and Chaim Shturman.

The terrible news soon spread throughout the country. Many who knew him recalled how they had warned him not to take risks and how he would answer: "We shall gain respect by our courage, or be scorned for our cowardice. We must not be afraid; we must be ready to even throw ourselves into their open jaws." Moshe Sharett, a future prime minister of Israel, came to Shturman's funeral. Wingate brought a wreath of flowers carrying the inscription: "A great Jew, a friend to the Arabs, killed by the Arabs." On his grave was laid a basalt tombstone, on which was inscribed: "Those who lead, fall first." His widow, Atara, the true heroine of the Shturman saga, wrote later, "I did not dare to interfere [with Chaim's dangerous work]. Deep in my heart I knew that what has to be done must be done at any price." When at the funeral people told her she must be strong, she replied, "We are strong!"

Atara needed all her strength for the years to come, because the Shturman legend actually was born the day Chaim died. From then and for the next thirty years, one of his descendants gave his life in each of Israel's wars.

Chaim Shturman's gun and binoculars were passed on to his son. Moshe was then sixteen years old. He was not separated from them for the next ten years, until August 1, 1948, when he fell at the head of a platoon in the battle for Mount Gilboa, in the War of Independence. Moshe died across from the spot where his father had been killed. One of his fellow commanders wrote, "His platoon was always the one that stormed ahead . . . and he was always in the lead."

On the anniversary of Grandfather Chaim's death and the twenty-fifth birthday of Ein Harod, the grandson Chaim (whose nickname was Chaimon) had been born to Ruchama and Moshe, to the joy of the whole family. When his own father, Moshe, was killed on Mount Gilboa in 1948, he was two years old. On July 19, 1969, Chaimon was also killed, in the raid on Green Island at the Gulf of Suez. (See "The Dark Shadow of Green Island.") The commander of the operation reported, "The battle was one of the most difficult and daring that the Israeli army had ever carried out. . . . Chaim died when, taking a tremendous risk, he boldly charged the enemy position." He was posthumously awarded the Distinguished Service Medal.

A year later, on September 14, 1970, the last day of the War of Attrition, the tank of Amir Brin took part in a military operation on the coast facing Green Island. Amir was the son of Tama Shturman and Shlomo Brin, the grandson of Chaim and Atara. The tank hit a land mine. A member of the tank crew wrote, "I heard a groan from the driver's cabin, a quiet groan, as if the person did not want to upset anyone, so modest was he, so shy and retiring." Amir breathed his last quietly and with the self-sacrifice typical of his family. He was nineteen years old.

Dr. Zeev Ibiansky is a historian and a member of Kibbutz Ein Harod.

GIDEON GOES TO WAR

ORDE WINGATE

by Avraham Akavia

"You are the first soldiers of the Jewish army." These words, spoken in faulty Hebrew with a heavy English accent, dropped like a bomb in the hut in Ein Harod. Those who heard them—the leaders of the Hagana, who sat in the front row, and the graduates of the Course for Jewish Sergeants who sat in the back rows—were dumbfounded. The Hagana was the Jewish defense organization in Palestine, which had taken the place of Hashomer, Bar-Giora, and other earlier groups. In September 1938 no one in the Hagana dared talk about a Jewish army. If anyone pronounced these words, he would be laughed at by everyone and considered delusional. But "The Friend," Captain Orde Charles Wingate, did not arouse such derision. Even the fact that he spoke in incorrect Hebrew, giving the masculine word "army" a feminine ending, did not cause any snickering among his audience. From his mouth the words sounded deadly serious, as a prophecy that was to come true in a very short time. None of those present forgot that Wingate was the only British officer in Palestine who was able to say such things, and in Hebrew as well.

Only a few of them knew that the whole thing had begun by chance. Some time earlier, before even dreaming of coming to Palestine, Orde Wingate had extracted a promise from the commander in chief of the British army that he would be given the first staff position available to an officer of his rank. Soon a position became available—intelligence officer in the Fifth Division. The divisional headquarters had been set up in Haifa in September 1936, because of the Arab riots that had broken out in the country a few months earlier.

Wingate was born in the northern Indian city of Naini Tal, at the foot of the Himalayas, on February 26, 1903. His father was a colonel in the Indian army, which at the time was considered part of the British military forces. The family belonged to the Plymouth Brethren, a small Christian community that recognized no order of clergy or ministers and whose main form of worship was reading chapters from the Old and New Testaments. In 1905 the Wingate family returned to England and settled near London. Here the seven children were given a full elementary education at home. This is how Wingate became so well versed in the Bible; in the future his knowledge of the Holy Scriptures was to amaze all of his acquaintances in Palestine. He later studied in a prestigious high school, and in 1920, at the age of seventeen, enrolled in the Woolwich College for Artillery and Engineering Officers. In August 1923 he became a commissioned officer and was posted at an artillery battery in the town of Larkhill.

As an officer he decided to broaden his horizons, and he began to study Arabic seriously. After a short time he met a relative who was serving as the high commissioner in Egypt and Sudan. Under his influence, Wingate decided to set out for the Middle East.

For the next few years, until the spring of 1933, he served in the Sudanese army on the border between Sudan and Ethiopia. During his stay he improved his Arabic, and went on research expeditions in the Libyan Desert.

When he was sent to Palestine, he studied the "Jewish Question." Later, when I became his assistant and interpreter, he told me that he had reached the Zionist solution on his own. He had come to the conclusion that it was necessary to establish a Jewish state. The Jews needed and deserved to have a sovereign state of their own in Eretz Israel, and he had decided to contribute to the best of his abilities to the realization of this ideal.

He began to fulfill this commitment in two ways. First, he dedicated all his efforts to helping the Jews in their fight against Arab attacks, and simultaneously he developed strong relationships with the leadership of the Jewish community and the Zionist movement and offered his services in helping them achieve their long-term goals. At a dinner with the high commissioner he became acquainted with Chaim Weizmann, at the time the president of the Zionist movement. A short time later he wrote to him about the need "to establish a Jewish defense force in Palestine . . . it should be efficient and organized in a special way. . . . Please consult me on this most important matter as I have a lot to say."

In his role as intelligence officer he cooperated with the intelligence forces of both the Jewish Agency and the Hagana. (The international, nongovernmental Jewish Agency promotes Jewish efforts to assist in the settlement and development of Eretz Israel.) He also spent a lot of time in the field. His journeys, both on foot and by car, brought him to many sensitive areas. He managed to discover the arms smuggling routes used by Arab gangs, as well as several of their bases. They were also attacking British targets, such as the oil pipeline running from Iraq to Haifa, which was blown up and burned time after time. Wingate initiated an active campaign against the gangs. Wingate was an excellent field navigator, who could reach his target easily with the aid of a map and a compass, without sticking to known paths and roads. He adamantly insisted that the rules of the game be changed. He claimed that the Jews should no longer hold back, dig in, and defend the settlements from within, but that they should set out to engage the enemy and attack him on open ground. And, of course, it should be done in the most unexpected places. To the members of the Hagana and to the British soldiers who were under his command he explained endlessly, around a sand table or in the field, the importance of a mobile ambush force that is not discovered until it opens fire. He himself often participated in night ambushes, at the head of mixed teams of soldiers and Jewish gendarmes. When Moshe Sharett (at the time secretary of the Political Department of the Jewish Agency) commented on how dangerous these missions were, Wingate answered, "One can't lead people in unorthodox directions without showing them how things must be done. How can I explain to a Jewish boy that it is not worth sitting behind a rock and only shooting back when he has been shot at? And that in night operations he must surprise the enemy, and attack him first? Only by personal example. I must do this until people understand what they have to do."

Wingate made a tremendous impression on the Hagana fighters. One of them was Itzhak Sadeh, who had launched, in Jerusalem, an initiative of his own of "coming out from behind the fence." That formula meant that the Hagana fighters shouldn't defend the settlements from positions dug behind walls and barbed wire, but get out in the field and confront the enemy in the open, or even in his own strongholds. Sadeh wrote, "For a certain period of time we were doing the same things that Wingate was doing, but on a smaller scale and with less skill. We followed parallel paths until he came to us and we discovered our leader." A young man named Moshe Dayan, who had participated in an ambush with Wingate close to his village, Nahalal, wrote, "We did not encounter any gangs. But I was deeply impressed by Wingate. . . . [First, I asked myself] what did he know about our Arabs and about the mountains of Nazareth? Toward morning, I had to admit that I was mistaken. This Englishman, this artillery captain, knew and understood what to do and how to do it better than I did. . . . Itzhak Sadeh had already planted in us the seed of this revolutionary spirit . . . but in Wingate there was something special, professional, decisive without any compromises, and a dominant personality."

In the summer of 1938 Wingate conceived the idea of the Special Night Squads (SNS) and convinced Brigadier Evetts, commander of the Sixteenth British Infantry Division, to take them under his wing. These squads were, according to Wingate, meant to be "government gangs, who with great resolve would destroy [the Arab gangs] . . . and thus, put an end to the terror, which was preventing the peaceful [Arab] peasants from cooperating with the government." He emphasized that "we can never succeed to do this with only the army. It is necessary to make use of the Jews; since enthusiasm, courage and perseverance are essential for such an activity, which will be exhausting, very dangerous and will require great bravery. Since the Jews are locals, they will adapt better, it will be easier for them to walk in the mud, to lie in the mud, not to sleep all night, not to eat for sixteen hours at a time, and in general overcome the physical hardships. The Jews are most suitable, since the most important characteristic of a soldier is not his body, but his brains and his will power."

After he convinced the British, he managed to also convince the leaders of the Jewish Agency and the Hagana. He later formed a group of seventy-five Jews and forty British, and under his command they carried out a series of unprecedented actions, terrorizing the gangs, and setting new standards of warfare for the Hagana fighters. In September 1938, after overcoming serious difficulties, some of which were with the Jews, Wingate opened a course for

Jewish sergeants in Ein Harod; this was where he talked about the Jewish army in the feminine (and where I was privileged to be appointed as his personal interpreter). The course's purpose was to enlarge the framework of the night squads. Again and again, Wingate spoke to the participants about one of his favorite subjects, the military history of the place. He never tired of mentioning to them his beloved biblical hero Gideon, and his three hundred men, who were chosen because they had lapped up the water when they drank and had not gone down on their knees (Judges 6:3–8). He also criticized the Munich Agreement, which had been signed at that time, and protested against British policy in Palestine.

He did not keep his thoughts a secret from his superiors, and soon the order came to disband the Special Night Squads and to get Wingate out of Palestine. When the Second World War broke out he was in London. He tried to promote the idea of the establishment of a Jewish army in the framework of the British army and dreamed of being its commander. But his dream was not fulfilled, and he was sent to Sudan in order to take part in the efforts to free the Ethiopians from the Italian conquest. Those who sent him realized that the qualities that he had displayed in his service in Palestine—creativity, originality, audacity—would serve him very well in commanding guerrilla activities in East Africa. He asked me to serve as his secretary, and I accepted the offer happily, after getting the blessing of the Hagana. Thus I had an opportunity to see him in action as the advisor, and in actual fact, the commander of the Gideon Force. In his typical fashion he managed, in Ethiopia as well, to combine his first-class military skill with his sharp political sense. Under his command more and more real victories were won, and Emperor Haile Selassie was allowed to claim that his men, the "patriots," were the ones who achieved these victories. When the fall of the Italians in Ethiopia was complete and the emperor returned to his palace, no one had any doubt, especially not the emperor, about Wingate's enormous contribution.

Wingate, who again encountered resistance from the establishment to his unorthodox activities, did not hesitate to circulate a document among the military that was typical of his style. He claimed in no uncertain terms that: "the essence of our mistakes from the beginning of the war was the deep-rooted tendency of the Central Command to see the means as the end. . . . The answer [of the officers of the Central Command to Wingate's suggestions] was not 'this action is essential as far as the general plan is concerned and therefore it must be carried out,' . . . but rather 'I do not have the authority to do what you are asking me to do; it is not written in the book.'"

Of course this did not make him popular among his superiors. But the necessity of war required that a man like Wingate be sent immediately to the Far East. In the middle of 1942 he left for Burma, to organize guerrilla activities against the Japanese, who were occupying the country at the time. In the midst of the chaos that prevailed, Wingate began to carry out deep penetrations and, in his words, to "inflict fatal blows to the soft lower belly of the enemy." Now he was the commander of an infantry brigade that organized the Chindits A Campaign, achieving the first land victory over Japan.

He continued to develop his own special methods of warfare, acquiring further experience and achieving continued successes. He became so well known that Winston Churchill himself considered promoting him three ranks at one time. He wrote of Wingate, "I maintain that Wingate should be the commanding officer of the army in Burma. He is a man of great genius and courage, and is rightly considered by all to be an outstanding figure, far above the usual."

The High Command thwarted Churchill's recommendation, but Wingate became a division commander, with the rank of major general. He managed to transport his division by air and land it behind Japanese lines, just as the Japanese had launched their attack on northern India. A high-ranking British officer later compared the importance of this campaign to what would have happened if the Germans had succeeded in parachuting two divisions into the heart of a populated area in England, two days after the beginning of the invasion of Normandy. "We are living history right now," wrote Wingate himself in his order of the day for March 7, 1944.

He did not manage to complete his work. Seventeen days later he was killed in a plane crash. Churchill eulogized Wingate in a session of the British parliament: "This was a man of genius who could probably have become the man of destiny." In a special order of the day published in Palestine, the leaders of the Hagana proclaimed: "In memory of Orde Charles Wingate, men of the Jewish Hagana, present arms! For the war hero who has fallen, bow your heads! For a faithful friend, stand at attention!"

In my archive I have a letter that I received from him in November 1943, while he was still preparing for his last great campaign. "I have been appointed to a new position," he wrote me from India; "I will never forget you and your cause." To emphasize his point he added, in Hebrew, "If I forget thee, O Jerusalem, may my right hand forget her cunning!" (Psalm 137:5).

Avraham Akavia was Wingate's interpreter in Palestine and his chief of staff in Ethiopia.

PART II

THE SECOND
WORLD WAR AND
THE HOLOCAUST

1939–1947

On September 1, 1939, the Second World War broke out.

During the war thousands of Palestinian Jews, men and women, joined the British army as regular soldiers, officers, pilots, and commandos. After a tenacious political struggle, the British government agreed that a Jewish Brigade should be established in the British army. In the meantime, in Palestine itself, the Palmach was created; this was the striking force of the Hagana. The chief of the Palmach was Itzhak Sadeh. His lieutenants were two handsome, charismatic young men, both Sabras (born in Palestine): Igal Alon and Moshe Dayan. Moshe Dayan was to soon lose an eye in the first Palmach operation, against Vichy forces in Syria.

As the war progressed, horrifying news about the Holocaust of the European Jews reached Palestine. In a desperate effort to help the threatened Jewish communities, the Yishuv dispatched a handful of paratroopers to occupied Europe. Many of them didn't return.

The Jewish Brigade took part in the bitter fighting in Italy, and later moved into Austria and Germany. Only during the last stages of the war did the Palestinian Jews learn the abominable truth about the systematic extermination of their people. Some Brigade officers engaged in secret revenge operations against Nazi criminals they tracked down in Austria and Germany. At the end of the war the Brigade soldiers became involved in the execution of two main projects: the Bricha—the escape of displaced Jews from Europe, and Aliya Bet—Aliya B—a huge enterprise of illegal immigration, whose goal was to bring the Holocaust survivors to Palestine.

BLESSED IS THE MATCH

HANNAH SENESH

by Aharon Megged

One wintry day in 1941, three young women arrived at our kibbutz, Sdot Yam, which at the time was located near Haifa. They were graduates of the Agricultural School in Nahalal. One of them was Hannah Senesh. The moment she arrived she stood out as a unique personality. There was something foreign and aristocratic about her pale face, framed by her dark hair. Her large, blue-gray eyes were very serious and made her seem mature for her age. We were a group of a few dozen young people who had belonged to the Hanoar Haoved and the Machanot Olim youth movements. These movements prepared their members for one main goal: form a kibbutz and settle on the land. But before we could actually settle at our permanent site at Caesarea, we had to overcome many obstacles. We were living in huts and tents, in a temporary settlement, and earned our living by doing hard physical labor at the Haifa port and fishing. Our living conditions were very difficult, and the level of education of most of the members was not very high. What made Hannah Senesh, a fine, educated, European young woman, who clearly came from a well-to-do home, choose, of all places, a kibbutz like ours?

"It was not by chance that my life developed the way it did," she wrote in her diary two years later. "It all came from some inner need, which at the time was beyond all reason, inevitable. Any other choice would have made me miserable." Anyone who reads Hannah Senesh's diary, which she began writing at the age of thirteen, and looks back over her life story—from her youth until the day she died—will in fact see how small a role chance actually played in her life. She herself chose her own direction in life, from a strong inner drive, without following the regular routes of political movements or other organizations.

Hannah—Aniko to her family—was born in Budapest on July 17, 1921, to a well-to-do, assimilated family. Her father, the famous author Bela Senesh, died when she was young. She was the outstanding pupil in her school in Hungary, well liked by her fellow students, and, since she was both good-looking and talented, she had numerous suitors. From a very young age she stood out as an extremely honest young woman, very demanding of herself, self-critical, with a strong sense of mission.

What mission would she take on herself, though? She excelled in many areas. She read a lot, attended concerts and theater. She had traveled in Hungary and the neighboring countries with her mother, Caterina, and her younger brother, Giora. She was also active in sports. What was she meant to become? Would she be a writer, like her father? One thing she knew she did not want to be, and that was mediocre. "To be a woman of letters is my dream," she wrote in her diary. When she was fifteen she wrote a poem:

> The stillness of night is falling slowly
> I know that this is the way of the world forever
> And every evening it returns again.
> A bird sings among the branches
> And if not from there, then from high in the sky
> The eye of God watches over me.
> Oh, how grand it is and limitless,
> And wonderful and marvelous and magical
> And sweet and pleasant,
> That here is a spirit, here is a soul,
> Watching over me my entire life
> On my way to forever.

Anti-Semitism in Hungary soared when the Nazis came into power in Germany. Hannah reacted by setting out to search her way back to Judaism. She joined a study group on Jewish religion. She became acquainted with the legacy of Theodore Herzl, discovered the Zionist Maccabia movement, began to take part in their activities, and took lessons in Hebrew from a private teacher. As an eleventh-grade high school student, she wrote in her diary: "One idea occupies me all the time—Eretz Israel. All that has to do with that subject interests me. Nothing else is important." Soon after that she wrote: "I am very weary of the assimilated world. Such emptiness! How could I have lived like this till now?"

And from that moment she prepared herself, alone, for her *aliya* to Eretz Israel. The only thing that aroused pangs of conscience in her was that she had to leave her mother, Caterina, with whom she had such a loving, understanding relationship. It was a hard decision, because her mother would be left completely alone, as Hannah's brother, too, had left home to study abroad. The mother let her daughter go in the end. She reached the conclusion that her daughter's overwhelming resolve and her idealistic fervor were more important than her own well-being.

If she was going to go to Palestine, Hannah thought, then she had to go as a pioneer. "Intellectuals are not what is needed in the country now, but laborers." She wrote a letter—already in Hebrew—to the Agricultural School in Nahalal, and asked to be accepted to study there. She was ecstatic when she received a positive answer after a few months. One day in September 1939, as the Second World War broke out in Europe, Hannah bid farewell to her mother and left for Palestine—on her own.

She spent two years at the agricultural school at Moshav Nahalal. Just as she excelled in her studies in the high school in Hungary, so she excelled in all branches of farming in the agricultural school. Just as she was popular there with the students and the teachers, she was popular here as well. The transition from the bourgeois way of life of a cultured, well-to-do family to the pioneering way of life involving physical work was not particularly difficult for her, because she chose this new life out of faith in an ideal and in herself. She sent constant letters to her mother describing her life in Palestine in vivid colors. But she did express concerns about the future, as the Nazis were winning one battle after another in Europe, and might also take control of Hungary. So confident was she of the direction she had taken in her life that she wrote in her diary, "Here, in Eretz Israel, I loved only this country. And even if I wanted to live differently, I wouldn't have been able to. I couldn't do anything but search for what I thought was right. I couldn't do anything but try to find it."

As this transition period came to its end, a very strong, almost mystical feeling overwhelmed her: she had to fulfill a mission chosen for her by her destiny. After a trip in the Galilee, she wrote in her diary: "In the mountains the question arises: 'Whom will I send?' Send me! To serve the good and the beautiful! Will I be able to do this?" And on the next pages: "God, if you have given me fire in my soul, let me be able to burn what is worth burning in my home, the house of Israel! And let these words be not just flowery formulas but a mission for my life. To whom are these words directed? To the goodness in the world, of which there is a spark in me."

A year after she had joined the founders of Kibbutz Sdot Yam, the kibbutz responded to her request and transferred her to its new site at Caesarea, which was at that time only a few tents, three huts, a stone cabin, and a fishing shed. There, in that poor but pure atmosphere, symbolizing a new beginning, she wrote the poem that after her death became forever connected to her name and to her image:

> My God, my God,
> Let there be no end
> To the sand and the sea,
> To the rustle of the water,
> To the shimmer of the sky,
> To the prayer of man.

The stranglehold around the Jews of Hungary was getting tighter and tighter, as the Nazis took further control of the country. Ruthless decrees were being leveled against the Jews: imprisonment, expulsion, discriminatory laws patterned after the Nuremberg Laws.

In a tent in Caesarea, by the light of a kerosene lamp, Hannah wrote in her diary on January 8, 1943: "It has been a shattering week. I was suddenly struck by the idea that I must go to Hungary. I feel that I must be there at this time, to help out the immigration of Jewish youth to the land of Israel, and also to get my mother out. Although I am aware how absurd this idea is, it still seems feasible and even necessary to me, and I intend to carry it out."

And she actually did carry it out.

A friend from Kibbutz Kinneret, who happened to be in Caesarea at the time, told her about a company of the Palmach that was training to parachute into Europe on a mission to rescue Jews. She immediately went to the Hagana headquarters and volunteered for the mission. Her candidacy was regarded with a great deal of hesitation. She was a delicate young girl, twenty-two years old, only four years in the country. Would she be able to parachute into enemy territory? Despite their hesitation, her determination and her persistence impressed the commanders at headquarters. They told her to wait awhile.

"I am waiting for them to call me. I cannot think of anything else," she wrote in her diary after three months of waiting. On June 12, 1943, a positive decision was made at Hagana headquarters. The kibbutz, therefore, decided to draft her officially. She went to a "seminar for emissaries" and later to a parachuting course. In January 1944 she was sent to Egypt. Now she was a British officer, under the command of the British Secret Service.

At the beginning of March 1944 a group of Jewish emissaries left on a British plane bound for Europe. Among them were Hannah Senesh, Enzo Sereni, and Reuven Dafni. They landed in Bari in southern Italy, and a few days later Hannah and Reuven were parachuted into Yugoslavia, in an area that was under the control of the Yugoslavian partisans. For two months they lived with the freedom fighters in the mountains and forests, and participated in combat against Nazi soldiers. Hannah inspired respect and admiration in her new friends. Not only did her self-confidence and her courage impress her companions, but also her good spirits, her cheerfulness, her sense of humor, and her infectious optimism.

But the fire in her heart did not let her rest. She impatiently waited for the day when they would let her cross the border to Hungary. Only on May 13, 1944—the day the transfer of the Hungarian Jews to the death camps began—was her wish fulfilled. Before taking her leave from Reuven Dafni she gave him a handwritten note, which had a prophetic ring to it, as if she had sensed what would happen to her:

> Blessed is the match that was burned in kindling a flame.
> Blessed is the flame that burned deep in those hearts.
> Blessed are the hearts that knew to stop in honor.
> Blessed is the match that was burned in kindling a flame.

A few hours after she crossed the border, hiding among the bushes, she was caught by the border guards. She was interrogated by the district police, and transferred to Budapest, to the Hungarian police headquarters. The interrogation, the torture, the imprisonment, and the trial that Hannah withstood during the next six months form one of the most heroic episodes in the modern history of our people. In order not to betray her mother, she gave her interrogators a false name—Maria Andi. Through cruel torture her interrogators tried to make her reveal the code of the transmitter she had with her, so that they could disrupt the movements of the Allied air forces. They also threatened that if she did not tell them her true name, they would kill, in front of her, the French partisan who had been captured with her. She could not bear this and told them her name: Hannah Senesh.

The Fascist investigators found her mother, who thought her daughter was still living peacefully in Sdot Yam. They didn't tell her that they were holding her daughter. They brought her into the room where Hannah was being interrogated. Both of them were in such shock that they almost fainted. They embraced each other in tears. Hannah's face was all bruised, and two of her teeth were broken. She could barely whisper to her mother, "Forgive me, Mother. I did not mean to harm you, believe me. . . ." Now the interrogators threatened to execute Hannah's mother if Hannah did not tell them the code. Hannah did not give in. She did not talk.

She was transferred from the Hungarian headquarters to the headquarters of the Gestapo, and was interrogated there as well, sent back to the Hungarians, and finally imprisoned in the municipal prison. In the same prison were her mother and another Jewish paratrooper from Palestine, Yoel Palgi, who had reached Hungary through a different route and had been caught in Budapest. Hannah inspired admiration and affection among the other prisoners and the guards. She used tricks to communicate with her mother by cutting out letters from paper, forming words out of them, and holding them up to the window of her cell so that her mother, who was in the cell across the courtyard, could see. One of the prison guards allowed the two to meet for a few minutes in the shower room and during the daily walk in the yard. On her mother's birthday she gave her a paper doll as a present. Meanwhile she was making converts to Zionism and the kibbutz idea among the Communist prisoners, and won their hearts with her strong faith.

The war was coming to an end. The Red army was getting close to Hungary, the decrees against the Jews were getting worse, and the deportation of the Budapest Jews to Auschwitz started. When Caterina Senesh was released from prison at the end of September, she asked the heads of the community and Dr. Rudolf Kastner, who had connections with Eichmann and the Gestapo, to try to get her daughter released from the clutches of the authorities. For reasons that have not been clarified to this day, they did not respond to her request. On October 28, Hannah was brought to trial before three Hungarian judges. In a brilliant speech she accused the Hungarian Fascists of betraying their people and all the high ideals that inspired the Hungarian freedom fighters and the eminent intellectuals and men of letters of the nation. The verdict was postponed to November 4, and later to November 7.

On November 7 an interrogation officer informed Caterina Senesh that that very morning, at ten o'clock, Hannah had been sentenced to death and executed by a firing squad. He praised her highly, saying that she had refused to ask for clemency, although she was given the opportunity to do so, and that she also refused to wear a black hood over her head when facing the firing squad. She stood erect, her eyes looking straight at her executioners. "She was a proud Jew," he said.

Hannah left behind two letters. One was to Yoel Palgi. It said, "Continue the struggle. Don't give up. Continue the struggle to the end, until the day of liberty, the day of victory for our people."

The other letter was to her mother: "My beloved mother, I don't know what to say, only this: a million thanks. Forgive me if you can. Only you can understand why words are unnecessary. . . . With endless love—Your daughter."

In a package that she left behind, was found the last poem she wrote about her life in her small prison cell:

> One—two—three . . . eight steps is the length,
> The width is just two strides across.
> Life hangs over me like a question mark.
> One—two—three . . . perhaps another week,
> Or next month may still find me here,
> But over my head hovers—nothing.
> This July I would have been 23 . . .
> In a risky gamble I stood on a number
> The dice spun, I lost.

Aharon Megged is an Israeli writer.

THEY WERE ALL HIS CHILDREN

JANUSZ KORCZAK

by Itzhak Navon

"A friend to children, a father to orphans"—that was the caption on the stamp that the State of Israel issued in memory of Janusz Korczak in 1962. And so he was, thanks to his amazing love, untiring dedication, great wisdom, delightful stories, and also to the heroism and daring he displayed until the very last moment of his life in the death camp of Treblinka.

He was born Henryk Goldszmidt on July 22, 1878, in Warsaw, the capital of Poland. The grandson of a well-known doctor, the son of a successful lawyer, he was exposed only to secular Polish culture, without any connection to Judaism. As a child he had daring dreams, which explain the future course of his life. In the Warsaw Ghetto, in its worst times, 1942, he wrote that when he was five years old, "I revealed to my grandmother in an intimate conversation my daring plan to change the world, which was, no more, no less, than to throw away all money. How to throw it away and where, and what to do afterward I did not know. Don't judge me; I was only five at the time and the problem I faced was perplexing and difficult: what to do so that there will no longer be children who are ragged, sick, and hungry, like the ones with whom I was forbidden to play in the yard."

He could not stop thinking about this maddening problem. His difficulties increased when he got to his strict, gloomy school and learned a bitter truth, which he described in his book *When I Am Small Again*: "In my days there were no good schools; they were strict and boring. Nothing was allowed. Alienation, coldness, and suffocation. Years later, when I would dream about school, I would wake up soaked in sweat, and be very happy that it was only a dream."

When he was eleven his father was institutionalized, due to a serious mental illness. The family's fortunes declined drastically. The boy was forced to give up all the luxuries that he was accustomed to and go to work in order to help out. He also worked hard to complete his studies, always setting aside some free time for reading, which he loved so much, and for writing, which was his escape from his hardships. At that time he came to the conclusion that when he grew up, he would not have any children of his own. His father's madness, he thought, was genetic, and he was afraid that he might pass it on to the next generation, if there was one. But he also wrote in his diary at the age of seventeen, "I have experienced a very strange feeling. I have no children and already I love them dearly."

His family prevailed upon him to study medicine. Presumably, he also had the feeling that as a doctor he would be able to reduce the suffering of mankind, all the more so of young children who were "ragged, sick, and hungry." In the meantime he kept up his literary writing. In 1898 he sent a play that he had written to a literary competition under the pen name of Janasz Korczak, after the name of a character in a story he loved. The play won an honorable mention, but in the announcement the name was misspelled and instead of "Janasz" they wrote "Janusz." Henceforth Henryk Goldszmidt became known as Janusz Korczak.

In 1901 his first book, *Children of the Street*, was published. Two years later he qualified as a doctor and began to specialize in pediatrics. He acquired a reputation as an excellent doctor. Many parents, Jews and Christians alike, sought him out in his clinic, willing to pay him any price. But he did not forget those who could not afford to pay. As he later wrote, "Since the older doctors can't be bothered to go out to treat patients at night, especially poor patients, I, because I am younger, have to help them at night. Do you understand? I am talking about dispensing immediate care. How can I not do this? Otherwise these children would not survive till morning!"

After serving as a medical officer in the Russo-Japanese War in the years 1904–05, and seeing the horrors of war firsthand, he returned to Warsaw to treat children and to write about them. He worked at the Jewish pediatric hospital and also continued to treat poor children (often not only did he refuse to take payment for his services, but he also left some of his own money, so that the poor parents would be able to buy medicines and food). But the most important thing he did was beginning to develop his own theory about children. His book *A Child of the Salon*, which appeared in 1906, was the first in a series of essays dedicated to the basic rights of children in a cruel world that does not smile upon these gentle creatures.

"A child, too, has the right to be treated with respect—respect for his lack of knowledge, his failures, his tears, his efforts, his possessions, his secrets and his hesitations in the difficult process of growing up." So wrote Korczak later in his book *The Child's Right to Respect*. In another book, *How to Love a Child*, he said:

> Medicine has shown me . . . the sensational surprises one experiences in discovering the secrets of nature. From it I have seen how a man dies; I have seen the merciless strength with which the fetus tears the womb of its mother and bursts out into the world, like a ripe fruit, to become a person. From it I have also learned to find connections between disparate details and contradictory phenomena and come up with a reasonable diagnosis. Rich in experimental knowledge of the enormous power concealed in the laws of nature and in the genius of human thought that investigates these mysteries, I confront the unknown—the child.

In the course of his strenuous work in the hospital and outside of it, Korczak came to the conclusion that the worst childhood diseases are neglect, poverty, and a lack of understanding by the adult world. As a result of this realization he began to develop a personal preference for neglected children who, although supposedly healthy, he believed needed more care than a child who was bedridden. He began to take more interest in the orphanage than in the hospital. At first he went to work as a counselor in a summer camp for poor children from Warsaw. He summarized his experiences in two books—*Moski, Joski, Srule*, which tells about a Jewish summer camp, and *Joski, Kaski, and Franki*, which tells about a Christian summer camp. Later he joined the Jewish organization Ezrat Yetomim (Help for Orphans). At the end of 1912 he was appointed director of the orphanage on 92 Krochmalna Street.

The transition was not simple for him. He later wrote, "During the years that have passed since then I have had the terrible feeling that I was a deserter; I deserted the sick child, medicine, and the hospital." But his orphans got his complete attention. He established himself in the attic of the orphanage and lived among the orphans twenty-four hours a day. He saw his role as that of a merciful father. He did what he could to pass on to them some wisdom and to prepare them for life, but he tried as best he could not to do it by giving orders and punishments. Among other things, he would cut their hair, weigh and measure them, keep detailed records of their development, and check on them at night while they were sleeping.

He also kept in close contact with the children's families. His institution, he emphasized again and again, did not wish to compete with the child's natural family but to complement it, if it had unfortunately been destroyed, to expand it and to provide the child with what the family had been unable to provide. Those orphans who had no family at all got special attention. The Doctor, as he was called in the orphanage, would take them to the movies and the zoo, buy them candy, and spend holidays with them.

He always emphasized the importance of a democratic society of children. Parliamentary-style organizations functioned in the orphanage, such as a parliament, a court, a legislative committee, and a committee to organize and allot the work. Each new child was assigned as a guardian one of the older students, who had volunteered for the position, and was considered suitable for it on the basis of a decision made at a general meeting of the children. "If you have enough goodwill, intelligence, and suitable qualities," said the letter that was given to every new child, "you will receive full rights from us, but you must earn them."

The children also had access to a mailbox, in which they could put letters with their requests, their doubts, and their problems. If they wished to complain about their teachers, even about Korczak himself, this was the place to do it. The teachers, claimed Korczak, could read the letters, at their leisure, whenever they had the time. In this way they would become aware of problems that a child perhaps might have found too difficult to express orally.

Writing was like second nature for Korczak, and also an important tool in his work. "I strongly believe," he wrote in 1921, "that there is a need for magazines for children and youth, but these must be magazines that they themselves write, that deal with subjects that are important and interesting to them, and not just weekly magazines that print stories and poems. And what are the things that are important for children and youths—that is what they themselves must say in their journals." Five years later he established and edited the children's journal *Maly Przeglad* (Little Journal), which appeared as a weekly supplement to the Polish Zionist daily *Nasz Przeglad* (Our Journal). Children were part of the editorial staff, dozens of children were included in all the other work, and they all received payment. Later, when Korczak discussed expanding the newspaper, he said that he wanted the paper to be one that "no adult will want to buy it for his child, but that the children will buy it themselves, with money they get from their parents."

In his attic room he wrote his essays on education as well as his literary works, first and foremost his children's books, which became classics. *King Matthew the First*, *Matthew on the Desert Island*, *Kajtus the Magician*, *A Stubborn Boy* (on the life of Louis Pasteur), and *Little Jack*— all stirred the hearts of many, young and old, not only in Poland but all over the world. In these books and in others, Korczak revealed again and again the great love he had for humanity and especially the child in him.

But heavy clouds hung on the horizon. Anti-Semitism was growing in Poland. The Nazis came to power in Germany and threatened to spread their reign of terror all over Europe. Korczak became aware of the dangers. The man who had grown up in an assimilated home, and who had never been interested in Zionism, now began to wonder whether he should not leave Poland, emigrate to Palestine, and realize his educational ideas on a kibbutz. Some of his pupils and his associates were already in Palestine and very much wanted to bring him there for good. He himself made two visits. On his return from the second visit he wrote to a friend in Palestine, "We belong to the past; you are the future. . . . we are tombstones and graves; you are cradles!" He added: "Right now, I would like to sit tomorrow in my small, narrow room in Jerusalem, and on the desk in front of me have my Bible, textbooks, a Hebrew dictionary, paper and pencil."

He wanted to do this, but he did not. The truth of the matter was that Korczak remained tied body and soul to the orphans on Krochmalna Street. Despite all sorts of plans and suggestions, he was not able to leave them. He was with them when the Nazis entered Poland and occupied Warsaw. He wandered among the Nazis wearing a Polish army uniform and refusing to put on a Jewish star, as he was ordered to do. Defiantly he hoisted the new flag of the orphanage—green with a flowering chestnut tree on one side, and white with a blue Star of David on the other. Now he devoted his superhuman efforts only to taking care of the children, assuring their physical survival, getting food, finding new living quarters (when it turned out that Krochmalna Street was not within the boundaries of the Ghetto), solving all the problems that kept popping up one after the other. He saw the end approaching rapidly and looked it straight in the eye, while taking his children under his wing.

"I would like to die fully conscious, with a clear head," he wrote. "I don't know what my parting words to the children would be. I would like to tell them that they had complete freedom to choose their own way." But this kind of freedom did not exist. On August 5, 1942, the Nazis surrounded the orphanage and ordered its residents to go to the railway station. Korczak did not reveal to the children what was awaiting them. He made sure that they wore clean, neat clothes, and had them stand in rows behind their flag and march as if they were going on an outing. He stood at the head of the line, as a witness said, "bent and stooping, holding a child in his arms and marching forward . . . to the sacrifice."

Along with him, inspired by his example, marched nine adult workers from the orphanage, among them Stefa Wilczynska, his devoted colleague. It was later told that the police of the Ghetto stood at attention and saluted while this awful, yet magnificent, procession passed by. It was also told that a German officer who had greatly enjoyed reading *Little Jack* suggested to Korczak that he get off the train at the last moment. On his own he would definitely have been saved. Even before that, some Polish friends had sent him false papers and prepared a hiding place for him. But a man of such courage could not escape the inevitable fate that awaited his helpless orphans. With them he reached Treblinka. With them he died. Let the story of his heroism be a unique and special symbol for us all.

Itzhak Navon is a former minister of education and president of the State of Israel.

DID YOU KNOW MORDECHAI?

MORDECHAI ANIELEWICZ

by Shevach Weiss

On May 23, 1943, a telegram arrived at Kibbutz Merhavia. It had already been rerouted through several addresses after having been sent from Poland ten days earlier. The telegram read: "I would like you to inform Grandfather Meir, that his dear children who worked for Mrs. Main—Tussia, Mordechai, Mira—went to Josef Kaplan. Did you know Mordechai? He was an extremely talented fellow. He is the grandfather of Hagana and loved it even more than his children."

The words "Grandfather Meir" referred to the leader of Hashomer Hatzair (a Zionist Socialist youth movement), Meir Yaari. "Mrs. Main" described the main leadership of the movement in Poland. Josef Kaplan, who was a member of the organization leadership, had been killed a few months earlier. In Palestine they already knew about his death. Those who were described as traveling to him, the readers of the telegram understood, were also now dead—among them, Mordechai Anielewicz and his friend Mira Pochrer.

"Did you know Mordechai?" the recipient of the telegram was asked, and it is doubtful whether he could have given a positive answer. Mordechai Anielewicz was twenty-four at his death in the Warsaw Ghetto. At the outbreak of the Second World War he was only in his early twenties and probably was not known to the leaders of Hashomer Hatzair in Palestine. When vague rumors began to spread that the last surviving Jews of Warsaw had gone down fighting, one could understand from the words "the grandfather of Hagana [literally, 'defense']" that this young man had led the fighters in that hopeless battle and had fought bravely until the end.

Mordechai Anielewicz was born to a working-class family that lived in Wyszkow, Poland, and later in Warsaw. He studied at the Labor High School. He was for a short time a member of Betar, a right-wing Zionist youth movement, and later joined the leftist Hashomer Hatzair. He soon emerged above the others as a beloved group counselor, a multitalented organizer, and a natural leader. Hashomer Hatzair became like a second home for him, an extended family.

He became a member of the central leadership and waited, like many others, for the day when he would be able to make *aliya* to Palestine and join a kibbutz.

The Nazi invasion of Poland on September 1, 1939, put an end to all his dreams. A few days later Anielewicz and a few of the other members of Hashomer Hatzair left Warsaw and went eastward. According to the rumors, the Poles were going to set up a defense line there against the invaders. From there they would launch their counterattack and drive the Germans back. But on September 17, it turned out that the invasion from the west was being supplemented by an invasion from the east: According to a previous agreement between Hitler and Stalin, the Red army took control of those areas of Poland that were not conquered by the Germans. In a final attempt to escape this trap Anielewicz went south. If he could manage to sneak across the border and get into Romania, he thought, he might be able to continue from there to Palestine. Unfortunately, he fell into the hands of the Soviet guards and was thrown in prison. When he got out, after a few weeks, he realized that all escape routes were blocked and that they would have to unite all the forces within the territory occupied by the Germans and fight for the honor of the Jews and for their very lives.

At first he wanted to see what the situation in Warsaw was like. He left the relatively safe Soviet territory, passed through several Jewish communities, saw what was happening there, and finally reached the capital. In Warsaw he found very few partners for the projected struggle. He therefore made his way to Vilna, which was still within the borders of semi-independent Lithuania. Many of the young Jews who had escaped from occupied Poland had found refuge there. He met scores of his friends from the youth movement and presented a strong demand to each of them. We have to return to German-occupied territory, he said, revive the branches of Hashomer Hatzair, and turn them into the core units of the Jewish combat. When the lists of volunteers for this project were drawn up, Mordechai and his girlfriend, Mira, were at the top of the list.

At the beginning of 1940 Mordechai became a full-time member of the underground, working twenty-four hours a day. He moved around from place to place, organizing cells, and urging them to acquire weapons and prepare for battle. He set up movement groups of teenagers and trained them himself. He ran seminars and conferences. He visited the various small groups that sprang up amid this terrible distress. He published a newspaper called *Against the Stream* and started other underground publications.

Besides all of this he also found the time to improve his education. Along with all his hectic activities, and his perpetual travels covering hundreds of kilometers, he worked on his Hebrew and read a lot of books on history, economics, and sociology.

In the meantime the Germans were tightening their grip on the Jews in the occupied lands. The program of the "Final Solution" had not been made public yet. The death camps had not been set up. But murders, expulsions, persecutions, and humiliations were more and more common, and ghettos were being established all over Poland. To Anielewicz it became clearer than ever that there could be no illusions. Something awful was about to take place, and no moderation or submissiveness would prevent it. All he could do was increase his activities and make it very clear to everyone he talked to that they had to prepare for the worst.

In the middle of November 1940 the construction of the Warsaw Ghetto was completed. An area consisting of 2.4 percent of the city was enclosed within a wall, and 30 percent of the population—between three and four hundred thousand people—was crowded inside. Anielewicz was theoretically among those locked in the Ghetto—theoretically, because he sneaked in and out incessantly. He went out to encourage and motivate Jews outside of Warsaw and to make contact with non-Jewish underground groups. He returned to work with his friends and disciples in the Ghetto. This included the Hashomer Hatzair "kibbutz"—a youth group modeled after a Palestinian kibbutz—that had been set up with his encouragement and help inside the Ghetto.

In the summer of 1941, after Nazi Germany launched a surprise attack against the Soviet Union, substantiated reports reached Warsaw and other places about the widespread slaughter of the Jews in the east. There were those who refused to believe these reports. But Anielewicz and his friends firmly believed they were true. They understood that the Nazis were determined to carry out the Führer's horrific plans to annihilate all the Jews just because they were Jews. Anielewicz and his friends swore that they would not go like sheep to the slaughter.

Their immediate conclusion was that they must establish an armed underground organization. But in their efforts to do so they encountered difficulties from within and without. Traditional political enmities, over matters that lost their importance considering the catastrophe that was about to befall them, prevented the Jews from consolidating forces. Zionists and Communists, right-wingers and leftists, were still not able to join together even when it was obvious that the jaws of the monster were wide open and ready to devour them. At the same time, attempts to make contact with the Armia Krajowa (the Homeland Army—the main Polish underground organization) were not successful. Anielewicz, who participated in these efforts, felt terribly frustrated. But he did not give up. In July 1942 he went as an emissary of Hashomer Hatzair to an area in southwestern Poland that had been annexed by the Germans. He began to spread the idea of resistance and of setting up an armed Jewish force. His friends, representatives of youth movements in Warsaw, carried out parallel missions in a number of areas all over Poland where there were concentrations of Jews.

Suddenly the Ghetto, which they had left behind, suffered a terrible blow. On July 21 the Nazis began a mass deportation of Warsaw Jews to some unknown location in the east, which soon turned out to be the death camp of Treblinka. At a ruthless pace and with fiendish efficiency, almost four-fifths of the 350,000 residents of the Ghetto were sent to their deaths. This *aktion* was completed in the middle of September. A week after it began, on July 28, the leaders of three youth movements—Hashomer Hatzair, Dror-Hechalutz, and Akiva—met and decided to establish the Jewish Fighting Organization (in Polish, Zydowska Organizacja Bojowa [ZOB]; in Yiddish, Yiddishe Kampf Organizatzia).

This new organization, unfortunately, had a very slight impact. Eight revolvers and a few hand grenades were all the weapons they had, and even those fell into the Germans' hands during one of their moves from one hiding place to another. Bit by bit the ZOB members began to take active steps to oppose the deportation of the Jews, and paid for their activities with their lives. One of them even managed to assassinate the head of the Jewish police force, who was collaborating with the Nazis. But beyond that nothing changed, except for one thing; now there was in the shrunken Warsaw Ghetto quite a large group of people who felt that their fight against the Nazis had become a central, positive goal in their lives. "People would be sworn in and loudly declare," wrote the historian Emmanuel Ringelblum, who was in the Ghetto; "'Never will the Germans move us from here, without paying the price. We will die, but the cruel occupier will pay with blood for our blood.'"

This was the new reality that Anielewicz discovered on his return from southwestern Poland in October 1942. He jumped into action with enthusiasm and started widespread organizing activities. Now almost all of the underground Jewish bodies joined the Jewish Fighting Organization. The Jewish National Committee was also set up, and in November, Anielewicz was chosen as the leader of its Central Command. The next three months were dedicated to creating fighting units, preparing bunkers, amassing weapons, and establishing contact with the Polish underground. The contacts with the Polish Resistance were limited. The Poles were not interested in helping. Until the beginning of 1943 all the Jewish fighters got from the Armia Krajowa, the Polish resistance organization, were ten revolvers and instructions on how to prepare homemade grenades. More than one request met with the response that the Jews would not fight anyway and that it was not worth sending them precious weapons. In other cases they were told that their rebellion against their assassins was liable to break out at an inconvenient time.

Then came January 18, 1943. The Germans started another *aktion* in the Warsaw Ghetto, and the ZOB decided to fight back. A few groups prepared for fighting from inside the houses, and one group, under the command of Anielewicz, purposefully sneaked into the rows of deportees. At the corner of Zamenhoff and Niska Streets, Anielewicz gave the signal, and he and his group opened fire on the Germans. The Germans were completely taken by surprise. Some of them were hit and others fled, but came back quickly with reinforcements. In the fierce battle that ensued, Anielewicz ran out of ammunition. He jumped a German gendarme, took his rifle, and continued shooting. He was one of the few fighters who came out of the encounter alive.

Four days later the *aktion* stopped. Everyone in the Ghetto said that the Germans had been taken aback by the resistance of the Jews. But Anielewicz and his friends knew that they had not seen the end of it, and that the real battle was still ahead. They also realized that the next confrontation would be much worse than what they had experienced until now. They speeded up their preparations, stockpiled arms—the Armia Krajowa had finally begun to take them seriously—prepared bunkers and attics, and coordinated their plans.

On the first evening of Passover, April 19, 1943, the Germans began the final *aktion* for the annihilation of the Warsaw Ghetto. The members of the Jewish Fighting Organization, under the command of Anielewicz, launched their rebellion. A large Nazi force, over two thousand well-armed soldiers, broke into the Ghetto with tanks and were met with sniper fire from several unexpected locations. A few hundred Jews, armed with light weapons, fought a battle with tenacious bravery, in which the Nazis suffered great losses. The Jewish fighters proved to the whole world that it was possible to resist this diabolical power with pride and courage, and that such a power could not rule forever.

The hopeless battle raged from bunker to bunker, from house to house. The Germans, livid with rage, systematically set fire to the whole Ghetto and destroyed everything in their way. But only on May 16, almost a full month after the uprising had begun, did they manage to take full control of the area, blow up the Great Synagogue, and send a gruesome message to Berlin: "There is no longer a Jewish quarter in Warsaw."

On May 8, 1943, exactly two years before the end of the war in Europe, Mordechai Anielewicz fell, in the midst of a battle, in his command bunker on 18 Mila Street. During the first days of the uprising he had sent a letter to a friend:

> Something has happened that is beyond our wildest dreams. . . . The Germans ran away from the Ghetto twice. One of our units managed to last for forty minutes, and another for over six hours. I cannot describe to you the conditions under which the Jews are living. Only a select few will survive. All the rest will perish, sooner or later. Our fate is sealed. In all the bunkers in which our men are hiding it is impossible to light a match for lack of air. . . . But what is most important is that my life's dream has been realized. I have been fortunate enough to see the Jewish defense of the ghetto in all its grandeur and glory.

And so he had.

Professor Shevach Weiss, a member of the Knesset, was the thirteenth Speaker of the Knesset.

THE MAN OF THE PLOWSHARE AND THE SWORD

MEIR "ZARO" ZOREA

by Arye Lova Eliav

If one were to sum up the life and work of Zaro in two words one could say that he was the man of "the plowshare and the sword."

As a lover of the Bible from his youth, Zaro read Isaiah's prophecy of peace: "They shall beat their swords into plowshares, and their spears into pruning-hooks; nation shall not lift up sword against nation; neither shall they learn war anymore" (Isaiah 2:4).

But another verse from the Book of Joel, with a completely opposite meaning, did not escape his notice either: "Proclaim ye this among the nations: Prepare for war; stir up the mighty men; let them come up. Beat your plowshares into swords, and your pruning-hooks into spears; let the weak say: 'I am strong'" (Joel 4:9–10).

So he read, and so he did. Meir Zorea lived his life between these two precepts. On one hand there was his love of the plowshare and the anvil, of agriculture and industry in his kibbutz, Maagan Michael. On the other hand, there was the call of the destiny of his people and his generation "to teach the children of Judah the bow" (II Samuel 1:18), in order to forge them into valiant warriors. This is the meaning of his very active life, which moved back and forth between the plowshare and the sword.

Finally, when he had had enough of this life of action (having reached the rank of major general in the IDF), Zaro said of himself, "My life has followed two interwoven paths that nurture one another: settling the land and the kibbutz way of life, and defense, from my youth until today."

Zaro was born in 1923 in Romania as Meir Zarodinsky. At the age of three he immigrated to Palestine with his parents. From childhood he was known affectionately to his friends as Zaro, a shortened version of his family name. This name stayed with him all his life, even after he chose his Hebrew name, Zorea, which means "to sow" in Hebrew, and testifies to his roots in the fields.

Zaro studied in the Reali School in Haifa. This school was famous for its high moral and ethical standards, and its strict and demanding regimen. These qualities were instilled in the pupils by its distinguished principal, Dr. Arthur Biram. There is no doubt that the education he received at that school contributed greatly to the shaping of young Zaro's character. The motto of the school, "Bear yourself modestly," guided him throughout his life.

Already in the upper grades at school Zaro was torn between the two loves of his generation. He joined the Scouts and went for agricultural training in 1941 to Kibbutz Ginegar, and later to Degania. There he learned to love working the land. But at the same time, he was even then a member of the Hagana. He learned how to use a gun and signed up as an auxiliary policeman in the police force of the Jewish settlements.

In 1942 Zaro volunteered to serve in the Jewish companies that were part of the "Buffs" Regiment of the British army. We have to fight the Germans, he said to his friends in the agricultural training camp. (The training camp was a prelude to the creation of their own kibbutz.) They refused to allow him to sign up, but he did so anyway, and left the training camp. He proved himself to be an exemplary soldier and was sent off to an officers' course. At the end of the course he came back to serve in what was now the Second Regiment and soon became part of the Jewish Brigade. When the Brigade sailed to Italy to fight on the Senio front, Zaro proved himself to be an outstanding soldier.

Zaro was awarded the Military Cross for his bravery. The British High Command was very spare in handing out medals of valor to Jewish soldiers in Palestine, but they could not ignore his courage in the battlefield. Among the reasons given by his commander for awarding him this medal were the following:

> Lieutenant Zarodinsky carried out many more duties and assignments in battle than those required of a platoon commander.
>
> Before crossing the Senio River he went out on continual reconnaissance missions, and whenever a difficult assignment came up he volunteered for it. After crossing the Senio the company was supposed to move forward and make contact with the enemy. Lieutenant Zarodinsky commanded the advance force, and, thanks to his courage, the platoon managed to capture the objective without any casualties. When he went out on a patrol, he encountered heavy mortar fire and was forced to take cover. Suddenly he noticed a platoon of another regiment that was moving toward open ground. He crossed the area under heavy enemy fire to warn the platoon commander.
>
> On the same night the enemy retreated, and Lieutenant Zarodinsky was ordered to head a patrol to find out the new disposition of the enemy troops. The patrol encountered heavy mortar fire. Lieutenant Zarodinsky left his men under

cover, moved forward on his own to an observation point on open ground, and found out the disposition of the enemy troops as well as the position of their mortar and artillery. This extraordinary courage and sense of duty in difficult situations, and throughout the whole time that the regiment was in battle, no doubt saved many lives and served as an example to all the soldiers.

After the victory over the Nazis and a heartrending meeting with survivors of the death camps, Zaro (who by now had been promoted to the rank of Captain) dedicated himself to three interrelated activities: providing the survivors with food and clothing, but mainly helping them to organize their future lives; purchasing and smuggling arms to the secret storerooms of the Hagana in Palestine; and carrying out acts of revenge against the Nazis, especially the SS, whom Zaro and his friends, "the Avengers," tracked down and executed.

In the ranks of the Brigade, Zaro developed a close relationship with Chaim Laskov, his "big brother." Laskov, a future chief of staff of the Israeli army, was from Haifa as well, a graduate of the Reali School, and an outstanding officer in the Hagana and the British army. Their remarkable friendship continued later in the High Command of the IDF, and lasted until Laskov's death.

In 1946 Zaro returned to Palestine and joined his friends from Group A of the Scouts. They were based near Rehovot and served as cover—as well as manpower—for the Ayalon Institute, the underground weapons and ammunitions factory of the Hagana. It was only natural that Zaro should be appointed the security officer of the factory. In addition he also did agricultural work, but not for long. He was soon conscripted into the permanent staff of the Hagana. An excellent, experienced officer like him was much in demand just before the War of Independence. From the beginning of the war, at the end of 1947, until it was over, Zaro was constantly part of the military action, especially on the road to Jerusalem and inside the besieged city as well. As a battalion commander, he was in charge of the capture of the Castel stronghold, which dominated the last leg of the road to Jerusalem. He also commanded some daring attempts to enter the Old City.

After the War of Independence, Zaro, now a high-ranking Israel Defense Forces officer, remained in uniform. He was appointed the first commander of the Officers' Academy. He brought with him to this position the battle tradition and fighting doctrine of the Hagana and the British army. To his dying day he continued to be proud of this tradition.

In 1950 Zaro asked to return to the plowshare. His new kibbutz was being set up at Maagan Michael, close to Caesarea, and Zaro, at the wheel of a tractor, took pleasure in digging the first furrows in the kibbutz fields.

But after no more than a year, the army called him back again. After many efforts a place had been allotted for the first Israeli officer at the Staff and Command College of the British army in Kimberley, England. Who was more suitable to go than Zaro?

He finished the school with honors. His final certificate said that he excelled in military judgment and that the officers, his fellow students, respected him for his personal qualities. He was found suitable for all staff positions in the ground forces and especially in the area of military operations. The commander of the school particularly emphasized that Zaro deserved special mention for his contribution to the course. When he returned from England, he was appointed head of the Training Division in the General Staff. He also played a central role in setting up the Staff and Command College.

Zaro again returned to work in the fields of his kibbutz in 1953. He was in charge of field crops and became an expert in a new crop in the country—cotton. But the army did not leave him in peace. In 1954 he took off his farmer's overalls and put on his uniform once more to serve as the right-hand man of his friend Chaim Laskov. Before the Sinai Campaign, the two of them developed a fighting doctrine that made the armored corps the main strength of the land forces, and was used no longer as a support force to the infantry. They encountered strong opposition from many of the top figures in the IDF, but they continued to build up the armored forces with diligence and perseverance. The clear proof of how right they were was the Sinai Campaign of 1956. In that lightning war, the Israeli armor pierced the Sinai peninsula and reached the Suez Canal in one hundred hours. From then on, no one in the IDF ever again dared to deny the importance of the armored corps.

In 1958, when Laskov was appointed chief of staff, Zaro was again appointed head of the Training Division. A short time later he became head of the Operations Branch and was promoted to the rank of major general. A year later he was made head of the Northern Command. At that time intense fighting broke out between Israel and Syria as a result of Israel's implementation of its sovereignty along the border and over sources of water in the north. As head of the Northern Command, Zaro led the Golani Brigade in battle against the Syrians, and turned it into a proud elite unit. When it was necessary to use force to establish Israeli sovereignty over lands that were in dispute with the Syrians, Major General Zorea got on the first tractor and plowed a furrow in the face of Syrian machine guns.

In 1962, crowned in glory, Zaro returned again to work in Maagan Michael. His family had grown, and his kibbutz had developed. Zaro went back to being a perfect farmer. His life was in tune with the changing of the seasons—plowing and planting, harvesting and gathering in the harvest. The warm home of Naomi and Zaro was open to his many friends from all the different stages of his life.

On the eve of the Six-Day War, in June 1967, he was called to the colors once again. On the first day of the war he learned that his son, the pilot Yonatan Zorea, had fallen on the Golan Heights. At the end of the fighting Zaro went to the Golan Heights to look for his son's body. While he was looking, wrote Uri Yarom, the pilot who flew Zaro to the Golan:

> I saw a lone figure walking bent over toward a scorched mud hut. Zaro told me to
> fly up to him quickly. When we came closer, we saw before us an old stooping Arab
> dressed in rags. Zaro jumped off the chopper and ran toward him, holding his sub-

machine gun in his hand. When he approached him, the old man got down on his
knees and began to kiss Zaro's feet. Zaro bent down, took the old man by the arm,
and helped him up. When he got up Zaro put his arm around his shoulder and led
him behind the trees. After no more than a minute, I saw the two again. Zaro was
carrying a wooden hand plow; he loaded it on the bent back of the old man, shook
his hand, and gave him a tap on the shoulder to send him on his way.

It was a sight I will never forget! An IDF general, while looking for the body of
his fallen son, meets an old man [who is an enemy civilian], forgets his personal
sorrow for a moment, and becomes a farmer again, who knows the value of a plow
to every farmer, whoever he may be!

Six years later, in the Yom Kippur War, cruel fate again struck the family. Their son
Yochanan, an officer of a tank battalion, fell in battle against the Syrian army in the Golan
Heights.

During the same war Zaro returned to the army as the head of the Training Division, and
worked hard at incorporating new weapons that had arrived during the fighting. Afterward he
was asked to head the Israeli Land Authority, a position that was close to his heart as a farmer
and a worker of the land. He tried to implement in this large, unwieldy organization the tradition of order and discipline that he had learned for years in the army. He did his best to keep
state land under government control, in order to prevent speculation.

In 1976 Zorea made a stab at politics for a short time. He joined the Democratic Party for
Change, a new party whose main aim was to prevent the political system from becoming fos-
silized and corrupt. He was elected to the Ninth Knesset, but he soon learned that even his
new party was becoming corrupt. He left the party in disgust, and in a demonstration of personal integrity uncharacteristic of the political arena he returned his mandate to the party and
went back to his kibbutz.

And once more he became a simple farmer. Later he went to work in the metal workshop,
but he was called back a few more times to serve in a public capacity, both as the comptroller
of the Defense Forces and as a member of various public and state committees.

In all his positions, his character and personality stood out again and again: impeccable
honesty, a penetrating and deep understanding of every subject that he dealt with, and the
ability to act upon his conclusions—no matter how difficult or painful—regarding any problem that he was faced with.

In the winter of his life Zaro returned to the metal workshop at Maagan Michael.
Until his dying day, in 1995, this bold war hero and lover of the fields continued working there.

Zaro was not an easy man, and in most of his jobs he had to be tough. But anyone who
knew him well—with his family, in his home, in his kibbutz, among his circle of friends
when he was out of uniform and free of the responsibility for the lives of those under his

command—saw a warm man, sensitive to the suffering of others, a lover of books and music.

When Chaim Laskov died Zaro eulogized him with these warm and moving words, which can be applied to him as well: "From his youth he always took the lead. To the call 'Whom shall I send and who will go for us?' he answered: 'Here am I; send me!' (Isaiah 6:8). In these few words is the essence of his life."

Arye Lova Eliav, a former Knesset member, is a teacher and educator.

Exposed in the Turret, in the Heart of Berlin

Arkadi Timor

by Yosef Argaman

On April 28, 1945, Lieutenant Colonel Arkadi Timor entered the heart of Berlin at the head of the Fourteenth Soviet Armored Battalion. For four and a half years he had been living in his T-34 tank. He already knew that the Nazis had wiped out his whole family—from his two-year-old sister to his ninety-six-year-old grandfather—but he ordered his soldiers to hand out soup to the starving civilians. He also set up the first kindergarten for German orphans. "That was my revenge," he would say fifty years later.

In occupied Germany, Arkadi met secretly with Shaul Avigur, one of the leading figures of the Hagana in Palestine. This meeting was to change his life. This brilliant and ambitious man was twenty-four years old at the time and thought to be the youngest officer of his rank in the Soviet Armored Corps. The hero Arkadi Timor, who had been wounded five times defending Moscow and Leningrad, and defeating the Third Reich, began to assist the Hagana.

In 1948, when he was recalled to the Soviet Union, he started working secretly to keep Judaism alive. In 1956, by then a full colonel, he was tried and sent to a forced labor camp for seven years. "I never acted against the Red army," he later said. "I just told Jewish officers that the Jewish homeland is in Israel."

After close to five years, and a retrial, he was released and went to Israel with his wife, Halena, and their son, Boris. The Ordnance Corps of the Israeli army was already waiting for him. From the Six-Day War on, Arkadi Timor became the "father" of thousands of Soviet armored vehicles, which the IDF had captured as booty in different wars. During the War of Attrition (1967–71), at the age of forty-seven, he crossed the Suez Canal in the Raviv Campaign, during which IDF Soviet-made tanks, camouflaged as Egyptian tanks, attacked army camps and positions on the Egyptian side of the Canal. Egypt's president, Nasser, had a heart attack after this campaign and never managed to recover.

In the Yom Kippur War, Arkadi was wounded on the Golan Heights. Nevertheless, within eight days he managed to repair hundreds of tanks captured from the Syrians, and to train crews and send them to fight on the Egyptian front. This arrival of fresh forces, after Israel had lost hundreds of tanks in the battlefield, changed the face of the war. "To Arkadi, the teacher of the soldiers of the Armored and Ordnance Corps. Our guide in Zionism and defense, in theory and in practice, with appreciation we salute you." So wrote Major General Israel "Talik" Tal on the shield given to Timor on his retirement in 1991. No one guessed then what lesson in Zionism Arkadi would give four years later.

In 1995, President Boris Yeltsin, who was intent on improving Russia's relations with Israel, decided to award Arkadi a medal for his contribution to the Soviet war effort. That was on the fiftieth anniversary of the Allied victory in the Second World War. Arkadi went to Moscow, but announced from the podium that he refused to accept the medal. He explained his reasons on the Russian-language program on Israel Radio: each of the half million Jewish fighters in the Soviet army deserved this medal. Two hundred thousand of them fell in battle, but the Russians had always chosen to cover up this fact.

Arkadi was born in the Ukrainian city of Dubossary. In 1939, while he was still a student at the Politechnikum (an engineering school), he was sent to the Academy of the Armored Corps. When the Germans invaded Russia, he was a tank officer and an engineer.

His first battle was in the area of Vitebsk, on June 25, 1941, four days after the Germans had invaded the Soviet Union. His good friend Major Moshe Rapoport fell in this battle. In the second battle, near Smolensk, the Red army began a panicked retreat eastward. According to Arkadi it was a difficult and shameful sight to watch. One battalion, to which Arkadi belonged, was left from the whole division. Hundreds of tanks were abandoned in enemy territory. Tens of thousands of soldiers were taken prisoner like a herd of cows, under the guard of a handful of German soldiers. Arkadi himself joined the long line of prisoners three times, trying to convince the soldiers to escape, but only thirty people listened to him.

In the beginning of August 1941 Arkadi was placed at the head of a unit of sixty tank officers. You must parachute into enemy territory, they were told, and render inoperative as many of the abandoned tanks as possible. The parachuting course was one night long. Only twenty officers survived the amateurish jump and the German gunfire from the ground.

For about two months they wandered around at night, hungry, thirsty, their clothes in tatters, removing perfectly good critical parts from tanks that had formerly belonged to them. They thus immobilized about 250 tanks and cannon. When they returned home alive, to the amazement of their officers, they aroused suspicion. Each of them was interrogated about possibly having collaborated with the Wehrmacht and was now an enemy agent.

Between October 1941 and April 1942, Arkadi participated in the battle for Moscow, and he was wounded by shrapnel in the chest. He was by now the commander of a company. "I saw German officers," he said, "wrapped in anything, including women's scarves. It was like a caricature." According to Arkadi, the winter and the fresh forces from Siberia gave the Red army back its most important weapon—hope.

The next front was Leningrad. During the long siege, Arkadi, who was now a battalion commander, repelled several murderous German offensives. He was wounded again. In August 1943 he was assigned to the First Army, under the command of General Yefim Katokov. Twenty months later, he saw the end of the war in Berlin. On the way he had managed to take part in several battles in Latvia and Poland.

In the spring of 1946, during a visit to an agricultural exhibition in Leipzig, he became acquainted with Zvi Netzer, one of Shaul Avigur's aides, and later one of the heads of Nativ, the Israeli secret organization that kept the contact with the Soviet Jews under the communist regime. Netzer told him about the activities of the Hagana in Palestine in preparation for the establishment of a state and asked if he could help. "I wouldn't ask anything of you that is against Soviet law," he said. Their next meeting was over lunch, with Shaul. The piercing eyes and serious face of the man from Kibbutz Kinneret were etched in Arkadi's memory forever. "Look," said Shaul in Russian, "we want a home and a state of our own. We only accept help from those who want to help us."

These words fell on fertile ground. Arkadi felt a kind of revelation at that table. Tears came to his eyes. "Wipe your eyes and we'll speak seriously," said Shaul, and Arkadi never forgot that sentence.

The Red army training brochures about armored equipment that Arkadi supplied were sent to Palestine and returned for clarification. There were more meetings, and also appeals from Arkadi to other Jewish officers. They helped, with their battalion trucks, to transport Jewish refugees and help them cross borders, in the framework of the Bricha (Escape) organization. The Bricha was an underground operation that took Holocaust survivors out of Eastern Europe and moved them to Central and Southern Europe between 1944 and 1948, in preparation for their primarily "illegal" immigration to Palestine. Even though Arkadi may have thought momentarily of joining these refugees, Shaul Avigur requested that he remain there until he gave him the signal.

But in 1948, before he was given the signal, Arkadi was sent back to Russia with his brigade to an unnamed area, far in the east. Two weeks earlier he had met with two of Shaul's messengers. "Meirov [Avigur] sends you his regards," they told him, "and he hopes that you will retain your feelings toward the Jewish people and help others to do so as well. . . ."

A few months later the establishment of the State of Israel was declared, and Arab armies invaded the country. Arkadi, far in the east, was beside himself. He organized a group of fourteen Jewish officers, volunteers, for the war in Palestine. Fortunately, his wife, Halena, hid his volunteer form, which saved him. All the other volunteers disappeared. After that episode he became very cautious, and almost always met with his Jewish friends in secret. In 1950 he was moved west, to Lithuania, and was given a new position as the chief engineer in the largest center in the western Soviet Union for the repair of tanks and motors. He later became the commander of this center, responsible for 3,500 people.

In Lithuania, which had the strongest concentration of Jews in the Soviet Union, he became acquainted, for the first time, with true Judaism. A veterinarian, Professor Eisenbod, became his teacher of Jewish and Zionist subjects.

In 1955 the repatriation to Poland began. Citizens of this country who had been stranded in the Soviet Union during the war were allowed to return home. Halena had been one of them, and the couple decided to take advantage of the opportunity. Zvi Netzer, Arkadi's old friend, who was now in the Israeli embassy in Warsaw, came especially to Kovna to give him the long-promised signal from Shaul Avigur. Arkadi filled out the forms, in the hope that he would be able to continue from Poland to Israel. Two months later he was arrested.

He was accused of encouraging Jewish officers to immigrate to Israel and reveal secrets. Taking his heroism in the war into account, the prosecution called for twelve years in a labor camp. The court decided that seven years was enough.

"All I did," said Arkadi, "was explain to people leaving for Poland that they should continue to Israel, because the Jews have no other homeland. I brought postcards from Israel, and told them what was happening. I organized meetings during the holidays, and told stories. If I received a postcard, I made sure that many people saw it. If it was necessary to travel to Moscow or Leningrad to show people a picture of a view in Israel, I did so. I was not a spy. My conscience is clear."

Halena was told that Arkadi was a traitor and that there was no chance she would ever see him again. For almost five years, this beautiful, delicate woman, a Holocaust survivor, lived in terrible anxiety. On her own, she raised their son, Boris, who suffered from kidney problems. The child was nine years old when his father was imprisoned.

But a miracle happened. Arkadi was released, apparently thanks to some secret negotiations on his behalf. In March 1960 he reached Haifa and began studying Hebrew in Ulpan Etzion, one of the centers for intensive study of Hebrew for newcomers to Israel. The Ordnance Corps quickly absorbed him. He worked on the installation of diesel engines in old Sherman tanks and tested the Soviet tanks that had been captured in the Sinai Desert during the Sinai Campaign. Later he worked on increasing the amount of time Centurion tanks could stay on the road, from two hours to eight. He also took part in a secret project that increased the shooting range of tanks during the 1965 fight with the Syrians over sources of water.

In the heat of the fighting during the Six-Day War, the chief of staff, Itzhak Rabin, called him in. "Should we consider using war booty in the Israeli army?" he asked. "I think we should," answered Arkadi in a heavy Russian accent. Within a few days the Armored Corps workshop, under the direction of Arkadi, had prepared a model for the Tiran 4, a Russian-Israeli tank.

"We put our hearts into something that was almost a dream, that we didn't believe we would manage to do," said Arkadi. And so within eight months a whole tank brigade was created from captured tanks. It was given the number 274, was stationed in Sharm el-Sheikh, and was used in the War of Attrition.

After the Raviv incursion into Egypt, described above, the converted Tiran tank became a regular IDF tank. At its high point the IDF had hundreds of active Tiran tanks. In the Yom Kippur War, Arkadi led his men out to collect Syrian tanks in the Golan Heights. "I told Dado [Chief of Staff David Elazar] in the pit [the underground center of operations during wartime] that there were a thousand Syrian tanks spread out all over the Golan Heights. This was half of the Syrian force that had attacked us. His eyes lit up. I said that three hundred of them were like new, because their crews had run away." Arkadi suffered shrapnel wounds at the Hushania junction, but did not stop working for even a moment. Within eight days they took two hundred tanks out of the Golan. These tanks provided the basis for a full brigade and were used on the Egyptian side of the Suez Canal.

Arkadi Timor continued this activity after the war as well. "We took out every screw," he said. "We learned things that we hadn't known before, and we produced a series of thousands of spare parts."

The tank was greatly improved. Even the Russians admitted eventually that the Israelis— that is, Arkadi—had introduced improvements in their tanks that they had never dreamed of. Arkadi also played an important part in the improvements made to the Israeli-made Merkava tank. A smokescreen that came out of the motor, components that allowed the Merkava to move in an enemy minefield, cast joints in armored personnel carriers—all these came out of Arkadi Timor's creative mind.

Since his retirement from the IDF, he has dedicated himself to the absorption of immigrants from Russia, but here and there he "steals" a few hours for writing. He has already written three large volumes about the Second World War. Jewish heroism in that war must be remembered, says the man who himself is an outstanding example of that heroism.

Yosef Argaman is a writer and a journalist. He is at present the deputy editor of the army magazine Ba-machaneh.

PART III

THE STRUGGLE
FOR
INDEPENDENCE

1939–1947

As World War II raged around the globe, David Ben-Gurion, by now the undisputed leader of the Yishuv in Palestine, reached a fateful decision. The time was ripe, he thought, for Jewish independence. The First World War had brought about the Balfour Declaration; the Second World War should result in the creation of a Jewish state. In the middle of the war, Ben-Gurion established the new goal of the Zionist movement. In May 1942, in a speech before the American Zionists at the Biltmore Hotel in New York, Ben-Gurion presented the Biltmore Program, calling for the creation of a Jewish state immediately after the war. The Biltmore Program soon became the new banner of the Zionist movement.

Still, Great Britian furiously rejected the idea of Jewish independence. Winston Churchill, who was sympathetic to Zionist aspirations, lost the premiership to Clement Attlee. Under the influence of Foreign Secretary Ernest Bevin, Attlee's government stubbornly refused to admit into Palestine even a trickle of Jewish survivors, who were just emerging from the most horrible ordeal in human history.

The Jewish community in Palestine launched a resistance campaign against the British. For the Hagana and the majority of the Yishuv, the struggle again was diversified: establishment of new settlements in spite of the British; a political campaign, mainly in the United States, intensified by a propaganda war in the world media; and armed operations against British strategic objectives. Aliya Bet, illegal immigration, was used to fight against the British blockade, to bring Holocaust survivors to Eretz Israel, and to alert the world's public opinion. That was how the Hagana ship *Exodus 1947*, whose plight made headlines in the world press, was to play a major role in the struggle for Jewish independence.

The Irgun Tzvai Leumi (National Military Organization, also called by the acronym Etzel), affiliated to the Revisionists, and a smaller splinter group, Lehi (the acronym for Lohamei Herut Israel Fighters for the Freedom of Israel, called by the British the Stern Gang, after its slain founder), launched incessant attacks, bombings, and other violent operations against

British and Arab objectives. One of the leaders of the Lehi, operating in the underground, was known only by his war name, Michael. His real name was Itzhak Shamir. A young Jew, recently arrived in Palestine with the Polish army, became the legendary leader of the Irgun. His name was Menachem Begin. Ben-Gurion and his party regarded Begin and the Etzel as dangerous and irresponsible people, and publicly condemned their deeds. Except for a short period of cooperation, the relations between the Hagana and the Etzel were utterly hostile.

The struggle against the British reached its dénouement on November 29, 1947, when the United Nations voted for the partition of Palestine into two sections and the establishment of a Jewish state and a Palestinian state. The Jews rejoiced and accepted. The Arabs angrily rejected the partition plan.

On the day after the UN vote, Israel's War of Independence began.

FATEFUL NIGHT IN HANITA

YAACOV BERGER

by Efraim Katzir

"What will night bring to Hanita?" asked a song that was very popular in Palestine at the end of the 1930s and 1940s. The answer: "There is a watch at Hanita / All night long." During the first watch at Hanita on the night it was established, Yaacov Berger died. Yaacov was my friend and commander in the Hagana in Jerusalem. I knew him as a brave man, dedicated with all his heart—to the bitter end—to Zionist ideas, a true hero of the times, of the stormy days of the 1936–39 riots, and the era of the "tower and stockade."

Yaacov Berger was born in Poland, in 1907, in the town of Jandzhov. He came from a wealthy family that maintained its Jewish heritage, and he was given a traditional Jewish upbringing. Later, since the Jewish community in his town was so small, he was sent to a Polish secondary school. He did well in his studies, but did not feel part of the Polish culture that predominated there. He tried to make contact with the new Jewish entity that was forming just after the First World War; eventually he found what he was looking for. At the age of sixteen he went to the district capital and joined the Hashomer Hatzair youth movement. He had already heard about this new movement. He knew that its members were young people, like him, who were fed up with the old ways and were looking for a different kind of society, which they planned to establish in Eretz Israel. Now he saw them with his own eyes and was very impressed. When he returned home he brought something new. He set up a Hashomer Hatzair branch there and became the life and soul of all its activities.

He became so involved in the youth movement that finally the Polish secondary school gave him an ultimatum: unless he stopped his activities in Hashomer Hatzair, he wouldn't be able to continue his studies. Yaacov Berger had no doubts about his choice. He had already decided to make *aliya* to Palestine and become a laborer, earning his living by the sweat of his brow. The school no longer had anything to offer him. He quit school and became totally involved in the activities of the movement. At the age of seventeen and a half, however, he led his friends into an adventure that was unheard of in the Jewish society of those days. He convinced a few other young Jews to quit their studies at the secondary school and to begin preparing for the life of pioneers, which meant agricultural work in Palestine. The group found a farm in a village near their town and began to do hard physical labor. The conditions were difficult; more than once they went hungry. But Yaacov Berger did not allow them to give up. He himself did all kinds of work, especially the jobs that others were not particularly eager to do, such as working in the farm garbage pit. He became a source of courage and perseverance for all his friends.

In the spring of 1926 he was given an opportunity to make *aliya* to Palestine. One of his friends begged him to wait for him so that they could go together, but Yaacov refused to wait. In June of that year he reached the port of Jaffa, and he discovered a grim reality. A serious economic recession had hit the Jewish community. He thought he could find a place for himself on a kibbutz and make use of the experience he had acquired in his training period, but he was unable to do so. In fact, he couldn't find any way to make a living. Things got so bad that for two weeks he had to sleep outdoors, on the Tel Aviv beach. He later found a stable for mules in the south of town where he could sneak in at night and sleep in the hay. But throughout this entire period he never lost hope. He was sure that everything would work out and refused to accept any help from his parents.

After a while he moved to Jerusalem, where he joined the Hagana. In those days this was not a simple matter. The Jerusalem branch of the organization was very cautious about the trustworthiness and loyalty of its members. Nobody was admitted to this secret organization without the recommendation of two senior members, or before he was warned that his only way out of the organization would be death. He was also questioned for hours about his opinions, and had to swear to observe the discipline and the secrecy rules of the organization. Those who were accepted, as Yaacov Berger soon learned, had to devote a lot of their time to the organization. The doctrine of the Hagana was learned in lessons during one evening in the middle of each week and on Saturday mornings. For security reasons the lessons were given out of town (in Atarot and Kiryat Anavim, among other places). Of course, transportation arrangements were not the best, and many had to get there on foot. One of his teachers had this to say about Yaacov and his two friends: "Their financial situation was very bad. Despite the fact that they were very good friends, all three of them never showed up at a lesson together. I noticed that from time to time one or the other of them would be missing. I demanded an explanation, and then I learned the real reason for their absence—the three of them together had only two pairs of shoes, and so one of them had to stay home and get the details of the lesson from his more fortunate friends who had been able to go."

Eventually Yaacov paid off this debt to the Hagana. He got a job in the government telephone department, and later became a permanent worker in the electric company. People would meet him at that time walking on stormy winter nights to Kibbutz Ramat Rachel for his courses and other activities. When questioned about his diligence he would answer, "I promised I wouldn't miss lessons when I had shoes." In the winter of 1929 there was a period of friction in the Jerusalem branch, which left it without a senior command. Most of the work fell to low-ranking officers, and Yaacov Berger emerged as one of the best. In the summer, when things were getting worse in the branch, these officers demanded that the national center of the Hagana send someone with authority. Avraham Ikar, one of the members of the Jewish Legion in the First World War and the commander of the Hagana in Tel Aviv, was sent to Jerusalem as a temporary commander and began to organize the forces. Yaacov Berger immediately stood out among the 250 members that he had to choose from.

Rachel Yanait, a labor leader and writer, and the wife of Itzhak Ben-Zvi, a future president of Israel, wrote about the events of the time: "In the whole country there seems to be a strained atmosphere. Around the Western Wall the tension is rising. . . . Everyone is waiting for Friday, the seventeenth of Av. Worrying rumors are spreading rapidly. The Arabs in the mixed neighborhoods are leaving their homes. Everyone says the Arabs are going to riot on Friday when they come out of the mosque. Our greatest worry is the Old City. Our best men—Avraham Ikar, Yosef Rochel [later known as Avidar, and a major general in the IDF], Yaacov Berger . . . have been sent there."

Yaacov Berger, considered one of "our best men," was in fact there on the Friday that the bloody riots of 1929 broke out. He was positioned at the fringe of the Jewish Quarter. When he heard that Arabs armed with clubs and knives were congregating around Zion Gate and planning to storm the Jewish Quarter from there, he hurried over there at the head of a small group of Hagana men and scared them off with a few shots. He then entrenched himself by Zion Gate and fought a long shooting battle with an armed group. "Four of them stood in front of the gate and blocked the road to the rioters," wrote one of the members of the Hagana who had been an eyewitness. "Four against hundreds! Among the four was Yaacov. With a daring and defiant look he inspired and encouraged his friends. For four hours the battle continued. The rioters' scheme was thwarted. They did not manage to get through the gate. Four defenders managed to fend off hundreds of rioters."

At one point the Arabs sent a small boy to check out the area and tell them what was happening. Yaacov Berger caught him and after a short interrogation told him to go back to those who had sent him and tell them that Jews don't murder children. Afterward, he requested from Avraham Ikar that he be moved into the New City, because there was greater danger there. Ikar described the exchange. "He spoke with tears in his eyes—'I can't sit around doing nothing. I don't want to be an officer. Give me something to do, no matter how difficult.' He knew that I had chosen him as my replacement in the Old City and that there was no way of letting him out of there."

The riots passed, but they left many casualties and scars. The Hagana was badly shaken up, and some members even broke away (forming the basis for the right-wing Irgun Tzvai Leumi). Yaacov Berger reached his own conclusions. He began to devote himself vigorously to the activities of the Hagana, more than once risking his job. He worked with determination to close the ranks after the split. He taught courses and purchased arms. Under the command of

Yaacov Pat, who was appointed the head of the Hagana in Jerusalem, companies of young men were set up. I had the honor of belonging to one of these. The city was divided into six areas, and Yaacov Berger was made the commander of one of them. In the beginning he was in charge of Area E (which included Tel Arza, Sanhedria, Batei Ungarn, Kerem Avraham, and the neighborhoods of Shimon Hatzadik and Mount Scopus). Later he was put in charge of Area B (which covered the south of the city as far as the southern end of Kibbutz Ramat Rachel).

During that time I got to know him well. I took part in a course for lieutenants that he organized in the basement of the university on Mount Scopus. The figure of this skillful, determined man, who always wore riding breeches and radiated authority, made a great impression on me. The impression became even stronger when I heard how, after being hospitalized in Hadassah Hospital in 1933, he ran away when he heard about the tension in the area under his command. And, of course, when he gave me my basic military training and taught me, for example, how to move around at night without fear, I felt that here was someone on whom I could depend. In 1934, when the Jewish institutions acquired the rights to the Hula Valley and there was a pressing need for guards on this swampy land, Yaacov Berger was one of those sent. (This meant that he was considered one of the best Hagana fighters in the whole country.) Two years later, when the 1936 riots broke out, he was again chosen to serve in the front lines, in the "spearhead" of the action, as it was later called.

On May 16, 1936, Arabs opened fire on patrons leaving the Edison Movie Theater in the middle of Jerusalem and killed three of them. The Hagana headquarters in Jerusalem decided on an immediate reaction, and Yaacov Berger was chosen to carry it out. He drove to an Arab café, Lifta, in the Romema Quarter, which was known as a meeting place for the gangs, and threw two grenades inside, killing three of the well-known rioters from the village of Lifta. He did the same thing in the western part of the city, in an area that was exposed to the fire of the surrounding villages. When he heard about Itzhak Sadeh's initiative in setting up the "Roaming Force"—the basis for all the future commando units of the IDF—he became very enthusiastic and set up a "roaming force" of his own.

He gathered together a group of young men and women. I was one of them, and so was Shoshana Gershonovitch, later the head of the Women's Corps in the Israeli army. He began to train us in guerrilla warfare. He taught us how to shoot revolvers quickly and with precision, how to move around in secret, how to tail someone, and other such things. We learned and practiced in the field. To this day I can remember the patrols I carried out under Yaacov Berger's command in the center of Jerusalem, armed with grenades and a revolver, well disguised, with a thick mustache and a big hat, walking past people I knew without being recognized. "Be prepared when you face your enemy," he would tell us over and over again.

It is hard to know what might have happened to this group, since Yaacov Berger never managed to actually take it into action. In the beginning of 1938, after the Peel Commission made public its intentions to establish a Jewish state in part of Palestine, it became necessary to increase the number of settlements on the northern border. As part of these efforts, land was bought in Galilee for a new settlement called Hanita.

The tower-and-stockade settlement that would be set up there was supposed to gain a foothold for the Jewish community in the area and serve as a springboard for further efforts. Everyone knew that this was a great and daring mission. The name Hanita aroused then the same emotions that the name Entebbe would arouse in 1976. As part of the detailed preparations that were being made, a "conquering group" of about ninety hand-picked people was set up. There was, in some cases, stiff competition among the candidates vying to be chosen for this group. It would be their job to stay in Hanita and defend it against the inevitable Arab attacks, after it had been set up by a larger group of four hundred people. It was clear that the conquering group would have to fight more than one battle to defend Hanita.

Yaacov Berger was among the first to be chosen for the group. He naturally also took part in the actual setting up of the settlement, helping to build the fortifications. At nightfall a storm broke out, which gave the Arabs cover for the fierce attack they launched on Hanita. Yaacov was among those who quickly returned fire, repelling the attack. But during the battle he was wounded. He told the medic who came to his aid that there were others more seriously wounded than he.

This turned out not to be true. He was transferred in a convoy to the hospital in Haifa, where, after great suffering, he died a week later.

Over the years, when I have visited his grave again and again at Ramat Rachel, I have thought of the song that the songwriter Yaacov Orland, also one of his students in the Hagana, wrote in Yaacov's memory: "For every thousand that have fallen/ A thousand others will rise/ Until a miraculous day will come to the mountains of Galilee./ If the hand of your enemy hurt and wounded you/ We would build, Hanita,/ Your walls for you."

Yaacov Berger was a living example of the promise: "For every thousand that have fallen/ A thousand others will rise."

Efraim Katzir, a scientist, is a former president of Israel.

I DIDN'T THINK TWICE

ZVI BRENNER

by Yosef Eshkol

"Once, in conversation with a son of the kibbutz I was asked, 'Did you do what you did because you were a Zionist?'" said Zvi Brenner, a member of Kibbutz Afikim. "I looked at him and answered, 'To tell you the truth, I didn't think twice about why I was doing it. Those were the conditions in the country, and if I wanted to play an active role, then that was what I had to do. I was aware of the consequences, I knew I could be wounded or killed.'"

This story of doing without thinking twice began in the town in Poland where Zvi Brenner was born in 1915. In his youth he joined the Hehalutz Hatzair Zionist youth movement and took part in its activities. He listened eagerly to the stories of the leaders about the building up of Eretz Israel. The Hashomer heroes became his heroes. After he finished elementary school, he went to live in Chicago with his mother, who had previously divorced his father, remarried, and started a new family.

In Chicago, Zvi joined a Zionist youth movement, and in 1930 he was one of the founders of the Hehalutz movement in the United States. Within a short time this movement set up four training groups—groups of young men and women who prepared themselves for a cooperative lifestyle and for agricultural work in Eretz Israel. Zvi himself joined a group in Parkville, Maryland. He and his friends worked a small plot of land and lived under crowded conditions in a ramshackle house, without running water. Once a week he and his friends would go into town, to a public bathhouse. They were not able to subsist from what they grew on the farm, and there were days when the group went hungry. In 1934 the Hehalutz movement in the United States got forty certificates—permits to immigrate to Palestine—and Zvi was chosen as one of the immigrants. Along with his friends he came to the newly founded Kibbutz Afikim, whose tents were temporarily located on the lands of Kibbutz Kinneret, while their permanent site was being built. (Afikim today is the largest kibbutz in Israel.) This new kibbutznik (kibbutz member) was assigned to work on the construction of the site. This meant that, besides his actual workload, he also had to walk daily back and forth between Kinneret and Afikim, in the stifling Jordan Valley.

He was soon co-opted by the Hagana and was given a special construction task. Along with another kibbutznik, he spent many nights digging the arms cache of Afikim under the storeroom of the new kitchen. He did not disclose the details of this job even to his wife.

As if the oppressive heat of the Jordan Valley and the hard physical labor were not enough, the American newcomers also had problems being accepted by the Russian kibbutz members. "Many times," said Zvi, "and not only during that period, but later on as well, I asked myself what was keeping us there, despite the difficulties. I think that mainly it was the feeling that we were part of something important. The longer I lived on the kibbutz the more I felt that the kibbutz system was the way to build up the country. You have the feeling that something is being built from scratch, and it all belongs to you. This gives you the courage to aspire to even greater things. The kibbutz was always my home."

During the riots of 1936, Kibbutz Afikim was asked to send two members to help out at Kibbutz Ramat Hakovesh in the Sharon plain, which was under attack. Zvi insisted on being one of those to go, and the kibbutz agreed. For a few weeks he took part in the defense of the place, either at positions inside the kibbutz itself or at small, isolated concrete positions in the orange groves. He also kept up communication—thanks to his knowledge of English—with the British military unit that was stationed in the area.

No sooner had he returned to Afikim than Zvi was asked by the Hagana to join the unit of railway auxiliary police that had been set up by the Mandate government. To that end he was sent on a course to Sheikh Abrek. The teachers of the course were English, and almost no one else taking the course understood the language, so Zvi became the interpreter. From time to time he would add things of his own that he had learned in the Hagana. But at the end of the course he did not join the railway police. The Hagana dispatched him to several training assignments, and he was even asked to take part in setting up a few of the tower-and-stockade settlements.

The most daring of these operations was the setting up of Hanita, which was built in the heart of hostile Arab land near the Lebanese border. (See "Fateful Night in Hanita.") Once again Zvi managed to convince his friends in Afikim to allow him to volunteer for the mission. On the day that Hanita was established, March 21, 1938, the Hagana commandeered four hundred of its men from all over the country, among them a hundred from the "field squads" under the command of Itzhak Sadeh, Igal Alon, and Moshe Dayan. A long convoy of trucks brought the people close to their destination. There they loaded on their backs posts and barbed wire for the fence, wooden frames for the wall, and material to build a watchtower in the center of the settlement. Then they climbed a wooded, rocky hill. By evening a few tents had already been set up on the spot, surrounded by a temporary barbed wire fence.

Most of the people went back home the same day, and of the "conquering group" only ninety men remained. After a few hours there was a fierce attack against the new settlement.

One of the defenders was killed; another was wounded badly, and died from his wounds a few days later. During the following nights further attacks were made, while in the daytime the construction of the settlement continued. The Mandate police arrived from time to time from a station that was ten kilometers away, and ordered the settlers to leave "for their own safety."

As opposed to this apathetic, and even hostile, treatment by the British, the sympathetic attitude of Captain Charles Orde Wingate was quite remarkable. (See "Gideon Goes to War.") Wingate, who came from a Christian background and was quite well versed in the Bible, supported the right of the Jews to establish their own state in Eretz Israel. After much effort he managed to convince his superiors to allow him to set up a small force made up of both British and Jewish volunteers. This force would carry out night patrols and attack Arab gangs in the areas that until then had been under Arab control.

Wingate visited Hanita often and used it as a base for patrols in the area. When he first arrived there he aroused the suspicions of the Hagana commanders on the spot. Zvi, the English speaker, was ordered to accompany him and keep an eye on him. Later, when Wingate asked the local commander for a few men to accompany him on short patrols in the area, Zvi was one of those chosen.

One of the targets of Arab attacks at the time was the oil pipeline from Iraq to Haifa, which passed through Ramat Isachar in the Jezreel Valley. In order to defend this pipeline, at the beginning of 1938 Wingate set up a unit made up of Jews and British soldiers. This unit was the basis for the Special Night Squads (SNS) which were formed soon after. The base of one of these squads was at Afikim, and Zvi Brenner was called back from Hanita to become its commander. Under the command of Wingate, Zvi took part in many night sorties, which often ended in violent clashes with Arab gangs.

The first large operation of the night squad that Zvi participated in was the night raid on the village of Daburia, at the foot of Mount Tabor, in July 1938. Wingate was wounded in this operation and as a result he was given a medal by the British and promoted. Two months later a large raid was organized on the Bedouin encampment in the southern part of the Jezreel Valley. In this raid the fighters in the night squad killed fourteen gang members who had been encamped in the area, without themselves suffering a single casualty.

One night an Arab informer requested an urgent meeting with a Hagana intelligence officer. He revealed that the Arab gang leaders were offering a large sum of money to whoever would murder Wingate. "The Friend," as he was called, therefore couldn't travel around without protection. But being surrounded with bodyguards was totally against his character and method of operation. He flatly refused to accept protection of any kind. In the end he agreed to have one bodyguard, and suggested Zvi Brenner for the job. For a few months Zvi traveled with Wingate all over the country. "Wingate was armed with an English rifle and a few hand grenades, and I always held a hand grenade in one hand and a revolver in the other," said Zvi. In Jerusalem he lived in Wingate's apartment and went out with him to return fire when an Arab gang shot at the houses in the neighborhood.

In May 1939 Wingate left Palestine. Zvi returned to the Night Squads, which continued to function on a limited scale. Later he went back to Afikim. From there he was called out from time to time for retaliatory raids against the Arab terrorist gangs.

Summer came, and Zvi was sent to a Hagana course for platoon commanders in Yavniel. The course, like most other Hagana activities, was illegal. The British found out where the course was to take place, so it was moved to Juara. The forty-three instructors and students who set out at night to the new location were spotted along the way. The British arrested them and took them to the central Mandate prison in Acre. Without Wingate, there was nobody to help the Hagana fighters. Like the rest of them, Zvi was interrogated that night and badly beaten by the British, but he gave away nothing. Years later he remembered that night: "All I wanted to do was faint. I waited for the moment when I would lose consciousness and no longer feel the blows. That moment actually arrived. I felt like I was diving, sinking into numbness. But not for long. A pail of cold water was poured on me and brought me back to reality. There I was again, standing against the wall with that blinding light in my eyes, being questioned again and beaten again."

The forty-three Hagana prisoners were brought to trial in a military court and sentenced to ten years in prison (except for one, Avshalom Tao, who was sentenced to life imprisonment). Due to the pressure of the Jewish establishment, and to the danger that Nazi Germany was about to occupy the Middle East, they were released after eighteen months.

Zvi went back to Afikim, but not for long. A few months later, he was in the Jordan Valley, training Hagana field forces. At the same time, the Hagana was organizing a commando unit of fighters to sabotage oil installations in Lebanon, which was then occupied by pro-German French troops. Zvi was supposed to join them, but his commanders in the Jordan Valley delayed his departure to the commando training camp. When he finally got there, the twenty-four saboteurs had already sailed in a boat called *The Sea Lion*. The boat disappeared in the Mediterranean, and none of the young fighters was ever seen again.

The early successes of the Germans aroused deep anxiety in the Jewish community. The Hagana leaders even planned to create a formidable redoubt in the Carmel mountains, where they would fight a last-ditch battle in case the Germans actually reached Palestine. For the same reason, more pressure was put on the British authorities to allow Palestinian Jews to join the British army and help fight the Nazis. Zvi had in the meantime married Ruth—his girlfriend from the days of Hanita, the Night Squads, and prison—and had become the father of a son, Eli. He asked the Hagana leadership to allow him to join the British army. When he didn't get an immediate answer, he announced that he would join anyway. For the first time in his life he disobeyed Hagana orders, in order to do what he believed was his duty.

"Those who joined the British army had two goals," said Zvi: "fighting the Germans, and strengthening our own independent forces. So we tried to learn as much as we could, and acquire arms secretly, both from the stockpiles of the British army and from the booty that was taken during the war. At a later stage, we added a third goal to our activities—to reach the European Holocaust survivors, organize them, and bring them back to Eretz Israel."

The British were in no hurry to send Jewish Palestinian volunteers to the battlefield, and for a long time Zvi's assignments were guarding arms dumps (as well as transferring some of these arms to the Hagana). When the Jewish Brigade was finally formed as part of the British army at the end of 1944, Zvi was one of its soldiers. After a difficult training period in the Egyptian desert, the Brigade went to Italy. There they were given further training under harsh winter conditions. In March 1945 they reached the front line in northern Italy, and finally got the opportunity to fight the Germans.

Each night the Brigade soldiers would go out on fighting sorties into the mined no-man's-land between the two front lines, and often come upon enemy patrols, at very close range. On one of these sorties Zvi was seriously wounded. He recalled:

> At nightfall we went out into no-man's-land, crossed the trench, and took up positions in the woods, as usual. Until two in the morning nothing out of the ordinary happened. There was mortar fire and fire from medium-sized machine guns, here and there the cry of a soldier who had been hit, but we were used to that. I was at a position with an officer, Asael Davidson. Suddenly we heard some rustling close by and immediately after that a burst of gunfire. The Germans had managed to sneak up and surprise us. They were very close. I could hear them shouting in German: "Damnation! A filthy Jew!"
>
> "There's no choice," I said to Asael. "Someone has got to get out of the fox-hole and throw some hand grenades."
>
> "Who?" he asked.
>
> "I'll go," I answered. "You cover me." At the same moment I jumped out, and as soon as I got out of the trench I was wounded in the shoulder by a burst of fire. I felt that I was getting wet, that some liquid was running inside my clothes. I said to Asael, "I'm wounded, but I can go on. Give me grenades, and I'll throw them." After I had thrown about twenty grenades a German grenade exploded beside me. The explosion knocked me down. About twenty pieces of shrapnel penetrated my leg. The bottom part of my leg was left hanging by a piece of skin. I saw bones sticking out of my flesh. The pain was awful, but fortunately I didn't lose consciousness. I decided to crawl backward, and in the meantime more soldiers arrived with a machine gun and started shooting at the Germans. I got to the edge of the trench and just rolled out of it toward the other edge. There they put me on a jeep and took me to the first-aid tent.

For a few very painful months Zvi was moved from one military hospital to the next. Aside from the pain from the wounds and surgeries, he also had to adjust to being disabled, even after he began walking without crutches. It took quite a few years for Zvi to find a proper work-place in the kibbutz after that.

A short time after the War of Independence broke out, Zvi was appointed head instructor of the Hagana officers' school. When the fighting intensified, the school was closed down, and he was put in charge of drafting new immigrants arriving in the country. And then came, to his great surprise, the order to leave immediately for the United States. He was to buy arms on the black market, since the American government had put an embargo on arms shipments to the Middle East. He also was to draft young American Jews as volunteers for the war.

Zvi and the other members of the delegation, which was headed by Teddy Kollek (later mayor of Jerusalem), bought almost anything, from explosives and ammunition to planes and warships. The equipment and people that were smuggled out of the United States made an in-valuable contribution to Israel during the most difficult war it has ever known.

The American authorities knew about this illegal activity and tried to prevent it. More than once Zvi risked being arrested for serious crimes. On the other hand, his contact with under-world figures—who helped him get arms and smuggle them out of the country—put him in great danger as well. But in these underworld circles there were also Jews, who wanted to con-tribute their share—in their way—to the creation of the State of Israel. In the end everything worked out for the best.

A little more than a year later Zvi returned to Afikim. Since then he has held central posi-tions on the kibbutz and in the kibbutz movement. He has refused all offers of jobs abroad, from an ambassadorship to undercover work for the Mossad (the Israeli Secret Service).

Over the years he became close friends with David Ben-Gurion, the first prime minister of Israel. According to Ben-Gurion's assistant, Chaim Israeli, he considered Zvi "the embodiment of goodness and camaraderie, a pioneering figure that represented more than anyone what is written in the book of Micah: 'to do justly, and to love kindness, and to walk humbly with thy God' [Micah 6:8]. . . . When we asked Ben-Gurion during the writing of his will who he would like to have as the executors, one of the first names he mentioned was Zvi Brenner from Afikim."

Yosef Eshkol is a writer and a journalist.

A GRENADE BETWEEN TWO HEARTS

MEIR FEINSTEIN AND MOSHE BARAZANI

by Arye Naor

Yes, the death cell soared that night.
At its sight
The heads of a conquering nation
Caught by the light, like a mouse, were drawn back into their holes
Like a thief caught in the act.
Natan Alterman—Davar, the 5th of Iyar, 5707 (April 18, 1947)

They were twenty years old.

Meir Feinstein wanted to be a writer. He had plans for the future, and he had a girl that he loved. Moshe Barazani was a blue-collar worker in a soft-drink factory. From an early age he had helped to support his needy family. Meir was born in the Old City of Jerusalem. Moshe was born in Baghdad, and immigrated with his family to Palestine as a child. Both of them grew up in Jerusalem; both of them were sons of learned Jewish families. Meir was the descendant of rabbis from Brisk (Brest-Litovsk) in Lithuania. Moshe came from a family of scholars in Baghdad. They met only in the central prison, wearing loose red uniforms. The color red meant they had been sentenced to death. Above all they both wanted the rebirth of the State of Israel, the liberation of the homeland, and the redemption of its people. Meir started off in the Palmach, joined the British army, and from there drifted to the Etzel. Moshe joined the Lehi.

Meir was wounded on October 30, 1946, during an Etzel attack on the Jerusalem train station from which the British army transported troops. The Irgun members arrived in the station—which of course was well guarded—in two cars. The first car carried fighters disguised as Arab porters, who would carry several suitcases; the other transported Etzel members disguised as the wealthy family of a bride and groom, on their way to their honeymoon, who owned the suitcases. Meir was the driver of the second car. The suitcases were filled with explosives. They arrived at the station as planned and unloaded the suitcases at the proper place. The "bride" started putting up warning signs for the public. An Arab who worked at the station tried to stop her. Her escorts shot at the Arab and ran to the cars. Soldiers and policemen chased after them, and before the Etzel members reached the car, the British opened fire on them at close range. Meir's left arm was wounded in several places, but he still managed to drive as far as the neighborhood of Yemin Moshe, not far from the station. There he looked for refuge for himself and his friend Daniel Azulai, who had also been wounded. While this was going on, the suitcases exploded, and the fortified station was destroyed. A police officer who had tried to defuse one of the bombs paid for his efforts with his life.

The blood dripping from the wounds of Meir and Daniel, while they walked through Yemin Moshe, made things easier for their pursuers. Meir was caught and taken to a hospital, where his left hand was amputated. The British moved him from prison to prison over a period of a few months, until he was brought to trial on March 25, 1947.

When Meir's trial began, Moshe had already been sentenced to death by hanging. He was caught by chance by the British on March 9, three days after the Etzel attack on the Schneller Camp, which was used by the British army in Jerusalem. In the nearby Mekor Baruch neighborhood three British policemen were on patrol. Their job was to track down people suspected of terrorism. They came across Moshe Barazani and ordered him to stop. While searching his belongings they found a hand grenade. During his interrogation at the police station Moshe tried to explain that a stranger had given him 100 mils—not an insignificant sum of money for a poor boy at the time—if he would hide the grenade until he returned. "I wouldn't have done this," he said innocently to his interrogators, "if I hadn't been hungry." But his performance did not help him. The military prosecutor decided to try him for carrying a weapon, a crime that was punishable, according to the emergency regulations, by the death penalty.

The minute the trial began Moshe changed his tactics. He refused to be represented by a lawyer, and during the whole trial he sat and read the Bible. When he was asked whether he pleaded guilty, he got up and said to his judges: "The Hebrew people see you as the enemy and a foreign ruler in its homeland. We, the people of Lehi, are fighting you in order to liberate our homeland. I have become a prisoner in this war, and you have no right to judge me. You will not frighten us by hangings, nor will you succeed to destroy us. My nation and all other subjugated nations will fight your empire till the end."

He finished what he had to say, which expressed in essence the view of Lehi about the war for the liberation of the homeland and the general struggle against Imperialism. He sat down and went back to reading his Bible. The trial began at 10:25 on the morning of March 17. It took his judges only ninety minutes to hear the witnesses, look over the documents, consider their verdict, and decide—ninety minutes, the length of a soccer game. At 11:55 the presiding judge announced their decision: "You will be hanged by your neck until you die."

Moshe Barazani was prepared for this. He stood up, repeated his cry: "You will not frighten us by hangings," and began singing "Hatikva," the Jewish national anthem. The policemen tied him hand and foot and dragged him out of the courtroom before he could finish singing. He cried out: "To the *Yishuv*—be strong and of good courage!"

Meir was tried a week after Moshe. The trial began on March 25 and lasted eight days. Meir was brought to trial with three of his friends. Two of them pleaded guilty, as they had been told to do by Irgun headquarters, and were eventually released for lack of evidence connecting them to the attack on the train station. Meir Feinstein and Daniel Azulai, who were caught wounded, could not deny their connection to the operation. They declared that they did not recognize the authority of the court to judge them. From that moment on they ignored what was going on in the courtroom, except for one incident on the sixth day of the proceedings. Meir demanded the right to interrogate one of the witnesses, a British policeman. He held out to him a book by Abba Ahimeir, a right-wing ideologue, which he had been given as a present from his girlfriend and his brother. He asked the policeman if he knew who had drawn a swastika on the cover. "Hitler is perhaps dead," he said, "but Bevin's friends [Ernest Bevin, the British foreign minister, was a staunch enemy of Zionism] do not put him to shame. . . ."

Toward the end of the trial Meir was allowed to speak. He read a written statement to the judges, in which he expressed, with impressive rhetoric, Etzel's ideology, which connected the war against the British to the lessons of the Holocaust:

> Officers of the occupying army:
>
> A regime of hanging scaffolds—this is the regime you want to impose upon this country, a country that is meant to be a source of inspiration to the whole world. In your foolish wickedness you assume that with this regime you will manage to break the spirit of our nation, a nation for whom the whole country has become a gallows. You are mistaken. You will discover that you have encountered *steel*. Steel, which is forged in the fire of love and hate—the love of our homeland and liberty; the hate of enslavement and occupation. We are made of burning steel, you will not break us. You will only burn your hands.
>
> How blind you are, you British tyrants. Are you still not aware who you are up against in this campaign, an opponent that has no equal in the history of nations? Do you really think you can scare us with death? We, who for years heard the clicking of the wheels of *those* carriages that led our brothers and sisters, our parents, and the best of our nation, to the slaughter, an act that also has no equal in the history of mankind. We, who asked and continue to ask ourselves daily, how are we better than they, the millions of our brothers? Why have we been allowed to live?

We could have been among them during those days of fear and those moments of dying.

To these questions, which arise again and again, there is but one answer in our conscience: We stayed alive not to live and wait, under conditions of slavery and oppression, for a new Treblinka. We stayed alive in order to promise life, freedom, and honor, to ourselves, and to our sons and grandsons, for generations to come. We stayed alive, so that what happened there would not happen again. What happened there is liable to happen under your rule, a rule of betrayal, a rule of blood. You cannot scare us. We have learned a lesson—at what a cost!—that there is a life worse than death, and there is a death that is greater than life. And if you have not yet understood this phenomenon of a nation that has nothing to lose but its chains of oppression and the prospect of a new Maidanek, then it is a sign that you have been struck blind and that you should get off the stage, from which the Almighty has removed all those who have risen up against our eternal nation. Assyria and Babylon, Greece and Rome, Spain and Germany have preceded you. But you will follow in their footsteps. It is the way of the world.

And as for me, I demand to be treated as a prisoner of war.

Meir and his friend Daniel Azulai were sentenced to death. They rose to their feet and declared, "In blood and fire Judah fell, and in blood and fire it will rise again!" The Barazani and Feinstein families tried to convince their sons to ask for clemency from the authorities, but they refused. "My fate will be the fate of the four other Jews who have been sentenced to death," said Moshe to his lawyer, Gideon Hausner (who was later to be the Israeli state attorney who prosecuted the Nazi war criminal Adolf Eichmann, and later a member of the Knesset, and a government minister). Hausner had been sent to Moshe by his family.

Meir was even more scathing. "What did you do," he rebuked one of his relatives, "when six million were being wiped out in Europe? The most you did was sigh. But now, when it is your own brother, you make such a fuss."

Two weeks after the trial of Feinstein and Azulai, the British executed Dov Gruner, Mordechai Elkahi, Yechiel Drezner, and Eliezer Kashani. The next day the British military commander approved Meir's sentence, and reduced Azulai's punishment to a life sentence. Apparently, immediately after that Meir and Moshe began to plan their last act. Their intention was to follow the example of the hero Samson, who declared, "Let me die with the Philistines," after which he brought down the house upon all of them together. They planned to smuggle explosives into their cell on death row. At the last minute, the two of them would set off the explosives, thereby killing themselves and their executioners together.

The underground managed to smuggle them "that"—as Meir and Moshe referred to it in notes that they smuggled out of the prison: a grenade that was hidden inside an orange. The prisoners in the next cell, to which outside access was easier, assembled the grenade and passed it to the condemned men. The two managed to smuggle out a last note of thanks for the package they had received: "Our final greetings, and do not lose heart because we are paying with our lives. . . . Carry with pride the banner of the revolt and continue until we redeem ourselves (and are redeemed). We proudly walk toward our death."

The execution was scheduled for April 22 in the central prison in Jerusalem, six days after Gruner and his friends had been hung in Acre. The police brought a rabbi to the death cell, to take the confession of the condemned men and to comfort them. They already knew why he was coming. For a long time they talked to him about Jewish martyrdom through the ages and about their love of the homeland, about their families and about their nation. Then they sang together the hymn "Adon Olam," a psalm of faith that ends with these lines:

> I place my soul in his hand
> Before I sleep as when I wake,
> And though I forsake my body,
> God is with me, and I will not fear.

No confessions were made at that meeting. The rabbi later said that he saw no reason to read to these two young men, who were going to the gallows, the list of sins that they had committed or not committed. The martyrdom of self-sacrifice transcends everything. The two young men tried to persuade the rabbi to leave, but he said that he would stay with them to the end. Finally, they convinced him to leave for a few hours—the hanging was scheduled for four in the morning—saying that they wanted to sleep for a while. The rabbi agreed to go, and when they took leave of each other they sang "Hatikva."

Immediately afterward they began their final preparations. They couldn't carry out their original plans and kill themselves with their executioners, because the rabbi had promised to return around the time of the execution, and they were not prepared to endanger his life. So the two of them decided to preempt the hangman.

Around midnight they faced each other, the grenade in their hands. They hugged each other, and pressed the grenade between their chests.

The whole jail echoed with the sound of an explosion. At first the British thought that the Underground had managed to break in, and only after a while did they become aware that the explosion had taken place in the condemned prisoners' cell. The police burst in and found the bloody bodies of Moshe Barazani and Meir Feinstein, lying dead in each other's arms.

As Meir Feinstein had said to his judges: "There is a death that is greater than life."

Arye Naor was previously the government secretary, and is now a lecturer at Hebrew University and at the Israeli college Michlala LeMinhal.

ON A DAY OF SERVICE I FEEL LIKE A COPPER ROD

DOV COHEN

by Yechiel Kadishai

"Did you kill many?" asks the officer.

"About 150 . . . maybe more."

"I heard that you also took prisoners."

"Prisoners . . ."—here the voice of Sharoni is a little shaky and unclear—"The prisoners carried our dead and wounded."

"I see that there are large bloodstains on your pants. Did you also hurt your hand?"

"It's only a small scratch. The large stains are German blood."

"One more question: how many bunkers did you destroy?"

"All of them."

It was not easy to surprise the commander of the Brigade, but this time the answer made a profound impression on him.

"Really? Why, that is an amazing feat! Without support fire I would not have dared to attack the mountain, even with the whole Brigade."

"That's true, sir, but I had to pay for the bullets. . . ."

The colonel opened his eyes wide. "Speak clearly, Sharoni. What bullets are you talking about?"

"Sir, it's a long story. . . ."

"I'm prepared to listen."

"It happened three years ago,"—Sharoni's voice was quiet, and full of sorrow—"in my hometown in Poland. The Germans murdered three thousand Jews, among them two hundred babies. After this mass murder the SS officer, the Obersturmführer Dofler, ordered my brother, who was a local lawyer, to collect from the surviving Jews the sum of a hundred thousand zloti to pay for the bullets that the SS men had wasted in the massacre. The Jews didn't have any money left because it had all been stolen from them during the first weeks of the occupation. My brother managed to collect only a part of the required sum; therefore, the Germans executed the rest of the Jews. From my whole family all that were left were my two younger brothers and I. We swore that we would also pay for the bullets. One brother joined the British commandos and fell in the battle for Keren, in Eritrea; my other brother served in the Polish army and gave his life for the capture of Monte Cassino, and I . . . I tried to pay for the bullets tonight." The colonel did not dare to ask anything more.

This was Dov Cohen's story "The Brothers Sharoni Paid for the Bullets. . . . ," which was sent to the Israeli newspaper *Ha'aretz* on December 30, 1945. This story was clearly autobiographical. A few days earlier Cohen had returned to Palestine, to be discharged from the British army. He was one of the first Palestinian Jewish volunteers in the British army during the Second World War. His ID number, 10182, showed that he was the 182nd volunteer. That was why he was also among the first to be discharged. By the end of 1945 he already knew that his family was dead. During the last few weeks of his stay in Europe he had traveled all over Poland and to all the displaced persons' camps looking for members of his family or people from his hometown of Grodzhanka, or the surrounding area, and found nothing. The information he gathered about the annihilation of the Jews of Poland left not the shadow of a doubt: not even one of his loved ones had survived the Holocaust.

A miserable and tormented man he was, determined to take revenge for those who had been killed. He also felt a dark fury, seeing how Jews were being forbidden entry into Palestine. During the war, he had fought the Germans in a British uniform. Now that he had been discharged, he was going to fight those who wore the same British uniforms in Palestine. The same British soldiers and officers who had been his comrades in arms in the struggle against Hitler were the enemies in Palestine—preventing the survivors from immigrating into Eretz Israel, imposing harsh restrictions on the Jewish community, and stubbornly opposing the Zionist dream of creating a Jewish state.

Dov Cohen therefore renewed his longtime ties to the Irgun Zvai Leumi (Etzel). Eitan Livni, the deputy commander of the organization, whom he had known for years, immediately appointed him to a command position. He collected his few possessions and left his hotel in southern Tel Aviv for Petach Tikva. Within a few days he became indispensable. There was hardly an operation of the Irgun that Dov, whose war name was Squadron Leader Samson, did not participate in, either as commanding officer or as one of those in charge.

Ten years earlier Dov Cohen had been the head of a small branch of Betar in the Galician town of Grodzhanka, in southeastern Poland. His parents, Sophia and Aharon-Leib Cohen, had given their four children a Zionist education, and all four of them found their way to Jabotinsky's youth movement. They took the seven-paragraph Betar oath, the first part of which stated: "I devote my life to the rebirth of the Hebrew State with a Hebrew majority, on both sides of the Jordan, east and west."

Dov took his oath very seriously. Having been an outstanding student at the Tarbut (Culture) School, he spoke Hebrew well. His enthusiasm and personal charm inspired many other Jewish teenagers from his town and brought them into the youth movement. At the same time he began planning his immigration to Palestine, in order to fulfill his oath. What can I do to be of most value? he asked himself, and found the answer. He signed up for the Navy School of Betar in the Italian port of Civitavecchia. He wanted to become a seaman so he could get involved in illegal Jewish immigration to Palestine. On December 25, 1936, permit no. 17 was sent from the Betar authorities in London, testifying to the fact that the Betar member Bernard Cohen from Grodzhanka had been accepted, and was to report to the commander of the Navy School no later than January 31, 1937. But in the meantime Dov had reconsidered. The news about the bloody riots in Palestine convinced him that young Jews should now be in Eretz Israel, defending the community. He decided to give up on his navy studies in Italy and make *aliya* as soon as possible. Within a few months he was in Palestine.

He reported to the recruiting unit of Betar in Rosh Pina. During the day he worked in the tobacco fields, and at night he was a guard. Later, when he was accepted to Hebrew University in Jerusalem, he joined the "road" unit in Nahalat Itzhak, near Jerusalem. In this unit, which he joined on January 20, 1938, Dov worked in the quarry during the day and spent his nights in defense and guarding assignments. At the same time he discovered the famous poet Uri Zvi Greenberg, one of the spiritual idols of Betar. Greenberg's fiery verses became Dov's Bible. From then on he would often quote the following lines:

> Your masters have taught you: The Messiah will come in generations to come
> And Judea will be reborn without fire, without blood.
> It will be reborn with every tree, with every new house.
> And I say to you: If your generation lags behind
> And does not force the issue by your own hand
> And does not get into the fire, [armed] with the shield of David,
> And the hooves of its horses are not bloodied—
> The Messiah will not come even in future generations
> And Judea will not be reborn.
>
> And you'll be an enslaved nation to every alien ruler.
> Your house will be straw to the spark of every fiend.
> Your tree will be cut down in full fruit.
> Your belly split open by the hand of a foe,
> And the life of a young man and the life of a baby
> Will be the same to the sword of the enemy.

And only your prattle will remain—yours . . .
And the testimony of your disgrace—in a library.
And an eternal curse in the lines of your face.

Dov did not want to be among those who "lag behind." He was determined to "force the issue" in any way he could. Since he was a born writer, he tried to make converts to his ideas through poems and stories that he published in the Irgun newsletters and in the periodical *Gazit*, edited by Gabriel Talpir. But above all he felt that he must learn the art of warfare, especially since the Second World War had broken out and the need to beat the Nazis left him no peace.

He got his opportunity when the Royal Engineers Palestinian Unit was formed at the beginning of 1940. He knew well that it was considered a support unit and would be given mostly dirty work to do. But this did not deter him, as it did many others. From the moment he put on an army uniform, he thought that he would find a way to get onto the battlefield. And he knew what he was talking about. In the summer of 1940 his company became the Fifty-first Commando, Middle East. Dov excelled both in military skills and in remarkable courage.

Dov's commando unit was absorbed into an Indian Division and sent to East Africa. The battles they fought in Amba-Alghi, Keren, and Gonder have entered the history books of the Second World War. Dov's courage and the daring of many of his friends contributed greatly to these victories. Some of them also fell in these battles.

Dov was promoted to the rank of sergeant for his personal contributions. When the unit was disbanded on February 18, 1942, the commanding officer praised Dov's outstanding behavior: "His promotion in the field resulted from his excellent bearing in action."

When the commando unit was disbanded Dov went on to serve in the "Buffs"—the infantry regiment of Palestinian Jewish volunteers—and later joined the Jewish Brigade fighting in Italy during the last months of the war.

The last eighteen months of Dov's life were filled with endless activity, planning, and risky operations. He had become one of the outstanding Etzel fighters against the British. From October 1945 onward he was involved totally in the activities of the Hebrew Resistance Movement, a combined force of the three main underground organizations: the Hagana, Etzel, and Lehi. The crowning achievement of Etzel and Lehi was the attack on the fortress of Acre on May 4, 1947. This was one of the most daring operations carried out by the united Jewish underground against the British: an attack on an apparently impregnable British fortress, in an Arab city, where the British had imprisoned many underground fighters. Some of them had been sentenced to death and were awaiting execution. The goal of the operation was to organize the prisoners' escape. Dov assisted the operations officer Amichai "Gideon" Faglin in planning the operation; later he was put in charge of carrying it out. During the attack he showed great resourcefulness, and when the operation ran into difficulties he did not lose his head.

With a Bren machine gun he covered the retreat of his wounded friends who were trying to escape their British pursuers—and he did not stop until he was shot dead.

David Niv, the editor of the book *The Campaigns of the Irgun Zvai Leumi*, described Dov's death:

> The death of Dov Cohen, the commanding officer of the operation, was a great loss to the Irgun Zvai Leumi, to his fellow soldiers, and to those who shared his beliefs. Cohen was one of the senior commanders in the fighting units of his organization. He was a member of the planning division and, since his release from the British army, he took part, in various command positions, in scores of daring attacks and penetration operations [into British installations]. From the war campaigns against the Germans he brought a lot of war experience to the anti-British struggle. In the Acre operation, the crowning glory of his extremely active life, "Squadron Leader Samson" demonstrated what was later passed on to the officers of the Israeli army as their traditional battle cry: "Follow me!"

Dov Cohen saved Matityahu Shmulevitch's life. Shmulevitch was one of the prisoners in dark-red uniform who awaited the hangman in Acre prison. He escaped during the operation, and later wrote, "The fire was heavy, but we heard Samson's cry clearly: 'Follow me!' " Shmulevitch added: "I did not know Samson previously. But from the first moment I saw him in action I admired him. His restraint and his courage were unmatched. Even when he saw that all was lost, he did not look for a way to save himself, but rather ran straight into the enemy fire to give us a chance to escape. . . ." Twenty-nine Etzel and Lehi prisoners escaped from Acre prison that day.

Dov Cohen reached Eretz Israel because of the first part of the Betar oath. Afterward, until his dying day, he faithfully kept two other parts of the oath:

> Glory:
> From the blood of Gideon I was sown,
> for those like me
> The glory of the descendants of a kingdom is in heart, in body, in all:
> Proud in the face of princes, humble in the face of the poor,
> Prevail—in order to forgive.
> Conscription:
> On a day of service I feel like a copper rod
> Like a lump of iron in the hands of a blacksmith who is called—Zion:
> Mold me as you will—as a scythe, a plow wheel
> Or as a sword and dagger.

Yechiel Kadishai was Prime Minister Menachem Begin's bureau chief

"IF YOU WANT TO SHOOT—SHOOT ME!"

MORDECHAI ROSEMAN

by Nissan Degani

Today we are boarding the ship that will fight the war of survival of the Jewish people. We will march tall with all the people of Israel, at their head and by their right side. We will come to their aid. We will march like our friends in the underground, in the ghettos, in the endeavor for the rescue of Jewish refugees, and in the war for the honor of Israel.

When we sail, we will demonstrate the pioneering and moral spirit of our movement and we will serve as an example to ourselves and to our fellow men.

We will faithfully fulfill our duty and take upon ourselves any task, any assignment and any mission. We will be ready to either reach our homeland, or be cruelly driven back. We will meet the emissaries of the White Paper with dignity and pride, befitting the tradition of our movement.

Be prepared for the final and decisive mission.

Be strong and of good courage!

This was the proclamation that Mordechai Roseman wrote at the port of Sète in France, in July 1947, when he was about to board the *Exodus*.

The readers of this proclamation were the members of Hashomer Hatzair who sailed on that ship. Roseman was a leader in the movement and a member of the Central Committee for Survivors. He organized these people in German refugee camps, brought them to the port of Sète, and led them throughout the days of the voyage and struggle.

He was in his early twenties, but he had already lived a stormy life. He escaped from Poland at the beginning of the Second World War; traveled all the way to Tashkent; returned to Poland in 1944 in a Polish army uniform; and took part in intensive activity for the Bricha.

Roseman's proclamation became a source of inspiration for all the *maapilim* (illegal immigrants), at all stages of their momentous journey: starting with the ramshackle, overloaded ship with its 4,600 passengers slipping out of the French port under the eyes of the British, through the sea voyage, to the bloody battle with the Royal Navy off the coast of Gaza, their dramatic entrance into the port of Haifa, and, in the end—their deportation.

Unlike those on previous illegal immigrant ships, the *Exodus* refugees were not taken by the British, after their capture, to relatively peaceful internment camps in the island of Cyprus. They were put on three British ships headed back to France.

Mordechai Roseman was locked up with 1,500 other refugees (and one escort from the Palyam, the naval arm of the Palmach) on the deportation ship *Runnymede Park*. After two days he realized they were being sent back to Europe. In the burning-hot hold of the deportation ship he had noticed that they were sailing and sailing and had not reached Cyprus. The food rations were bad and inadequate. Roseman became very anxious about the uncertain future, and immediately began to organize the refugees into groups. Later a secretariat was chosen with Roseman at its head. They confronted the commander of the ship and demanded clear answers to their questions. The commander refused to answer, and Roseman declared a general hunger strike.

The colonel was taken aback. He knew that the conditions on the ship were very difficult. This had been done on purpose, in order to wear out the refugees before their arrival in France. But now he feared that a hunger strike under these conditions would have disastrous results, for which he would be blamed. So he agreed to a first concession: the refugees now became responsible for the preparation and distribution of the food. The hunger strike ended. But Roseman started to prepare for the next stage in the struggle. As he said, "The minute we knew that we were headed for Port-de-Bouc, in France, and before we knew what was going to happen and how it would happen, we had already all made up our minds: 'We are not getting off! Absolutely not!' We didn't know if that meant that they would take us off by force or not— but we were not getting off!" He got down to work in earnest, what he described as "a tireless effort to build up our strength." He saw to it that "no one among us went hungry, that order was maintained, and that lectures, speeches, and social gatherings took place without any disturbances."

He said to the commander of the ship, with whom he met regularly: "You claim that we are a gang of terrorists that have taken over the ship, that everyone wants to get off and that we are preventing them from doing so. All right, then, all the other members of the secretariat and I have nothing more to do with the refugees for as long as you want. We won't talk to them. You'll see the reaction. After a short time a new secretariat will be set up with new people and they will also say: 'We are not getting off!'"

The colonel was convinced. Apparently he had found out that on the other two deportation ships—*Ocean Vigour* and *Empire Rival*—the refugees had reacted in a similar way.

The ships dropped anchor in Port-de-Bouc. A French-British delegation boarded the *Runnymede Park* to try to convince the refugees to disembark. Roseman refused to talk to this delegation in private. "You want to talk to all the refugees," he said, "then it's fine; come downstairs." The delegation went down to the hold where the refugees were imprisoned, and when the French representative finished making his promises, Roseman got up and said, "Ladies and gentlemen, France of the French Revolution, with its freedom, we love you, but we are not getting off!" All the refugees stood up and sang "Hatikva."

The reactions of the refugees in the two other ships to the delegations that came to them were essentially the same: "We are not getting off!"

The scores of journalists that gathered at Port-du-Bouc reported on the heroic stand of the refugees, but the deportation ships did not move. At the headquarters of the Mossad le-Aliya Bet (Hagana Institute for Illegal Immigration) they began to fear that the refugees would not be able to endure such difficult conditions for long. They therefore decided to send Israeli emissaries onto the ships. One of them, Avner Giladi, wrote: "The crowding is terrible, people sleep with their legs folded for lack of space. The sanitary facilities are awful, there is filth all around them. . . . Miri, the guy from the Palyam, was very happy to meet with me, but when I told him why I had come, he burst out laughing. He said that they didn't need any help. . . . The man in charge of everything is Mordechai Roseman; everyone does what he says. . . . The mood is very good. Everyone is just waiting to get going again, and they hope it will be to Eretz Israel. . . ."

Seventeen days later he wrote: "Tonight there was an Oneg Shabbat [Friday night service] that finished with a lecture, or actually a speech, by Mr. Roseman. He 'pounded' Zionism into them and had all the Jews in tears. He talked again about our troubles, and that the Jews and the Jewish nation had no other place in the world but Eretz Israel. Whoever wanted to get off here could do so, but he should know that the Jewish people would judge him as a traitor and a deserter from the battlefield, because this is the battle of the Jewish people now."

Roseman's bold, heartfelt words made a strong impression on his friends, since he was one of them. Women in an advanced state of pregnancy refused to disembark and announced that they intended to give birth only in Eretz Israel. Only 130 of the 4,500 refugees responded positively to the French requests. That number included a few dozen whose physical condition was extremely bad, and they had been explicitly ordered by the secretariat to leave.

The ships did not budge. The refugees decided on a hunger strike, which began on the night of August 17. Everyone complied, except for children, sick people, and pregnant women. The strike brought the struggle of the refugees at Port-de-Bouc back into the headlines and gave them political leverage. Representatives of the Jewish Agency in Jerusalem and London had one response to all British appeals: "The Agency can advise the Jewish immigrants to disembark only in Palestine."

These answers and the pressure that American and European statesmen put on the British government did not help. British Foreign Secretary Ernest Bevin decided to send the refugees to Germany, and on August 21 the refugees were given an ultimatum: "Anyone who does not get off the ship by 18:00 on August 22, will be returned by sea to Hamburg."

Roseman responded to this forcefully: "Anyone who wants to can get off," he said to the refugees, "but we will all spit in their faces, as will the whole Jewish nation. Our war is the war for the survival of the Jewish people and there is no retreat. The scoundrels, the murderers, want to destroy us and send us back to the hell we came out of. We cannot accept that. They will only take us off these ships by force. We cannot go back to that country. We must collect and keep every bottle and anything else that can be used as a weapon in our resistance."

The commander of the *Runnymede Park* had good reason to report to his superiors: "The presence on this ship of strong, fanatic leaders of Polish extraction has created a different problem here than on the other two ships. The negotiators on the other ships are Americans; they have taken a much more rational approach and are cooperating. Mordechai Roseman has stirred them up and incited them to rebel ever since they left Port-de-Bouc. . . ."

The deportation ships sailed to Hamburg, and the whole way Roseman prepared the refugees to resist being taken off the ship. He still emphasized, though, that all of them could decide for themselves whether they wanted to get off or only show passive resistance, which would mean that it would take quite a few soldiers to remove each refugee, and the whole process would take a long time. To make things harder the refugees decided to take apart the staircase that led to the upper deck. When they started doing this the captain appeared, drew his gun, and threatened them: "If you take those stairs apart I will shoot you." Roseman, who was immediately called over, announced: "Sir, you want to shoot, go right ahead. I'm your first candidate! Whether you want it or not we are going to take these stairs apart. . . . One staircase is still intact; anyone who wants to disembark is welcome."

"Are you in charge here?" the captain asked. "I'm in charge," answered Roseman, and the captain walked off.

The confrontation that occurred later, at the port of Hamburg, was hard, as the British commander's report shows:

"The first Jews who were taken fought ferociously, all the way. . . . They bombarded us with bottles. . . . It was very frightening to go down into the hold that was full of raving maniacs, six or eight on each soldier. . . . In the first confrontation soldiers were knocked down with a half dozen Jews on top of them, hitting them and going wild. The soldiers used clubs for self-defense and firehoses as well . . . to stop this group of fanatic resisters. It was a tough battle. . . ."

Thirty refugees, Roseman among them, were taken to the hospital. The British beat him up badly. When he got a little better they moved him to the refugees' detention camp at Poppendorf.

Here the refugees got reorganized, based on the experience they had gained on their travels at sea and on land. Their main activities were on the social and educational levels. Small groups even managed to escape. On September 17 the British colonial secretary, Arthur Creech-Jones, announced the British intention to leave Palestine. But Bevin's war against the refugees did not stop. He could not accept the fact that the refugees had not been tempted to go out to work in Germany; he demanded of them that they return to France. The refugees reacted with furious demonstrations. In the Am-stau camp they burned the office in charge of their return to France, and in the Poppendorf camp Roseman called a press conference and said:

". . . The refugees of the *Exodus*, who were dragged by force onto German land, showed themselves to be a new category of oppressed people. We could easily define them as 'displaced people,' but with one small difference. Until today the world has known only about people who were persecuted by the Germans. Now there's a new category, people displaced by Great Britain. I think that the whole world knows and understands that the only solution for the 'displaced' Jews, the old ones and the new ones, is the Land of Israel. . . . We appeal to the United Nations—put an end to our suffering!"

On September 9, 1947, the refugees on the *Exodus* had been forced to disembark in Hamburg. Exactly a year later, on September 9, 1948, a coded report reached Shaul Avigur, head of the Mossad le-Aliya Bet: "We have taken the last of the *Exodus* refugees out of Germany. Except for the sick, there is no one left. Since the last seventy boarded the *Kedma* we have now fulfilled our promise to bring the people from the *Exodus* to Israel. Please inform all those who were involved in the affair." Mordechai Roseman himself had managed to reach the country before that, in May 1948, and join Kibbutz Haogen.

In 1994 the Youth and Pioneer Department of the Jewish Agency initiated a new educational project. Rented ships renamed *Exodus* took Jewish youth on their summer vacations from Italy to Israel. During the voyage they were told the history of the amazing illegal immigration activities. During the last sailing, in the summer of 1995, one of the youth took sick and had to be hospitalized immediately. The air force sent a helicopter to carry out the assignment. "The pilot of that helicopter," said Roseman with pride, "was my grandson!"

Nissan Degani is an Israeli writer.

THEY CALLED HIM DOV, THE BLOND ONE

YAACOV GRANEK

by Itzhak Shamir

Legend has it that the Messiah will be born on the ninth day of Av, the traditional day of mourning for the destruction of the temples in Jerusalem. Yaacov Granek, who later became known as Dov, the "tall blond guy" from Lehi, was born in Lodz, Poland, on the night of the 9th of Av, 5683 (1923). He was not the Messiah, and neither were his ancestors nor his descendants, but there is no doubt that he was one of those who have brought us closer to redemption.

He was from a family of well-to-do cattle merchants. A strong, healthy fellow, he studied in a Jewish-Polish school. He was athletic, energetic, a talented student, quick on the uptake, and had yearned from a very early age to make *aliya* to Eretz Israel. At bar mitzva age he became a member of Betar, and joined one of the Etzel cells that were being set up at the time in Poland. He also signed up to the military training brigades of the Polish authorities. All this he did to learn the art of warfare.

In September 1939, with the outbreak of the Second World War and the German invasion of Poland, Yaacov ran away to Warsaw and volunteered for the Polish army, which was defending the capital. He soon found himself on a train that was transporting prisoners to Germany. He managed to jump off the train and get back to his home in Lodz. Later, after some risky attempts, he reached Vilna, the capital of Lithuania. Many Jews who had escaped the Germans and were trying to find their way to Palestine congregated there. It was there that he met by chance his leaders and future commanders, Natan Yellin-Mor and Dr. Israel Eldad, who a few years later were to become members of the Central Committee of Lehi.

Yaacov, and the group of young people he was with, were lucky enough to find their way to Palestine on the first night of Passover, 1941, after having wandered around Russia and

Turkey. On the way he heard that a split had occurred in Etzel, and that a young man named Yair had founded a new organization, Lehi. He did not know the details, but his heart went out to Yair (code name for Avraham Stern) and his men. Within a short time he was drafted into an auxiliary police unit in the Jezreel Valley, and there, with the help of friends, he joined Lehi. He was given the code name Dov. His girlfriend, Leah, who was soon to become his wife, joined along with him.

Both of them joined the underground at the most difficult time in its history. Immediately after the split in Etzel, Lehi was subjected to terrible persecution. The British secret police fiercely attacked the newly formed underground, which they named the Stern Gang, and arrested almost all its members. A few of them were murdered without any interrogation or trial. Among these was Yair, the founder of Lehi and its commander. He was shot "while trying to escape."

The British authorities were sure that these cruel blows would put an end to Lehi, once and for all. But they were wrong. A few experienced fighters managed to escape from prison and joined up with a small group of supporters who had survived outside. They were soon joined by newcomers who had recently arrived in the country. Together they managed to get the organization back on its feet and renew their activities. Dov became totally involved in the Lehi struggle.

His first assignment was an attack on a group of British soldiers in Tel Aviv, which was carried out in retaliation for the murder by the British of a freedom fighter called Elisha (Yerachmiel Aharonson). Elisha had been in charge of the mobilization of supporters and sympathizers, who could be of help. Dov's skill and resourcefulness in this action drew the attention of Yehoshua Cohen (later the loyal companion and close friend of Ben-Gurion, the first prime minister of Israel). Dov was co-opted onto the team that organized the assassination attempt on the life of the British high commissioner in Palestine, Harold McMichael, a staunch opponent of the Zionist enterprise. The attack did not succeed. McMichael was wounded slightly and left the country. The wide scope of the operation and its daring execution, though, impressed the Jewish community and lifted the Lehi fighters' spirits. Soon afterward Dov participated in a special Lehi course on guerrilla activities, sabotage, and street warfare tactics. This course took place in Ramatayim under the direction of Yaacov "Yashka" Eliav, who had taken a similar course in a military school in Poland before the war.

Some of the course participants were to form the operations department that was in charge of Lehi's military activities until the British left the country. Dov demonstrated his talents and inventiveness in the course, and immediately after the training ended he became involved in a series of operations.

As usual, the first operations were not particularly successful. An attempt to steal arms from the military camp in Tel Litvinsky failed. But failures did not deter the fighters. Two days after the unsuccessful attempt in Tel Litvinsky, Dov took part in an attack on the Jerusalem-based headquarters of the CID, the British secret police, as second in command of the operation and head of the attack unit. The unit broke through the gate of the building and placed the explosives inside. Unfortunately, the explosive charges went off before Dov managed to get away. He was injured but ignored his wound, and continued attacking until the operation was completed. While retreating he encountered a British officer who happened to be there by chance. The officer shot him in the chest. Despite his wounds, Dov managed to kill the officer. His friends then moved him to a safe place, and from there to the Sharon plain, where he could rest and recover. Within a few days he took part in a successful raid on a British paratroopers' camp on Hayarkon Street in Tel Aviv.

One operation followed another. In the meantime the world war ended, and the Hebrew Resistance Movement (Tenuat ha-Meri ha-Ivri) was established. This was a combined front of the Hagana, Etzel, and Lehi. This new force was supposed to carry out coordinated activities on British targets, under the overall command of the Hagana. In this framework Lehi was given an assignment to attack the military airport in Kfar Sirkin, and blow up all the planes there. Dov was the commander of the action, which was crowned with complete success. Eight fighter planes were destroyed, and those who had participated in the action returned to their bases unharmed, after a dangerous and complicated retreat.

Dov was particularly pleased with the operation that led to the release of "the doctor," Israel Eldad (Scheib), a member of the Lehi Central Committee and the organization's ideologist. Eldad himself was arrested at Ben Yehuda High School in Tel Aviv, where he was working as a Bible teacher. When the British police burst into his class, Eldad ran toward the window and tried to climb down the drainpipe, but, unfortunately, he fell and broke his hip bone. He lay in a cast for a long time in the Jerusalem prison hospital. Eventually, when his condition improved somewhat, the British began to take him regularly, under heavy guard, for care to an orthopedist. The underground decided to kidnap Eldad during one of these visits, and the job was assigned to Dov. He worked out all the details of the operation. On the chosen day he and his men stationed themselves outside the clinic. Some of them, disguised as stretcher bearers, entered the building, disarmed the policemen, and kidnapped Eldad, without even removing his handcuffs. They then drove him by roundabout ways to a hiding place in Tel Aviv. Dov played an important role in this operation and was absolutely delighted with its success. This was his way of repaying "the doctor" for the help he had given him during his wanderings from Poland to Palestine.

For Dov all these activities were his way of fulfilling the basic Lehi commandment to fight a "constant war." Among other operations, he was also responsible for blowing up the Intelligence building in Jaffa and for a series of mining actions on the roads. The movement of the British army on the roads was almost totally paralyzed at the time, due mostly to Dov's activities.

His tall figure and his abundant blond hair became famous because of the major role he played in what were called "financial operations." The underground needed a lot of funds. As its activities increased, a greater and more urgent need for money developed. Purchasing arms, renting apartments to be used as safe houses, supporting people who were in hiding, buying gas, maintaining storerooms—all these cost a fortune. Here and there the leaders of Lehi managed to get contributions from well-to-do people and pay for some of their needs, but this was not enough. The only thing they could do then was to rob banks.

Not only did banks have money. The main consideration was (as it was for many other revolutionaries in many other places) that the loss to the bank would not have a direct effect on the deposit of any individual. Therefore this was not really robbery, especially when one considered the sanctity of the purpose it was going to serve. Besides that, the Lehi fighters tried to concentrate on British banks in order to minimalize the damage to Jews. That meant that the expense would be borne by foreign capitalists or the British government. That was how the branches of Barclay's Bank became Lehi's main targets.

The "financial operations" had to be daytime surprise attacks, during the banks' working hours. Consequently many people would come to be "acquainted" with Dov. The figure of this tall blond man, appearing like a storm and escaping quickly with his loot—sometimes exchanging fire with the police—became a common sight in the streets of Tel Aviv. Dov was in charge of a number of these operations, and his remarkable, quick coups became legendary. He often risked his life, and was once wounded very seriously. He underwent surgery in a hospital under the guard of many friends, who then whisked him away and brought him to a safe spot to rest and recover. There was not the slightest doubt that neither he nor the other fighters who took part in these operations ever touched a penny of the money taken, or even considered putting any of it in their own pockets. All of them lived frugally and modestly and made do with the absolute minimum.

The British authorities in Palestine had had more than they could take by the end of 1947. On November 29, 1947, the United Nations General Assembly held a historic vote, declaring the end of the British Mandate and the establishment of the State of Israel. Inside the country, animated discussions and preparations for the Declaration of Independence began. Simultaneously, bloody confrontations broke out between Arab and Jewish forces. It now became clear that a single Jewish army had to be set up, despite the difficulties. The various underground forces had to be disbanded and replaced by a unified national army.

On May 29, 1948, a final military parade of Israeli freedom fighters took place at the Lehi base in northern Tel Aviv, on the grounds of Sheikh Munis (today the campus of Tel Aviv University). For the first time the three members of the Lehi Central Committee, whom many members did not know, were seen in public—Gera, Eldad, and Michael. I was Michael. Gera read out the last order of the day, which ended with the words of Yair in the anthem "Unknown Soldiers": "From our ranks only death can release you." The Lehi underground had ceased to exist.

Many of the ex-Lehi members now joined a new unit of the newly formed IDF (Israel Defense Forces). It was the Eighth Brigade, or the raiding and striking brigade, under the command of the famous General Itzhak Sadeh. In the beginning this was the brigade that combined tank and commando forces for special assignments. Dov was made the commander of Company A of the Eighty-ninth Battalion, the commando battalion of Moshe Dayan. The transition from underground activity to a regular army was not easy, but the frank, open relationship that was built up between the men and the brigade commander, Itzhak Sadeh, helped greatly to get them through crises and problems.

Dov quickly adjusted to the military framework and carried out his tasks with excellence from the very beginning. The other Lehi people were sent for training when possible. The officers were taken into officers' training courses. A notable episode was the transfer of Moshe Dayan from his border command to the Jerusalem front. Many soldiers, among them Lehi men, became bitter and rebellious, because they thought that this would lower the status of the battalion. A delegation of officers went to Ben-Gurion to demand that either Dayan stay with the battalion or that the whole battalion be transferred to Jerusalem.

Ben-Gurion turned down their requests, but was curious to hear what these men had to say. Dov was introduced to him. Ben-Gurion knew perfectly well who the tall officer with the rebellious blond locks and the bushy mustache was. He asked Dov if he would always be ready to obey Dayan's orders in Jerusalem. Dov's answer was not surprising: "Yes," he said, "according to my conscience." Ben-Gurion was not pleased with this response.

Dov continued to take part in the military activity of the battalion, showing outstanding leadership qualities and courage. He commanded the attack on the Iraq-Suweidan fortress near Negba in the Negev, and seized this murderous stronghold from the Egyptians. He proudly delivered the flag of the fortress to Itzhak Sadeh. Dov also excelled in a typical commando raid on an Egyptian unit near Nirim. This unit was completely taken by surprise and totally wiped out.

In December 1948 he led his men in his last attack, to capture Awja al-Hafir, which is today Nitzana, in the Negev. To this day some still feel that the operation was not planned properly. There is no doubt that the intelligence had not done its job. In any case, Dov sat erect in the armored truck that moved quickly ahead. Suddenly they encountered a superior Egyptian force, and a fatal bullet hit Dov in the neck. He slumped forward in the truck. He was killed instantly.

He had had premonitions before he died. He believed that December was going to be a catastrophic time for him; in previous years he had always been hit by calamities during this month. He knew that something bad was going to happen to him, but his sense of duty and discipline made him go ahead. Dov was deeply mourned by his friends, his loved ones, and all those who knew him. His friends, the Lehi freedom fighters, said in his obituary that their "hearts were broken," and this was indeed how they felt.

The poet and visionary Uri Zvi Greenberg wrote on Dov's headstone: "We mourn the *sicarius* Lieutenant Dov of the Israeli army. He was a burning tree that all the water of his enemies could not put out." (The *sicarius* were Jewish secret fighters in the late Second Temple, so called for the dagger—*sica* in Latin—that they used to kill those who collaborated with the Romans.)

Afterward, a very experienced officer wrote about him: "Dov anticipated the concepts and development of the IDF by twenty years. Today our typical response, when fired upon, is to attack the source of fire. Dov did that instinctively. He was the only one, and probably the first one, to do that."

That was our Dov, always first, always leading.

Itzhak Shamir was Michael, one of the three Lehi commanders, and is a former prime minister of Israel.

PART IV

THE WAR OF INDEPENDENCE

1947–1949

ecretly, systematically, the Yishuv prepared for its independence. In 1945, long before
the United Nations vote, Ben-Gurion had reached the conclusion that the neighboring Arab
states would try to prevent the creation of a Jewish state, by invading its territory with their
regular armies. Therefore, he had to prepare his people for war. Ben-Gurion himself took
charge of the defense portfolio, and studied the basics of warfare. As the British army was still
in Palestine, all military preparations had to be carried out in utmost secrecy.

With funds Ben-Gurion had obtained in America, underground weapons factories were established. Officers of the Jewish Brigade, the Hagana, and the Palmach formed a nucleus for
the future army. But Ben-Gurion knew well that without establishing a regular army, equipped
with tanks, cannon, and aviation, Israel would be doomed. Golda Meir, a rising leader in Ben-
Gurion's party, Mapai, flew to the United States and raised $50 million from the Jewish com-
munity. "One day," the grateful Ben-Gurion said to her, "when history comes to be written, it
shall be said that there was a Jewish woman who found the money that enabled the establishment of the State." This money was used by Ben-Gurion's young assistants, Ehud Avriel,
Munia Mardor, Yehuda Arazi, Teddy Kollek, and others, who fanned out throughout the world,
buying large quantities of heavy weapons, and stockpiled them in Europe. The weapons could
be brought to Israel only after its Declaration of Independence.

The United Nations vote of November 29, 1947, heralded a series of military setbacks for
the Jewish community during the winter of 1947–48. Many Jewish leaders in Palestine and
the United States started worrying that the Hagana, which had trouble dealing with gangs of
local Arabs, would not be able to withstand the attack of the regular armies of the Arab states.
The United States which had supported the idea of a Jewish state, made an about-face. Secretary of State George Marshall told Jewish leaders that the partition had been "an error." On
May 8, 1948, six days before the State was to be proclaimed, Marshall received Moshe
Sharett, the future foreign minister of Israel, and pressured him to delay the proclamation of

the state. Sharett left Marshall's office deeply disturbed. He arrived in Tel Aviv on May 11, and advised Ben-Gurion to accept Marshall's suggestion. Ben-Gurion refused and finally convinced Sharett to support his point of view.

In the People's Administration (the provisional government) Ben-Gurion had to put the question of independence to a vote. This was the most dramatic and fateful vote in Jewish history. Of the ten leaders present, six voted for Ben-Gurion's motion to declare Israel's independence right away; four voted against.

Forty-eight hours later, on May 14, 1948, Ben-Gurion publicly read the Declaration of Independence in the Tel Aviv Museum. A few days later the army of Israel was created, and became known by the acronym Zahal—the Israel Defense Forces (IDF).

The Arab countries invaded the territory of the young State of Israel. The first twelve days were desperate. The Syrian army reached Kibbutz Degania. The Iraqis thrust deep into the West Bank, aiming to reach the Mediterranean and cut Israel in two. The Arab Legion (the army of Trans-Jordan) overran the Etzion bloc, massacring or capturing its defenders, and besieged the Jewish part of Jerusalem. In the south, the Egyptians reached Ashdod, a short distance from Tel Aviv.

But then the first ships carrying weapons reached Haifa. The first aircraft arrived from Czechoslovakia. Ironically, these were German-made Messerschmidts from World War II. During the following days they took off, adorned with the blue Star of David, the emblem of the Israeli air force. The tide turned, and Israel took the initiative, reaping victories and enlarging her borders, far beyond the UN partition plan.

A parallel combat was simultaneously waged inside the Jewish community: Ben-Gurion's battle for establishing a unified state army, to replace the former underground organizations, which were affiliated to various political parties. The Etzel was disbanded following the bitter, painful affair of the *Altalena*, an arms ship that was brought to Israel by Menachem Begin. After Etzel's refusal to surrender the ship to the army, Ben-Gurion ordered that it be bombed. The *Altalena* was sunk off the coast of Tel Aviv. Fourteen Etzel men and one Palmach soldier were killed. This incident was to poison the political scene in Israel for decades.

In September of the same year, Lehi fighters murdered the UN mediator, Count Folke Bernadotte, in Jerusalem. The assassination caused the disbandment of Lehi, and Etzel in Jerusalem as well. Finally, in October, Ben-Gurion disbanded the separate Palmach command, attracting the wrath of the left-wing party, Mapam, to which most of the Palmach was affiliated. Ben-Gurion also had to face the anger of the Palmach rank and file, his best officers and troops, many of whom declared they would leave the army as soon as the fighting was over. But he stood firm. When the War of Independence ended, the "private armies" didn't exist anymore. Zahal, the Israel Defense Forces, was the only army in the State of Israel.

Sarah Aharonson: "I strove for my people"

Joseph Trumpeldor: A man of mystery

Alexander Zeid: In blood and fire Judea fell

Chaim Shturman:
Founder of a dynasty of heroes

Orde Wingate: The British officer dreamed of a career in the Jewish army

Janusz Korczak: The ghetto police saluted

Meir "Zaro" Zorea:
A hero of the British army

Mordechai Anielewicz:
"My life's dream has been realized"

Arkadi Timor: The Red Army hero dreamed of emigrating to Israel

Yaacov Berger: "For every thousand that have fallen a thousand others will rise"

Zvi Brenner: A hand grenade in one hand and a revolver in the other

Moshe Barazani (above) and Meir Feinstein:
A grenade between two hearts

Dov Cohen: "I had to pay for the bullets"

Mordechai Roseman:
The leader of the Exodus immigrants

Yaacov Granek:
They called him Dov, "The Blond One"

Yosef Damst (left) and Shalom Karniel:
A model and an emblem

Gur Meirov: Where he fell, an olive tree is growing

Eliezer Feig: A number was tattooed on the boy's arm

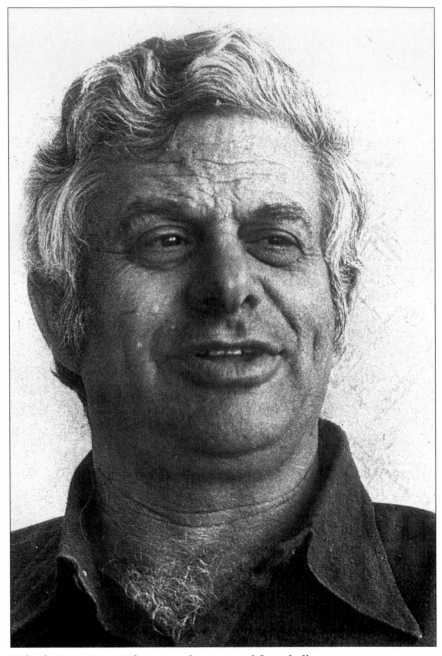

Yehuda Tajer-Tagar: The man who returned from hell

THE WAR OF INDEPENDENCE

WE ARE THE SILVER PLATTER

by Uzi Narkiss

"A state is not handed to a nation on a silver platter."
—Dr. Chaim Weizmann, first president of the State of Israel

—From the darkness appeared
a young girl and a young boy
and slowly they stepped to face their nation.

Their fatigue had no limit; they had known no rest,
And drenched in the dew of a Hebrew youth,
Silently they approached, and stood quite still
And nobody could tell
If they were living or had been shot to death.

Then the nation spoke, choked by tears and by wonder
And asked: Who are you?
And the two quietly answered her:
We are the silver platter
On which you were given the State of the Jews.

So they spoke, veiled in shadow, and at her feet they fell,
And the rest will be told in the Saga of Israel.

In this poem, published on December 19, 1947, the poet Natan Alterman paid tribute to the young Israelis, dead and living, whose sacrifice in the War of Independence became our "silver platter." And when this poem stirred the small Israeli nation, nobody knew how costly the silver platter would be. By the end of our War of Independence Israel had lost six thousand lives, one percent of the Jewish population of Palestine.

When Alterman wrote his verses, the War of Independence had barely started. On November 29, 1947, the General Assembly of the United Nations, meeting at Lake Success, decided on the partition of Palestine into a Jewish and an Arab independent state. Immediately afterward Jamal al-Husseini declared, in the name of the Supreme Arab Committee, that "what was written in ink in Lake Success will be erased by blood in Palestine."

The first drops of blood were spilled the following day, when Arabs ambushed a Jewish bus, killing and wounding the passengers. After that day, the attacks and the clashes didn't stop for many months. In the long, bitter war that claimed so many victims, fought by so few people and such limited resources, the small Jewish community in Israel was offered a unique historic opportunity, coupled with a terrible danger to its very survival: to become an independent nation, or to be annihilated. The outcome of the war proved once again that the courage of the fighting man was the country's most valuable weapon. "The most important asset I found was the man," said the leader of fighting Israel, David Ben-Gurion. Again and again, on all fronts, Alterman's young boys and girls proved—by risking their lives, by rushing into battle courageously against an enemy with superior power and equipment—that they could win the war and bring about the renewal of Jewish sovereignty after two thousand years—and after the Holocaust of Europe's Jews.

The War of Independence ended in the spring of 1949. On the twentieth day of the month of Tamuz, 5709 (July 17, 1949) twelve men were awarded the title Hero of Israel, the equivalent of what was later to be the Medal of Valor.

There were many acts of bravery in the War of Independence, and it was hard to measure them. Did all the heroes receive the honor they deserved? Were there heroes whose deeds were not recognized? These are gnawing questions, but they do not diminish the greatness of the twelve heroes who were chosen to symbolize the courage of the reborn nation of Israel. The number twelve was a symbol as well, as if each of the chosen fighters represented one of the ancient tribes of Israel.

Their common trait was that all of them carried out their exploits without being ordered to do so, risking or sacrificing their lives for their friends without being asked. They transcended their orders, assumed crazy risks, and kept fighting even when all hope seemed lost. Even if they were not the only heroes of their generation, even if there were others like them, there is no doubt that they were true representatives of our silver platter.

Our twelve heroes were Yair Racheli, Emmanuel Landau, Avraham Avigdorov, Zerubavel Horowitz, Yizhar Armoni, Emil Brig, Zvi Zibel, Ben-Zion Leitner, Ron Feller, Yochai Ben-Nun, Siman-Tov Gana, and Arye Atzmoni. We shall describe their acts of courage according to the chronology of the war.

The War of Independence had two main stages. The first was from November 29, 1947, the day of the UN resolution creating the Jewish State, until May 14, 1948, the day of the

Declaration of Independence. During this period, the British army and administration were still in Palestine. Officially, the British were in charge of security. In practice, the British army actually had retreated from most of the country, concentrating in bases and around cities, and worrying mostly about its own safety. The country was left wide open to a struggle between irregular forces from both sides. On the Arab side there were mostly irregular gangs and groups, some of them local, some of them infiltrated from the neighboring countries, that acted either independently or under a vague Palestinian command. The Jewish units, mostly Hagana and Palmach companies and platoons, operated under the general command of the Hagana. This first stage of the war was mostly focused around the isolated Jewish settlements, and the roads to the different parts of the country. In this struggle, the Jews were trying to maintain the communications with each kibbutz and village, and the Arabs attempted to cut and surround them, starting with tiny settlements in the Negev and Galilee—and ending with Jerusalem.

The second stage of the war began on May 14, 1948. After the creation of the State of Israel, it was invaded by the armies of all the neighboring states, with forces also coming from Iraq and other far-off Arab states. Israel established her army, the Israel Defense Forces, which fought against the invaders, and eventually repelled them, also conquering large chunks of territory from the lands that the United Nations had allotted to the Palestinian state. That state was never established, because of internal Arab infighting, and because of the desire of Israel's neighbor from the east, the Kingdom of Jordan, to annex the territories of the Palestinian state, which would be known in the future as the "West Bank" of the Jordan River. This stage of the war ended with the signing of separate armistice agreements between Israel and its neighbors.

THE FIRST STAGE: NOVEMBER 29, 1947—MAY 14, 1948

Yair Racheli

On January 18, 1948, a unit of the Palmach left the training camp at Ramat Yochanan in Galilee to attack a house on the outskirts of Shefaram, an Arab village. In Shefaram were concentrated several gangs that had been attacking Jews traveling along the roads in the area; they had also attacked the neighboring settlements a number of times. The Palmach raid was one of several reprisal acts carried out all over the country in retaliation for the massacre of thirty-five Jews who had tried to reach the besieged Etzion Bloc, south of Jerusalem. Palmach headquarters wanted to make it very clear to the gangs, as well as to the disheartened Jewish community, that they were still capable of launching far-reaching raids.

The fighters left their truck in the outskirts of the village and approached on foot, to surprise the enemy. But it turned out that the enemy was ready and waiting. The Arabs opened fire on the Palmach fighters even before they had begun their attack. One was killed, a few others wounded. The attack was repulsed. The situation seemed desperate. Nobody could move, as the entire unit was under sustained machine-gun fire. Another disaster was in the making. But the commander of the company, Yair Racheli, nineteen years old, did not panic.

He crawled among his soldiers, and collected grenades from all the wounded. Then he ran toward the house, under murderous fire, and with the five grenades he threw he silenced all the machine guns. During the short lull the soldiers managed to regroup, gather up the wounded and the dead, and retreat in the direction of their truck, which was waiting nearby. They were no longer in danger from gunfire from Shefaram.

Emmanuel Landau and Avraham Avigdorov

Two months later, on March 17, 1948, three trucks loaded with arms and ammunition, along with two escort cars, confidently moved on the northern road connecting Beirut in Lebanon to Haifa in Palestine. The convoy carried an important passenger: Muhammad el-Huneiti, the commander of the Arab force in Haifa. When Moshe Carmel, commander of the Hagana in the area of Haifa and the north, heard about this convoy, he gave the order to ambush it. The mission was assigned to a Palmach company from the training camp at Ramat Yochanan, which immediately took up positions near Kiryat Motzkin, a Jewish suburb north of Haifa. The soldiers hastily filled a few barrels with stones and sand, which they intended to roll onto the road to block the convoy.

The commander of the ambush had been given a description to identify the convoy—up to five cars, and among them trucks that were unusually overloaded. Besides that he had been assigned a motorcyclist, who had a blurred photograph of el-Huneiti, to help him identify the convoy north of the ambush and to warn the Palmach fighters of its arrival. At 3:30 P.M. the motorcyclist noticed a suspicious convoy that fitted the description he had been given. He drove into the convoy and passed the five cars, one after the other. In the first car he saw soldiers of the Arab Legion, armed with Bren machine guns; he recognized one of the men in the car as the man in the picture. He then raced ahead to the ambush and shouted: "Get ready! They're behind me!" The fighters coolly rolled down the barrels. The convoy stopped, and immediately an exchange of fire broke out.

Emmanuel Landau darted to one of the trucks. All that mattered to him was to seize the weapons it carried and bring them to his badly equipped comrades. In spite of the fierce exchange of fire, he tried to get the truck off the battlefield in one piece and pass its precious load on to our forces. A grenade hit the truck, and it exploded. Landau was blown up beside it. Avraham Avigdorov, his friend from the training camp and the son of an old-time Hashomer watchman, attacked the convoy as well. Shooting his submachine gun from the hip, he destroyed two Arab Bren machine guns at close range. When the truck exploded, he was wounded. But this last attack determined the outcome of the battle. The convoy was stopped, and Arab Haifa did not get the arms and ammunition it was expecting. This battle probably sealed Haifa's fate. Soon after this, the Jews took control of the entire city.

Zerubavel Horowitz

Saturday, March 27, 1948. A Jewish convoy that had brought supplies from Jerusalem to the Etzion Bloc, a cluster of settlements south of Bethlehem, was preparing for its return journey. At first the area seemed quiet, but at the last moment the convoy's departure was delayed. A light observation plane reported that Arab gangs were beginning to block the road at the southern entrance to Bethlehem. Tensions were rising, but the members of the convoy assumed that the "barrier breaker," the armored truck at the head of the line, specially equipped for breaking through road blocks, would do its job. In the past, it had always cleared the road for them, and it did so again at the first six barriers. The armored vehicle, under the command of Zerubavel Horowitz, a member of Kibbutz Tel Yosef, broke through the barriers one after the other, but he got stuck at the seventh barrier near the village of Nabi Daniel. The Arabs immediately surrounded the convoy, and directed their fire mainly at the driver of the armored truck. Its tires were punctured; its back wheels got stuck in a ditch. The Arab fire got heavier, and the other armored trucks were hit as well.

The commanders of the convoy decided to send all the vehicles that could be pulled off the battlefield back to the Etzion Bloc. Inside the barrier breaker Zerubavel Horowitz stayed calm. He encouraged his friends, some of whom were badly hurt, and tried to find a way of evacuating the wounded. During the next seven hours, no way was found to do so. The truck was under constant fire, and the soldiers couldn't even open a slit to get some relief from the stifling heat. In the meantime, Zerubavel monitored the radio and managed to hear some fragmented messages. From them he learned that some of the soldiers had managed to leave their disabled trucks and reach a deserted house at the side of the road.

At nightfall he took stock of the situation: In the truck there were seven fighters who were badly wounded, and couldn't escape; the remaining three, beside him, were slightly wounded. He ordered the three who were slightly wounded to escape and reach the Etzion Bloc, which they eventually did. He then decided to fight back, even if it cost him his life. He would at least take as many enemy soldiers as he could with him. Samson had said, "Let me die with the Philistines," and so would he. When he heard the voices of the Arab attackers approaching the vehicle, he set off all the explosives inside it. He and all the wounded were killed, and along with them several Arab soldiers. His courage shone as a bright light amid the great pain at the heavy losses in human lives, and the bitter defeat in the battle of Nabi Daniel.

Private Yizhar Armoni

In the very north of the Galilee, the fortress of Nabi Yusha commands a view from the top of the Naftali mountain range of the whole area. It also dominated large parts of the Hula Valley and of the eastern part of the northern road, which follows the line of the Lebanese border. It was essential to conquer the fort. The first attempt, on April 15, 1948, failed. Five days later a Palmach force got ready at Kibbutz Hulata for another attack. The plan was simple. A holding and diversionary force would act south of the fortress to divert the enemy's attention, and the main attack would be launched from the north. After a number of hitches the attack began.

It seemed that everything was going according to plan. The barbed wire fences were cut by sapper scissors. There were too many fences, though, and a bangalore torpedo was fired, breaking a large gap through the wires. The demolition squads moved forward and reached the wall of the police station. Again they faced a problem. The wooden stand on which they were supposed to place the explosives, due to the height of the outside wall of the fortress, got lost. The sappers hurriedly piled up a bunch of stones to place the explosives on. Yizhar Armoni, a machine gunner, lay behind a rock and covered his friends during the whole attack. He was under heavy fire from the fortress, but he hung on tenaciously. His closest friends from the kibbutz were out there; he was not going to let them down.

In the meantime the enemy fire got heavier, and most of the Israelis were hit. Two of the three gunners covering them were also hit. The third one, Yizhar Armoni, kept returning fire. He did not give up even when it became clear that the attack on the fortress had failed and the order to retreat had been given. He didn't budge from his position, although he could have done so. He kept covering the retreating soldiers and the wounded left on the battlefield. He continued to do so until he was killed—at the age of eighteen.

The Nabi Yusha fortress was captured finally on May 17. It was then renamed the Fortress of the Twenty-Eight, for the number of fighters—Armoni among them—who fell in the battles to capture it.

The capture of Nabi Yusha was one of the first victories of the Israeli army after the State of Israel was born on May 14, 1948, and the second stage of the War of Independence began.

THE SECOND STAGE: MAY 14, 1948–APRIL 3, 1949

Sergeant Emil Brig

On the very day of the Declaration of Independence, Emil Brig became a hero. Born in Poland, Emil Brig, at the age of twenty-five, was a demolition sergeant in the Barak battalion of the Golani brigade. At the beginning of May 1948 he was sent with an officer from the battalion's demolition unit to stop the advance of the Arab Legion—the formidable Jordanian army—and the Iraqi expeditionary forces. They both knew that during World War II the British had planned to blow up the bridges on the Jordan River. They now looked for the holes left from the British sappers' preparations among the stones of the first bridge. They couldn't find the holes, so they left without blowing up any bridge.

On May 14 the battalion commander ordered Brig to blow up the bridge at all costs. Kibbutz Gesher is depending on you, he told him. Emil, a Holocaust survivor, called upon all his courage and wartime experience as a partisan in Poland.

At his request, the tractors of Kibbutz Naharayim started moving in the daytime so as to distract the guards on the bridges. He himself crawled in broad daylight, through a field of thorns and thistles, and reached the bridge right under the noses of the guards. He carefully attached the explosives to the huge posts of the ancient bridge, and to the other bridges as well, connected all of them with electric wire, retreated, and took cover. He tried to set off the explosives. Nothing happened. The battery that was supposed to send an electric current through the wires was too weak.

Emil was determined to blow up the bridges, come what may. He crawled back to Naharayim and returned at night with a simple ignition wire that was only a few meters long. He knew that the wire would burn at the rate of a few centimeters a second. He connected the wire, struck a match, and lit it. The match briefly flared, but that was enough for the enemy to open heavy fire on Emil. At the last second he managed to roll to cover, and from there he watched the bridges explode one after the other. His courage and perseverance prevented the Jordanian tanks from crossing the river.

Private Zvi Zibel

Zvi Zibel, known to his friends as Chibi, learned how to fly in the Palmach, in a clandestine course at Kibbutz Naan. When the war started he moved to Sde Dov airfield, north of Tel Aviv, and from there went out on patrol, liaison, and supply missions, as well as on air attacks. Among other operations he participated in a highly improvised attempt to help the fighters of the convoy that got stuck at Nabi Daniel at the end of March 1948.

On June 25, 1948, he was assigned to bring supplies to the agricultural school of Ben Shemen, which was under siege. Ben Shemen was situated about two and a half miles from the large Arab town of Lod. All the roads to this small youth village had been blocked from the beginning of the war. Arab forces stationed in the towns of Lod and Ramle, as well as in the neighboring villages, thwarted every effort to break through. There was, therefore, no alternative but to airlift supplies to Ben Shemen in the so-called Primus light planes and land them on the short runway that had been laid out for this purpose. It was now Chibi's turn to do this, and at first it seemed quite an easy job. After all, since June 11 the first truce had been maintained, and the chance of being shot at was relatively small. Nevertheless, when he began to lower his plane onto the runway, it turned out that the Arabs from the village of Hadita didn't care very much for the truce regulations. They opened heavy fire at him, with rifles and machine guns. He managed to land, but the fire got much worse, and was now aimed at the landed plane.

In a desperate attempt to put an end to the attack and save the plane, Chibi feverishly loaded a heap of heavy sandbags onto a platform. He then attached the platform to a tractor and, braving the enemy's fire, drove the tractor toward the enemy positions and placed it in front of the plane. The aircraft was now sheltered from the fire. Chibi jumped from the tractor, ran to his plane, took off, and returned to Sde Dov. A few months later he was killed in an air battle with Egyptian planes on the southern front. He was then twenty-three years old.

Private First Class Ben-Zion Leitner

On July 19, 1948, the Givati Brigade set out on its fifth assault on the Iraq-Suweidan fortress in the Negev, near Kibbutz Negba. A reinforced platoon was charged with the main part of the operation. The platoon was a new one in the battalion. It was made up of men who had not been drafted until then because they were married, with children. They had acquired some battle experience in capturing several enemy positions at the Negev road junction. Intelligence officers reported that the Egyptian force in the fortress was small, and its morale was low. That was the reason for giving the assignment to a platoon whose soldiers were relatively old and lacking in battle experience. An early patrol approached the fortress and did not discern any signs of life.

But around midnight, when the platoon began to move toward its target, it was met with heavy fire from all the positions in the fortress. The platoon commander decided to continue. The sappers darted forward and broke through the first fence. In front of them was a bunker from which heavy fire spurted. At first, an unsuccessful attempt was made to blow up the bunker with PIAT bombs. Later, a squad of soldiers was launched toward it. They were stopped by the murderous fire. The machine gunner was killed, the squad commander was wounded, and the attack stopped.

It was at this point that Ben-Zion Leitner went into action. Leitner was a former scout in the Red army, who had come to the country as a refugee on the illegal immigrant ship *Af-Al-Pi*. He attacked alone, shouting "Hurrah!" as was the custom in the Red army. Shooting incessantly, he managed to silence the bunker. The attack on the fortress was renewed, but it finally failed, and Leitner was seriously wounded.

Iraq-Suweidan, which later became known as the Yoav fortress, was captured only during the eighth attack, in November 1948.

Ron Feller

On the morning of July 19, 1948, a company from the Givati Brigade captured the Arab village of Kartiya, in the south, and immediately regrouped, expecting a counterattack by the Egyptians.

The antitank weapons of the company, a pair of PIATs under the command of Ron Feller, were set up on the east side of the village, on the assumption that the Egyptian attack would come from that direction. But, in fact, the Egyptians had concentrated their infantry and tank forces on the west side, and the PIATs were quickly moved. The Egyptian tank force began to advance through the sorghum fields, under cover of artillery bombardment, and, at first, encountered no resistance. The Israelis opened fire only after the tanks had gotten within five hundred meters of the village. Their fire was very effective; the Egyptians hastily retreated.

A second Egyptian attack, of two infantry companies, covered by fifteen armored cars and four tanks, was more successful. The Egyptians managed to get within 150 meters of the village.

Under the circumstances Ron Feller decided to make a flank attack on the Egyptian tank forces. He rushed up to the company commander under heavy fire, and got his permission. Then he began to advance toward the enemy, exposed to Egyptian fire, and completely alone.

The first bomb he fired hit a tank and slid off it. Heavy fire was opened on the lonely Israeli soldier from all sides. He fired a second bomb immediately, the tank went up in flames, and the Egyptian attack was halted. The other vehicles retreated in haste.

The second truce, which began a few hours later, recognized the *fait accompli*—Kartiya was in the hands of the IDF.

Yochai Ben-Nun

At the end of October 1948, during Operation Yoav, an operation to capture the northern Negev, the newborn Israeli navy went out to block the supply routes and reinforcements of the Egyptians in the Mediterranean. On October 22, close to the end of the campaign, the navy sappers went into action. Their commander, Yochai Ben-Nun, undertook an ambitious mission: destroy two Egyptian boats, the flagship *Emir Farouk* and the minesweeper that accompanied it. The mission was assigned to five soldiers in three boats carrying explosives. One boat was meant to attack the *Emir Farouk*, the second one the minesweeper. The third boat, commanded by Yochai himself, was in reserve, ready to move in where necessary. The boats sailed off into the night. At their starting point, facing the bow of the *Emir Farouk*, Yochai gave his final orders.

The first boat moved out and hit the *Emir Farouk*, its crew managing to get away in time. The commander of the second boat also moved forward, but made a mistake and directed the boat at the *Emir Farouk*, which was already sinking, instead of at the minesweeper. Yochai, who saw the mistake, attacked the minesweeper. While he was doing this he was caught in the minesweeper's searchlights and hit with heavy fire, but he kept on going. At that point he also realized that his boat wasn't functioning properly, but the thought of turning back didn't even cross his mind. He remained on it almost until it hit the minesweeper. He jumped into the water at the last second and saw nearby the cloud of smoke and the column of water rising at the spot where the minesweeper had sunk. The daring operation achieved complete success.

Yochai Ben-Nun eventually became the commander of the Thirteenth Flotilla, the naval commando unit. In 1960, a major general, he was appointed commander of the Israeli navy.

Siman-Tov Gana

Siman-Tov Gana was a soldier in the tank force that carried out the eighth attack on the legendary Iraq-Suweidan fortress. He was an armored-car driver in the diversionary force that attacked the village of Iraq-Suweidan, near the fortress. During the attack he was hit by an antitank shell and was severely wounded in both legs. There were several wounded soldiers around him, among them the other three occupants of his vehicle, but unlike the other wounded soldiers, Siman-Tov continued fighting with his last bit of strength. Among other things, he grabbed a machine gun and covered the retreat of other soldiers for six hours. He actually fought alone against large Egyptian units, repelling their attacks. During that time he also encouraged and cheered up his wounded friends and dressed their wounds as best he could.

When the gunfire let up sometime after the fortress had been captured, Siman-Tov Gana managed to contact his unit, and to inform it of his whereabouts. Only then was he rescued and taken to the hospital, where both of his legs were amputated.

Arye Atzmoni

In the last stages of Operation Horev, at the beginning of January 1949, the Golani Brigade made an attempt to capture Rafiah, on the southern edge of the Gaza Strip.

On the night of January 3, after an earlier patrol in the area, a company reinforced with medium-sized machine guns, mortar, and artillery conquered an enemy position near the town cemetery. The position was properly entrenched, with deep communication canals and bunkers, and even a special sleeping bunker for the commanding officer, but the Israeli force managed to take the Egyptians completely by surprise. The weak resistance of the stunned enemy soldiers was quickly overcome. By dawn, before they had a chance to organize their defense, the Israelis sighted a number of Egyptian tanks and armored trucks at a distance of a thousand meters. The Egyptians opened fire and wounded many of our soldiers.

The Golani soldiers had brought along an artillery gun, but it turned out that one of our trucks was blocking the gun's field of vision, and it could not be used. The company sergeant major, Arye Atzmoni, acted immediately. On his own initiative he jumped out of his trench, ran to the truck, and jumped into the cab. After several attempts, under heavy fire, he managed to back the truck out toward the Egyptian tanks. This opened the area to the artillery crew, and five Egyptian tanks were destroyed, one after the other. The Egyptians retreated.

A combination of circumstances, though, prevented the Israelis from capturing Rafiah until the Six-Day War, eighteen years later.

The twenty-two-year-old Atzmoni, who had fought as a boy with the partisans in Europe, and had even served for a short time in the Jewish Brigade, was the last in the long line of national heroes in the War of Independence. He also became a symbol of the continuity of Jewish heroism, from the snow-covered forests of Eastern Europe, through the bitter battles of the Jewish Brigade in Italy, and finally to the scorching battlefields of the Negev, where Jewish independence was won.

Major General (res.) Uzi Narkiss was the head of the Central Command of the Israeli army during the liberation of Jerusalem.

A MODEL AND AN EMBLEM

SHALOM KARNIEL AND YOSEF DAMST

by Zevulun Hammer

They were studying Mishnah [a collection of oral Jewish laws, which forms the basis of the Talmud] in Shoshana Karniel's room. Shoshana was the young widow of Shalom, who had fallen, with nine other young men, in the bloody Arab ambush of the "convoy of the ten" during Chanuka 5708 (December 1947). It was crowded in her room. The students who sat there were armed. They wore peaked caps and work clothes, khaki uniforms, or winter overalls. Crowded in together, leaning over their books eagerly, they looked like some surrealistic gathering from another time and another world. Through the window they could see the view of the mountain; the edges of the dark clouds glowed slightly from the light of the setting sun hidden behind them.

Perhaps Shoshana was remembering what Shalom had written only a year and a few months before. Perhaps for a moment she had lost track of the lesson, and an echo from days before all this fighting rose like a divine voice laden with pain. Memories invade the mind of a person who is trying to concentrate on something. "Dusk," wrote Shalom, "is like a crimson-azure veil that envelops the mountains from afar, a time of calm and harmony." What irony that was! The mountain was swarming with mortal enemies. They would never be satisfied until they destroyed all of Gush Etzion, this bloc of Jewish settlements clinging to the rocky slopes south of Jerusalem. The enemies would not rest until they had broken off the hinges of the doors of this humble house built into the mountain, until all its defenders had fallen at its threshold. Shalom had already gone to the mountain and not returned. Calm? Harmony? When they had laid the bodies out in the dining hall and walked past to identify them, someone said that Shalom's face looked peaceful; Shalom, who had been killed in such violent circumstances. Perhaps they should have said Shalom's face looked harmonious, because harmony was a basic part of his being. "It seems as if the trees and all of nature are locked in a silent prayer, a prayer of thanks. My heart overflows with feelings of joy and confidence. Anxiety because of the days to come is fading. There is no fear and no apprehension. . . ." When these lines were published in *Alonim*, the journal of the religious kibbutz movement, a few days after Shavuot 5706 (June 1946), his friends read them as lines of poetry. The pioneer, the religious scholar, the poet Shalom Karniel, knew that it was not possible to settle the Judean hills between Kibbutz Ramat Rachel and Hebron without faith, and that it was not possible to live there without anxiety.

The voice of Yosef Damst, the teacher of the lesson, sounded like it was coming from inside a seashell. His thin face, framed in a black beard, gave him a saintly appearance. Shoshana looked at him, and saw Shalom. Damst was teaching the laws concerning the martyrdom of the Jews. The prayers were not about the souls of those who had already died, but about the souls of those who were going to die in the future.

When he had asked permission to teach in her room, he said to her, "Difficult trials lay ahead of us. They will be much worse than anything we have known till now. How can a person bear them? How can he not break down before the end comes?" She looked at him without saying a word. He had not tried to comfort her for the loss of Shalom. His friends were already climbing the same ladder that had taken Shalom up to heaven. They must learn how to climb.

"We'll learn the laws about the martyrdom of the Jews," he had said. "Every Jewish family must sanctify His name, but this kind of martyrdom does not come to all. But to us it has come. . . ." He knew they were going to die. He taught his friends how to be worthy of dying. "A lesson in the laws of sanctity," he told her. "That will be the name of the lesson." She was silent. "When?" she asked. "Between the afternoon and the evening prayers," he had said. She nodded and whispered, "At dusk . . ."

There was a lesson every day. Anyone came who was not guarding or at his post or escorting convoys or at work. They all knew what they were learning, and whoever could, joined the small group. Yosef, who was studying agronomy so he could be of service to Kfar Etzion in some practical way, was a spiritual man. He was so serious, perhaps too serious for his age. The psalms he had carefully chosen spoke of a common grave. After a thorough study, he had selected verses that were read to describe events that should not be canceled because of the fighting. Even for tree-planting on Tu Bishvat in the heat of a battle—as if the battle would end and the trees would still blossom and give fruit—for this too Yosef found a verse.

Yosef was a fighter, and a hero, but so different from the famous fighters and heroes who had become widely known. Shoshana knew that he was going out alone to Massuot Itzhak and Ein Zurim, the nearby kibbutzim. Even in driving rain and bitter cold he would tie up his army coat with a rope or a belt, hang his Sten submachine gun on his shoulder, put a Jewish law book in his backpack, and go out to teach.

What would Shalom have said to Yosef if he were here with him? This young man used to gather flowers in the mountains, find out their names, and display them to warm the hearts of others and strengthen their ties to the good, fertile land. Would Shalom have understood how Yosef made the heroic transition from a time for living to a time for dying? Would he have reproached him? Or perhaps he too would have gone with Yosef to dedicate his life to the study of martyrdom, in God's name.

One day, Shoshana pondered, when all this terrible preparation would be only a memory, when these who taught our boys the art of war would save them, when we would live and not die—would today's lesson be one of despair or a lesson of unparalleled faith? She believed that life would win out. She believed that Yosef also believed it. She opened her house to the lesson, even in her widowhood. This unwavering stand in the face of death was at the same time an honest, courageous stand in the face of life. Shalom would have known this as well.

Was Shalom a hero? If he had not fallen in battle, would his memory have been so strongly etched in the hearts of his friends and loved ones? What is a hero? Does climbing the mountain mean as much as fighting for the mountain, or is it only the fighting that counts?

In 5687 (1927) Jews first settled on the Hebron Mountain and established Migdal Eder. The settlement lasted until 5689 (1929). Migdal Eder was deserted after the massacre in Hebron. Six years later Jews returned to settle the same spot. The El Hahar (To the Mountain) association built a settlement, but the bloody events that occurred all over the country (in 1935–36) also destroyed this second settlement at Kfar Etzion.

In 5703 (1942) Kfar Etzion was reborn in the Hebron Mountains. Two years later Massuot Itzhak was founded; Ein Zurim followed, in Tishrei 5705 (September 1945), then Revadim in the month of Shvat (January 1946) of the same year, according to the Hebrew calendar. The earth is very dry. The winter winds and the snowstorms freeze the earth and turn the thousand meters (three thousand feet) of altitude into a hostile obstacle. Young men and women who had not inherited the skills of working the land from their ancestors came here to build themselves a home. Shalom wrote: "We dreamed of this for years—to build, to plant, to establish our homes so that they would be a shelter for those homeless people who so thirsted for a land of their own. Their lips whisper a song of thanks. Thank you, God, that you have enabled us to reach this time and place." What was this time? A lull between two periods of rioting? A time when the railway cars were bringing the Jewish people to the platforms of Auschwitz? A time when redemption had to come from the depths of an almost extinct Diaspora? And what was this place? A place of jagged rocks, arid hills, and driving rain, or the place about which Shalom's friend Zvi Lipshitz wrote: "Our friends did not ask to be heroes. They wanted to turn a desert into a paradise for the people of Israel. Those who died hoped that our place would be a fertile garden and not a gloomy valley."

Thank God, therefore, that we had reached the beginning of redemption and the end of the gloomy valley. If only this evil war had not occurred. If only Shalom could have kept plowing, sowing, and planting; if he could have stayed in Beit Ovadia, which was built as a house of study for those seeking relaxation and healing, for those who came from all over the country to take pleasure in the mountain and in the friends who built it up. If only he had continued weaving his poems so full of yearning and faith, and lived to a ripe old age. Would then his sons and daughters, his friends and descendants have known that he was a hero? "My God, only You will never leave me," he wrote in one of his wonderful poems, and went on:

> I have loved you for your truth, your light and your courage,
> I have loved you for your forests, your fields, your harvests,
> For your heavens, your clouds, your mountains, your valleys, your rivers, your seas.
> I have loved you for every spark of truth you have passed on to me.

From where did this young man get the poetic wisdom of old age, the ability to handle a hoe, a rifle, a pen, and to stand fast with all three of them before his God, and say to him: "Only you will never leave me"?

Shoshana could no longer follow the lesson. It passed her by. Perhaps it was not Shalom who was the hero, perhaps not Yosef, perhaps not one of the many who were with them. Perhaps it was all of the Etzion Bloc: its four settlements; the men, women, and children; the fighters in the field units that came to stand by the settlers; the company of the thirty-five Palmach members who were slaughtered on their way here. All of them were one, one soul. And perhaps this one collective soul was the embodiment of heroism.

On November 29 a vote was taken in the United Nations, and it decided to partition the country and create a sovereign Jewish state. The Etzion Bloc belonged, according to the partition plan, to the area given to the Palestinian Arabs.

Despite the fact that these settlements were, supposedly, no longer part of Israel, the settlers were all wild with joy. The hand-printed internal bulletin of Kfar Etzion rejoiced: "Joyful song rose up and spread over the whole area. The circle of dancers grew and exulted." But before the night of celebration was over, the Bloc was under siege. The road to Jerusalem was cut. People were killed. The bulletin stated: "There is now an awareness that our blood is not being shed in vain. The blood shed now is the blood of a covenant, the birth pangs of the redemption of the homeland." And Shalom, the man of faith, said in a eulogy for one of the fallen: "A homeland is the value without which we are all doomed to destruction and constant degradation—we, in the land of our fathers, and even more so the millions of our brothers in the Diaspora who seek redemption."

The first convoy was attacked; ten were killed. Shalom was one of the ten.

On Saturday night a hasty letter arrived; it was written by the chief rabbi of Israel, Rabbi Itzhak Isaac Herzog: "In tears and sorrow I write these words of solace to you. Be strong and of good courage! Whatever you think necessary to do for your defense on the Sabbath, feel free to do. Not only is it allowed, it is your duty. God will protect you, and hasten your salvation." The letter showed a strong awareness that the battle for the mountain, in the hands of these sons of the Torah, needed the assistance of the authorities of the Torah. In the kibbutz they studied the letter carefully. A committee for religious matters in time of war was set up. "What will be allowed, will be allowed on the basis of the law of the Torah," wrote Dov Knohall. "We will do this with the feeling that we are carrying out a *mitzva* [a religious precept], and we will know to give up those things that are only for our comfort."

In Jerusalem they knew that the defenders did not have the strength to hold out against all their foes: the Palestinian rioters, the Egyptian army that was breaking through from the south, and the Arab (Jordanian) Legion arriving from the east. It was impossible. They also knew that the Etzion Bloc was the last stronghold against the capture of Jerusalem. They felt that if the Bloc fell, the city would fall. No one could take the responsibility for sacrificing one life for another. So the leaders suggested that the Bloc consider whether to give in and be evacuated, or face the attackers and pray for salvation. Shalom was no longer with us, thought Shoshana, when they gathered for an evening meeting to discuss matters of life and death, of the sacrifice of Isaac and of another ram caught in the thicket.

That night was their greatest trial. "Everlasting night is Jerusalem," said Rabbi Akiva. In Kfar Etzion there was only one interpretation for this statement. Without their holding on until the last drop of blood was shed, this nation, fighting for its sovereignty, would not have a capital in the holy city. The enemy would break through the walls of the besieged city, and it would fall. The blood of Kfar Etzion would keep it alive. Thirty-five Palmach boys had left Jerusalem to strengthen the ranks of the defenders of Kfar Etzion. They did not arrive. On their way they had met an old Arab shepherd. They had pitied him and let him go, unharmed. He had run back and raised all the neighboring villages. The thirty-five were suddenly surrounded by a huge crowd of enemies. They all fell in a battle that became a legend and a miracle—thirty-five wicks in one torch.

Today we look back to those distant heroic days. Shalom and Yosef are no longer with us. Many of their friends and brothers are also no longer alive. Only the memory of that hour at dusk—between the afternoon and evening prayers—stays with us. The Etzion Bloc held out so that Jerusalem would not fall. The sun set and the sun rose again and they were still there, fighting, until the bloody conclusion.

Two hundred forty died. They will remain forever our heroes and saints. And a soft whisper will keep repeating gently: These boys won everlasting life for Jerusalem.

Zevulun Hammer is a former Israeli minister of education, culture, and sports.

LIKE A BLAZING STORM

GUR MEIROV

by Ruth Sapir-Nussbaum

The legend of Gur was born with him. Like a blazing storm he swept through our lives for all of his seventeen years, and he remains with us yet. His youthful image keeps flashing in our memories, in our dreams, and in all the other Gurs that carry his name.

Sarah Solichenski, an ardent pioneer who arrived in the early Twenties from Vilna to Kibbutz Kinneret, decided to improve her Hebrew. Her friends told her that Shaul Meirov, a member of the kibbutz who was a graduate of the Herzliya Gymnasium, could help her. She went into the dining hall to look for him, and when he turned to face her she saw only a pair of eyes. From that moment she knew that, more than Hebrew, she wanted to get to know those eyes. Their older daughter, Ruta, and Gur were the fruit of this love.

But even before that, said Sarah, "in 1923, when I just met Shaul in Kinneret, he was a man of mystery. He would appear and disappear." And later, "we only managed to live together for short periods, and when he was home he was usually exhausted."

Shaul—whose extremely active life has been recorded in history books under the name Shaul Avigur—wrote:

> I had a bit of an argument with Sarah about what we would name the baby. . . . The figure of King David appealed to me. The combination of physical beauty, courage, spirituality, and love of music made it seem the perfect choice. Sarah had some objections to the name, and I grudgingly gave in to her. We called him Avraham, but the name didn't stick. It was almost forgotten completely. Our daughter, Ruta, who was so happy to have a brother, as a child called him Gur [Puppy], Guri, Gurile [diminutives of Puppy], and this name remained with him to his last day. . . .
>
> Sarah did not have an easy time with Gur. He was independent, daring, sharp-tongued, impulsive. He did not like people making too much of a fuss over him,

nor did he like them interfering in what he wanted or chose to do. Since I only saw him once a week or every two weeks, I could never get my fill of his antics. . . . I enjoyed his playfulness, and even his wildness and his unkempt appearance. I saw only his positive side—his effervescent, vigorous love of life, his beauty, his strength, his natural drive. . . .

. . . Gur, full of strength and energy, was a never-ending source of inventive pranks. "Gur, the prankster," Ruta used to playfully call him when she wanted to provoke him. Sarah called him "Tarzan" after the film character, or "the little Bedouin," or "Gur-Hamsin," after the burning, restless desert wind. . . .

As a child he played the violin well, especially when he played "from his head," as he called it. After a while he gave up the violin, and turned to the mandolin. He was considered an excellent player in the string orchestra. Playing music used to calm him down. This boy, who usually couldn't sit still for a minute, would become totally absorbed in the world of music. His face would radiate joy more than ever. He was happy to be playing and to be a part of this community of musicians, the musicians of Kinneret, of whom he was so proud. On the way back to his room [in the children's house] from the weekly rehearsal he would stop in, often with Dan, a friend whom he loved like a brother; they would pick up their instruments, and music, sometimes gentle, sometimes more intense, would float throughout the balmy Kinneret evening. . . .

One day I arrived home in the later afternoon. It was a burning hot summer; there was not the slightest breeze. I found him on the eastern field that borders on a steep slope down to the Lake of Tiberias. I walked up to him quietly. With a sure, quick, experienced hand he was spreading chemical fertilizer from a sack tied to his waist. His head, as usual, was bare. A broad smile spread across his sweaty face when he realized I was there. He was very thirsty. In a flash he disappeared behind the hill, ran down, drank some water from the lake, and scampered back up. Again he smiled at me with his unforgettable smile. I grabbed hold of his front lock of hair, as I used to, pulled his sweaty forehead to my mouth and kissed him. I can still feel in my mouth to this very day the salty taste of his sweat. Right before my very eyes I see my hope being realized, I thought to myself. A new generation is growing up in this country, a generation of children who are part of nature, of the land, of work. Simple. Natural.

When he was in the tenth grade, in the summer of 1947, the boy took part in a student journey to Aqaba. Shmueli, the biology teacher, described how Gur was the first to unload the baggage, to light the kerosene stoves, to cook, to push the buses through sand and rocks and clear paths for them. At the same time he would run to every new plant, every new find, collect them, arrange them, take notes. Shmueli also wrote about the nights at Aqaba:

The sky turned silver and the high granite rocks stood out prominently. Suddenly the moon appeared between two cliffs, and by its light I saw Gur standing by our driver, totally absorbed by the granite cliffs and the moon rising between them. We were approaching Aqaba. The full moon rose above the sloping granite mountains and poured its silver light on the quiet waters of the gulf. The buses stopped. Gur jumped off first and walked silently toward the illuminated gulf, which was shimmering and sparkling.

Eleventh grade. November 29. Night training began. On March 15, 1948, school ended. Meir Hadash, the Hagana commander of the Kinneret district, wrote:

> We decided to put all the boys in one section . . . we felt their need to be together, and there was nothing more important to us. They were a very closely knit group. A small pride of lions. . . . The young boys were impatient to get going, eager to go into battle, while the older ones had an aura of seriousness about them and a gentle sadness. In the prewar days there was an atmosphere of merriment and mischievousness in the section. This jovial confidence seemed to be what kept them going.

About Gur's battles Aharonik Israeli, the section commander, wrote later to Shaul, who was abroad at the time, on a secret mission:

> One Friday evening (April 27) we gathered all the men in a hurry—one was on his way home from work, one in the shower, one playing with his son on the grass, and one just fooling around. How unprepared we were! . . . We did not know anything about warfare. We jumped into the armored car, and drove to the police station of Zemach, which the Arabs had taken previously when the British left. We had one goal—to take the station. After a difficult hand-to-hand battle that went on for about four hours, we succeeded. Later I saw the ardor and the pride in your son's face, his black eyes, glistening with a feeling of brotherhood for all those around him, his black head covered with a captured *tarbush* [the tasseled cloth or felt hat usually worn by Moslem men], which he wore with an air of arrogance and ostentation. . . . On May 6 we were the spearhead of the platoon that went out to block the connection between the Zubh Arab tribe and the village of Ein Mahal. Gur was the scout, guiding us up the mountain, through tall wheat fields. The climb was very hard, and when we reached the high ground we immediately encountered Arabs. For two hours we lay there and held back their reinforcements. . . . Gur was the contact between us and the platoon commander. His

shouts echoed through the wadis, amid the thunder of the explosions and the whistle of bullets. At the end he asked to be sent to the front line.

The Arab reinforcements kept coming. They rushed toward us. We were ordered to retreat, but the platoons stationed in the village were rescued from there only after a few hours, exhausted and depressed, leaving behind seventeen dead.

Then came May 15. The State of Israel had just come into being. Again we found ourselves unprepared. Again, when we were called in, the Syrian army, with all its arms and vehicles, was already at the gates of Zemach. And again the same group was gathered together—the three boys, Danik Kinnarti, Zamir Dahan, and Gur—and all the others, and they were sent to Zemach. (This scene always reminded me of a frenzied rush to put out a fire.)

We stayed at Zemach for two days, with little equipment, without commanders and without instructions . . . Dan, Zamir, and Gur were at a front position of our sector, a position of machine guns and Molotov cocktails. They would duck every time there was the boom of a shell on the ruined stone house behind them, straighten up again, and wait impatiently for the enemy to come closer. If there were doubts about other positions, I knew this position would not disappoint us. The three of them were always together, until they fell, one after the other. Two days later we were replaced and went to Tiberias to rest.

And then came the bitter day, May 18, the day of the withdrawal from Zemach. Early in the morning we were again called in suddenly, to 'put out another fire' in Zemach.

The Syrians had circumvented our lines, broken through between Kibbutz Shaar Hagolan and Zemach, and come from behind. When we reached Kibbutz Degania the situation suddenly became very clear to us. We were running in one direction, and toward us ran old men, children, women with babies in their arms, fear and shock on their faces. We kept on running to Zemach. We had not even managed to take up our positions when we were surrounded by tanks. A hasty retreat began, with shells and fire beating down on us. We were the last ones to retreat, and suddenly Dan was injured, and the tanks were after us. He made an effort and ran on his own another hundred yards—and then he fell. Gur and I grabbed his arms, and we began to drag him (you should know that the wounded were not carried away during the retreat from Zemach . . .). We didn't have the strength to run. We walked and stubbornly kept on dragging him without looking back. One glance between us made it clear that we weren't going to leave Dan behind—we would escape with him or we would stay with him (this is what Gur told me afterward)—and we escaped. . . . "Kinneret, shalom," said Dan as we put him into the car, and while we were still attending to him. . . .

We heard the noise of a motorcycle and the bump of someone falling to the ground. We jumped down to see what had happened—Tulik from Degania had fallen wounded, with a bullet in his chest. While we were dressing his wound he started shouting; "I have a dispatch; it must be delivered immediately." In a flash Gur jumped on the motorcycle and rushed directly to headquarters. From then on he became a liaison soldier, carrying out his duties faithfully and bravely.

If it was necessary to call a midnight patrol from Menachamiya to Kinneret, Gur rode in the darkness and brought it. If it was necessary to deliver a message quickly, Gur got there swiftly on his motorcycle. We were worried about him, because he used to vent his enormous energy, his unexpressed feelings of revenge on the gas pedal of his motorcycle. This was not enough for him. He asked to be transferred to a front position along with his friends in the section, but headquarters would not give him up. In the end, as you know, the Syrian attack on Degania failed. But we returned home tired and depressed about those who did not come back.

The daily battles continued, and all the time we worried about Dan. . . . One night we were informed that Dan had died. Gur was the only one who was released for the funeral. He stood at the graveside and cried bitterly, with the huge tears of a boy for a brother-friend . . . The next day he returned with a more mature look in his eyes, a tight expression of stubbornness and determination at the corners of his mouth. He was silent; he didn't say a word.

After a while, everyone went back to his work at home, since we weren't professional soldiers. And again the section was called up, this time to the aid of Kibbutz Ein Gev, at the foot of the Golan cliffs. Again Gur excelled, as he moved with his Spandau machine gun outside the fence, beyond the line of field positions. He alone held the front for a long time.

When the Jordan Battalion was established, Gur was assigned to it, but with his stormy temperament he couldn't find a place for himself, and "escaped" with two of his friends, Yaacov M. and Natanel, to join a commando unit of this battalion. Natanel told about his last day:

In the evening we went home for twenty minutes by jeep. I was with Gur when he said good-bye to his mother. I saw him fall on her neck and kiss her warmly and lovingly, and Gur was not the type to show his emotions. Toward morning we attacked the position that had been occupied by the Arabs, and they ran off in panic. We held the position with the Arabs facing us about thirty to forty yards away. There was constant shooting and sniper fire. Eventually we got so tired that we couldn't keep our eyes open anymore. Gur tried some sniper fire with his machine gun but was unsuccessful. "Let's trade places," said Eitan from Afikim; "you're so tired." Gur answered: "One more shot and I'll give you the gun." Just as he finished saying that, he fell to the ground. The bullet had hit him in the forehead, below his helmet. He died on the spot. His last words were: "Everything looks dark; I can't see anything, but I must be strong. Natanel, you must be strong too."

This was on the 5th of Tammuz (July 14, 1948).

Sarah wrote to Shaul, who was on a vital mission for the Israeli army: "I have buried the hope of my life, the source of my joy and pride in a grave. . . . Everything around me has been orphaned—the fields that he loved so much, the sea, his musical instruments, his school bag; the whole country has lost his enormous strength, which he had not yet managed to give. And we aren't even allowed the chance to mourn our child together."

And later: "Spring has come, nature is renewing itself, life bursts out of every crack, on the pile of stones on the eastern field nothing moves, nothing stirs. . . . On his eighteenth birthday we planted an olive tree on the former strong point at Sejera. At least the tree will continue to flourish at the place where his short life came to an end." In memory of his son, Shaul Meirov changed his name to Shaul Avigur, Father of Gur.

Ruth Sapir-Nussbaum was born in Kibbutz Kinneret.

THREE WOMEN IN BATTLE

MIRIAM BEN-ARI, SHULAMIT DORCHIN, AND DEVORAH EPSTEIN

by Zvika Dror

One of the most heroic battles in the War of Independence was the battle of Nitzanim. This tiny kibbutz, in the south of Israel, resisted with amazing tenacity and courage the assault of large Egyptian army forces. Into the epic story of Nitzanim's sacrifice were interwoven the exploits of three young heroines—Mira, Shulamit, and Devorah.

The military situation of the young State of Israel at the beginning of June 1948 was difficult, but the situation at Nitzanim was especially hard. This small kibbutz, which belonged to the Zionist youth movement, had been established five years earlier. It lay on the main road between Gaza and Ashdod, surrounded by Arab villages. The area was hard to defend. At that time, a few weeks after the establishment of the state, there were 150 fighters there, half of them members of the kibbutz, half of them new recruits to the Givati Brigade. Many of both groups were new immigrants. Among the fighters there were also ten women who had chosen not to leave Nitzanim when all the children and the other women had been evacuated in Operation Baby in May. Three of these women—Miriam "Mira" Ben-Ari, Shulamit Dorchin, and Devorah Epstein—fell in the last battle of Nitzanim on June 7, 1948.

The Arab attacks on Nitzanim and the supply convoys that tried to reach it began back in December 1947, right after the partition decision of the United Nations on November 29. But the kibbutz members gritted their teeth, continued working, entrenched themselves as best they could, and hoped for the best. Their situation worsened after the Egyptian army invaded the country. The large Egyptian force that was moving northward up the coast, toward Tel Aviv, surrounded Nitzanim. When the Egyptian advance was stopped near Ashdod, it turned back to attack the tiny besieged settlement at its rear, with full force.

"At times like this we have to overcome everything!" wrote Mira Ben-Ari after the big siege began. She was then twenty-two years old. She had immigrated to the country in 1934 from

Germany, with her parents. The well-to-do Glazshniev family settled in Tel Aviv, and Mira soon showed her independent spirit. During her studies at the Ben-Yehuda secondary school she developed radical views and began to severely criticize city life that she deemed "degenerate." She joined the Maccabi youth movement and excelled at fencing. At the same time she was also active in the Lehi (Stern) youth movement. She gave vent to her stormy nature in her journals and in the poems she wrote; "Jewish blood will not be free," she often stated. She even hinted that she was willing to pay with her life to be a part of the struggle for a just cause. After she finished her secondary school studies she decided, against her parents' wishes, "to fulfill the pioneering idea," which meant settling on a kibbutz. A short time later she wrote about it to a friend: "I felt in my heart a terrible emptiness. I had been thinking about my future, my studies—medicine, bacteriology, teaching, clerical work. I did not know which direction to go in, and finally I found the solution in the kibbutz."

This pretty, intelligent, competent young woman found a way to fit in, with her European manners, in the Roots group of the Young Maccabi movement. At first she settled with the group in the Lower Galilee. There she also met Eliakum Ben-Ari, whom she married. Within a short time they moved to Nitzanim, in the northern fringes of the Negev. She worked at different jobs, depending on where she was needed, but became most involved in gardening. With great dedication she planted and hoed and weeded. She took pleasure in every green patch and every flower bed that grew in the sand. In time, when the war broke out, she suffered greatly when the digging of the communication trenches and defenses destroyed her handiwork.

In Nitzanim, Mira and Eliakum had a son, Danny. Caring for him did not prevent her from taking an active part in the defense of the settlement. At the beginning of 1947 she went out as a radio operator to Kfar Uriya. When she returned she was put in charge of radio communication at Nitzanim. On March 12, 1947, she found herself in a very special situation. At the time, the British army, which still occupied the country, was trying to prevent the immigration of refugees at any price. The refugee ship *Shabtai Luzhinski* was approaching the coast and was directed to the area of Nitzanim. Mira, who tried to establish contact with the boat, moved from place to place in order to avoid the intensive interference activity of the British. Finally, she shouted joyfully, "I've done it!" Shortly afterward a large black mass, the refugee ship, materialized in the sea, and Mira guided it until it got stuck in shallow waters and the refugees began to disembark. Her heart was full of joy at her part in the successful operation. The refugees mixed in with the many Hagana members who were quickly rushed to the spot. The British were unable to trace them and deport them to Cyprus. Two of the refugees from the *Shabtai Luzhinski* joined Nitzanim and later fell in its final battle.

When the battles of the War of Independence became harsher and bloodier, the IDF command decided to evacuate the Nitzanim mothers and children in Operation Baby. During the evacuation Eliakum Ben-Ari was on duty outside the kibbutz. Mira, the radio operator, was the only mother who remained behind with the defenders of the kibbutz. She put a note into her son's clothes that was meant for her husband. The note said:

I will only write a few words, and I'm sure you'll understand that I can't write more. It's just a little difficult, more than a little. I have never felt this way before, but I'll get over it. At times like this, we have to overcome everything! Perhaps because of the ability of our people to suffer and not give up, because of our stubborn will to survive despite the fact that we are few in number, because of all of this, we will get what we deserve after two thousand years. There is nothing worse than the separation of a mother from her child. I am leaving my child so that he will grow up in a secure place, so that he will be a free man in his country! Visit him often. Give him all my love when you go to see him! Give my father and mother many kisses and ask them to forgive me for not writing them, but I really couldn't do it!

To one of her friends, who left with the babies, she said: "Tell Danny that he had a mother."

Two days before the decisive battle, Mira's radio, which ran on batteries, broke down. A squad that went out to the battalion command in Beer Tuvia brought back a radio that could only be run by an electric current from an emergency generator. But then it turned out that the noise of the generator interfered with the wireless connection, so cables were connected between the generator and Mira's radio. Contact was renewed for a while but broke down soon when the cables were hit in the shelling. One of the fighters volunteered to go out and fix the cables under heavy fire, but after a few hours the radio itself broke down. After 8:00 P.M. on Sunday, June 6, there was almost no radio contact between Nitzanim and the headquarters of the Givati Brigade.

That same night, after midnight, the Egyptian forces launched the final assault. Mira did not stop trying to make contact, but only at 10:00 the following morning did she manage to send an SOS call, which was received in Beer Tuvia. Later she tapped out the last message: "The Egyptians are in the kibbutz. I am destroying the radio and the code. I'm going out to fight."

The Egyptians stormed the small kibbutz with large forces. When the commander of Nitzanim, Avraham Shwartzstein, realized that they no longer had a chance to repel their attackers or break through the Egyptian lines and join our forces, he consulted with a few members and decided to surrender. He intended to negotiate a cease-fire with the Egyptian army officers and thus avoid falling into the hands of the disorderly gangs of local Arabs. His voice thundered above the din of the battle: "It's not worth continuing! This is a slaughter! We are surrendering!"

One of the members stood up in the trench and shouted: "Who says we're surrendering? We will never surrender!" At that very moment he was hit by a shell and killed. At Shwartzstein's order one of the Israelis raised a piece of white cloth on the end of his rifle, but he too was killed. Then the commander of Nitzanim got up on a mound of earth, took off his shirt, and waved his undershirt slowly, ignoring the bullets that were flying all around him.

After a few attempts he calmly walked back to his place and took over. All signs pointed to the fact that the Egyptian officers knew Nitzanim was surrendering. Avraham Shwartzstein decided to walk out toward them with Mira, who was holding a white handkerchief in her hand.

They approached the Egyptian lines. An Egyptian officer suddenly drew his revolver and shot Avraham, who collapsed, dead. Mira could have assumed that the Egyptian officers weren't going to shoot at her, but she drew her revolver and shot the Egyptian officer who had hit Avraham. At that very moment she was shot to death.

A few minutes later, at 4:00 P.M., the enemy fire stopped. The last battle for Nitzanim had gone on for fifteen hours.

When the tired prisoners were rounded up, covered in blood, dust, and sweat, they recognized the bodies of Mira and Avraham, which were lying beside each other. They knew that Mira's friend, Shulamit Dorchin, was also among the dead.

Shulamit Dorchin was born in Poland in 1925, studied in a Hebrew school of the Tarbut network, and had been a Zionist from her youth. During the Second World War she was exiled with her family to a remote area in Central Asia, deep in the heart of the Soviet Union. There she worked hard to help support her family, continuing with her studies as best she could.

After the war the family returned to Poland, knowing that this was only a stopover on their way to Palestine. Shulamit was active among the children and youth of the Zionist youth movement. She was also a counselor and leader in the Children's Kibbutz in Poland, and in displaced persons' camps in Germany. Later, she participated in the operations of Bricha, the underground organization that helped Jews escape Europe and get to Palestine. In 1947, immediately after immigrating to Palestine, she started traveling, to get to know the landscape and the ambiance of her country. Her parents, who were well aware of her talents and her high intellect, tried to convince her to continue her studies. She agreed, and enrolled in the math and physics departments of Hebrew University, and even studied there for a while.

But there was already a feeling in the air that war was imminent. During a vacation Shulamit visited her friends at Nitzanim, and when she returned home she announced that she had definitely decided not to return to the university. In November 1947, a few days before the UN decision, Shulamit joined Nitzanim and immediately started to work and take part in Hagana training. She tutored immigrant youth during the grim days of the continuous siege. She also took a quick course in first aid. She had a very optimistic attitude toward life, always cheerful and willing to perform any task. "So I'll go," she used to say whenever there was need for a volunteer. The Givati fighters, who admired her greatly, named one of their armored cars after her.

She wrote to her brother, who was fighting in the north, "We should be happy that our fate is to fight this holy war, this war of independence." When the attacks on Nitzanim began, Shulamit moved from one position to another in the courtyard under heavy fire, encouraging the fighters. During temporary lulls in the fighting she arranged parties and community singing. She even tried to put out a newspaper.

As a field medic she went from one wounded soldier to the other with her first-aid kit. One day she wrote: "I have just ended guard duty and have rushed to take care of a wounded soldier. It's awful. Only a few hours ago we were joking together, and now he is dead. I take care of the wounded, I, who hated and was so afraid of the sight of blood, am now busy dressing the wounds of friends and acquaintances. How strange fate is. The nausea has passed, as if I was born to do this."

On the day of the last battle, around noon, she was called to the "shoemaker's" position, which was no longer functioning. Two men lay there wounded, and Shulamit, who realized they were in critical condition, ran to get the doctor from the clinic. He gave her bandages but did not go with her. He later said he could not understand how she managed to get through the living hell of the enemy fire and return to the position. Friends who saw her there said that she bent over the wounded, talked to them, and dressed their wounds. "Shula tore off a wounded soldier's undershirt and used it to stop his bleeding wound," said an eyewitness. "She didn't say out loud that their condition was critical, but the smile that usually accompanied her gentle talk had disappeared." After a few minutes she herself was hit and fell beside the wounded. Someone from the next position heard her whispering: "Shoot me; I can't take it anymore. . . ."

Carmela Gur-Reichman, a new immigrant who had arrived in Nitzanim via Cyprus, said:

> As dawn was approaching we already had many casualties. I felt helpless. The gunfire was terrible. Members who came to the aid of the wounded were themselves hit. Some of my best friends were wounded. I was in shock. . . . I felt so alone, a girl facing Egyptian soldiers and officers, armed and ferocious. I did not know what awaited me; I only understood that I was going to my death. I wanted to die. I ran into a burst of gunfire, and not one bullet hit me. I kept going until I got to the edge of the trench, and I fell straight into the arms of an Egyptian officer. An Egyptian soldier grabbed my watch and tore the chain from my neck. The officer took me to where the other prisoners were being held. On my way I saw Shulamit, who had a serious stomach wound. I couldn't even stop for a minute beside her.

The prisoners were taken to the Majdal police station, which was in the hands of the Egyptians. The women were separated from the men. Among them was Devorah Epstein, who had been badly wounded in the stomach. Devorah, eighteen years old, a member of a group from Zionist youth in Uruguay, had arrived in the country around the time of the UN partition vote. Her dream to work in agriculture was realized for only a few days. The fighters called her "the flying liaison officer" because she ran like a gazelle between positions. A good friend of Mira and Shulamit, she was hurt while bending over a wounded friend. She died in prison and was buried in the yard of the Majdal police station. After the IDF captured this position her grave was discovered, and she was buried in a communal grave in Nitzanim.

A week after the fall of Nitzanim a special memorial service was held in the prisoners' camp. The deputy commander of the reinforcement platoon said:

> My soldiers were simple boys, who had gone through a lot of pain and suffering, the survivors of exile and hell. Most of them, survivors from Europe who had just recently arrived, were almost anonymous. I hadn't even got to know them and didn't even remember all their names. We were together for only a few days from the time they were drafted. They were supposed to get training in the use of firearms, but were not deterred when they learned that they would not be trained because the enemy was at our doorstep. An example is the boy who came with us to Nitzanim in a terrible mood because the people at the recruiting center at Tel Litvinsky had lost all his family photographs. I helped him look for them, but unfortunately we didn't find them.
>
> The boy was terribly depressed. "If I die here," he said, "please write on my gravestone in clear letters: 'Here lies the soldier Schwartz from Romania, who fell for his homeland.'"

Zvika Dror, a researcher and writer, is a member of Kibbutz Lohamei Hagetaot.

FROM THE DEATH CAMPS TO THE BATTLES OF 1948

ELIEZER FEIG

by Naftali Yaniv

"The cloth they wove that day was the cloth of hope for a day to come." Thus did the poet Shaul Tchernichovsky eulogize the Jews fallen during the Arab riots of 1936–39 in his well-known poem "Land, Behold." The cloth Eliezer Feig wove day after day was surely "the cloth of hope for a day to come." Less than nineteen years did he live on this earth, and some of those were filled with the painful, shocking experiences of the horrors of the Holocaust. With this kind of past, what was left for him, if not to hope for a better future? He waited for this day to come, but it did not arrive. This young man, who had barely escaped the concentration camps, did not hesitate to go out onto the battlefields of the War of Independence. He had escaped the Nazi death machine only to meet his fate in Tel Arish, between Holon and Jaffa, before the IDF had even come into being and before the Declaration of Independence.

"Elik was born of the sea," wrote the great Israeli writer Moshe Shamir about his brother Eliahu who fell three months before my cousin Eliezer, on the road that passed through the Arab village Yazur, a few kilometers from Tel Arish. "That's what Father used to say," added Shamir, "when we used to sit together at dinner on the porch of our small house on summer evenings." My cousin Eliezer, or Leizer as his family called him, was not born of the sea, did not grow out of the sands of the country, did not even manage to enjoy the sun of Palestine. When I met him he didn't even have a father who could sit with him at dinner on the porch and talk about his birth.

He arrived at our house in Rehovot completely by surprise during the summer months of 1945. One day my late father returned home for lunch and told us that he was planning to go to the center of town. In his bicycle shop he had heard about a group of a few dozen young boys and girls "from the camps" who were about to visit the town. "Perhaps," he said, "I will find someone from our family."

"The camps" for us meant something gloomy and dark. As a small boy I didn't know all the details, but I knew that in "the camps," during World War II, which had just recently ended, the Nazis had killed many Jews. From time to time, in response to questions about uncles who were not around, we heard, my friends and I, cryptic hints about "the camps." Occasionally, I heard a restrained sigh from Father or Mother when they remembered their relatives who had ended up in "the camps" and who knows what had happened to them. Now there was talk at home, in the street, in the kindergarten, about the few people who had gotten out alive, and even reached Palestine. Would one of them "belong" to us? I asked myself. Would I suddenly find some relatives from there?

I don't know if my father had any other information about this group of young boys and girls. When I think back on it, it was clear that without some clue the chances were very slim. My parents had immigrated to the country from Transylvania. A large number of Jews from that area had perished in the German death camps. If there were a small number of young survivors, and if someone from my family was among them, how likely would it be that he should be here? How likely would it be that he was among the youths who had reached the country as part of the religious quota of Youth Aliya and settled in Kfar Yavetz and were arriving for a visit that day in Rehovot?

But what then seemed so unbelievable, actually happened! My father came back from town with a young boy who looked a grown-up to me. He certainly was not a grown-up, but I was only six at the time. The blond hair of the young boy was curly and combed back. His blue eyes examined us with curiosity. He had a tattooed number on his forearm. Now I know that he was very thin. "This is Leizer," said Father, and he went on to explain: "He is the son of Benzy, whose mother was my cousin." The excitement was, of course, tremendous. Neighbors were called in to hear the news, which had spread. There were tears and conversation, mixed in together. We were of course dying to know how Father had found him.

Father told us that he had approached the group from Kfar Yavetz and had been struck by the familiar face of one of the boys. He asked him if his father was called Benzy Feig, and when he said that he was, Father went on to ask him if he was born in the town of Bistria. Yes, the boy answered, and Father was probably getting very tense when he asked the next question, which was meant to remove any further doubt: "Do you have an older sister whose name is Leah?" The sixteen-year-old boy, who had managed to escape the hell of the Holocaust, answered directly, without any emotion: "I had a sister. Her name was Leah. I think that she's dead like all the rest."

"Your sister is alive," announced Father, who was deeply moved. He had already learned previously that Leah had landed in a displaced persons' camp in Italy, and was planning to immigrate to the United States. "And besides that," he added, "you, Leizer, will not return now to Kfar Yavetz. You will come home with me, to your family. You will live with us, and be like our son." And that was how I suddenly had a cousin, "from there," a sort of older brother of a new kind.

A sort of older brother, because our relationship could not be a simple one. There were language problems as well as a ten years' difference in age between us. I was a boy who grew up in Palestine, in a warm home, without ever having any real worries, and he was a survivor, snatched from the burning flames, who had already seen so much killing and evil and escaped. What did he think when he saw me playing innocently near him? Would he be able to tell me something about his wretched life? Had he told anyone else? Did he tell my parents?

Small bits of his story came out from time to time. Over the years we also heard the stories of other survivors whom he had happened to meet along the way. Now I know that he had been through a few death camps, which were (in an order that was not clear to me): Auschwitz, Dachau, Bergen-Belsen, and Mauthausen. When was he taken from his home? When was he separated from his parents and his sister? How did he manage to survive in those atrocious camps, so young, so vulnerable? I still don't know the answers. But from the details I managed to piece together it seems that he had survived by calling up his amazing inborn resources. He had gone through a few of the so-called selection tests of the Nazis and come out alive. He would stand on tin boxes to make himself look taller than he was. He would pinch his cheeks hard so he would not look too pale, or too weak. He used all kinds of other tricks, which he discovered at the last minute, when he was literally on the edge of the abyss.

And now he was here, in a small town, in the house of distant relatives, who took him in with great love, but who could never be a substitute for his real parents, who were gone. He wanted to plan a life of his own, and he felt too old to go back to school. Father arranged an apprenticeship for him in a workshop at the Ziv Institute, the scientific institution that Chaim Weizmann had set up in Rehovot in the mid 1930s and from which the Weizmann Institute developed. Here, in a workshop that dealt with precision mechanics, he was supposed to learn a trade and find work, and make the best use of his "golden hands." He quickly fit in, enjoyed what he did, and earned the trust and understanding of his fellow workers.

I remember how he came home one day waving a photograph with enormous pride. The photograph showed him, together with a number of workers from the Institute, standing with the great Chaim Weizmann, who had come to visit the country. We old-time residents of Rehovot used to look up at the "palace" on the distant hill, among the orange groves, knowing that there lived "the king of the Jews." And here, in this picture, was Leizer, who had just come from far away, standing right beside him. "He knows me," he bragged; "he called me Feigeleh [Little Feig—a form of endearment]."

What did he do in his spare time? Who were his friends? Did he have something to talk about with boys his age, the rough Sabras [native-born Israelis] of the town? Father, who belonged to the volunteer fire brigade, got him into the brigade too. He was happy to go. He soon also joined the firemen's orchestra, which had a very good name in town. One of the members of the orchestra taught him to play the trumpet, and he learned how to play it well. I was very proud when I saw him marching in a procession in the firemen's blue uniform and peaked cap, playing with the youthful enthusiasm that apparently still remained in him despite everything.

I also know that he joined the ranks of the Hagana field corps. Often he would come back from work late because he had gone out to do training. More than one night and one Sabbath he spent in unknown places. Often I would see Mother bend over him with love and devotion, and nurse his feet, which had been wounded from treks in the field. That was, actually, the only sign of his activities. I never heard him complain, or try to skip out or avoid it, or claim that he had already suffered enough. I remember also the look on his face on Black Sabbath, in June 1946. A curfew was imposed on the town, and British paratroopers in red berets—we used to call them the Poppies—moved from house to house. They were looking for illegal arms, and rounding up all the men, Leizer among them, for interrogation at the Maccabi Stadium.

Father and Leizer came back after a short while, and Leizer was depressed. I'm sure that not-so-distant memories of other arrests in another country had come back to haunt him.

On the night of November 29, 1947, Leizer wasn't at home. He had gone out for Hagana training and came back after the die had already been cast: the United Nations General Assembly had decided on the establishment of a Jewish state in Palestine. We were all ecstatically happy. I will never forget that he did not join in our celebration. The eighteen-year-old boy had come back worn out from his night training, knowing that he would have to go out to work in a few hours. He heard the exciting news and sadly concluded with these words, which have remained etched in my mind: "We will have a state, but I will probably not live to see it." I remember that Father got very angry when he heard that, and Mother cried.

A few days later Leizer found out that he was going to be drafted for full service. In the meantime he went off each morning to the workshop at the Ziv Institute, but very often he was called away by the Hagana in the middle of the day. At the same time preparations were being completed to set up the battalion that was later to be the IDF Fifty-second Battalion of the Givati Brigade. In this battalion there was a company of field soldiers made up of Rehovot youth, including Leizer. The battalion was supposed to defend the whole area south of Tel Aviv, down to the line of settlements of Nitzanim–Gat–Galon–Kfar Uriya–Gezer, and to also secure the transportation routes to Jerusalem and the Negev. Anyone with eyes to see understood that this was a unit that would take part in many battles and suffer great losses.

I have no doubt that Leizer understood exactly how things stood. Even if he was only a private, a new immigrant, his life experience was great and his senses were very sharp. I also have no doubt that he could have arranged things differently, without any difficulty. Despite the lack of manpower of those days, I'm sure that with his resourcefulness he could have found a sympathetic ear and managed to get released from combat service as a young Holocaust survivor, the last of his family, a "graduate" of the death camps. And I have no doubt that he decided not to choose this direction. Whatever he knew or did not know about those who evaded their national duty—among them the children of the country's well-to-do, who had not gone through a fraction of the suffering he had endured—he did not think for a moment about not being drafted. Boldly, without making a fuss, without using the flowery language from lectures he had never had the chance to hear, without the support of a group of friends of his own that he had grown up with and with whom he could face the new dangers, he put on the uniform of the Hagana that had still not become an army— and became a soldier.

His first battle was on Mount Castel, as part of the Nachshon Operation, which opened the road to Jerusalem. During the week of Passover, in April 1948, he was sent to Mikve Israel, in order to take part in the first battalion operation, to capture the area between Tel Aviv and Holon. Leizer's company was supposed to capture the Arab stronghold of Tel Arish and the concrete pillbox at the top of it. The operation was successful, but the fighters were quickly exposed to a murderous counterattack from the direction of Arab Jaffa, and many of them were wounded. A bullet hit Leizer in the temple. This brave youth, who had managed to survive the Nazis' death machine, collapsed in front of Tel Arish.

He was not even nineteen years old at this time. David Ben-Gurion declared the establishment of the Jewish State only seventeen days later, and Leizer, as he had known in his heart would happen, did not get the chance to see it. At the end of the war, Tel Arish's name was changed. Whenever I remember Leizer, I feel that it was a just decision to rename the small hill Tel Giborim (The Hill of the Heroes), in memory of those who fell there.

Naftali Yaniv, a relative of Eliezer Feig, is the media advisor to the minister of agriculture.

PART V

THE STRUGGLE
FOR SURVIVAL

1949–1967

This period is known as Israel's "heroic years." The heroism was not military; it characterized the astounding effort made by the tiny state to bring back to Eretz Israel hundreds of thousands of immigrants, in spite of its precarious economy. The immigrants came from all over—Eastern Europe, India, North Africa, Yemen, Iraq, Iran. . . . Many thousands lived in tents and crumbling huts, exposed to lashing rains and raging storms. The country was often on the edge of hunger. Aid from abroad was practically nonexistent, except for the Jewish contributions to the State of Israel. Yet, step by step, Israel overcame the obstacles. In 1952, over the bitter opposition of the Herut party, led by Menachem Begin, an agreement was signed with Germany for reparations payments of $822 million over twelve years. This transfusion alleviated Israel's desperate situation and allowed it to invest heavily in infrastructure and heavy industry.

Israel's hopes to make peace with its neighbors, once the War of Independence was over, were soon abandoned. The Arab states declared they were preparing a "second round." Moderate Arab leaders who considered making peace with Israel, like King Abdullah of Jordan and Riad Sulh of Lebanon, were assassinated. Infiltrators kept crossing the armistice lines—Israel's borders—to steal, to sabotage, and to assassinate civilians. The Israeli army was weakened by the departure of many fine soldiers and officers.

But then new men arrived at the helm, and carried out a revolution in the IDF. On the top level, it was the new chief of staff, Moshe Dayan, who introduced an original strategy and new standards of fighting. At the level of field commander, a young captain named Ariel "Arik" Sharon founded the legendary Unit 101, which would metamorphose into the Israeli army. At the fighting level, the one who carried the burden of operations was Meir Har-Zion, a 101 veteran and a paratrooper, who trained and led into battle the boldest Israeli soldiers.

Ben-Gurion himself resigned from office in December 1953, and moved to Kibbutz Sde Boker in the Negev, hoping that the Israeli youth would follow him there and "make the desert bloom." Moshe Sharett became prime minister and minister of foreign affairs. Pinchas Lavon became minister of defense. But after a sordid sabotage affair in Egypt, in which lives were lost, Lavon was forced to resign, in February 1955. Sharett called Ben-Gurion back from Sde Boker. Ben-Gurion returned as minister of defense; after the August 1955 elections, he became prime minister again.

Winds of war were blowing again in the Middle East. In September 1955 Egypt signed an arms deal with Czechoslovakia for the supply of huge quantities of tanks, cannon, jet fighters and bombers, warships and submarines. Egypt also closed the Straits of Tiran, which led to the port of Eilat, to Israeli shipping. Israel felt threatened. The United States and other Western powers refused to sell Israel the weapons necessary for her defense. The young director-general of the defense ministry, Shimon Peres, steered his country toward a secret alliance with France. The French government was engaged in a bitter war in Algeria, trying to crush a revolt by Algerian nationalists against the continuation of French rule. Egypt's president, Gamal Abd el-Nasser, Israel's archenemy, was also the patron of the Algerian rebels, whom he supplied with money and weapons, and trained on his territory. Nasser became therefore the common enemy of France and Israel.

In 1955–56 France started to supply Israel with important quantities of weapons, mainly tanks and aircraft. Senior officers of the two countries started discussing the possibility of a common operation against Egypt. A preemptive war against Egypt was approaching. Ben-Gurion forced the dovish Sharett to resign and appointed the hawkish Golda Meir as minister of foreign affairs.

In July 1956, Nasser nationalized the Suez Canal. The British and French governments decided to intervene against him. On October 22, 1956, Ben-Gurion, Dayan, and Peres flew secretly to France and were lodged by the French government in a villa in Sèvres, a suburb of Paris. In the following two days, secret negotiations between Israel, France, and Great Britain took place in Sèvres. An agreement was reached about a coordinated attack on Egypt, which would be triggered by an Israeli invasion of the Sinai.

Israel launched its attack on October 29, 1956. A week later, it had achieved an astounding victory over Egypt. That victory showed that since the War of Independence, the gap between Israel and her neighbors had grown. The Sinai Campaign reopened the Straits of Tiran to Israeli shipping. It also resulted in almost eleven years of peace for Israel, a golden age of prosperity, economic development, and absorption of new immigrants. In 1963 Ben-Gurion resigned from office. Levi Eshkol took his place.

THE MAN WHO RETURNED FROM HELL

YEHUDA TAJER-TAGAR

by Shlomo Hillel

"Dan and Dror have been missing since the morning. Their car was found abandoned in the main street. We assume that both Dror and Dan have been caught." These were the words of the telegram that was sent on May 25, 1951, from an underground wireless station in Baghdad to the Tel Aviv headquarters of the Aliya Bet. They signaled the beginning of a remarkable, heroic affair. Dror was the code name for the Aliya Bet emissary Mordechai Ben-Porat. Dan was the code name of another emissary by the name of Yehuda Tajer-Tagar. Soon it was established that the two Israelis had indeed been arrested by the Iraqis. The news caused utter distress at the Aliya Bet headquarters. Iraq was an implacable enemy, still in a state of war with Israel. The two Israeli agents might suffer beatings, torture, and an atrocious death. There seemed to be almost no way to save them.

Mordechai Ben-Porat managed, fortunately, to escape quickly and get to Israel. Yehuda Tagar was sentenced to death. Later, his sentence was reduced to life imprisonment with hard labor. It took almost ten years until a dramatic reversal brought about his release and his return to Israel. The trials and tribulations that Yehuda Tagar endured during those years, and his survival, are part of the amazing Zionist struggle of the Iraqi Jews. This also makes Yehuda one of the most exemplary figures that Israel has known in its fifty years of existence.

Yehuda Tagar reached Iraq during a transitional period. The Zionist movement had been active in that country since the early Twenties. It worked openly at first, but from 1929 onward it went underground. It was about to end its activities with an incomparably dramatic climax. On Purim 5711 (March 3, 1950) the Iraqi parliament passed a special law that allowed Iraqi Jews to leave the country and fly straight to Israel. This was the culmination of a long struggle for the exodus of Iraq's Jews. At the end of the War of Independence, a tough struggle of young men and women from the Zionist movement had brought about a mass escape from Iraq to Iran, and from there to Israel. As a result more and more members of the community were swept up in the Zionist struggle for immigration to the Jewish State. This situation, along with a unique combination of circumstances, brought about the passing of the special law. What was called "the largest emigration by air in history" was now well under way. The vast majority of the community, more than a hundred thousand people, accepted the challenge and joined the immigration in the framework of Operation Ezra and Nehemiah. Twenty-five hundred years of Babylonian exile, the most ancient dispersion of our people, was coming to an end.

As a result the need arose for the reorganization of the Israeli activities in Iraq. Up until that time secret emissaries from Israel had worked in the framework of the Zionist youth movements primarily in education, self-defense training, and illegal immigration; they took part in a few other activities as well. Now it was clear that the Zionist movement would cease to exist, and all the Israeli secret organizations that wanted to function in Iraq would have to work on their own. Yehuda "Yudke" Tagar was the man chosen to coordinate these operations, and to function, according to his definition, as "a kind of Israeli underground consul."

He was twenty-seven at the time, the son of a longtime Jerusalem family. He had been one of the first Palmach fighters and had served in the Jewish Brigade in the Second World War. In the War of Independence he was the commander of a supporting company of the Sixty-second Battalion on the Jerusalem front. When the Israeli intelligence community was first set up, he joined the Institute for Intelligence, which later became the Central Institute for Intelligence and Security—Mossad.

When it was decided to send him to Iraq, he was given a passport and a cover story. He was to pose as an Iranian merchant by the name of Ismail ben Mahadi Salhun, a representative of the Kashanian Company. Perhaps this was the source of all his troubles. I was sent at the same time on a secret mission to Egypt posing as an Iranian merchant as well with a passport from the same series. But before that I had managed to spend a year in Iran, and I also spoke Persian quite well. Yehuda Tagar's situation was completely different. He had no Iranian background, he did not speak Persian, and he was sent to, of all places, a country that was a neighbor of Iran, where his assumed identity could be checked out easily. Moreover, he spoke a Palestinian dialect of Arabic, which could be easily detected the minute he opened his mouth.

In Israeli activities in Iraq there was no compartmentalization at all, and this was also a great hindrance. When Yudke arrived in Iraq he was in close contact with some of the emissaries of the Hehalutz Zionist pioneering movement and was even considered as a candidate to coordinate their immigration activities if it turned out that the movement's head, Mordechai Ben-Porat, had to leave the field. This was also the time when this organization had been partially exposed, due to its deep involvement in Operation Ezra and Nehemia. A Jewish Communist had also betrayed the organization to the Iraqi authorities.

And if that wasn't enough, a coincidence occurred that could not have been foreseen. Shortly after the War of Independence, a Palestinian Arab had worked for a week filling in for his cousin in the offices of the military administration in Acre. His cousin had a small coffee shop, and every morning he would come to the military administration offices, carrying small cups of coffee on an ornate plate, and serve them to the Israeli officers. This took place at the same time that Yehuda Tagar served there. The Palestinian left Israel after a while, wandered through the Middle East, and finally ended up in Baghdad, where he became a salesman in the Uruzdi-Bak department store. One day, looking up from his work, he saw a familiar face, the face of an Israeli officer he had served in Acre! He reported this astounding fact to the Iraqi police. There was another man with Tagar whom he didn't know. The other man was the second Israeli emissary, Mordechai Ben-Porat.

On May 22 "Dror" and "Dan" (Ben-Porat and Tagar) were arrested while walking out of the department store and were taken to the offices of the secret police. While Tagar was still worrying about the results of the verification of his Iranian identity he discovered that he was not going to need it anymore. Within forty-eight hours the Iraqi secret police had arrested another Israeli agent, Peter Rodney, a German-born Jew who had a perfectly good British passport. Rodney broke down under interrogation and told the Iraqis about Yehuda Tagar and even identified him in a lineup. From then on Tagar's Israeli identity was exposed, and he was considered an agent in the service of an enemy country.

The Iraqis not only incriminated him as a Zionist spy; they also decided that he had been involved in two other affairs. The first one was the affair concerning the arms caches of Hashura, the defense arm of the Zionist underground in Iraq. The second one was the wave of mysterious bombings in Baghdad in 1951. The bombs actually had been set off by local provocateurs. Out of this affair terrible blood libels arose that have not died to this very day.

Over many years Hashura had laboriously collected arms and ammunition to be used when the order was given. This operation was launched after a bloody pogrom against the Jews of Baghdad during the Second World War. Zionist leaders had decided then to train young Jews in the use of weapons, and to store firearms and ammunition in Jewish neighborhoods, so if there were another attack on the Jews they would be able to defend themselves. The arms were stored in hidden caches in the houses of some Hashura members. When the wave of immigration grew and Jewish houses were left empty, the caches had to be moved from place to place. Unfortunately, in the process two men were caught by the police. One of them was Shalom Salah Shalom, one of the members in charge of the caches, and the other was Yosef Basri, a lawyer. The "confessions" that were wrung out of Shalom by terrible torture made it possible for the Iraqis to accuse Basri of being a leader of a sabotage network that had stockpiled arms and supposedly set off the famous bombs. Another thirteen local Jews were added by the Iraqis to the list of members of this network, as was Yehuda Tagar, who had been arrested even before them.

All of the prisoners underwent terrible torture, at which the Iraqi security forces were experts. Tagar suffered twice as much because he was an Israeli. Besides being given what he described as "every possible kind of beating," he was strung up by his hands in various positions, and submitted to other kinds of physical torture. He was also forced to spend scores of nights near the interrogation room of the central jail in Baghdad and to hear again and again the screams of those being tortured. "My whole lower lip," he later said, "was one big sore, because I would bite it with my teeth out of nervousness, anger, and pain. Every effort to block my ears did not help. I could easily have gone crazy."

Later on, psychological pressure was added to the physical abuse. The examining magistrate made sure to show Tagar the Iraqi newspapers every day and to point to the articles and reports that demanded again and again that he and his friends be condemned to death. While looking at these newspapers Tagar happened to see that the immigration to Israel was going as planned. When the judge noticed this he also attacked him from this angle. If he saw that there was a temporary delay in the immigration he told Tagar that the government had ordered the emigration of the Jews to stop until he would reveal the names of his partners, especially that of Mordechai Ben-Porat.

It was a terrible dilemma. "On one hand, if I gave away his identity he would definitely be sentenced to death and hanged. On the other hand, he was just one man, and who was I to take upon myself the blame for stopping the immigration of the Iraqi Jews?" Fortunately, the delay was short, and a week later, while Tagar was still searching for a way out of his quandary, he saw a newspaper article saying that the immigration had been renewed. The examining magistrate himself admitted that the trick had not worked.

Now the Iraqis chose to use a diabolical trick. One night, right after the weapons caches had been discovered, Yehuda Tagar was told straight out, "Tomorrow morning you will be hanged." When he asked how they could hang a man who was still being interrogated, he was told that there was no need for a trial. They showed him the weapons. The Iraqi secret police knew everything, they said; the weapons had been found, he had been caught—end of story. On the spot they made it clear to him that the plans to hang him were entirely serious. He was dragged to a room full of military police, and toward midnight a bearded Jew, escorted by police officers, came to visit him. He introduced himself as a rabbi. The rabbi sat beside him for hours and read chapters from the Book of Psalms, to purify Tagar's soul before he was taken to the gallows.

At 3:30 A.M. Yehuda Tagar was escorted to the gallows cell. The hangman tied a heavy sack of sand to his feet and tried to cover his face with a black hood. Tagar refused to wear a hood. They didn't insist, and they placed a noose around his neck. Under the circumstances, when "I was convinced that this was serious and that I was going to be hanged," Tagar demanded that they send his body to Israel. His tormentors decided to add a bureaucratic touch to his suffering and made him sign official forms so that his supposed last wishes could be carried out. Then they kept him for a quarter of an hour on the trapdoor of the gallows, with a noose around his neck, his face to the wall, and his back to the handle of the gallows. Only when they realized that even this did not break him did they take him down from the gallows and tell him that he would stand trial, after all.

When he realized that the hanging had been a trick, after all, Tagar of course felt great relief, but he also knew that even if he stayed alive terrible years awaited him. "I knew from the beginning," said Tagar afterward, "that the minimum sentence I would receive would be life imprisonment with hard labor." What he perhaps didn't know from the beginning and only understood in retrospect was what he would go through until this "minimal" sentence was passed. He was returned to his cell on death row and spent about a year there without a trial. In the meantime the Iraqi authorities concocted another torturous intrigue. The regular court refused to try the men of the "Zionist network," claiming the evidence was too weak for a case that demanded such heavy punishment. So the authorities had no choice but to set up a special court and to distort all the procedures that were carried out in its sessions. The defense counsels were limited, or limited themselves, in their interrogations; the witnesses recited their texts quickly and were not asked to explain obvious contradictions; the arguments of the accused were ignored. At the end of the trial, which went on for a half a year, the presiding judge announced that three of the accused, Shalom Salah Shalom, Yosef Basri, and Yehuda Tagar, had been sentenced to death. Only after he read the verdicts for three quarters of an hour did the judge add that Yehuda Tagar would "only" get a life sentence.

Only after the results of the trial were made known, and after Basri's and Shalom's appeals had been rejected, did the Israeli government begin to make extensive diplomatic efforts to convince the Iraqi regent Abd El-Illah to cancel the harsh verdict. The foreign minister, Moshe Sharett, conveyed a personal telegram from President Chaim Weizmann, who was on his deathbed, to U.S. president Harry Truman, to urge him to use all of his influence in the matter. But it was to no avail. The Iraqis would not give in. On January 19, 1952, at dawn, Shalom Salah Shalom and Yosef Basri were hanged in the Bab Al-Moazem Square in the heart of Baghdad. Their hanging was accompanied by the jubilant cheers of the masses of people who gathered in the square. Their last words were: "Long live the State of Israel!"

Yehuda Tagar spent the last night of their lives with them. A rabbi sat at the back of the cell and read from the Book of Psalms, while the three of them sang Zionist songs. "Both of them were calm and amazingly brave. They held up extraordinarily well to the very end. I was the one who cried all night."

By that time Yehuda Tagar had won a special status in the prison. The criminal offenders knew that he had been taken to the gallows and brought down again still alive, and they related to him as if he had superhuman powers. The guards respected his strength of character. He became a kind of "elder of the prisoners" and also a trusted friend of those condemned to death. The latter would deposit with Tagar a sum of money, as a bribe to the hangman so that he would carry out the hanging quickly, without the torture of their being choked to death. Tagar had to witness the hanging, and only if he was convinced the hangman had fulfilled his part of the bargain would he remit the bribe money to him. When the turn of Shalom and

Basri came, Yehuda Tagar tried to negotiate with the hangman to ease their pain. He discovered, though, that in their case no sum of money would help. Those who had refused to pardon them made sure that they would suffer their full measure of cruelty, and had given to the hangman explicit instructions in the matter.

Tagar's status among the prisoners grew even more thanks to the kerosene stove that he had managed to get hold of, on which he cooked his food and heated water. He would use the water to massage the bodies of prisoners who had been badly beaten. These massages were often given to the most serious criminal offenders, who were naturally beaten the most. The prisoners didn't forget his good deeds. One day, fanatic Shiite prisoners threatened to kill Tagar because he supposedly had contaminated with his Jewish lips the only water jug available to them. Suddenly, a huge thug jumped up, one of his "patients," and announced that whoever touched Tagar would not go unpunished.

After many months around ordinary criminals, someone decided that the Zionist spy belonged with the political prisoners, most of whom were Communists. And so Yehuda Tagar was moved from Baghdad to Nugarat Salman, a relatively roomy prison, on the Saudi Arabian border. New trials awaited him there. In his youth in the Machanot Olim youth movement he had read Karl Marx's *Das Kapital*, but now he had to deal with long, serious ideological debates that sometimes became violent. Tagar said that "after Nugarat Salman I became an expert in all the Marxist-Leninist theories."

It was the time of the Korean War, and the Communist prisoners were constantly writing petitions against the Americans. Anyone who did not identify with them totally was soon considered an enemy. In the end Tagar became, against his will, the anti-Communist focus of the prison, and when things got worse he had to fight for his life, along with ten other "non-Red" prisoners against over a hundred men. When the prison guards managed to separate them, they had no choice but to keep Tagar and his friends in the courtyard for four months, out in the open air. There was no way they could run away. "There was no way to escape and no place to go," said Tagar later. One of the guards became friendly with him and suggested that he take two camels and escape to Saudi Arabia. Tagar answered him, "Come on, they almost hanged me here, so all I need is Saudi Arabia."

Over the years the Communist prisoners became less hostile and began to show respect for this proud, upstanding Israeli. In the end they became real friends. Perhaps an interesting ethnic phenomenon had something to do with it. The Iraqi Communist Party had many Jewish members, some of whom landed in Nugarat Salman and discovered their fellow Jew. Most of them eventually found their way to Israel.

In the autumn of 1956, during the Sinai Campaign, Tagar was moved to Akuba prison. One day he was called to the prison warden and shown a lineup of camel riders. The warden said, "You see, this is how we are going to capture Tel Aviv." After a discussion, during which Tagar valiantly defended the first Jewish city, the two parted as friends. Their friendship grew when the extent of the Israeli victory became known. In fact he was given respect by the entire prison, because everybody assumed that such a resounding victory was won thanks to men of Tagar's caliber. The headquarters of the Third Division was near the prison. Two of the officers in charge were Generals Kassem and Arif, the future instigators of the 1958 revolution. Since Tagar had won a name for himself in the area, a series of "seminars" were organized in the prison, during which Tagar gave lectures to senior officers about the State of Israel and its security problems.

"Sometimes," Yehuda Tagar said about his lectures, "they would bring up the matter of the 1948 massacre in the Arab village of Dir Yassin, purportedly perpetrated by Jews. They would say: 'You Zionists are cruel and bloodthirsty!' I divided my answer into two parts. First, I said, you as army officers can understand that there was a strategic need to capture that position on the road to Jerusalem. Second, as for acts of cruelty, who are you to talk?" The officers did not take offense.

Tagar's conditions were improved somewhat. Five years after he had been imprisoned he received his first letter from Israel. It included a message saying that he had not been forgotten, and that efforts were being made to free him. He was also told that he could ask the Christian mission in Baghdad for a copy of the Old and New Testaments in English, Arabic, and Hebrew so that he would not forget the Hebrew script. Later, in July 1958, a bloody revolution broke out in Iraq. The young king and the prime minister were among the dead. The new government began to free prisoners who had been imprisoned on the basis of the subversion clause (which included Communists and Zionists).

Tagar, who had been imprisoned on the basis of this clause, was not released because of interference by an intelligence officer. In his situation he also could not know about other developments, which were taking place far away from the prison. The Israeli Secret Service discovered a plot by President Nasser of Egypt to assassinate the Iraqi president, Kassem. They warned the president in time through a third party. After a while this third party reminded the president of the need to return the favor and presented Tagar's case to him. Tagar himself, who did not know about the plot, had also written a personal letter to Kassem, which was passed on to him by the commander of the Third Division. This letter, which was cleverly formulated and made use of quotes from the speeches of Kassem himself, probably also contributed to laying the groundwork for the next step.

On December 23, 1959, on his thirty-sixth birthday, the Israeli prisoner was taken to the presidential palace and escorted to the office of the dictator himself. There was a short conversation between Kassem and Tagar. The Iraqi president asked Tagar, among other things, what he would do in the future if a war broke out between Israel and Iraq. The Israeli prisoner answered that every man must fight for his homeland. At the end of the conversation Kassem called out to him, "Tell them back there that Iraq is now a completely independent country and no longer dependent on imperialism!"

"Tell them back there?" Tagar was stunned. He suddenly realized that Kassem's words meant that he was soon to be freed. Yehuda Tagar was taken from the presidential office to the headquarters of the secret police. After a few days he was flown to Beirut and then to Cyprus.

After Tagar took off from Baghdad, a very strange announcement was published in the Iraqi newspapers, saying that the dangerous spy Yehuda Tagar, who was a danger to the Arab world, had been released from prison the day before. Anyone seeing him, the announcement continued, should report this to the nearest police station. . . .

By then Tagar was safely back in Israel. He later became a professor at Tel Aviv University. The story of his proud and daring stand, and his miraculous survival, became an important chapter in the Israeli heritage of heroism.

Shlomo Hillel, cabinet minister, ambassador, and Speaker of the Eleventh Knesset, wrote the book Eastern Wind *about his work in the Iraqi underground.*

TO LIVE ON ANOTHER PLANET

MARCELLE NINIO

by Hannah Zemer

Lieutenant Colonel (res.) Marcelle Boger lives with her husband, Eli, who is also a reserve lieutenant colonel, in an area of private houses in Ramat Hasharon. Two large arches at the front of their house give it a unique, Eastern style. The house is surrounded by a pleasant garden, a yard, flower beds, and fruit trees. The two-story house is well equipped and furnished with conservative taste. Everything radiates affluence, not necessarily wealth.

The mistress of the house is well groomed, dressed with elegant restraint. During the week she is an MA student in art. On the Sabbath she entertains her grandchildren. There is nothing in Marcelle's appearance, in her surroundings, or in her lifestyle that would point to anything unusual in her life history or her personality. Actually her ability to live like everyone else, without being like them, is one of the unique qualities of this impressive woman.

For she is definitely not like everyone else. Marcelle Boger is Marcelle Victorine Ninio, known in the underground as Claude. She spent fourteen years in an Egyptian prison for having spied for Israel.

In July 1954 one of the most tragic affairs in the history of the clandestine war between Israel and the Arab states took place. In Cairo and Alexandria the Egyptian Secret Service captured two groups of young Jews who had placed primitive homemade bombs in the mailboxes of private homes, and American cultural institutions, and in movie theaters. These surprising acts of sabotage, which caused almost no damage, were part of an absurd plan concocted by Israeli Intelligence.

At the time the British government was about to evacuate its armed forces from the huge bases it had held along the Suez Canal in Egypt. Israel was afraid that the withdrawal of the British would cause the Egyptians to feel free to launch aggressive operations against it. Israeli intelligence experts decided to initiate a series of sabotage acts in Egypt's capital city, which would create the impression of dangerous ferment against the government and the West. England would be faced with proof that the Egyptian government was unstable and that it was doubtful whether it would ever fulfill its commitments according to the evacuation agreement with the British. Thus—the intelligence experts maintained—England might change its plans and leave its army in Egypt.

The plan was amateurish and criminally stupid. It was certainly catastrophic for Israeli Secret Service agents in Egypt. It was especially so for a group of dedicated Jewish young men and women who had carried out without question the orders they received, in complete faith that they were serving the security of Israel. This was the most criminal part of the plan. The golden rule of Israeli Intelligence, until then, had been never to employ local Jews in its operations in enemy countries. They were defenseless, they were always under suspicion or surveillance, and if captured they were expendable; the local authorities were also inclined to carry acts of revenge against the entire Jewish community.

This time, nevertheless, this rule was brutally broken. Several young Egyptian Jews, who had secretly visited Israel and were deeply devoted to it, were launched into the foolish bombing operations. They were instructed to assemble rudimentary bombs made of condoms filled with chemicals and stuck in eyeglass cases; when the chemicals corroded the condom and leaked into the eyeglasses case, they would come in contact with another substance, and that was supposed to produce an explosion. Several of those "bombs" never functioned. Some of the young people were caught in the act, and as a result of their arrest the networks collapsed like a house of cards. Eleven Jews were arrested, among them Meir Bint (Max Bennett), an agent of the Israeli Intelligence, who was only loosely connected to the network. Meir Bint (Bennett) and another Jewish Egyptian, Edmond Carmona, committed suicide in their cells as a result of the torture they underwent.

Of the other prisoners, six were given long prison sentences, from seven years to life, and two of them, Shmuel Azar and Dr. Moshe Marzuk, were sentenced to death and hanged in the prison yard in Cairo. In Israel the news of the hanging caused a terrible political storm. On the pages of the ruling party's newspaper, *Davar*, the national poet, Natan Alterman, demanded an explanation for the criminally stupid act that cost human lives. The affair became known as the "rotten business," and as a result of it the defense minister, Pinchas Lavon, was forced to resign from his job. Lavon claimed that he hadn't given the order to carry out the operation in Egypt. He pointed an accusing finger at the chief of military intelligence, Colonel Binyamin Gibli, and maintained that Gibli had acted without authorization. Binyamin Gibli fought back, accusing Lavon of ducking responsibility. Their mutual accusations, and the innuendos Lavon cast upon the army and the defense ministry, grew into a gigantic scandal, the most devastating in the history of Israel until this very day. The Lavon Affair shook up the Israeli political establishment, resulted in dramatic crises, and split the ruling Mapai Party. It indirectly contributed to the fall of David Ben-Gurion in 1963.

The effects of that affair are still felt in the country to this day. A definitive answer has not yet been given to the question "Who gave the order?" to carry out that catastrophic operation.

The only woman arrested in this unfortunate affair in Cairo was Marcelle Ninio. One day

Marcelle's full story will be published in a book that she herself intends to write. But it is doubtful that she can describe what five thousand days and nights of loneliness, suffering, anxiety, and despair do to a young woman.

A person who has been through what Marcelle has been through is not like other people. Besides the physical handicap, there is an emotional price. A new personality is created. The nightmares of the past, even if one supposedly gets over them, thanks to the passing of time and a satisfying present life, are not erased from the memory, and surely not from the subconscious. When I mentioned this in a private conversation with Marcelle, with her knowing that I had myself been a prisoner, she told me what she might not have told others. In her everyday life, in encounters with other people, and even with her friends, she certainly feels that they come from another planet. But when they talk to her, no one can tell that she is from another planet. Marcelle is a very special person.

Let's start from the beginning. Marcelle was born in Cairo to a Turkish mother and a Bulgarian father. The parents spoke Ladino [Judeo-Spanish] between them, as a result of which she knows Spanish today. In the Jewish elementary school where she studied, the language of instruction was French. She attended a Catholic mission high school where nuns taught her in English. She, of course, speaks Arabic, since that was the language of the country she grew up in, and in prison she had plenty of time to learn more. She first heard Hebrew from songs when she was in the Hashomer Hatzair youth movement in Cairo. Later, during her years in prison, when she managed to get hold of a radio, she listened secretly to Voice of Israel broadcasts in easy Hebrew, aimed at the new immigrants. Eventually she improved her Hebrew in Israel, in an ulpan and at the university.

For a period of time, in Cairo, she was a jailmate of a blond German woman who was called Teddy. Her full name was Waltrud Lutz; she was the German partner of the Israeli agent Wolfgang Lutz (Zeev Gur-Arye), who was captured in Cairo in 1965. She learned a little German from her. She also had a German dictionary there. "In prison you have to try to do something, to learn something, otherwise you begin to degenerate," says Marcelle. Later, when her husband, Eli, was sent for five years to Frankfurt for the Koor Company, her German improved. Today she speaks six languages fluently, and there is a seventh—Italian—that she can get by in. She had Italian neighbors. "Cairo," she reminds me, "was a cosmopolitan city."

She did not come from a religious home, but she was observant. While her father was alive, he would say the *kiddush* prayers on Friday night, and they would go to synagogue on the holidays. Her father died when she was ten. Marcelle considered the two children from his first marriage as full brothers. One of them came to Israel in 1952; when she was imprisoned he was no longer in Egypt, and he is now no longer alive. The second brother emigrated to France while Marcelle was in prison. While still in Cairo he did everything he could to visit her, but he himself was being followed because he was a Communist. It took a year from the day she was arrested for him to get up the courage to visit her—a year of total isolation, without visits, without letters, without packages, while she was sick and lonely, surrounded by prostitutes and murderers.

Actually Marcelle had no direct connection to the "rotten business." Her underground activity belonged to an earlier period. In 1951, when she was twenty-two, an Israeli spy who went by the name of John Darling (his real name was Avraham Dar) arrived in Egypt to set up a spy network without defining what its activities would be. Marcelle was at the time the secretary of the director of a British import company. She spent her spare time taking care of her sick mother. One of her friends from her days in the Hashomer Hatzair youth movement approached her. "We need you," she said, and she hinted that she would be asked to do something for Israel. "Are you willing to help?"

She didn't need to hear more than that. Marcelle had always felt that she was an Israeli. All her friends had been in the youth movement, and most of them had gone to Israel. Also her boyfriend, whom she planned to marry, had gone to Israel while she stayed behind to take care of her mother. She agreed to help without knowing what it entailed. Within a short time she became the communications operator of the network between Cairo and Alexandria. Later, when Max (Meir) Bint (Bennett) got to Cairo, she worked for him as well, but she didn't have anything to do with the operations that led to the exposure of the underground network. She doesn't know how the Egyptian secret police got her name; she has no idea who turned her in. Even today she isn't interested in knowing. She didn't try to find out then and hasn't tried since. There is no one who knows as well as she what it is like to be interrogated and what the effects can be.

Marcelle suffered terrible tortures that started the very night of her arrest. The interrogation by the Egyptian secret police was accompanied by slaps on the face, hair pulling, blows to the back of the neck, whippings on the soles of her feet. She would faint, and then they would start from the beginning. After a day she was moved to Alexandria and submitted to torture again. Besides the terrible pain, the degradation, and the nights without sleep, she was also threatened with gang rape. She couldn't bear it anymore, and all she wanted was to die. She jumped out of the window into the paved yard from a height of eighteen feet.

She paid a high price for this suicide attempt. She had fractures in her skull and her joints, eleven fractured ribs, a crushed hip, internal bleeding, and a concussion. For a long time after being hospitalized she couldn't stand up. To this day she still suffers from the results of this act of despair, which was intended to put an end to her suffering.

Like Victor Levi, Robert Dassa, and Philip Nathanson, Marcelle was also released from prison and reached Israel in February 1968, as part of a prisoner exchange after the Six-Day War. During the fourteen years of their imprisonment, the men were together. Marcelle was alone. Her brothers had left the country, and her mother had died. She had no one left in the world. Besides all her other problems she also had a kidney ailment, for which she was hospitalized again and operated on. Every one of her five thousand days in prison was a battle—for her life, for her health, for the small things that make life bearable. Above all, she struggled for her humanity.

Events that had nothing to do with her had an effect on her life in prison. Changes in the prison service, in the prison management, in the composition of the guards and of the prisoners all caused her renewed anxiety from time to time, requiring her to cope in a new way. There is no need to elaborate on what happened to her as an "Israeli spy" during the Sinai Campaign and the Six-Day War. During those days, all the Egyptian propagandists were talking about the deeds of the Zionist enemy and of the heroism of the Egyptian soldier, and all the political and criminal prisoners decided to demonstrate their patriotism at her expense.

When she finally reached Israel, she remained in the underground. Egypt's president Gamal Abd el-Nasser, who authorized the exchange of prisoners, had been promised that everything connected to the release of those sentenced in the affair would be kept secret. Does she feel bitter about all the things that have remained unexplained, which caused her such indescribable suffering? In other words, does she have anything against Israel or those who acted in its name?

I believe that I can fairly summarize what I heard from her by saying that she has not forgiven to this day—and the same goes for the other prisoners in the affair—one unexplained thing. Why were they not freed in the prisoner exchange after the Sinai Campaign? It is clear, according to them, that the Israelis didn't even try to get them released at that time. Israel had five thousand Egyptian prisoners. Egypt expected such an offer, says Marcelle, and it was not even asked. This was also a time of crisis for her and her friends. In 1956, when they were not released, they lost all hope that they would get out of prison alive.

Why were they not released after the Sinai Campaign? Some people suspect that this was a Machiavellian manipulation by certain Israeli groups that did not want to renew the public discussion about the "rotten business." Many furiously deny this theory, but they have no other explanation. Others say that Israel just forgot about the young people, rotting in some Egyptian jail. But an effort to get them released in the framework of the prison exchange after the Sinai Campaign would have saved Marcelle and the three men twelve years in prison. Nothing can justify such a foul-up, say the prisoners, and nothing can compensate them for it. Marcelle is "angry and hurt."

When she got to Israel, Marcelle felt, despite all the bitterness and pain, that she was coming home. But she had to remain anonymous for a while longer. She went to an ulpan and later to Tel Aviv University, where she finished a BA in English literature. This period was counted as a postarmy leave period. The Israeli army, indeed, considered all the time she spent in prison as full military service. In 1972 Marcelle was officially released from the army, and given an officer's pension. That year she married Eli Boger. The prime minister, Golda Meir, was the matron of honor at her wedding. Only then was the presence of the Egyptian network members made public for the first time. Four years after they had become free, their presence in their land was finally acknowledged.

Eli, Marcelle's husband, was a Viennese *yekke* (a Jew of German origin). He had come to Israel with the Youth Aliya, lived on a kibbutz, served in the Jewish Brigade, the Hagana, and the regular Israeli army. He had been in uniform for twenty-five years. He later went into business. When he married Marcelle he already had a son and daughter from a previous marriage. The grandchildren who visit Marcelle on the Sabbath are their children. It was too late for her to have children of her own. "When you get married at the age of forty-two," with a feeling of terrible weariness, she says, "giving up on children is a price that one has to pay to the past. For me it's a very heavy price." And this, of course, is not the only price.

Over the years the effects of the wounds she incurred during her suicide attempt have gotten worse. She suffers from head pains, from weakness in her muscles, and one of her hands is bent. In 1979 she was granted 56 percent government disability. She continues to exercise at the Beit Halohem rehabilitation center.

Trauma is also part of the price she pays. Marcelle tries not to dramatize her situation. She emphasizes that "I don't experience the trauma twenty-four hours a day." But the past leaves its emotional mark. For example, to this day Marcelle is not able to sleep behind a closed door. You don't have to be a psychologist to understand the reason why.

The discipline that she had to impose upon herself in prison has remained with her until today. She functions properly, calmly, and affably, but she doesn't expose herself, open herself to others. She naturally feels real closeness and identification when she meets, for example, with her Greek friend Marie, who was with her in the Egyptian prison as a political prisoner. It was Marie who, after she had been released, sent Marcelle a small radio, which kept her going during her last three years in prison. Marie knew how to pass this forbidden object to her. With Marie, Marcelle opens up, feels free. They're from the same planet.

But Marcelle feels that she belongs here completely. Israel is her country, and she doesn't want to live anywhere else. Her suffering did not cause her to feel alienated or fanatic. She has moderate opinions, and doesn't feel hatred. She doesn't even hate the Egyptians. "They are a good people, but it is easy to influence them and manipulate them," she says. She hasn't visited Egypt even since the peace agreement. She has no reason to do so. Friends whom she asked to find her parents' graves couldn't find them. She has no other reason to go there.

At the end of September 1987, when the events celebrating the fortieth year of the State began, the defense establishment remembered the Cairo prisoners. Marcelle was elevated to the rank of lieutenant colonel in the office of Defense Minister Itzhak Rabin, as were the male prisoners and (posthumously) Moshe Marzuk and Shmuel Azar. Max Bint was elevated in rank in a separate ceremony. This was a symbolic demonstration of gratitude and appreciation for what they had done and for what they undertook for the State of Israel. The defense minister expressed only the facts when he said at the time they were awarded their ranks, "There is no compensation in the world that can be given for the long years in prison, for the difficult days, and the hellish nights, for the never-ending winters and summers, for the physical and mental torture, for the loss of freedom, for the years of youth that were lost in prison."

It takes a lot of courage to carry out underground activity in a hostile country, but it takes real heroism to pay the terrible price. Of all the prisoners of the affair it was Marcelle that needed the greatest amount of heroism. She was a woman alone. In a certain sense she will always remain a woman alone.

I thought a lot about Marcelle's story from my point of view as a Holocaust survivor. I went through the hell of the Nazi period, its persecutions and its concentration camps. I know what suffering is, and in the light of this experience I maintain that what Marcelle went through was worse than what Holocaust survivors experienced. We dealt with a collective danger; she was alone. We suffered four or five years; she suffered for three times as long.

Hannah Zemer is a journalist, and is a former editor of the newspaper Davar.

THE BEST FIGHTER WE EVER HAD

MEIR HAR-ZION

by Ariel Sharon

There are few fighters who have influenced the spirit and the fighting methods of a whole army over a period of several years. One of these fighters is Meir Har-Zion. Through his leadership, his determination, and his actions during the days of the courageous reprisal raids of the IDF during the 1950s, Meir Har-Zion contributed greatly to the revolutionary change not only in the army's approach to special operations, but also in its fighting spirit.

There are fighters who shine in one battle. There are legendary commanders who have excelled in one war. Meir Har-Zion is a fighter and a commander of an era. From 1953 to 1956 he fought as a soldier and an officer, leading scores of operations, from which he returned only after they were successfully completed.

A single Jordanian bullet ended his activity during that period. That night in September 1956, we rushed to the hospital in Beersheva after having captured and totally destroyed the Jordanian police fortress at A-Rahawa on the Beersheva-Hebron road. Our action had been a reprisal for the murder of Jews by Palestinian terrorists. I remember the worried face of Chief of Staff Moshe Dayan, who must have also noticed a similar expression on my face. We were waiting for the doctor's report on Meir's condition. He had been wounded badly in the neck, and only immediate medical care on the battlefield had saved him. The bullet had hit Meir when, as usual, he was leading the fighters in breaking through the gate and attacking the Jordanian fortress.

That same night, in the corridor of the hospital, anxious about Har-Zion, who was twenty-two years old at the time, I again thought about the high price that we were paying in dead and wounded in this endless battle against the Palestinian terrorists.

If Meir Har-Zion could have stayed on in the army, I am sure that he would have reached higher positions in the IDF command, if not the highest. In a speech in the summer of 1955,

Chief of Staff Moshe Dayan best defined the conditions in which the military combat of the Zionist revolution in Israel was waged. These words hold true also for the more than one hundred years of settlement in the country. Dayan said, "We cannot protect every water pipe from being blown up, nor every tree from being uprooted. Nor can we prevent the murder of workers in the orchards, nor of families in their beds, but *we can exact a high price for our blood* [Dayan's emphasis], a price too high for the Arab community, the Arab army, the Arab governments to pay."

In the paratroop units under my command, Meir Har-Zion stood out when we went to "exact a high price" in special operations against Jordan, Egypt, and Syria. In his army diary, which he wrote secretly at the time, Meir Har-Zion started his description of a reprisal raid in Azun against the Jordanian Legion with these words: "In June 1954 a squad of 7 soldiers infiltrated the Legion's camp in Azun, and in retaliation for the murder of a Jew in Raanana killed 3 soldiers and wounded 3 others. An Arab citizen who happened to be in the area and endangered the mission was stabbed to death. A wounded Israeli soldier was left in the field. The squad covered 30 km [about 19 miles] that night. . . ."

The murder of one Jew in Raanana was enough to have us immediately "exact a price" as punishment. The philosophy of David Ben-Gurion and Moshe Dayan had made its mark on all of us—the murder of a Jew, even one single Jew, must not go unpunished. That is how we were educated, and this is how we must continue to educate. Unfortunately, Dayan's statement is likely to hold true for the situation today as well.

These days we are faced with renewed waves of Palestinian terror inside and outside the country. Only if we can explain to the Palestinians that they have no chance of winning in this way can we achieve peace with them.

We have been in worse situations—at the beginning of the 1950s, for example, when the Jewish population in Israel was barely over a million. At the end of the War of Independence, Arab infiltration increased. From 1949 until the end of 1952 the Arab acts of sabotage and terror were disorganized, and directed at first against economic targets and later against Israeli civilians. By the years 1953–54 these random acts of sabotage and terror turned into small-scale warfare.

The year 1952 was the height of border activity. There were three thousand incidents that year, which included all kinds of actions. These hostile acts were carried out both in the central areas of the country and on the borders. Facing the terrorists were mainly civilians, most of them new immigrants. Unlike today, the army usually faced these attacks along the borders. The tension in the border settlements was great, and regular daily life was seriously disrupted. There were many murders in settlements around the country and in urban centers.

The IDF after the War of Independence was powerless in the face of the situation that developed. The army, which had held fast against all the Arab armies in the War of Independence, was helpless when faced with this kind of warfare and regularly failed in actions over the border. The reasons for this were many. The army was in the midst of getting organized, and most attention was given to operations in large military frameworks.

The reprisal acts carried out during peacetime were limited by serious political constraints. It was necessary to carry them out exactly according to instructions and not to fail. Great efforts were made to prevent casualties, more so than in times of war. These special conditions meant that reprisal acts had to be carried out as an immediate reaction to enemy activities, and often as their direct continuation. This required a constant state of alert, readiness to act on any front against any enemy within a few hours. Only a unit that understood and sensed the intentions of the military and political authorities could deal with such a state of alert. Therefore, a decision was made to set up a special unit that would be responsible for carrying out actions over the border.

I set up Unit 101 in August 1953. It began to function immediately and proved within a short time that there was no mission it could not accomplish. The most outstanding operations were in Kibia and Hebron. These operations brought about a conceptual change in the IDF's approach and renewed its confidence in its strength. This had an immediate effect on the enemy. In the area of Lod, where there had been a lot of enemy activity that had cost us many casualties, things became peaceful, a peace that was not disturbed for many years. A similar result was achieved in Jerusalem.

In January 1954, Moshe Dayan, upon his appointment as chief of staff, decided to combine our unit with Paratroop Battalion 890, of which I became the head. Moshe Dayan knew the sweeping effect that this small unit had on the paratroopers, and later on all of the IDF.

The small Unit 101, which numbered barely twenty fighters, soon became an excellent paratroop battalion, and was later turned into a fighting paratroop brigade capable of carrying out any mission. And we were assigned many difficult missions. Between 1954 and 1956 the paratroopers were responsible for all the reprisal raids, which numbered dozens of operations. The army gained experience and self-confidence. Political powers gained confidence in the operational ability of the army, and there is no doubt that more than a few decisions were influenced by these achievements.

The paratroopers did not stop at these operations. During those years they also took part in determining objectives and determining the pace at which these actions were executed. They suggested targets and operations and urged that they be carried out. One can say that the ideology of the reprisal raids was formed to a great extent in the paratroop units.

The paratroopers' accomplishments were not easily achieved. Great efforts were invested in the planning and development of new means of warfare, in training soldiers, in getting to know the country and its borders, in constantly learning lessons, in an attempt to understand what motivated the soldiers in battle, and in training officers able to carry out any operation. A lot of work was invested in educating soldiers to make accurate reports, in exhaustive training, and in hundreds of reconnaissance patrols over the border. There are military doctrines and especially military values that are learned in the battlefield at the expense of human lives. In those years it was mainly the paratroopers who paid with their lives for these lessons.

The paratroopers who worked for years on their own influenced the IDF and swept it along with them. They imparted to the IDF the basic values of perseverance, resourcefulness, and volunteerism. Their achievement-oriented approach and their high level of performance were passed on to all of the IDF units. The paratroopers soon reached the level of Unit 101, and the rest of the army units in time followed suit, never resting on their laurels.

The IDF is an excellent army. It has wonderful forces—the air force, the armored corps, the infantry—and in all of them one can find the spirit of the paratroopers; when one examines the achievements of the IDF today, it is impossible not to notice their influence. When one talks about perseverance, which is today one of the basic values of the army, one cannot help remembering operations like the raid on Hebron in 1953, the raid on the camp of the Jordanian Legion in Azun, or the raid on Kuntila—operations that were the best model of willpower and perseverance. Meir Har-Zion played a central role in carrying out all of these raids, completing every mission I assigned him.

One of the basic characteristics of the IDF is its readiness and ambition to enter into hand-to-hand combat, a face-to-face confrontation with the enemy. This quality of the IDF was nurtured in the paratroopers. In the capture of an Egyptian post across from Kissufim in 1954, where for the first time the methods for fighting against fortified targets were tried out, in the attack on the headquarters of the Egyptian forces in Gaza, and in the paratroop raid on the Syrian posts east of the Kinneret in 1955, one could see how these fighting methods developed.

In 1967, during the Six-Day War, the enemy forces were overcome by a combined attack from the rear, from the flank, and from the front at one and the same time. This was done by bringing troops in by helicopter to attack the enemy artillery and by combined attacks of armored forces, infantry, paratroopers, and the air force. We crossed the Suez Canal in the same fashion in the Yom Kippur War.

This sophisticated means of warfare was developed by the paratroopers. Its roots can be seen in the motorized raid on Khan Yunis, in the Gaza Strip, in the capture of the Egyptian compounds in Sabha, which were overcome in a surprise attack from the rear, and in the attack on Syrian positions on the Kinneret, in which combined forces moved on foot, by water, and across the Jordan River. One could add to that the action in Kalkiliya, carried out on the eve of the Sinai Campaign, which included paratroopers, armored forces, and artillery.

The technique of warfare we use today, which has proven itself again and again, was also born in the paratroopers' battles. Fighting fortified objectives, ambushes, and raids—all these were developed in the paratroops and were adopted by all of the IDF. Standards of warfare, of command, of the viability of operations, which have now become the standards of every unit in the IDF, were set in the paratroops.

And above all, the daring that typifies and unites the IDF, more than any other army, came from the paratroopers and became a permanent, standard asset of the IDF. Besides military achievements, the paratroops also established ethical standards that influenced the character of the army. These included the role of the commanding officer in battle, the personal example he provided, the policy with regard to the wounded, and the concern for soldiers taken prisoner. The paratroopers formed and developed a war camaraderie that has no equal in the world.

The scores of operations that were carried out, besides being stages in the advancement of the army, were, in themselves, in their level of planning and performance, achievements that any army would be proud of. The reprisal acts of the army during the period before the Sinai Campaign cut down the extent of Arab terrorism and turned it from disorganized activity that was wide in scope into much more limited action. On the other hand, it became more organized and directed by the Arab governments. Terrorism became more a means of political warfare both for them and for us. That was also the reason why the objectives of our retaliatory actions were government targets—military and police compounds. This had a significant effect on the Arab governments. When they began to feel that our reprisals were endangering them, they themselves took care of stopping the attacks on us, launched from their territories.

The men who over the years bore the brunt of this reprisal activity, almost completely on their own, were not tough fighters out for blood, as they were often described, or as portrayed in legends that grew out of their activities at the time. These were young men who had belonged to youth movements, kibbutz youths from all political camps, settlement and moshav boys, from development towns, from Haifa and the suburbs of Tel Aviv and Jerusalem. This was a group of excellent young men with great faith and courage. In short, this was a group of men that cared.

The most outstanding paratrooper at the time was Meir Har-Zion. Meir came to us when Unit 101 was established. He had been a corporal in the Nahal who could not find peace there for his stormy spirit, for his desire to be active, for his belief that we must and could find a way to overcome the Arab terrorist activity. Within a short time he became the most daring fighter in Unit 101 and in the paratroopers, and an excellent scout, perhaps the best that the IDF has ever known.

He outshone the others by far in leadership qualities. His achievements in the battlefield were many. He commanded several operations himself, and played a major role in others. Meir Har-Zion became a symbol of a fighter in the paratroop units and in the army as a whole.

Combat commanders are tested mainly when they are asked to carry out an assignment independently, when there is no officer of a higher rank around to help and rescue them if necessary from the battlefield, an officer who will notice them during a battle. The greatest effort is demanded of an independent officer. He leads his men, fights himself, heads the attack, and brings his men back to their base safely after the battle. An officer in this situation decides whether or not the mission will be carried out and decides how it will be carried out. His influence is greater than any order or briefings given beforehand.

Meir led many paratroop operations as the senior commander in the field. While still a sergeant he commanded the forces that attacked Shukba, Solomon's Pools, and Hebron. As a platoon and company commander, and a commander of the brigade commando unit, he took on the most difficult missions, for the most part independent missions that demanded special courage and resourcefulness.

One of the tests of a good commander is his ability to groom other commanders. Meir Har-Zion trained a generation of commanders that were influenced by his leadership qualities, his courage, and his tactical methods. Many of them served, and are still serving, in high-ranking positions in the paratroops and in other units in the army. Many others, among them senior officers, fell in the battlefield.

Meir Har-Zion was very skilled in tactical planning. He was involved, more than others, in planning and determining the fighting methods of the paratroopers. He was blessed with the most excellent natural leadership qualities. There are many ancient and modern legends about the heroism of our people. Fortunately, during the last forty years we have had extraordinary fighters. Many of these soldiers and officers have fallen in the battlefield, several in campaigns they commanded.

I have often wondered what made Meir Har-Zion, or Har, as we call him, into such an outstanding hero in a generation of heroes. How did he become such an outstanding member of this outstanding group? Where did he find the superhuman strength to carry out the most difficult missions?

There are many answers to these questions, but I will mention only a few. First of all, as a human being he was honest with himself and with others. Despite his successes he behaved modestly and simply. He never demanded of his fellow man anything that he wasn't willing to do himself and in fact did.

Second, his accomplishments didn't come easily to him. He invested enormous efforts until he could perform perfectly. Har was a man in constant struggle with himself. He was a man who had to overcome obstacles and succeeded in doing so, and not only as a fighter. When he decided to rehabilitate himself after he had been seriously wounded (80 percent disability) he did this first and foremost with his own strength and was not satisfied until he had replaced the sword with the plowshare. He set up a model farm at the windswept plateau of Kochav Haruchot (The Star of the Winds) near Beit Shean. He named the farm Shoshana's Estate after his sister, who had been murdered by Bedouins on Mount Hebron. In his personality, Meir combined the valiancy of the warrior and the hard labor of the farmer, the worker of his land.

Moshe Dayan called Har "the greatest Jewish fighter since Bar-Kochba" (the ancient hero of the Jewish rebellion against the Roman Empire). But Har's secret was above all his endless love for his country. He loved every crook and cranny, which he knew like the palm of his hand. He loved its flowers, whose scent intoxicated him, and its animals, who were his friends during his travels. "A strange madness has got hold of me," wrote Har-Zion in his travel diary in the spring of 1949 when he was fifteen years old. "To learn to know the country, to know it firsthand, to hike through the wadis and the mountains, the Galilee and the Negev, and take pleasure in the experience of the journey. . . ." Only someone who loved and knew the country, as he did, could be able to fight for it as he did.

Meir Har-Zion was not a sociable man. He was not made for lavish receptions, or good at public relations. He was a true fighter, the greatest fighter we have ever had. His activities spread over a relatively short period, but they left a strong impact on the IDF and its soldiers for many years, for generations.

The Israeli nation is fortunate. Today, after fifty years of independence, the Israelis still can see with their own eyes that their hero Har is not a legend, but a flesh-and-blood man of the land, living up there in the heights of Kochav Haruchot, his Star of the Winds.

Ariel Sharon, Minister of the Infrastructure, set up Unit 101 and was a major general in the IDF.

LARGER THAN LIFE

ITZHAK "GULLIVER" BEN-MENACHEM

by Michael Bar-Zohar

"The darkness in the mountains never falls, but rises. It comes up from the valleys and ravines, crawls along the mountain slopes like a winding snake, until it overpowers the sun. The greatest deeds are carried out at night. In the middle of the night God struck down every firstborn child in Egypt. The children of Israel left Egypt at night. Gideon and his boy went down at night and hit the enemies in the camp of Midian and Amalek. The night abounds with magic and splendor. It bestows upon its heroes legendary strength. I simply love the night." The man who said these words did not surprise his audience. This poetic description of the night and the use of biblical verses fit his size—larger than life. He was a gigantic Sabra, twenty-four years old, a handsome, strong boy with a rebellious lock of hair, a big heart, a romantic soul, and a burning love for his land. They called him Gulliver.

Gulliver seemed to have come down straight from a Zionist poster praising the new generation of Jews born in Palestine. He was known, indeed, as one of the most impressive young men in the settlements of the Sharon plain, with a glorious record in the War of Independence. He had his feet firmly planted on the ground, but at the same time it was clear to his friends that the streak of poetry that often sneaked into his words was his natural style, without being pretentious, without being artificial in any way. Even the irregular circumstances of the time and place, when he praised the magic of the night, did not cause his listeners to be surprised at his words. It was August 11, 1953, in one of the rooms at the Schneller Camp, the headquarters of the Jerusalem Brigade. One of the reserve battalions of this brigade was under the command of Major Ariel Sharon, a student of the humanities at Hebrew University, located at the time in the building that had formerly been the Franciscan Terra Sancta College. A day or two before, at the height of his exam preparations, Sharon was called to an urgent meeting with his battalion commander, Colonel Mishael Shaham. He thought it was going to be a discussion about administrative and logistics matters, but Shaham opened with this question: "Have you heard of Mustafa Samueli?"

"Yes," Sharon said. Despite his studies at the university, this young man, who had distinguished himself during the War of Independence, kept up with army material enough to know who Samueli was. This Palestinian Arab, a resident of the village of Nebi Samuel, had sworn to massacre a hundred Jews to avenge the blood of his brother, who had been killed in one of the battles in the War of Independence. Sharon even knew that Samueli had begun to carry out his threat and had already committed a few murders. Nebi Samuel was across the border, on the West Bank, which was under Jordanian rule. Samueli had only to sneak across the border (actually the 1949 cease-fire line), which was close to his village, carry out his bloody design, and retreat to his village with impunity.

Sharon did not understand why he had received this sudden summons to his battalion commander. Shaham's sphere of military responsibility included the area of Nebi Samuel. He was well aware that troubles for Israel were liable to originate there. Now he explained his idea to Sharon. He had requested permission from his superiors to carry out a deterrent action against Samueli, and had been given permission in principle. "We have to get there and blow up his house," he said, "and I want you to do the job."

Sharon muttered something about his exams, but Shaham cut him off. "A man has to choose between two options," he said, "to study about the deeds of others or to leave it to others to study about his deeds."

From the way Shaham was talking it was clear that the blowing up of Samueli's house was not a matter for all of Sharon's battalion, but an operation for a small, select unit, the kind of commando team that did not yet exist in the IDF. It had to cross the border, penetrate into enemy territory, reach Nebi Samuel, plant explosives at Samueli's house, blow it up—then retreat over the border. To put together a commando unit able to operate swiftly and effectively under the cover of night, Sharon was given a free hand to recruit whoever he wanted. The first name that came to his mind was that of an old friend, Itzhak Ben-Menachem, whom everyone called Gulliver because he was so huge. Gulliver, at the time a law student in Jerusalem, agreed immediately.

On August 11 he arrived at the Schneller Camp with five other old army buddies whom Sharon had recruited, and they began to prepare for the operation. It was in this context that they heard Gulliver's praises of the night. Through the window, on the northwestern range, they could see the village of Nebi Samuel. They then armed themselves with tommy guns (British-made submachine guns), knives, and grenades; put on ammunition belts over their civilian clothing; and crossed the cease-fire line under cover of darkness. They moved forward slowly, and after three hours they managed to reach the olive groves, which were downwind from and on the outskirts of the village. No dog barked at the intruders. No one even noticed them.

Gulliver, Shlomo Baum, and Saadia, the Palmach demolition expert, worked their way toward Samueli's house. The other four took up cover positions. Baum laid a charge to break through the iron door. There was an explosion, but the door was not dislodged. The silence was over. Gunfire burst around them; many of the villagers were shooting rifles. Gulliver did not lose his head. He immediately found a window that was closed by two heavy shutters, stuck his fingers between them, pulled with all his strength, and managed to open them. One of the fighters fired a long burst of submachine-gun fire inside the dark room; another one tossed a grenade. Saadia got down to work. "This is not the Palmach," Sharon quipped, urging him on. Saadia smiled, and lit the fuse. The three joined their friends, and they all turned back toward the border. While retreating they heard a thunderous explosion; Samueli's house had been destroyed. Someone whispered to Sharon that Shlomo Baum and Saadia were falling behind, but before he had the chance to react he saw the huge shadow of Gulliver running toward them, to offer help. All seven reached the border together, shook hands, and each went his own way.

A few days later Sharon told Mishael Shaham that what they did was all very well, but it seemed to him that was not the way to do things. If the army wanted further deterrent actions, then a suitable unit should be set up for this, and they should not depend on calling in these great guys from all over at the last minute. As a result of this conversation a new, half-irregular unit was established. It was given the code number 101. Gulliver did not join the unit, but none of his acquaintances had any doubt that he would be a part of any operation that would need an extraordinary sense of duty and resourcefulness.

Itzhak Ben-Menachem—Gulliver—was born in 1929 in Ramatayim. He grew up close to the land and the trees, raised by parents who were very special people. His father, Yechezkel, had come to the country at the beginning of the Third Aliya (1919–23) after all sorts of adventures. Along with his wife, Gita, he set up an outstanding farm on a plot of land he bought. "I didn't want to live off of others or exploit anyone," he later said. "Even on a kibbutz or a moshav there is hired labor and exploitation. I thought that only on a plot of land of my own would I be able to make my living from the earth by myself."

Gulliver learned from him, respected and loved him. At the age of thirteen he got involved in an event involving his parents that was typical of his personality. Along with his classmates, he was called upon to join the youth battalions of the Hagana. At the first meeting he was told that these activities were secret and that he shouldn't tell a soul about them, not even his parents. Gulliver calmly informed the instructor that he considered his father completely trustworthy and that he would never keep anything from him. He was rejected outright by the Hagana. But, being loved and accepted by his friends, he soon was told all the "secrets." He came back after a month to the people who had rejected him, pointed out the absurdity of the situation, and was accepted into the organization without any problem. This faithfulness to principles without the loss of the love and sympathy of those around him, this combination of wisdom, courage, and charm, was to come up again and again in Gulliver's short life.

Gulliver was very active during the three years between the Second World War and the War of Independence. He studied at the Beit Hinuch Gymnasium in Tel Aviv, worked on the family farm, read a lot, and took full part in the training and exploits of the Gadna (a youth movement that trained teenagers in defense and national service) and the field companies of the Hagana in the area. Sometimes he would find interesting ways to combine his various activities. One of his friends remembers that he found him watering the orchard and at the same time eagerly reading the poems of Chaim Nachman Bialik. Noticing his friend's astonishment, Gulliver explained: "Bialik is the greatest poet we have ever had."

He always stuck to his guns—when he went out as part of a "special section" to fight "dissenters," when he devotedly took care of the arms cache and was ready to defend it from the British police, when he joined patrols or did guard duty. His battalion commander at the time also remembers how impressed he was one day, when "this overgrown boy, with the face of a child and the expression of a poet," appeared before him, and asked to be appointed the battalion cultural officer. "Our youth," Gulliver said, "do not understand well enough the importance of the challenges they are facing." The battalion commander promised to find out if that would be possible, but he never managed to get around to it. The challenges, in the form of the War of Independence, soon arrived.

In December 1947 Gulliver was drafted to full service in an armored corps company, which soon became the core of the Thirty-second Battalion of the Alexandroni Brigade. Although he was a private, his direct superiors used to consult with him and take his opinions into consideration. He was a trained gunner who got the most out of the Bren machine gun he had been given. Often Gulliver provided the main firepower of his platoon and his company. So it was, among other attacks, in the capture of the huge army camp east of Tel Aviv, in Tel Litvinsky (which later became Tel Hashomer); so it was in the bloody, unsuccessful assaults on Latrun, the Arab fortress that dominated the road to Jerusalem. Ben-Gurion, eager to open the sealed road to Jerusalem and free the besieged city, launched several attacks on Latrun, ordering the commander of the Israeli forces, Shlomo Shamir: "Attack at all costs!" But the cost in human lives was too high, and the attacks on Latrun failed. (Jerusalem was finally relieved when the Israelis secretly built a road in the mountains that bypassed the Latrun death trap.)

The company commander, Asher Levi, reported after the controversial battle of Latrun: "The gunner Gulliver managed during the heat of battle to advance somewhat and take a position on the western flank . . . and from there he stopped the advance of the infiltrating enemy forces with machine-gun fire. . . ." When the order to retreat was given, Levi said, "Gulliver and a few other fighters . . . volunteered without being given any order to cover the retreat. . . . Gulliver the gunner and Tishler, the section commander, continuously covered the retreat of the forces. Both of them deserved a citation . . . both of them played their machine guns like violins, and caused a lot of enemy casualties." By some miracle Gulliver left the killing fields of Latrun without a scratch, and in the most natural fashion carried out the retreat without panicking and without losing his head. In the course of the retreat he took care of the wounded and collected valuable equipment. He also never stopped asking himself why things had turned out so badly.

Six months later, when the war was virtually over, Gulliver participated in an officers' train-

Marcelle Ninio: Fourteen years in an Egyptian jail

Meir Har-Zion:
Not a legend,
but a man of flesh and blood

Itzhak "Gulliver" Ben-Menachem: The face of a child and the expression of a poet

Natan Elbaz:
With his heart's blood,
a soldier in the army of Israel

Uri Ilan: The symbol of a generation

Shula Cohen:
The Mata Hari of the Middle East

Chaim Zarfati:
He stayed by his radio even
as the ship began to sink

Eli Cohen: The greatest Israeli spy in the Arab world

Esther Arditi: The "White Angel" of the paratroopers

Yechezkel Avi Shabi Maor:
Exiled for life to Siberia

Zorik Lev:
A silent landing in a hidden airport

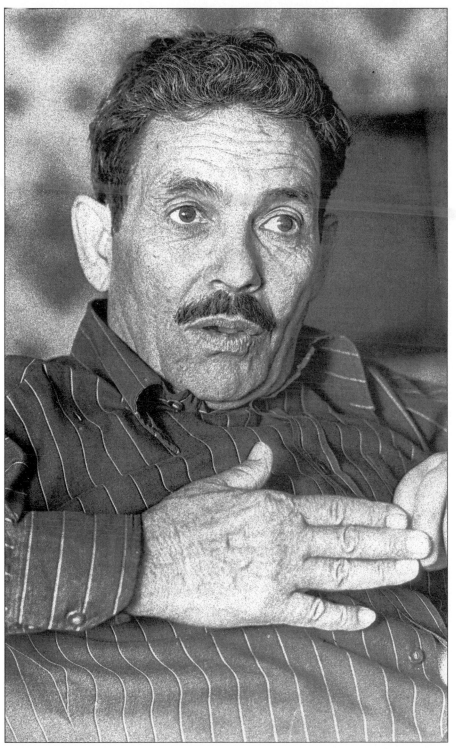

Amos Yarkoni (Abd el Majid Hadr el-Mazarib)

Ami Ayalon: The knight of the ground floor

Yoni Netanyahu: He loved Alterman's epic poetry

Mordechai Goldman (left) and Moshe Kravitz: A fortress of fire and stone

Muki Betzer: He always rushed into battle

Avida Shor:
"I am not prepared to kill women and children"

Ismail Kabalan:
"You are my brother,"
Moshe Dayan told him

Abd el-Karim Abd el-Rani:
"Ramadan! Ramadan!"
he shouted at the killer

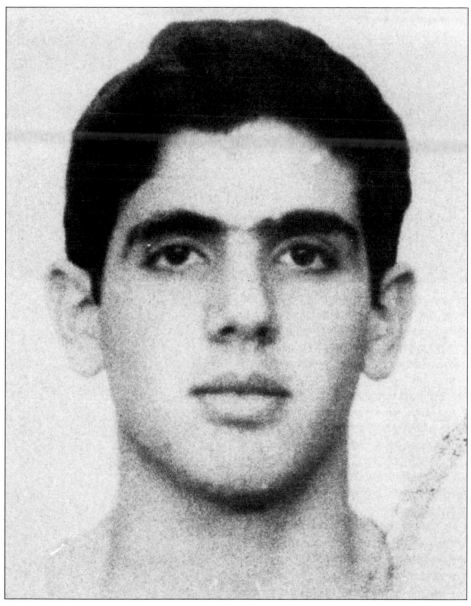

David Delarosa: "And you'll love thy brother like thyself"

Nir Poraz: Both father and son were heroes

ing course. During the course he heard a lecture given by Shlomo Shamir, the commander at Latrun, on the lessons learned from the battles. When it came time for questions, Gulliver stood up and sharply criticized his superiors. Why was the attack put off from the night until dawn? Why wasn't there artillery support? Why didn't they prepare enough water supplies for the troops? Why were untrained new immigrants, just off the boat, sent into battle? Has someone paid for these foul-ups? Gulliver's criticism was hushed up, but it made a great impression on many of those present.

Between Latrun and the officers' course Gulliver managed to join Moshe Dayan's commando battalion and prove himself as a gunner and a section commander in a series of daring operations. He became so well known that at the end of 1948 he was chosen to be part of an IDF delegation that was sent to the United States, to get support and raise funds. What an unusual sight this was! A nineteen-year-old, who a short time ago had taken leave of his friends, still in full uniform and wearing heavy army shoes, standing in front of crowds of Jews and declaring, "You aren't giving the money for 'someone,' but rather for yourselves. How will you be able to look your children in the eye, knowing that by not giving money you are endangering the lives of the young men and women who are fighting Israel's battles?" At the same time he complained in his letters about not being able to take part in the triumphant offensive in the Negev.

He made up after the war for a lot of what he had missed. At first he was a very dedicated reserve officer who invested much more in his unit than he was required to. He also thought about what direction to take in civilian life. He never stopped working on his farm and carrying out all sorts of agricultural experiments. At the same time he began his studies at the university (although he kept asking himself, again and again, whether he really wanted to be a lawyer). While he studied he taught Hebrew to new immigrants in the Jerusalem area, showing goodwill and friendship to all those around him. He also showed sincere concern for all developing issues of national importance. He was strongly opposed to negative phenomena, like the official tolerance for young people who had evaded combat service during the war, while their friends were shedding their blood, and started their careers afterward.

In the end he decided to go back to the army full time. He wrote to a friend, "I don't think that a period of calm—even if it lasts awhile—will prevent a confrontation within the next two to three years." Faithful to his words, he joined the career army and found himself training officers. As usual, he did this with thoroughness and dedication, and won over the hearts of his students. They admired and praised him, and knew that everything he taught them was based on hard personal experience in the field. But he still wasn't satisfied. This was the time of the Reprisal Raids (1954–56) when, as a response to every murderous infiltration by terrorists over the border, the IDF attacked Jordanian, Egyptian, and Syrian military bases. "I don't feel good about myself," wrote Gulliver, "because I am not one of those taking part in the reprisal operations."

Here and there he managed to take advantage of his influence with students and friends to join them in operations. In the Black Arrow raid on Gaza, in 1955, he joined his student Mordechai "Motta" Gur (later to become the chief of staff), serving as his personal runner. But he wanted more than that.

In November 1955 he finally succeeded in getting released from training courses and joined the paratroopers. He was given command of Company D, whose previous commander, Motta, had been wounded. The soldiers received him with suspicion, among other reasons because a dislocated shoulder had prevented him from completing the parachuting course and getting his red beret. But within a day all of them were won over by his charm and were willing to follow him anywhere. He served in this position for only three weeks. At the beginning of December he led his company in Operation Kinneret—a raid on the Syrian positions above the Lake of Tiberias—and was killed by a grenade that exploded near him.

"There was no mission that seemed too hard for him," said Chief of Staff Moshe Dayan, at Gulliver's graveside.

Professor Michael Bar-Zohar, a former Knesset member, is a writer and lecturer.

WITH HIS HEART'S BLOOD

NATAN ELBAZ

by Yossi Walter

Kiryat Yovel in Jerusalem—a neighborhood with drab porches and narrow stairwells. The neighbors don't know Rachel, the mother of Natan Elbaz. They have also never heard about Natan. After some effort I track down the apartment of his sister, Simcha Atias. Like the rest of the people in the neighborhood she also lives in one of those forlorn-looking long housing projects. Simcha climbs up to her apartment on the third floor, her arms laden with shopping baskets. She is a full-bodied woman, in her mid fifties, with kind eyes. She has eight children, some of them married, three still at home. One of them, Natan, is a soldier.

An old woman comes to greet us. She is a small bent-over figure. This is the mother, Rachel Elbaz. She is eighty-four years old. She knows no Hebrew. When Simcha explains the purpose of my visit she bursts into tears, and clutches to her heart an old, yellowing picture, a portrait of Natan, her beloved son.

"I dreamed about Natan last night," she says in Mograbi, the Arabic spoken in Morocco. "He told me, 'Mother, there's nothing to worry about; you live with my sister and she takes care of you. I want you to know that I am happy.'"

The dream is a direct link to her son. A night doesn't pass without her beloved Natan appearing in her dreams and talking to her. From the picture on the wall a young man clad in an IDF uniform looks down on us. He is chubby, round-faced, with a youthful smile, dressed in khaki. On his head he wears a soldier's beret with the emblem of the infantry, on his feet high boots and gaiters, typical of a combat soldier of the Fifties.

Rachel had six children. Natan was the third, her favorite. They had a special relationship. More than the other children in the family, he showered his mother with affection. Natan Elbaz was born in Morocco in the town of Sufro, a remote town with winding lanes and a ghetto surrounded by a stone wall, which protected the Jews from their Arab neighbors. And, above all, it was a place where it was hard to make a living. From his youth, Natan had a dream. One day he would go beyond those walls into the wide-open spaces. "Natan," says Simcha, "was a good quiet boy who showed a lot of respect to his parents. He studied the Gemara every day. My brother had a warm heart. He always helped Mother."

As a child he was sent to the Em Habanim yeshiva in the town, where he studied Torah and Hebrew. It was there that he acquired Jewish values and his yearning for Zion. He did well in his studies. He especially loved the Torah. But because of financial problems at home he had to leave the yeshiva and became a porter. He gave his wages to his father. Later he became a shoemaker's apprentice. And throughout that whole period his yearning for Zion grew. His childhood dream to leave this remote town turned into a desire to immigrate to Israel.

At that time the illegal immigration organization that was to bring Jews to Israel was being established. Natan, fifteen at the time, would sit for hours and listen open-mouthed to the stories of the emissaries about the War of Independence, about the acts of heroism of the Moroccan-born boys, some of whom he knew well. He was burning to go to Israel. But his parents told him that at fifteen he was still too young. Natan did not give up. He tried to go without their permission but was caught and sent back home. At the age of seventeen he tried his luck again, this time in the framework of the Youth Aliya organization. His parents were still against it, but he hugged them, cried on their shoulders, and went his own way.

Rachel Elbaz describes the scene: "He kissed my head and asked for forgiveness. I cried and begged him not to do it, to wait a little longer, and then we would all go to Israel. In my heart I had a feeling that something was going to happen to him. There were wars in Israel, and I was afraid that something would happen to him. Natan said to me, 'Mother, I'm going to Israel to build a better life for you. Don't be afraid that I will die. If I die it will be for *kiddush hashem*' [the sanctification of God]."

Natan managed to get to Israel, but his sweet dream turned sour in the difficult reality of immigrant life at the beginning of the Fifties. He moved from kibbutz to kibbutz, but couldn't find a place for himself. As an observant Jew he had thought that everyone in the Holy Land studied Torah. On the kibbutz he found a totally secular way of life without any religion. His first letters to his parents were full of longings for home and feelings of guilt for deserting his family. Between the lines he hinted at a lot of difficulties as well, which raised doubts in his mind as to whether he had made a mistake by not listening to his parents' advice. But as the days passed he became more optimistic. He gained control of himself, felt an increasing happiness, and in every letter urged his parents to plan to come to Israel where he was "preparing a better life" for them.

A short time after he came to the country Natan joined the army. He had no papers, and since he looked younger than his years, the military authorities demanded that he provide papers verifying his age. Natan asked his mother to send them. "You will die, my son," she answered him in desperation, but Natan insisted. He wrote, "I want to do this for my country."

Natan was drafted and joined an infantry unit. As a youth on his own he experienced a lot of disappointments in this alienating, sometimes threatening, reality. But he was very proud of his determination not to be different from others, to be like everyone else and even better. He remained an observant Jew and did all he could to avoid breaking any religious laws during his service. He never asked to be released from the morning run or from standing in the line for food because he had to pray.

But his strong feelings of loneliness and alienation throughout his basic training reached their peak during a series of exercises near Beit Guvrin. It was the eve of a holiday. The company soldiers completed their training for the day and awaited their releases for the holiday. Before the furlough passes were handed out there was an arms inspection, and it turned out that the shooting wheel in Natan's mortar was missing. When the platoon sergeant handed out the passes, he didn't give one to Natan. Natan was deeply hurt by the punishment. He clenched his fists, and withdrew into his bitterness. He felt that he had suffered an injustice. Many times he had complained to his commander that the shooting wheels would often fall, but nothing had been done about it. In the end his feelings of frustration burst forth. He announced to his platoon commander that he would disobey the order and not remain on base.

Natan was brought before the company commander but stood firm in his refusal. While he was standing in front of the commander he could no longer control himself and burst into tears. "They always get me in trouble and make me the scapegoat," he said bitterly.

The officer was a sensitive man. He calmed Natan down and explained to him that he was not alone, and that there was always someone who would listen to his problems. He asked Natan to apologize to his commander for his refusal to obey an order and to explain the circumstances under which he had lost the shooting wheel. Natan softened. The commander explained that no one wanted to do him an injustice, and that the pass hadn't been canceled but delayed until the matter could be looked into. The next day, indeed, Natan received a pass, but remained on base because in any case he had nowhere to go. He had fought for his right to go out on leave only because he had felt that he had been unjustly deprived of this right.

A few days after this incident he was tried before the battalion commander. On his way to the officer's office he prepared himself for the possibility that he would be sentenced to several days of detention. To his surprise, the commander let him off with a reprimand and then comforted him. "You are among friends," said the commander, smiling at him.

These words made a big impression on Natan. For the first time since he had come to Israel he felt that he belonged. A new man left the commander's room. From then on there wasn't a soldier who volunteered as much as he did.

If another soldier went out on leave and didn't have clean laundry, Natan would lend him his shirt. In any case he wasn't going out on leave, and he had a lot of clean shirts. When he was asked why he didn't take leave, he answered with a smile, "What do I have to do in the city? The army is like a five-star hotel."

In time Natan began to excel as a soldier. When the company was asked to carry out a difficult mission, he was the first to volunteer. He loved to handle weapons and explosives. He wanted to get to know all the different kinds. He was especially good at throwing grenades. His achievements as a soldier soon brought him a promotion to deputy commander of his squad. He became a happy man. He became known as the best mortar-crewman in the battalion, as a soldier who wasn't put off by any assignment.

His letters to his parents were full of optimism. In his last letter he wrote, "Father, Mother, my dear parents. I will not die until I see your faces again."

February 11, 1954. On this day the company was ordered to stop all activity and get ready for a parade in honor of a visit by the chief of staff. Natan's platoon was ordered to prepare the camp for the visit, even though they had gone out the night before on a security patrol against infiltrators. The platoon sergeant gave everyone a task and asked for volunteers to disarm hand grenades and store them in the armory. Two soldiers volunteered, Private Zeiss and Private Elbaz. They began to collect the grenades and bullets and put them in Natan's tent. When Zeiss entered the tent he saw that Natan had disarmed some of the grenades and was putting them into a box. Suddenly there was a click, the threatening click of the safety catch of a grenade being released. Zeiss ran out of the tent in a panic, holding six grenades in his hands. Behind him he heard Natan shouting, "Grenade! Grenade!" In the IDF vocabulary this was the warning that a grenade was about to explode.

Natan held the grenade whose safety catch had been released and ran out. He had four seconds. If the grenade had exploded inside the tent it would have caused a serious disaster. His fellow soldiers were working near the tent at the time. Natan knew that the rest of the grenades would also have exploded and that for sure there would have been casualties. Natan came out of the tent intending to throw the grenade as far as possible. But then he saw that most of the company soldiers were all around the area. Some of them heard his shout and ran for cover. Others were frozen to the spot.

Two seconds were left. No one will ever know what went through his mind at that moment. His friends watched in amazement as Natan ran with the grenade, jumped into a ditch near the tent, and pressed the grenade close to his chest. An explosion was heard. A cloud of black smoke billowed up.

When the smoke cleared Natan's mutilated body was lying immobile in the ditch. A long moment of stunned silence followed. Then one of the soldiers turned to the commander and said, "Sir, that was an act of heroism."

Natan Elbaz, a Jewish boy from Morocco, who had wanted to go to Israel all his life, died sanctifying the name of God.

The next day the IDF spokesman made an official announcement: "Private Natan Elbaz, twenty-one, sacrificed his life in order to prevent a disaster and the loss of his friends' lives from an exploding grenade. The deceased has no address, and there is no one to inform of his death." The IDF authorities made an effort to find some address but were unsuccessful. Natan Elbaz remained alone in the country, but his heroic deed did not go unnoticed. The story spread around the country. An inquiry commission was appointed whose conclusions were made public by the chief of staff in the order of the day:

I would like to praise soldier no. 228639, the late Private Elbaz Natan, Infantry, who in an extraordinary act of heroism sacrificed his life for his friends.

Moshe Dayan
Chief of Staff

Natan Elbaz was buried in the military cemetery in Kiryat Shaul. He was twenty-one years old at his death. It was said of him that he died to sanctify God's name, and that beyond his act of heroism, which left the people in the country dumbfounded, he spoke out on behalf of the whole Moroccan community. His cry was like an accusing finger pointed at all of Israeli society for the injustice done to a whole community, which had been stigmatized and prejudiced against with expressions like "Morocco—the—knife." (Some Moroccan Jews were said to be uncouth, violent people, who would not hesitate to draw their knives and stab their enemies.)

Simcha Atias tells her story:

> We didn't know that Natan had died. No one told us. The Israeli authorities didn't know our address. One day we got a letter from Mother's cousin, who had gone to Israel with Natan. The night before Mother was suddenly in a bad mood and began to sing mourning songs. I asked her, "Mother, why are you singing songs like that? It makes me feel terrible." Mother cried all night. At six in the morning we woke to the shouts of my grandmother, who lived one floor below us. She called Mother and told her, "Come and see the letter that has arrived." It was a letter from Israel. I saw an article from a Hebrew newspaper with my brother's picture.
>
> We went to Mother's brother, who knew how to read Hebrew. He began to read the article and we said to him, "Come on; tell us what it says already!" My uncle answered sadly, "Can't you let me finish reading in peace?" Then I knew that something had happened to Natan. I knew that my brother was dead.
>
> Later an emissary arrived from Israel and told us what had happened. We also got a letter from Ben-Gurion. But all of this did not give us Natan back.

Eight years later the family decided to move to Israel. When they arrived, no one they met knew anything about Natan's act of heroism. They lived in miserable asbestos huts and went hungry. Volunteers from the Jerusalem Labor Council tracked them down and found them in a rundown shack, wearing patched clothing, with broken furniture; and in the middle of all this was an old woman, Natan Elbaz's mother. The Ministry of Defense gave the family an apartment and a monthly allowance.

Rachel Elbaz lives in her daughter Simcha's house. Few of the residents of Kiryat Yovel know her. Fewer still know the story of Natan Elbaz. All that is left are albums full of yellowing pictures and a bundle of letters. Beside them is a poem that Israel's national poet Natan Alterman wrote about the soldier Natan Elbaz:

> With a stylus on a tablet as in days of yore,
> A nation will write its history,
> Looking for the heart of hidden times,
> Searching for it with a torch in her hand.
> And those times, like a heart, are broken
> Into your four seconds, Elbaz.
>
> To them it kneels as it must,
> To this African root, a son of Morocco,
> In them it rages like the sea
> And the Lord will be its witness.
>
> It seems that not all is spelled out,
> Because there is still a secret.
> Look, the time kneels.
> As his reward it will be praised and slandered
> But his eternal value remains—
> The passing seconds of Elbaz.
> Oh, he falls to the dust as he must,
> The African root, the son of Morocco.
> Oh, lying there open-mouthed and stunned
> God is witness to you and to us.

Yossi Walter is a former military correspondent of the newspaper Maariv.

I Did Not Betray
My Country

Uri Ilan

by Ran Edelist

A nineteen-year-old boy he was, slim and quiet, with the sunburned face and callused hands of a kibbutz youth. He had grown up in Gan Shmuel, located in the fertile lands of the Sharon plain, facing the rolling hills of the Jezreel Valley. The Sharon is one of the most beautiful areas in Israel, and Uri Ilan lived most of his life in this lush little piece of Eden. But on that night in January 1955, Uri Ilan was squatting, shivering in the damp cold, in a cell of the el-Maza prison in Damascus, laboriously weaving a rope out of thin threads he had pulled from his stinking mattress. Every few minutes he would test the rope. It had to be strong enough to support his body weight.

That night, the most lonely, desperate night of his life, he must have thought back to his childhood, his friends, his family. Uri was born on Gan Shmuel in 1935. The kibbutz belonged to Hashomer Hatzair, a left-wing Zionist movement that advocated tolerance and brotherhood between Jews and Arabs. It was represented in Israel's political life by the Mapam Party. The kibbutz members believed in hard life and hard work. For them the needs of one's society and community took precedence over one's individual needs. The individual's goals and aspirations must, therefore, be sacrificed for the sake of the common struggle. That was how the country had been built, they said. That was how Uri's parents, Shlomo Ilan and Faiga Ilanit, had educated their son. They instilled in him the belief in absolute truths, in a life dedicated to Zionist-Socialist ideals. Uri's mother was very active in Israeli political life. She was a member of the Knesset and one of the ideologues of her party.

Uri's character was shaped in the early 1950s, in the years following the War of Independence and the establishment of the State of Israel. During the War of Independence, Uri was thirteen years old. He was a smart, curious boy who grew up in the free atmosphere of the kibbutz. He read avidly any book or newspaper he could lay his hands on, and was deeply influenced by the strict ideological atmosphere in his home. His mother was the dominant personality in the house. Uri's teacher was Benio Greenbaum, the son of Israel's first interior minister, Itzhak Greenbaum. Greenbaum passed on to him the radical ideas of the Socialist revolution. Throughout his youth he would hear the slogans calling for a binational Jewish-Arab society that were the basic principles of the Mapam Party. Yet, despite the idealistic speeches and pamphlets, Uri knew that these utopian ideals would not be realized in the near future. Israel was still surrounded by Arab states that had vowed to destroy it, and he knew he would have to fight for its survival.

That struggle was felt even in the daily life of the kibbutz. Uri had been drawn to a huge, powerful man on the kibbutz by the name of Niumka, who was a kibbutz guard. At night, Niumka would drive around the fields in his gray pickup truck, armed with a heavy machine gun strapped to the roof by a steel cable. Infiltrations by Arabs into the kibbutz fields and stealing were a common occurrence, and Gan Shmuel had to be protected. Slogans about Jewish-Arab brotherhood were fine for speeches, pamphlets, and articles. But in Gan Shmuel, night after night, burly Niumka would wage the ancient, brutal war of farmers defending their land against the inhabitants of the nearby Arab village of Cherkess.

That was how Uri learned back then that Israelis must be ready to fight for their survival. He realized that if they were not prepared to take whatever risks were necessary and to make painful sacrifices, they had no chance of overcoming the dangers that threatened them.

In 1953 Uri was drafted into the IDF. He joined the Golani Brigade, a famous fighting unit that had participated in all of Israel's major battles and was traditionally charged with securing the northern front. On December 8, 1954, Uri was ordered to join a small squad of five men who were to cross the Syrian lines near Kibbutz Dan for an intelligence-gathering operation. Israeli Intelligence had tapped the phone lines connecting the Syrian bunkers overlooking the Dan region. They had used a small compact listening device that needed servicing every couple of months. The operation was code-named Grasshopper. For Uri, the boy who had grown up in this battle for survival, it was clear that the security of Israel largely depended on the snatches of information intercepted by the listening device.

The select team that crossed the border that night was composed of five elite soldiers. Three of them were paratroopers who had been trained by the legendary Meir Har-Zion—Gad Kastelanetz, Meir Yaacobi, and Jacky Lind. (See "The Best Fighter We Ever Had.") The other two, First Lieutenant Meir Moses and Uri Ilan, were Golani fighters. They had experience in this kind of operation; they had already crossed the border in the past to install such devices and service them. The order always came at the last moment. Uri was at home in Gan Shmuel, on leave for the Sabbath, when an urgent phone call to the kibbutz office summoned him to join the Grasshopper team immediately. He put on his uniform and hitchhiked north.

The moon was rising as the five men crossed the border. Silently they moved toward their objective. Suddenly they were caught in a deadly outburst of fire from the Syrian positions. There were Syrians behind them as well. The Israeli soldiers realized that their escape route was cut off. An IDF backup squad in the area was supposed to come to their rescue if they were detected by the enemy, and pin down the enemy while the Grasshopper team retreated. But the backup squad had lost contact with Lieutenant Moses's men and they didn't go into action. The five men were surrounded by the large Syrian forces, and were called to surrender. Meir Yaacobi, from Kibbutz Beit Alfa, realized that there was no alternative. "That's it, guys," he muttered. "There's no choice. With these bastards it will take forever." He meant that a long, difficult period of captivity awaited them. The five soldiers were taken prisoner, stripped of their weapons, and imprisoned in the Kuneitra jail, in a huge army camp on the Golan Heights. Soon after, they were transferred for interrogation to the el-Maza prison in Damascus.

The year was 1954. The Syrian interrogators were sadistic and brutal. The soldiers were isolated in tiny cells, without any contact between them. They were hungry, exhausted, cold. They were subjected to terrible beatings. None of them knew what had happened to their friends. Uri maintained a stubborn silence, despite the savage beatings. He didn't know that his fellow soldiers had already broken down and revealed almost all they knew. He believed that the enemy was entitled to know nothing but his name, rank, and serial number. He believed that the secret device they were sent to service was crucial to Israel's security. And, above all, he was firmly convinced that if every soldier fulfilled his duty as he should, Israel would remain secure and its society would be better off.

He had no doubt that he was doing the right thing. The thought that he should save his life by revealing what he knew was totally alien to him. He was brought up to believe in the sacrifice of the individual for his community, for his ideals, for his country. He knew that in the el-Maza prison he, Uri Ilan, represented the entire Israeli people in this confrontation with its vilest of enemies, and if he broke down, so would his country. And he didn't break down.

Uri didn't know that the "wars of the generals" surrounding the Grasshopper fiasco were already well under way. Senior officers were hurling accusations at each other for the failed operation. Prime Minister Moshe Sharett angrily wrote in his diary that the squad was captured because of the sloppy planning and execution of the mission. He blamed military intelligence for the failure. But on the other side of the border, in el-Maza Prison, five teenage soldiers, almost children, were paying the price. And Uri held his tongue.

Later many would say that he was a naive fool. But at the time it was naive fools like him who took the risks, carried out the dangerous missions, and gave their lives so that Israel could survive.

Uri Ilan was brutally tortured by the Syrians, but he kept his mouth shut. Finally, when the torture became unbearable and the lonely prisoner felt that he might break under the pressure, he made his fateful decision. He was determined that the Syrians wouldn't learn from him about the secret listening device. He didn't know what had happened to his comrades. The interrogators told him they had killed them all, and that he was the only one left. When the dread of breaking down and betraying his country grew too strong, Uri Ilan wove the threads of his mattress into a rope and hanged himself.

January 13, 1955. The office of Major General Moshe Dayan, chief of staff of the Israeli army. Thirty-five days after the capture of the squad, Dayan's aide scribbled an entry in his log: "An IDF intelligence unit has been ambushed in Syria. The boys have been taken prisoner. One of them, Uri Ilan, has committed suicide. We are going this evening with Moshe [Dayan] to the Bnot Yaacov bridge. The Syrians will return Uri's body."

In the darkness, the Israelis were watching the Syrian army truck that stopped by the narrow bridge, escorted by UN observers. Several stony-faced enemy soldiers handed over a wooden casket to the Israeli honor guard. The body was brought to a bare room in Kibbutz Mishmar Hayarden and laid on an oblong table. Moshe Dayan watched in silence. There was a blue welt on Uri's neck. The medic examined the body, and suddenly stopped short. A tiny piece of paper was fastened to Uri's toes with a piece of string. It had been perforated by a pin or a sharp, fine piece of straw. The tiny holes were arranged in the form of letters. General Moshe Zadok, OC Northern Command, raised the note to the light and read: "They have killed all the others. I am waiting to be sentenced. I know nothing about the rest. Bury me beside Gabi. Take revenge. Uri Ilan."

Under his name he added, "There are pieces of paper in my clothes."

At that late hour, in the yellow light of the single bare bulb that hangs above them, officers and soldiers bent over their comrade's remains, examined his body, carefully unstitching the seams of his clothing. It was a horrific night. The dead body of a nineteen-year-old was laid out before them. There were other notes concealed in Uri's clothing: "Look for my will in the clothes," one of them read. "Shalom, Uri Ilan." "Revenge!" read another, also written with pinpricks.

Moshe Dayan picked up one of the perforated pieces of paper and raised it to the light. He read in a loud voice: "I did not betray my country."

Moshe Dayan, Israel's hero, had been through a lot in his military career, seen everything, done everything. But on that stormy night in the grim room at Mishmar Hayarden he experienced one of the most painful moments of his life. It would have a profound effect on him. When he stepped down as chief of staff more than two years and many battles later, he spoke of Uri Ilan in his parting speech. When he resigned from the position of foreign minister in Menachem Begin's cabinet in 1979, he mentioned two young men, Roi Rotberg of Kibbutz Nahal-Oz, who had been murdered by Palestinian infiltrators from the Gaza Strip, and Uri Ilan, who had not betrayed his country.

The four other soldiers captured with Uri Ilan had not been killed. They were exchanged for Syrian prisoners a few months later.

Uri's note, "I did not betray my country," became the symbol of a generation. Scores of children were named after Uri Ilan after his death.

One of Uri's friends at Kibbutz Gan Shmuel said, "Uri had a code of honor. For him being a soldier meant being Orde Wingate, at the very least [see "Gideon Goes to War"]. It was not the torture that broke him but the fact that he, Uri Ilan, had been taken prisoner and the fear that he wouldn't be able to withstand the torture, that he would talk and betray his country."

Uri was buried beside Gabi, according to his will. Gabriel Wald had been an orphan, a Holocaust survivor brought to Gan Shmuel through Youth Aliya. In February 1954 he had been murdered by Bedouins in the "wild west" of Beit Guvrin, not far from Jerusalem.

Moshe Dayan said, "Most of our soldiers fall . . . for a reason . . . but few fall for [a principle] . . . like Uri Ilan."

And the poet Natan Alterman wrote:

> This nation will remember that it has sent the fallen to their fate,
> And not from the enemy alone should their blood be redeemed.
> Time will turn many poems with morals into flying dust,
> But there are crumpled paper notes
> That will be sealed in the nation's heart.

Ran Edelist is a former editor of Monitin *magazine.*

The Heroes of the Reprisal Raids

Yaacov Mizrahi and Pinchas Noi

Gulliver's death occurred during the period known as the Reprisal Raids. It started in 1954, and ended in October 1956, with the launching of the Sinai Campaign against Egypt. For more than two years, the Reprisal Raids dominated the scene of the conflict between Israel and its neighbors. Jordan, Egypt, and Syria either would send groups of terrorists and assassins across the Israeli border, or would tolerate such groups, which acted in coordination with their armies. The infiltrators carried out acts of bombing, sabotage, and murder inside Israeli territory, attacking the civilian population. Israel retaliated by launching deadly raids on her neighbors' military camps, strongholds, and police fortresses, located close to the border, mainly in the area from which the terrorists set out for their operations.

Most of the operations were carried by the small, highly trained paratrooper battalion, which became in those stormy years the main guardian of Israel's breached borders. Many of the paratroopers got killed in these operations, and some brave and capable officers rose from fighting in the Reprisal Raids to the top echelons of command in the IDF. Among them were future generals like Rafael "Raful" Eitan, Motta Gur, Ariel Sharon, Aharon Davidi, and others—and the younger generation that is still at the helm of the Israeli military establishment today—Itzhak Mordechai, Amnon Lipkin-Shahak, Matan Vilnai.

The Reprisal Raids also had their share of heroes, and two of them were awarded the highest decoration of the IDF. They were Yaacov Mizrahi and Pinchas Noi.

Yaacov Mizrahi was the hero of the Kuntilla battle. At the beginning of October 1955 the first shipments of weapons began to reach Egypt, as part of a huge arms agreement with Czechoslovakia. In the middle of the month a military pact was signed between Egypt and Syria to establish a common command with one aim—to attack Israel and threaten its existence. A few days later the Egyptians began to heat up the demilitarized zone of Nitzana, and even attacked the Israeli police station at Ketziot and took a policeman prisoner. The IDF decided to respond with Operation Egged—an attack on the police station at Kuntilla in Sinai, twelve kilometers (7.5 miles) west of the cease-fire line, across fields of quicksand and stones. The goal was defined—to take prisoners. The attack force was made up of two hundred paratroopers.

On the night between October 27 and 28 they set out, completing the last part of the march on foot. This last part consisted of three hours of hard trekking before the battle. Finally they reached their attack positions. Around 2:00 A.M. the paratroopers opened fire, and both sides were in shock—the Egyptians because of the unexpected attack, and the Israelis because of the size of the defending forces, which were much bigger than Intelligence had reported. Two machine-gun positions, set on high ground, showered the paratroopers with heavy fire. Rafael "Raful" Eitan, the future chief of staff, attacked one of them and destroyed it. Meir Har-Zion, the man who had led the force to the target and himself a living military legend, silenced the second machine gun.

Private Yaacov Mizrahi was an eighteen-year-old young man with thick, curly hair, burning black eyes, and a square jaw. He had just begun his service in the paratroopers, and had been assigned to a secondary force that was not supposed to fight, but to capture prisoners. During the battle he saw that a group of Egyptian soldiers was still putting up a resistance. Some of them ran away. He would not let that happen. He went after them, fighting them alone, with a daring and efficiency that amazed his friends and officers. He ran ahead, straight into the enemy fire, when a bullet hit him and mortally wounded him. On the way back, on the shoulders of his friends, he died from his wounds. He received a posthumous citation from the chief of staff, who later awarded him a Medal of Valor.

The second hero of the paratroopers was Pinchas Noi. Operation Shomron—a reprisal action in Kalkiliya on the night of October 10, 1956—was unique among the reprisal actions of the IDF that preceded the Sinai Campaign. This was the largest and most complicated operation, but only one day had been devoted to its planning. The target was a fortified compound in Jordan, which at the time was an ally of the British. The British government, however, was engaged in secret preparations of a military invasion of Egypt, in cooperation with France (and as it later turned out, with Israel as well). The raid was launched and immediately ran into trouble. During the action a blocking unit was cut off, and was in a desperate situation. Its rescue almost caused an international incident. The cost in lives—eighteen dead and sixty-eight wounded—was so heavy that in spite of its success, it caused a revision in the entire reprisal policy. Chief of Staff Moshe Dayan later wrote that the Kalkiliya operation put an end to the era of the Reprisal Raids.

During the battle itself there were many acts of resourcefulness and bravery, but evidently the most outstanding were those of Pinchas Noi-Naidik, best known by his nickname, Alush. A slim, oval-faced boy, Noi, who was twenty-one years old, was born in Poland after World War II to a survivor couple. He was deputy commander of a paratroop company. He was sent at the head of a support unit to cover the attack on the police fortress at Kalkiliya from the western side of the building.

While the paratroopers were moving toward their target, they were spotted by Jordanian soldiers, who opened heavy fire on them. Noi and two of his men were the only ones who managed to cross the road, which was within firing range, on the way to their cover position. Suddenly they realized that they were facing an enemy entrenchment of which no one had been aware in advance. The fire from this fortified position endangered the whole platoon. Noi crawled alone toward the enemy position, threw a grenade into it, and put it out of commission, killing five enemy soldiers.

At the same moment three Jordanian soldiers darted toward him, and he fired and killed them at short range. Immediately afterward another Jordanian soldier jumped up in front of him with an unloaded PIAT missile. Noi intended to shoot him, but discovered that the magazine of his Uzi was empty.

The two of them jumped on each other and started wrestling with their bare hands and their useless weapons. The Jordanian hit Noi's hand with the PIAT, injured him, and tried to bite him. During the struggle, though, Noi managed to reload his Uzi and kill the Jordanian. The enemy position was cleared, and the platoon could now cross the road and cover the attack of the police fortress. In many respects, Noi, who killed nine Jordanian soldiers, was the one who made the attack possible. For that the chief of staff awarded him a citation, and a Medal of Valor.

Amos Carmel

ONLY A BURST OF GUNFIRE IN THE CHEST

ZVIKA OFER

by Amos Carmel

"Zvika Ofer was one of those soldiers that only a burst of gunfire in the chest could stop. He was one of those soldiers who looked around him and knew what he was seeing, and the sights he saw in over twenty years of service in the IDF were not pleasant sights. What he observed throughout those years and in the years after was neither easy to look at, nor to bear. Nevertheless, perhaps thanks to his clear-sightedness, Zvika was a mainstay for us, a senior officer, from whom his men derived a sense of security and inspiration." With these words Minister of Defense Moshe Dayan eulogized Lieutenant Colonel Zvi Ofer, the commander of the Horev Commando Unit, who fell while in pursuit of terrorists at the end of 1968.

Ofer was thirty-six at his death. How was it that he served over twenty years in the army? The story begins with his birthday. Gingi (Red), as many of his friends called him, was born in 1932 to parents who came to Israel in the Third Aliya (1919–23) and who were among the founders that year of Kfar Azar. This small moshav, which today has become part of the Dan Region, was once a small Jewish island in hostile Arab surroundings, and its members had to devote a lot of their energy and time to the defense of their home. An "illegal" rifle, hidden under the bed during times of tension, was a common sight in Kfar Azar. Zvika himself became a part of this while still a small child. When the women were asked to take part in a course about first aid during battle, he was chosen to be one of the "wounded." For his bar mitzva, which took place during the last year of the Second World War, he got a very special present— the right to shoot thirteen rounds from a small rifle, a first step toward his joining the Gadna and the Hagana a year later.

As a boy he delivered the Hagana newspaper *Eshnav* to its subscribers in the Ramat Gan area, put up posters in the middle of the night, and enthusiastically cleaned and oiled the guns in the arms cache of the moshav. He also liked to roam around the country, preparing himself for his job as a scout. His physical strength, along with his love of outdoor life, made him a perfect field fighter.

When the War of Independence broke out Zvika was a sixteen-year-old student in the agricultural school in Moshav Nahalal. He ran away from the school, made his way to the Third Battalion of the Palmach, in the Yiftach Brigade, and became a soldier in the regular army. At the end of the first truce he took part in Operation Dani, whose objective was to capture the Arab towns of Lod and Ramle, off the road to Jerusalem. The talent he showed made him a natural candidate for a section commanders course during the second truce. Again he ran off, in October 1948, in the middle of the course, when he found out that the Third Battalion was preparing for Operation Yoav, which was to break through the road to the Negev. He didn't hesitate, but grabbed his things and rushed to join his unit and his friends.

By the end of the war Zvika had reached the rank of sergeant. His classmates had not even enlisted in the army yet. After his discharge, he worked for a while for the Mekorot Water Company, took an officers' course during his reserve duty, and decided that his place was in the army. "I felt a need to return to the army," he said. When he reenlisted he was first assigned to a unit that followed and chased after *fedayeen*, Arab terrorists who infiltrated from the Gaza Strip. In the 1950s the *fedayeen* worked for Egyptian Intelligence, carrying out terrorist activities all over the country. This was the time of the Reprisal Raids, and Zvika had to be there. He soon joined a paratroop battalion, which was responsible for most of the reprisal operations, and took part in many of them. "In the paratroops," he said later, "I found again the spirit of the Palmach."

In the Sinai Campaign, in 1956, Zvika Ofer was the commander of a paratroop platoon that reached the Mitla Pass over land. He took part in the famous, very bloody battle that was fought there and later participated in the taking of the Sharm el-Sheikh Egyptian military base, whose huge cannon controlled the Straits of Tiran. His officers and men soon discovered during this war that although this redhead was stubborn and spoke very slowly, his thoughts and reactions were fast. He carried out every assignment he was given thoroughly and to perfection. In the early 1960s he took off the red beret of the paratroopers. The General Staff had decided to further improve the Golani Brigade with the addition of paratroop officers. Motta Gur was made commander of the brigade, and Zvi Ofer, who had managed in the meantime to finish a company commanders' course, became the brigade intelligence officer.

"He was an excellent intelligence officer," said Gur. "He had the ability to analyze situations objectively, based on intensive study of the problems and on his own experience. He was very good at remembering the material he studied and at understanding the basic goals and problems of any assignment." He didn't want to sit in an office. At the first opportunity, he jumped on the chance to set up the commando unit of the brigade, which became known as The Flying Tiger, and became its commander. The soldiers assigned to him had come directly from basic training, but he soon had them toeing the line. In February 1962 it was already very clear that if a battle assignment was given to the Golani Brigade, Zvi Ofer's unit would play a major role in carrying it out.

The assignments soon came. From the beginning of the year the Syrians had increased their attacks on Israeli fishermen on the Kinneret, and they had opened fire more than once on civilian and military boats sailing on the lake. In March, Syrian recoilless guns hit a guard boat and wounded two of its men. It was then decided, at the highest government level, that enough was enough, and that it was time to respond with force. Operation Swallow was given the green light. This was the first large reprisal action since the Sinai Campaign.

The designated target was a Syrian company stronghold near the village of Nukeib on the eastern front of the Kinneret. It stood on a hill four kilometers north of Ein Gev.

On the afternoon of March 16, Ofer was informed that his unit would serve as the main striking force to attack the position itself. Other forces of the Golani Brigade would capture the village and put up road blocks, from the east and the north. He was not surprised by this order. A few days before, when tensions were already rising, he had gone out with a few officers from the brigade to look over the area on their own. "We will soon reach Nukeib," he told them confidently.

He knew that they were dealing with an all-round defense post built according to Soviet doctrine, 300 m long and 150 m wide. Ofer also knew in advance that the crucial area was in the southwest section—two trenches with five concrete pillboxes between them. Before going out to battle Ofer remembered the 1955 Kinneret Operation, in which he had taken part, when enemy civilians had been killed as well. So he said to his men: "The IDF is not an army of murderers. We are not going out to kill the enemy but to destroy its positions. But don't hesitate to shoot Syrian soldiers who aim their guns at you. Whoever surrenders will be taken prisoner. I want decisiveness and speed in carrying out the assignment, and perfect fire discipline."

According to the plan of action, the members of Zvika's unit were supposed to attack the position from the rear, from the east, after making their way there under cover of night, and this is what they did. But before they even got started, a number of mistakes were made in other places, by other Golani units. The element of surprise was lost. Zvika's unit found itself under heavy fire before it had a chance to attack, and its commander had to adapt to the new circumstances and change the original plan. This was when the truth of Motta Gur's words was demonstrated: "I relied on Zvika's ability to improvise and on his leadership qualities, and I knew that he would carry out his assignment, come what may." Ofer assigned a small force to take care of the wounded. Then, instead of sliding down the side of the wadi, which bordered on the position, and attacking up the other side, straight into enemy fire, he disengaged himself from the enemy, circled around, and quietly reached a new attack position.

Within a short time the men under his command began to clear out the two trenches. Ofer himself rushed to the southern trench and took a position in the middle of the line. Suddenly he realized that they were no longer advancing. He quickly moved to the head of the line, discovered that one of the officers had been wounded, and dressed his wound. The moment was captured by a photographer accompanying the force and was immortalized in a picture that received worldwide coverage. From then on he stormed ahead first, leading his men, shooting in all directions, replacing his gun from time to time with one passed up to him from behind, tossing grenades, sweeping along with him all the soldiers who could still fight. When he approached the pillboxes, he opened with bazooka fire, went on to grenades, and even tried shouting to them in Arabic: "Surrender; you don't stand a chance." In the end he silenced them with antitank missiles.

In the debriefing after the battle, he said: "The first critical moment was at the beginning of the battle, when the Syrians opened fire on us before the assault, which meant that we had to change our plans. The second critical moment was close to the end of the battle, when we had to overpower the block of pillboxes at the western end of the enemy compound. At this point I had to take charge of the battle alone, since my subordinate officers had been wounded. I also had to coordinate the entry of the second force into the battle." He didn't forget to pay tribute to his men. "The boys are wonderful. They . . . went into the battle as trained soldiers and came out as superb fighters."

Operation Swallow was later criticized for planning errors, but no one expressed any doubt about Ofer's contribution, his daring, and his resourcefulness. He was given a citation by the Chief of Staff Zvi Tzur "for determination and perseverance in carrying out his mission and for serving as a personal example to his men." He later received the highest medal for bravery, the Medal of Valor, after a law was passed establishing the practice of awarding such medals.

On receiving the medal Zvi Ofer said: "I did what every other commanding officer in my position would have done." But he did not live long enough to wear that medal. After the battle of Nukeib he underwent retraining to join the Armored Corps, and he studied in the Staff and Command College. A few days before the Six-Day War he was promoted to the rank of lieutenant colonel and was assigned to be an instructor at the Officers' School. When the war broke out, he was given a battalion in the Jerusalem Brigade. He was eager to get into combat, but at first there was nothing for his battalion to do. On Wednesday, June 7, 1967, he was ordered to take Bethlehem, but the city surrendered to the Israelis without a fight. The next day they were sent to capture Hebron, and again found a city covered in a sea of white flags.

Ofer was very surprised. Having been born in the country and fought in the War of Independence, he remembered well the riots of 1936, the religious fanaticism of the people of Hebron, and their part in the heavy attacks on the Etzion Bloc. But he ordered his men to hold their fire. "As fate would have it," he later explained to his sister, "of all battalions mine was the one that finished the Six-Day War without firing a single shot." He organized the surrender ceremony, took control of the Tombs of the Patriarchs in the Machpelah Cave, collected arms from all the city's residents, and hoped that he would still get a chance to take part in the war on the Golan Heights. But then he was informed of a new direction in his military career. He was appointed military governor of Hebron and was ordered to bring life back to normal there. How does one do that? he asked himself. His answer: However you think it should be done.

His approach to the matter was considered exemplary. Author Shabtai Tevet wrote in his book *The Curse of the Blessing*: "He did everything thoroughly. If he was given the job of military governor and asked to bring life back to normal, then he would be a model governor. . . . By noon he already had a plan of action for the first two days. . . . With the help of the mayor and the leading citizens of Hebron, he became the only military governor in all of the occupied territories . . . who had all services functioning within a few hours of the occupation." Among other things, he punished looters severely, compelled doctors to take care of the poorer patients, and did not hesitate to visit a seven-year-old girl who had been wounded by gunfire and hospitalized.

His success in Hebron resulted in his being appointed military governor of Nablus in August 1967, to his great displeasure. He had wanted now more than ever to command a regular combat battalion, but he acquiesced. He served in that position for over a year and, according to Moshe Dayan, "was the best governor; he was openminded, he saw what was happening, and understood the situation." In the middle of October, everyone knew that Ofer was going to get what he wanted and that he would soon be leaving his job. The Arab mayor of Nablus, with whom he had had more than one disagreement, asked the minister of defense not to let him go.

Immediately afterward he was made commander of the Horev Commando Unit. He made great efforts to strengthen the select team of commando fighters. A month after he arrived, they received information about a terrorist group that had infiltrated Wadi Kelt, a dried riverbed in the barren hills dominating the Jordan Valley. The Horev unit and other forces closed in on the terrorists and drove them into a cave at the top of the wadi. As usual, Zvika Ofer approached the enemy at the head of his men. A burst of gunfire from that cave put an end to Ofer's life.

"The figure of Zvika, the country boy, the youth from the Palmach, the scout, the commander, and the instructor, will remain engraved on our hearts," said the OC Central Command General Rechavam Zeevi at his graveside.

Dr. Amos Carmel is a scientist, a publicist, and an editor.

The Mata Hari of the Middle East

Shula Cohen (The Pearl)

by Hannah Zemer

On the walls of Shula Cohen's Jerusalem apartment are hung many framed certificates—the citation of the Council of Women's Organizations in Israel for her "contribution to saving the Jews of Arab lands and for her heroic stand for the security of Israel"; certificates of merit from several military units to which she lectured, sharing her vast experience; and, most important of all, a certificate declaring her "an honored member of the intelligence community," which was given to her in 1992. The certificate says: "To Shula Cohen, a secret fighter who risked her life and contributed with all her heart to the undercover activity of the State of Israel."

The undercover activity referred to took place in Beirut and lasted for fourteen years, from 1947 to 1961. During this period Shula Cohen arranged to smuggle to Israel Jews who had escaped to Lebanon from Syria and other Arab countries. She also drafted intelligence agents into the service of the State of Israel. She herself passed on information to Israel collected from the highest sources, with whom she had cultivated a relationship. One could say that she was a spy, but there is no doubt that she was more than that. She was a volunteer who took upon herself every task necessary and useful to Israel or to the Jewish community, without considering the dangers involved.

How dangerous it all was became clear in 1961. Shula was arrested, kept in prison without trial for two years, and underwent repeated interrogations. She was then tried and sentenced to death. The sentence was later commuted to twenty years' imprisonment with hard labor. Shula was released after the Six-Day War in a prisoner exchange, after having spent six years and a few months in prison.

The story of Shula Cohen's activities is so incredible that even a writer of spy stories would not dare to use it. The woman whom the newspapers called the "Mata Hari of the Middle East" was an observant Jew, the wife of a conservative cloth merchant, a housewife, and the mother of seven children!

In the mornings she helped her laundress who worked in her house, and in the afternoons she met with a senior officer in Lebanese Intelligence. She cooked kosher meals and acquired secret documents with the same skill. She conducted herself with the same naturalness in her home in the Jewish Quarter as she did in the palace of the president of Lebanon. And so she lived in two worlds and was an expert in combining her contradictory lives.

Almost thirty years after being released from prison and having settled with her family in Jerusalem; after having given birth to Yaffa, Bertie, Meir, Arlette, Isaac, Carmela, and Dudu— who all married, and who gave her twenty grandchildren—at the age when most women have been retired for fifteen years, Shula Cohen is still an unusual woman, full of energy. Every day she goes out to work in an antique store across from the King David Hotel, meets tourists from all over the world, and has no problem communicating with them. Shula Cohen, it should be known, speaks French, Spanish, and English, as well as Hebrew, Arabic, and Ladino.

She grew up in Jerusalem, in the Mekor Baruch neighborhood, a seventh-generation Israeli on her mother's side (Algara, née Harosh). She studied at the Evelina de Rothschild Girls' School. In the eighth grade she went to Buenos Aires with her father, Meir Cohen-Arazi, an Egyptian Jew who had established a chain of clothing stores in Argentina with his brother. Her father spent most of the year at his place of work, and around Passover he would come home, loaded down with presents, and stay for two or three months. His wife adamantly refused to live in Argentina. From time to time he would take one of his children with him. When he returned to the country for good, Shula was fifteen.

So Shula did not have a typical childhood. She saw the world, learned languages, and read novels voraciously. When her father's business in Palestine did not go well, and her parents decided to marry her off to a much older man for the *mohar* (the money paid for a bride), everything was carried out in the most conservative fashion. No one asked her opinion or asked whether she agreed to the marriage. Shula Cohen-Arazi became Shula Cohen-Kishik. From the Mekor Baruch neighborhood in Jerusalem she moved to Wadi Abu-Jamal, the Jewish Quarter of Beirut.

And so she found herself at a very young age separated from her friends and family, in alien surroundings, where she was looked upon as a foreigner. "The Palestinian" was what the members of the community called her. She had a loving husband, but her mother-in-law ruled the household with an iron fist. Shula was homesick for Jerusalem. She was also bored. Even when she moved into her own home and the children were born, one after another, she was still dissatisfied. She was unwilling to make do with being just a housewife, so she assembled the Jewish children in the Quarter and taught them Hebrew. But she was still restless.

One day, after the United Nations vote on the partition of Palestine on November 29, 1947, she was visiting her husband's shop. She overheard a conversation between three of his customers, peddlers from southern Lebanon, who bought merchandise in the capital and sold it in the villages. The three were talking about the preparations being made for the war against the Jews, who were about to declare the founding of a sovereign state. One said that in his village ten men had already been drafted and were in training as they were soon to be sent over the border. Another one boasted that he had met Fawzi el-Kaukji himself, when he had come to his village of Tibnin to draft soldiers. Kaukji was a famous Arab warlord who was setting up a large paramilitary force, the Rescue Army, that intended to invade the Galilee and participate in the destruction of the future Jewish state. The third merchant reported that in his village, Bint-Jebel, a shipment of arms had already arrived from Iraq, which would be transferred to Sassa, in Galilee. This route, he said, would be the regular route to transfer arms to the Rescue Army of Kaukji.

When she heard this conversation Shula became very tense. She pleaded with her husband to help her relay this information home. He agreed in the end, despite his doubts. He had a customer from Kafr Adisa, a Lebanese village close to the Palestinian border, who also was a true friend to the Jews. Shula entrusted him with a letter to be delivered to the small Jewish town of Metulla. In the letter she introduced herself as "a Jew who wants to help." She described what she had heard, and noted down her address, as well as her parents' address in Jerusalem. The letter was delivered and soon was passed on to the right people.

That was how the first contact was established. It was later to develop and become more intense. No one drafted Shula; she drafted herself. This beginning was quite typical of what was to come. Later on as well, she was the one who took most of the initiatives. Nor did her husband ever stand in her way, despite his doubts. In fact, he helped her with interim funds for her activities, especially for paying bribes. "The Arabs wanted money immediately, while the Jews wanted to pay after the transaction had been completed," explained Shula in a documentary in the archive of the memorial site of the Intelligence community, "and so my husband was a sort of bank for interim funds." In the long run, Joseph Kishik paid a heavy price for his help. He was also tried along with Shula, accused of abetting her activities, and sentenced to ten years' imprisonment, which were later commuted to two. He won his appeal, but sat in prison for eight months. In the meantime he had gone bankrupt. The forced neglect of his business, the cost of his defense, the large sums he had to pay to bribe those who could speed up the proceedings, lessen the sentence, and improve his prison conditions—all this cost him a fortune. At the same time he lost his respected position in the community. Like his wife, he fell from the greatest heights to the lowest depths.

During her years of intelligence work Shula organized the transfer to Israel of thousands of Jewish refugees from Arab countries—by land, by air, and by sea. To move them by land, through southern Lebanon and northern Israel, all she had to do was develop connections with the smugglers. But to get them out by plane via Europe, as it was necessary to do when there was tension on the border, was much more complicated. Shula had to pay off a senior clerk in the Ministry of the Interior to provide her with false passports, as well as a clerk at the airport, so that his men would not look too closely at the passports. Transferring them by boat also required forging special relations. Shula thought up the ideas and succeeded in carrying them out. She found the right people and secured their cooperation.

Besides the framed certificates on the wall of her apartment, there is also beautiful Gobelin tapestry that she made herself, even though it is hard to imagine when she found the time for it. She gave presents of tapestry to Lebanese President Kamil Shamoun and to Pierre Jemayel, the head of the Christian Militia—the Phalangists. Her connections reached the highest levels, not only among the Christians, but also in the upper echelons of the Moslem leadership of Beirut. When a Moslem gang kidnapped a group of local Jews, Shula was the one who got them released. It was she who found out to whom it was worth talking, it was she who made the contact, and it was she who entered the lion's den to meet with the leader of this hostile group—a woman alone, at night, in the Moslem Quarter.

In the material she sent to Israel she also included secret information about what was going on in Damascus. If the Syrians had suspicions about the matter, they were certainly not unfounded. But they also suspected, which was not true, that Shula Cohen had a hand in organizing the escape of Jews from Syria. In any case, Syrian Intelligence took a great interest in her, and at one point during her arrest its agents also interrogated her.

Many years later, in 1980, a book came out in Israel called *Code Name: The Pearl*, which described her exploits. If she in fact had such a code name, she was not aware of it. Most people called her Um Ibrahim (Mother of Abraham), from the name of her oldest son, Avraham-Albert, who was nicknamed Bertie. There were others who called her Monsieur Shula, not Madame Shula, to emphasize her position of authority, which far exceeded that of a married woman in those surroundings at that time.

What motivated her? First and foremost, she says, it was love of her homeland. She always considered herself an Israeli and even sent three of her children to the country when they were still young, so that they would grow up where she had grown up. But she admits that there was something else that spurred her on—the challenge. She enjoyed the challenge of secret missions, of facing danger, of testing her ability to open up new paths, defuse land mines along the way, and reach her objective.

Time after time she stood the test, in one operation after another, year after year, until she was forced to deal with a different kind of test—the test of suffering. For 2,300 days and nights she went through hell in prison. Her interrogations were accompanied by physical torture, but she did not break. She admitted only to helping refugees leave Lebanon, but to nothing else. Nevertheless, she was found guilty of treason, of aiding an enemy country, and of "dangerous spying." When she began serving her long sentence, she would read the Book of Psalms most of the day to keep up her courage and her humanity among hardened criminals, pickpockets, prostitutes, drug dealers, and murderers.

There were two thousand prisoners, and she was the only Jew among them. They were hostile, especially during the Six-Day War. Even when they left her in peace, she couldn't fall asleep in a large prison cell that held dozens of prisoners. When she was in solitary confinement she wasn't allowed to listen to the radio or read the newspaper. She suffered terribly from the loneliness. And she was in solitary confinement often, because the head prison guard, who was pro-Nasserist by inclination and Syrian by marriage, treated her badly, often inflicting punishments on her.

She was also very concerned about her family. From the moment she was arrested and suspected of spying, the members of the community broke off ties with the whole family, and ordered their children to stay away from hers. They were friendless, and found themselves ostracized from a community to which they had contributed so much. Only Israel did not forget her and never stopped making efforts through various channels to bring about her release. The Israeli efforts succeeded only with the prisoner exchange after the Six-Day War.

When they brought Shula to the border crossing, an Israeli officer received her and took her to Haifa. On the way she asked him to stop at a beauty salon in Nahariya so that she could come into town with a proper hairdo. That was Shula, and she hasn't changed much now that her hair has turned white.

Hannah Zemer, a journalist, is a former editor of the newspaper Davar.

FACING MOUNT SINAI

THE SINAI CAMPAIGN

by Shimon Peres

The Sinai Campaign started on October 29, 1956, at 5:00 p.m., when a special force of paratroops, led by Rafael "Raful" Eitan, jumped over the Mitla Pass, in the vicinity of the Suez Canal. It lasted for less than a week, but had a tremendous impact on Israel's security for over a decade.

More than once the claim has been made that the Sinai Campaign, or Operation Kadesh as it is officially called in the IDF, was a war that could have been prevented, a war that Israel chose to enter. I firmly believe that this was not the case. At the time, October–November of 1956, I was serving as the director general of the Ministry of Defense and had the privilege of assisting the prime minister and defense minister, David Ben-Gurion, in the negotiations and activities that led to the launching of the Campaign. I promoted the cementing of the alliance with France and worked toward equipping the army with excellent French weaponry. I initiated the secret conferences of Saint-Germain and Sèvres and took part in the formulation of the secret agreement between Israel, France, and Great Britain for combined action against Egypt. I was thus closely familiar with the political and security issues, and on the basis of this knowledge I can unequivocally state that under the circumstances and conditions that prevailed in 1956, it would be necessary, even today, to take the same action.

Operation Kadesh was unavoidable for four reasons:

First: The activities of the *fedayeen* (terrorists sent by the Egyptian Intelligence to perpetrate acts of sabotage and murder on Israeli territory) had reached such proportions that Israel had no choice but to react. In retrospect it can be said that in this respect the Campaign achieved its aim—for almost eleven years after the war, until the 1967 Six-Day War, there was peace and quiet in the country.

Second: The Israeli government announced unequivocally that the blocking of the Straits of Tiran at the southern entrance of the Gulf of Eilat would be considered a declaration of war (*casus belli*). The government would have lost its credibility if it had not kept its word. And the proof is that the Straits of Tiran were opened to Israeli ships by the Sinai Campaign. A further attempt by the Egyptians to close them, in 1967, justified, in the eyes of the world, our right to launch the Six-Day War.

Third: The clashes between us and Jordan (from whose territory the Egyptians were sending out *fedayeen,* as well as from the Gaza Strip) were increasing. The climax came when, after an Israeli reprisal raid in Kalkiliya, on the night of October 11–12, 1956, the British ambassador informed Ben-Gurion that his government would come to the assistance of Jordan if Israel took military action against it. It was therefore necessary to prevent a full-blown confrontation between us and the Jordanians. The only way to do this was by attacking Egypt, the source of the conflict.

Fourth: Egypt had purchased enormous amounts of up-to-date arms from the Eastern Bloc—including hundreds of jets, tanks, submarines, artillery, and other advanced military equipment—and did not hide its intentions to use them against Israel. We had to check these terrible intentions before this modern equipment was absorbed into the Egyptian army.

Thus, not only was it not an unavoidable war; there were, in fact, four reasons why we had to go to war. Those four constraints forced Israel to carry out a three-point plan that Moshe Dayan, the chief of staff at that time, had suggested a few months earlier—to capture the Sinai Peninsula, the Straits of Eilat, and the Gaza Strip. We believed that tiny Israel,which had been under constant threat, would find itself in a completely new strategic situation when these objectives were met. The belligerent intentions of the Arab states, under the leadership of Egyptian President Gamal Abd el-Nasser, would be held in check for a long time, and we would be able to consolidate the existence of Israel without being afraid of what each new day might bring.

The Sinai Campaign was carried out, as is well known, in partnership with two European states, France and Great Britain. It was, however, made clear that Israel alone would fight its own war. Under the circumstances this was the only reasonable option open to us. Compared to the huge stocks of weapons and ammunition of the Egyptians, Israel had almost nothing. If not for the preliminary agreements with the French and the British, we would have faced the danger of almost certain intervention by the British on the side of Jordan. We also would have been exposed to attacks on civilian targets in the heart of the country, and we would have found ourselves completely isolated in the United Nations. But worst of all, we would have suffered from a very serious lack of arms and equipment. All these things together were prevented, thanks to the mutual agreement. In war it is also important to consider what has been prevented. What is prevented can also be considered an accomplishment.

The alliance with the French and the British, although criticized by Third World nations, was also a great accomplishment for Israel. Up to that point our country had been isolated in the world and threatened with destruction. And overnight, we became the ally of two great powers, France and England. And the cooperation, especially with France, later brought us unexpected gains, which I will not go into here.

Besides the importance of the alliances and the equipment, the most important element to be taken into consideration was the fighting man. Ben-Gurion could decide to wage this necessary war since Dayan had promised him that under the given circumstances the IDF was well prepared and could carry it out successfully. Dayan could promise what he promised because he knew his fighters well. In the meeting of the expanded General Staff, on October 26, 1956, three days before the Sinai Campaign began, Dayan said, "During the last year the army has attained a high level of fighting spirit. Complaints heard from the unit commanders toward the General Staff were not about the large number of missions they had been asked to carry out, but that they had not been given enough missions. The units considered themselves deprived not because they hadn't been given enough vehicles or more manpower, but because they have not been a part of the battles. This kind of spirit in an army is a great asset, and we should foster it and strengthen it."

Therefore, the IDF that went into the Sinai Campaign was different—in its equipment, its organization, the structure of its forces, and the professional training of its officers—from the IDF that fought the War of Independence. But, on the other hand, there were still certain distinct similarities between the two armies. As in 1948, so too in 1956—daring, resoluteness, as well as knowledge and the ability to improvise, were evident in most of the army's operations. On the first day of the campaign, Dayan was told that the Seventh Brigade of the Armored Corps had gone into action too soon, against explicit orders. He wrote: "With all the displeasure I was feeling . . . I could not deny the sympathy I felt when the tank brigade went into action before it was given permission. It is better to struggle with powerful steeds when the problem is how to restrain them, than to have to prod oxen that refuse to move."

This image of powerful steeds rushing into battle was a fit description of many of the fighters in the Sinai Campaign, on all fronts. It was an especially fitting description for Company A of the Eighty-second Battalion, which stormed the Rawafa Dam near Abu Aweigla, for which the whole battalion was given a citation. It also fit the Ninth Brigade, which moved all along the Gulf of Eilat, through mountainous and rock-strewn areas where there were no roads, until they reached Sharm el-Sheikh. Then there were the air force pilots who flew dangerously low and cut the Egyptian telephone lines with the blades of their planes. And of course, the paratroopers were very brave steeds when they found themselves in a problematic battle at the Mitla Pass, and despite all difficulties, managed to come out as winners.

Later, when the citations for the Sinai Campaign were handed out, many were found worthy of them. And when the recipients of citations were later given medals, four of those given citations received Medals of Valor, the highest medal of all. Others were given the Gallantry Medal and the Distinguished Service Medal. As in other wars, here too one had a discomforting feeling when deciding between "supreme heroism during battle in the face of the enemy at great risk to life" (which is the description of the first medal) and "heroism in carrying out combat duties at great risk to life" (the description of the second), and between those two and "exemplary courage" (the description of the third). In any case, considering the limited scope of this chapter, I shall focus on four men, the first of which is the paratrooper Yehuda Ken-Dror.

The paratroop unit under the command of Ariel Sharon carried out many of the reprisal raids before the Sinai Campaign. During these operations certain norms were established with regard to efficient and determined fighting, without compromise, as well as to tenacity of purpose. They set the standards of behavior and resoluteness for other combat units as well. It was only natural that the paratroopers were a central element in the plans being made for the Sinai War, especially since the intention was to begin the war with a deep penetration into enemy territory and the seizure of an objective near the Suez Canal. In secret talks between Ben-Gurion and French and British leaders in October 1956, it was agreed that Israel would start the war by attacking an objective close to the Suez Canal. This would trigger a joint French-British ultimatum to both Israel and Egypt to retreat from the canal. Egypt would probably refuse, thus furnishing a pretext for the French and British to attack and seize the canal And so it was that Battalion 890, the paratroop battalion of the regular army, carried out the first parachute drop "after two thousand years" near Parker's Memorial, at the eastern entrance to the Mitla Pass, thirty kilometers from the Suez Canal.

The drop took place in the early evening of October 29. At the exact same time two other battalions of the paratroop brigade—the Nahal airborne battalion and the reserves battalion—began to move overland from Ein Hotzev in the Negev toward Parker's Memorial, crossing three hundred kilometers of enemy-held territory. Actually the operation began at its end. The plan was not to move forward toward the Suez Canal but backward, so that they would return home while mopping up the area from the Egyptian border.

After twenty-eight hours the two forces met up—the paratroops at the Mitla Pass, who had already managed to entrench themselves close to where they had landed, and the forces coming from the east, who had to overcome a lack of equipment, transportation problems, and a number of Egyptian positions along the way. The next morning Sharon realized that the paratroopers were located at a spot that was difficult to defend, especially considering reports that an Egyptian tank force was located not far away. He asked for permission to advance westward and capture the Mitla Pass, but his superiors allowed him to send only a reconnaissance patrol that would move in quickly and return the same way. According to reports from air force pilots, there was no reason to worry.

The patrol set off around noon on October 31 under the command of Mordechai "Motta" Gur, who later commanded the paratroop brigade that liberated East Jerusalem, and who was to become the tenth chief of staff of the IDF. This force included two companies of half-tracks (armored troop carriers), a paratroop commando unit, three tanks, and a battery of heavy mortars. When they entered the winding pass between the mountains the paratroopers found a terrible surprise awaiting them—an Egyptian battalion had managed to advance into the pass and had taken positions in natural and man-made niches overlooking the road, setting up a deadly ambush.

The Egyptians opened fire. At first it seemed that there was no need to stop the advance of the patrol, but the fire soon got heavier. The front part of the column managed to get through the pass and reach its western end, but the back of the column was exposed to an Egyptian air attack. Those in the middle were trapped. Moshe Dayan wrote:

> All that the paratroopers could do was to assault the Egyptian niches above them, and in hand-to-hand combat to capture one position after the other. This was the only way to end the battle successfully and at the same time evacuate the dozens of wounded and dead lying at the side of the road among the burning cars. And that was what they did. I don't think there is another unit in the IDF that under such conditions would have been able to overpower the enemy and wipe him out. The paratroopers who had managed to free themselves from the trap, and two other companies, sent as reinforcements, bypassed the Egyptian positions, climbed the mountain ridge, and from there came down again and penetrated the positions dug in the slopes of the Mitla Pass.

Aharon Davidi, one of the outstanding paratroopers (himself awarded the Gallantry Medal for his part in a reprisal raid in Gaza in 1955), commanded the force that was at the eastern end of the Mitla Pass. He received dispatches from the fighters who were stuck in the heart of the pass and heard about the many casualties. He also heard that the ambulance had been hit and that all the field medics had been killed. He tried to use the mortars but discovered that mortar fire was not efficient in these field conditions. He sent the commandos on three assaults on the northern mountain ridge, and discovered several problems that made all action difficult. The sources of the Egyptian fire were still not clearly identified, so it was impossible to attack them. At 4:00 P.M., under the pressure of urgent, grim dispatches from the pass and the large number of wounded commandos, he had to take desperate steps.

"I need a volunteer," he said, "who will drive into the pass and draw the fire in his direction. This is the only way to discover where it's coming from." A few of the senior paratroop officers who had gathered around Davidi said that they were willing to take on the challenge. Davidi figured that he would need them, so he chose another volunteer, his personal driver for the past two years, Yehuda Ken-Dror. Davidi knew him well; he knew that he was a quiet youth, shy and retiring, a nature lover, and brave. "He had always wanted to see action in some dangerous place that would be meaningful," Davidi remembered years later. "He had a desire to fight, to do something brave. This desire came to a large extent from the feeling that everyone else was doing much more than he was because he was just a driver."

Davidi also said:

> During the two years that we were together, we spoke very little. He was a quiet person. He sat behind the wheel, and did what he was supposed to. Maybe that

was why I chose him, and why I loved him so much. Quiet, shy guys like him don't always come into their own. Who knows, he could have been sitting a hundred yards away that day and not heard the request for a volunteer. Someone else might have stayed out of it, and continued to live his life without ever showing his character and extraordinary courage. He was very introverted and amazingly stable. I don't know what made him do it, but it came from very deep inside him. He never did anything to make an impression, so that others would see; he did it so that he would feel that he had done the right thing.

Yehuda looked over the area and saw what the situation was. It wasn't as if he was volunteering for some unknown assignment. He had been following the terrible battle for hours and definitely knew that he didn't have much chance of coming out of this alive. When he volunteered, I looked at his face. It was strangely pale, but there were also strong lines of determination. He was tense before he went, resolved to carry out this act of suicide. He didn't hesitate; he didn't think twice. He only asked quietly how he should drive and what exactly he was supposed to do. Then he got into his jeep, started it up quietly, and set off to carry out his fatal mission, so that he could save the lives of many others.

A cloud of dust rose up behind the jeep as it sped into the Mitla Pass. A shower of bullets began drumming upon the jeep from all sides. "It was the heaviest fire I have ever seen in my life," said an experienced commando soldier who was looking on from above. First a bullet hit the front window and scratched Yehuda's forehead. He continued moving—and was hit by more bullets, in his arm, his foot, his stomach. But he did not lose consciousness, and he still sped ahead quickly, until a burst of machine-gun fire hit the motor and put it out of commission. With his last bit of strength Yehuda jumped out of the jeep and, covered in blood, hid behind one of the wheels. There he lay until it was completely dark, fighting his pain and waiting for the moment he could get into the jeep, take out his weapon, and shoot at whoever came near him.

At night, after the battle was over, he was evacuated and flown to the hospital. For two months he fought to stay alive, suffering terribly, also worrying about his family, who were quite poor. Finally, he lost his last battle. With his death the number of paratroopers killed in the battle for the Mitla Pass reached thirty-eight.

Shlomo Nitzani, a platoon sergeant and the commander of a half-track, was part of the spearhead force of the patrol that entered the Mitla. This is his personal testimony, told simply and faithfully:

Our unit went through the pass first. It was one in the afternoon. Suddenly we were fired upon from both sides. The men inside the half-tracks were completely exposed to the fire. The half-track in front of me got stuck and stopped the convoy. Within a short time the first vehicles in the convoy managed to get beyond the enemy fire and pass through, but three half-tracks and the ambulance got caught in the ambush and were unable to move forward or back. There were about thirty of us trapped there. Many were killed or wounded in the first round of gunfire. Almost everyone in the half-track in front of me was killed. All of the medics in the ambulance were killed. But by some miracle the doctor wasn't hit. I was in the second half-track. When we saw we were stuck, we decided to get out of our vehicle and head for cover. We lay the wounded down close to the rocks. Those that hadn't been wounded continued fighting the Egyptians. During the exchange of fire our men were killed, one after another. Within a short time there were only a few of us who had not been wounded. The Egyptians knew we were trapped. They tried to get close to us, but another soldier, the battalion signal operator, and I stopped them. Actually only the three of us were fighting. The rest were either wounded or taking care of the wounded. We kept on fighting till nightfall, when we were evacuated by our forces.

Shlomo Nitzani did not forget to add in his statement: "If someone deserves a citation, it's the signal operator of the unit, a soldier named Gideon. As soon as we entered the ambush at the beginning of the battle, his transmitter was hit, and he had no way of reporting to his superiors about our difficult situation. Gideon volunteered to run ahead, under enemy fire, and tell the commanders about the vehicles trapped in the pass. Actually he could have stayed outside the pass after that, but he chose to risk his life and come back through the gunfire."

Shlomo Nitzani did not mention what was written about him on the scroll that came with his Medal of Valor: "During the battle his half-track was subjected to heavy fire. His driver was killed immediately. Sergeant Shlomo Nitzani took the wheel of the half-track and under heavy fire moved forward, rescued a number of the wounded who had fallen from the half-track in front of him . . . and all of this under heavy enemy fire. Later he fired various weapons, which belonged to the wounded, against enemy positions and silenced them."

It is worth mentioning as well that on October 6, 1973, the first day of the Yom Kippur War, Shlomo Nitzani, who was by now a lieutenant colonel and the commander of a tank battalion, found himself at the Egyptian front again, facing the city of Ismaliya. The Egyptians had crossed the Suez Canal to Israeli-held Sinai, in several points, and were establishing entrenched lines of defense in the sandy terrain. The force that Nitzani was commanding carried out repeated assaults on the Egyptian bridgehead in that sector, and thus aborted the Egyptian attempt to cross the bridge. The battalion commander Shlomo Nitzani did not forget the heritage of Sergeant Shlomo Nitzani. Despite heavy enemy fire, he made great efforts to evacuate the wounded and did not stop until he himself was wounded seriously. He was awarded the Distinguished Service Medal for his leadership ability, his resoluteness, his courage and coolheadedness, which gave his soldiers confidence and kept up their spirits.

Two other fighters who received the Medal of Valor for their deeds in the Sinai Campaign were the paratrooper Dan Ziv and the tank driver Uzi Bar-Tzur. Dan Ziv, from Kibbutz Ayelet Hashachar, was a platoon commander in the forces called in to the aid of the trapped soldiers in the Mitla Pass. According to the scroll that came with his medal, he volunteered "to go in to evacuate the wounded. He drove a half-track through machine-gun fire, Bazookas, and rifle grenades at a distance of 50 meters. During the day he carried out his duties to perfection and continued to lead his unit in evacuating the wounded."

Uzi Bar-Tzur's scroll stated:

> In Operation Kadesh, Corporal Uzi Bar-Tzur reached the battalion as a volunteer driver. During the battle he asked to be given an assignment. The company commander took him on as his jeep driver. At the most difficult moments of the battle communications broke down in the company. Corporal Uzi Bar-Tzur ran around the area, passing on the orders of the company commander under a shower of bullets and bombs. He continued to do this after his jeep was hit. Endangering his own life, he evacuated the wounded and took them to the evacuation point. After the commander's jeep was hit, he quickly got another vehicle and continued to evacuate the wounded.

The political negotiations that began immediately after the war were not heartening. The two superpowers, the United States and the Soviet Union, used heavy pressure against Israel, to force it to withdraw as soon as possible from Sinai. The Soviets even threatened to intervene militarily in the Middle East, if their demands were not met immediately. Finally, Ben-Gurion gave in.

The decision of the Israeli government to withdraw aroused a great deal of criticism inside the country. Only after some time did the first fruits of the war become evident. They were in fact many, even if they did not meet expectations. But the achievements of the IDF in battle were indisputable. An American military expert, General Marshall, wrote about them: "The Israeli shock troops covered quite a distance over very difficult terrain in a shorter period of time than any other fighting force in history." The well-known British commentator Liddel Hart wrote that "the Sinai Campaign was as far as quality goes one of the best examples of circumvention strategy in the modern age. The strategic plan of the IDF was a work of art."

This may be true. But none of that praise would have ever been earned if it had not been for the exemplary heroism of the Israeli fighters.

Shimon Peres, a member of the Knesset, is a former prime minister of Israel.

PART VI

VICTORY, ATTRITION, AND A BITTER BLOW

1967–1973

On May 15, 1967, while a carefree Israel was celebrating Independence Day, large units of the Egyptian army suddenly moved into the Sinai Peninsula and deployed along the Israeli border. Israel was stunned, even more so during the following days, when a totally unexpected sequence of grim events followed. President Nasser of Egypt expelled the UN observers stationed in the Sinai since 1956, closed the Straits of Tiran to Israeli shipping, signed a military pact with Jordan and Syria, announced the forthcoming war for the liberation of Palestine, and challenged Israel to strike back if it could.

Israel felt as if it were living through a nightmare. A few days earlier nobody would have imagined a new war; today a bellicose coalition threatened to destroy the Jewish State, gaining enthusiastic support in the Arab world. Israel's friends backed off. France's president, De Gaulle, warned Israel not to fire the first shot and decreed an embargo of arms shipments to the Jewish State. The United States, which had officially guaranteed free navigation through the Straits of Tiran, refrained from action. It dawned upon Israel that it should act alone. General Itzhak Rabin was chief of staff of the IDF, but the people turned toward Moshe Dayan, now a Knesset member from a small splinter party created by Ben-Gurion. Under tremendous public pressure, Prime Minister Levi Eshkol appointed Moshe Dayan minister of defense. Eshkol established a Cabinet of National Unity, in which Menachem Begin became a minister, for the first time since the creation of Israel.

On June 5, 1967, Israel attacked. In a lightning air strike it destroyed the Egyptian, Syrian, Jordanian, and a part of the Iraqi air forces on the ground. Israeli armor rolled into the Sinai in a three-pronged attack, soon annihilating the Egyptian army. Four days later, the first Israeli tanks reached the Suez Canal.

Despite Israeli assurances that it had no aggressive intentions against Jordan, King Hussein ordered his army to attack Israel. Jordanian cannon shelled Israel's cities. The IDF reacted by occupying the West Bank and liberating East Jerusalem. On the fifth and sixth days Israel attacked Syria and occupied the Golan Heights.

When the war ended on June 10, the Middle East had changed dramatically. Israel now occupied huge territories taken from Egypt, Jordan, and Syria. It had assets that it could exchange for peace. But an extraordinary summit meeting of Arab heads of state, hastily convened in Khartum, shattered any hope for peace by adopting a resolution of three Nos: No to recognition of Israel, No to negotiations with Israel, No to peace with Israel.

Israel's nightmare, though, had turned into a dream. The nation was stunned by its tremendous victory. The war had proved that the gap had grown between Israel's military force and the combined strength of the Arab countries. Israel's existence was no longer in danger. Israel also gained an important international standing. In the ruthless conflict between the United States and the Soviet Union, Israel's victory was viewed as the triumph of its close ally, the United States. A warm relationship developed between the two countries, and America replaced France as the main weapons supplier to Israel.

The frustration of the Arabs, though, had several far-reaching results: The Suez Canal became the theater of the cruel War of Attrition between Egypt and Israel, which lasted for several years. Egypt and Syria, deeply humiliated, started preparing their revenge. And a little-known terrorist leader launched his men into bloody attacks against Israeli civilians, emerging in the eyes of many as the only Arab who kept fighting the Zionist enemy. His name was Yassir Arafat.

In 1969, Levi Eshkol died of a heart attack. He was succeded by Golda Meir.

But Israel tripped into the dangerous trap that had proved deadly for many a victor in history. Confident, drunk with power and self-admiration, it fell asleep on its laurels. It disregarded the precursory signs of an enemy attack. It let out a breath of relief at the death of President Nasser and didn't think highly of his successor, Anwar el-Sadat, or the Syrian president, Hafez el-Assad. Golda Meir rejected a halfhearted initiative of Moshe Dayan to withdraw the Israeli troops twenty miles from the canal, allowing the Egyptians to reopen it for shipping and rebuild their destroyed cities.

Six years after the Six-Day War, the Arabs launched their revenge. On October 6, 1973—Yom Kippur—Syria and Egypt simultaneously attacked Israel. The small Israeli forces protecting their positions in the Golan and Sinai were swiftly overpowered. The Egyptians conquered the Israeli strongholds along the canal, taking hundreds of prisoners. A Syrian officer, moving in his tank across the Golan Heights, wildly shouted into his radio: "I see the Lake of Tiberias!"

But he never lived to reach it. Paying a terrible toll in blood and tears, Israel pulled itself together and won the war.

It was a different Israel that emerged from the killing fields of the Golan and the Sinai. A nation that had sobered up, after the painful defeats of the first few days of the war. A nation that had learned the hard way it was not invincible, and for the first time had come to doubt the judgment of its leaders.

Shortly after the Yom Kippur War, David Ben-Gurion died, at the age of eighty-seven.

OUR MAN IN DAMASCUS

ELI COHEN

by Shmuel Segev

At sunrise on May 18, 1965, a force of Syrian police and soldiers surrounded the Marja Square in the heart of Damascus and blocked off all vehicle access to the square. In the center a gallows was built, guarded by two rows of police and paratroopers. A battery of projectors lit up the scene. The preparations testified to the fact that, after recently having witnessed the hanging of two "American spies," the residents of Damascus were again being invited to witness a similar event. And on the news broadcast at 1:15 a.m. Radio Damascus called upon the residents of the city to gather in Marja Square and witness the hanging of the man who is even today considered "the greatest Israeli spy in the Arab world"—Eli Cohen.

A few hours earlier, the Syrian president, Amin al-Hafez, had approved the death sentence for the Israeli spy. Eli Cohen was moved from an armored brigade's camp in Kabun to the condemned prisoners' cell in the el-Maza prison. Handcuffed, dressed in the gray suit he had worn the day he was arrested—January 18, 1965—Eli Cohen was taken to the police station in el-Marja. There awaited him the presiding military judge, Colonel Salah Dali, who had sentenced him to death, other judges, the head of the Damascus police force, a military doctor, the director of the president's office, the director of the government press office, and three journalists. Dali read the Israeli spy his death sentence and asked if he had anything to say. In a choked, quiet voice Eli Cohen said that he had nothing to add to what he had said at the trial.

Haham Nissim Andebo-Cohen, the old rabbi of what was left of Damascus Jewry, said the Prayer of Justification with Eli Cohen. After saying the *Kaddish* prayer for the soul of his father, Shaul, Eli Cohen asked Haham Nissim to call his family and tell them that he had carried out his duty fully and remained faithful to his people and his country to the last moment.

Then the judge asked the condemned man what his last wish was. In the presence of Haham Nissim and the foreign journalists, Eli Cohen answered that he would like to write a farewell letter to his wife and children. He wrote two letters, one in Arabic and one in French. The letters were passed on to Israel through the headquarters of the UN armistice observers, and were later checked by a graphologist who verified that they were authentic and that while writing them Cohen had been in control of his faculties. There was no sign of nervousness in his handwriting.

At 3:02 A.M. a prisoner guard arrived and handcuffed Eli Cohen's hands behind his back. He was led to the gallows under heavy police guard. The hangman removed his handcuffs, wrapped him in a white shroud, and ordered him to climb the six stairs to the gallows. There he put a noose around his neck. Eli Cohen cried out: "Shma Israel," but before he finished saying it the trapdoor dropped open under his feet.

Ninety seconds later the military doctor pronounced him dead.

Although more than forty-two years have passed since Eli Cohen was caught and put to death, his deeds still stir the imagination in Arab countries, and his activities as a spy serve as study material in all the intelligence services in the world. His ability to penetrate the centers of power and influence in Syria shook up the self-confidence of that country's rulers and increased their suspicions toward all those around them. During the forty-two years that have passed since he was captured, and even before that, Israeli secret agents have continued to work in Arab countries. Most of them have completed their assignments successfully, and few have been caught and executed. Eli Cohen represents these anonymous heroes.

Eli Cohen was born in 1924 in Alexandria, where he was active in the Zionist movement. The anti-Jewish feelings that spread over Egypt during the War of Independence prevented him from completing his university studies. He worked in an import company and ran a clothing store. After the Sinai Campaign he immigrated to Israel, following his parents and seven brothers and sisters. At first he worked in the Hamashbir department store. He applied to the intelligence service and worked for a short time as a translator. He was fired, and after only a few years, he was drafted again. In 1960 he married Nadya, with whom he had three children.

Eli Cohen was drafted for a second time into the Israeli Intelligence on May 24, 1960. On June 10 he was informed that he had passed all the tests successfully. He was drafted by a senior intelligence officer who went under the name of Salman, a man to whom the State of Israel owes a great deal for his continuous and dedicated service.

As a candidate for a position as an agent in an enemy country Eli fulfilled two basic conditions—a suitable external appearance and a knowledge of Arabic. Now it was necessary to teach him to forget not only his Jewish identity but his Egyptian past as well. The building up of his new identity was done cautiously and painstakingly. Everything was planned and well thought out to the last detail. His training was difficult and strenuous. At first he was taught how to sharpen his memory, then how to use and evade surveillance tactics, and how to take photographs.

After he had finished his basic training it was time to test his ability to adapt to his new identity. Eli was given a French passport under the name of an Egyptian Jew who had immigrated to Africa. He was sent to the King David Hotel, and with this false passport he had to pose as a tourist "who had come to the country to check out his options for immigrating to

Israel and settling there." During the test Eli Cohen turned out to have a captivating personality. He was completely fluent in French and had a very active imagination. When he sat in the bar of the King David or in a café in the center of Jerusalem he could strike up a conversation easily and endear himself to those sitting near his table.

After he passed this test successfully as well, Eli Cohen was given an identity card under the name of Kamal Tabet and eighty Israeli pounds for expenses. He now began an extended period of study of Islam, Arab customs, and history. Eli studied selected verses from the Koran, learned the five prayers that every Moslem must say every day, visited mosques, listened to the sermons of the imams and adopted the customs of the Shafiite Moslems, who were also common in Syria. It was clear that Eli Cohen's ability to assume the role of a Moslem would be one of the most important elements of his success in Syria.

His new story was planned carefully. According to his cover story he was born Kamal Amin Tabet in Beirut on January 6, 1930, to Syrian parents, Amin Tabet and Saadaya Ibrahim. He also had an older sister. In 1933 the family immigrated to Egypt and settled in Alexandria. In 1934 his sister died. In 1946 his uncle Kamal went to Argentina and urged his brother to join him in Buenos Aires. The father at first refused to emigrate to South America, but in 1947 he gave in to his brother's urgings and went with his wife and son to Italy. In 1948 the family moved to Argentina. The two brothers went into partnership with an Argentinian merchant dealing in the sale of textile products. The partnership was unsuccessful, and the business went bankrupt. In 1956 the father died, and six months later the mother died as well. Kamal was left alone and went to live in his uncle's house. At first he helped his uncle in business, but because he knew French he got a job in a local tourist company. A few months later his uncle moved to Brazil and took Kamal with him. The uncle, who was childless, got rich, came back to Beirut and left his property in South America to his nephew. Kamal preferred Argentina to Lebanon, and so didn't go with his uncle to Beirut but returned to Buenos Aires. As a well-to-do businessman, who expected a large inheritance, he could finally realize his lifelong dream to visit his homeland, Syria.

At the end of January 1961 "Kamal Amin Tabet" was ready for his mission. After a few days' vacation he left for Argentina in order to establish his cover story and put down roots in the large Syrian-Lebanese community in Buenos Aires. He told his wife, Nadya, that he was going to Europe for three months on an assignment for the Defense Ministry. He said he was "almost sure" that this would be a one-time trip.

On February 3, 1961, Eli Cohen took off for Zurich. He had $500 with him. According to the instructions of the commander of Unit 131, in the Israeli Intelligence Corps, he was supposed to go by bus from the airport to the passenger terminal in the heart of Zurich. There a tall, gray-haired man would be waiting for him. He would take his Israeli passport and give him an Iraqi laissez-passer in the name of Kamal Amin Tabet. Eli Cohen's contact in Switzerland bought him a plane ticket to Santiago, the capital of Chile, which would make a short stopover in Buenos Aires. The immigration authorities at the Buenos Aires airport usually didn't make a list of the passengers in transit. Eli was told to leave the airport by taxi, rent a small room in a hotel in San Martin Street, and meet his Argentinian contact, "Avraham," the next day in one of the cafés in the town. "Avraham" would give him instructions about his stay there.

Eli and "Avraham" met at the designated time in the La Paz café on Corrientes Boulevard in Buenos Aires. "Avraham" gave him an address where he could rent a furnished room for three months and also the name and telephone number of a Spanish teacher. During the whole period he stayed in Buenos Aires he was forbidden to meet Jews or visit the Israeli embassy or any other Israeli institution. He had to keep his letters to his wife short and to the point and not mention where he was living or give details about things that might disclose what he was doing.

After three months, when he could speak Spanish fluently, Eli Cohen moved to another apartment in the heart of the Syrian-Lebanese quarter of Buenos Aires. In order to give validity to his image as a "wealthy Arab merchant" he bought a large American car, opened a bank account in a local Arab bank, frequented Arab restaurants and clubs, and contributed to Palestinian charity organizations. Within a relatively short time he acquired a reputation as a "great Arab patriot" and a "philanthropist who was always willing to help out the Palestinians."

Abed al-Latif al-Hassan, a sixty-year-old Syrian emigrant, was the owner and editor of an Arabic and Spanish weekly in Buenos Aires called *El-Alam el-Arabi*. One of his two sons owned a grocery store in the Jewish ghetto of Damascus. This connection was eventually used to help Eli strike roots in the local Arab community, but mainly in the target country of Syria.

Toward the end of August Eli Cohen was ready for his next assignment in Damascus. On August 30 he took an El Al plane from Zurich to Israel. After spending the holidays with his family he underwent additional training and briefings about Syria. Among other things he learned how to use a Morse code device and invisible ink.

He was supposed to send his telegrams in French. He was given a three-digit identity number and ordered to send only short telegrams, to prevent the Syrian security services from tracking him down. Rules for reading and identification were established, as well as alternate times for transmission. He was also given instructions to destroy the paper on which he wrote telegrams and not to keep even the smallest piece of paper that might give him away if he was arrested. He would receive the Morse transmitter from his contact in Europe, concealed in a small pack of cigarettes. He was told to buy the radio for receiving transmissions from Israel at a duty-free shop in Munich or Switzerland.

Toward the end of December 1961 Eli took off from Israel for Zurich, and he continued by car to Munich. His contact in Europe took his Israeli passport and gave him an Argentinian one. Before he left, "Kamal Amin Tabet" was told that he would serve as the commercial agent of the Refimax company, with headquarters in Brussels and branches in both Munich and Rotterdam. His contact gave him a packet of stationery with the company logo printed at the top. He was also given an address in Brussels and its telephone numbers, as well as his Morse transmitter, concealed in a small pack of cigarettes with a false bottom, and two bars of Yardley soap.

The bars of soap were actually very powerful explosive devices that he might be ordered by Israel to place in public buildings in Damascus. After he had opened a Swiss bank account in the name of Kamal Amin Tabet, he traveled to Italy. On January 1, 1962, in Genoa, he boarded the *Astoria*, which sailed for Beirut.

On board ship he met Majd Sheikh el-Ard, a fifty-two-year-old Syrian citizen, who owned a farm near Damascus. He took him into Syria in his private car, and introduced him into the Damascus upper-class community. On January 10, 1962, "Kamal" entered the Syrian Republic with the help of Abu Haldun, a friend of Majd Sheikh el-Ard who served as security officer at the Jedida border station, on the Syrian side of the border with Lebanon. Abu Haldun got an electric shaver from Majd Sheikh el-Ard for his trouble, and in anticipation of future contacts "Kamal Amin Tabet" lent him four hundred Syrian pounds. Over the next few months Abu Haldun received five thousand Syrian pounds in cash as well as presents from "Kamal."

According to the instructions given him in Israel, Eli Cohen rented a luxury apartment in a high-rise building that had a view of the Syrian general headquarters. He hid the Morse transmitter in the lampshade of one of the rooms. With the aid of the letters of introduction that he had brought from Argentina, he began to develop connections as a "rich merchant" who dealt with the import, and mainly export, of Syrian products to Europe. The special conditions that existed in Syria at the time helped "Kamal Amin Tabet" establish his credentials in Damascus in record time. After the Syrian-Egyptian union (the United Arab Republic) collapsed in September 1961 the new government was involved in consolidating its power and in persecuting the pro-Nasser circles and other enemies of the new regime. Therefore, the secret services were quite busy, and didn't have much time to investigate other foreign agents.

Within a short time "Kamal Amin Tabet" managed to infiltrate Syrian high society. Among his friends were army officers, wealthy merchants, activists in the ruling Baath Party, and foreign diplomats. His great "wealth" served as a temptation to wealthy unmarried women who wanted to marry him. There were also the amateur matchmakers who wanted to marry him into the privileged families in the Syrian capital.

It didn't take long before "Kamal Amin Tabet" began to pass on material regularly about what was happening in Syria, as well as a lot of information about its leaders and army officers, about the deployment of the Syrian army in the Golan Heights, and about the Arab plans to divert the sources of the Jordan River. During his three years of activity in Damascus, Eli Cohen demonstrated great skill. His ability to get information soon amazed his superiors. "Eli Cohen was like a telephone. I asked him for certain information in the morning, and by the afternoon I would have an answer," one of his commanders later said.

As a result of the internal conflicts in the Syrian leadership the authorities began to more seriously investigate opponents in the internal political arena and gradually became more vigilant. At the beginning of January 1965, while Eli Cohen was transmitting a message to Israel, Syrian security agents burst into his apartment and caught him in the act. At first "Kamal Amin Tabet" tried to pretend he didn't understand why he had been arrested. After he was tortured during interrogation he admitted that he was an Israeli secret agent and that his name was Eli Cohen.

For a few months the Israeli government made enormous efforts to get him freed or to put off his trial in the hope that they would be able to exchange him for Syrian spies. Israel offered money, information on the opponents of the government in Damascus, medicine, and various kinds of machinery and equipment. It also used all its connections with heads of states, kings, and even with the Pope—but to no avail.

Eli Cohen was sentenced to death in a show trial in which he was not allowed to defend himself; nor was his French lawyer allowed to observe the proceedings. On May 18, 1965, he was hanged.

Israel regards him as a national hero.

Shmuel Segev, a member of the editorial board of the newspaper Maariv, *has written a number of nonfiction books on the Middle East, including a biography of Eli Cohen.*

THE LAST VOYAGE

CHAIM ZARFATI

by David Levy

"My heart is in the East, and I am in the distant West," wrote the poet Yehuda Halevi in the twelfth century while living in Toledo, Spain. If Toledo was "the distant West," then how much more so were Casablanca and the Straits of Gibraltar, which lay even farther west. In this "distant West," at the beginning of 1961, the bitter fates of forty-four Jews were sealed. Their hearts were truly in the East, and they followed their hearts. These Jews—men, women, and children—who could not immigrate to Israel openly, became part of an illegal immigration program. They died in the *Egoz* boat disaster, sharing the fate of other Jews who had lived in the Diaspora for hundreds of years and longed for Zion. All of them were born in Morocco. Forty-three of them were still the subjects of King Mohammad V. One of them, Chaim Zarfati, had been an Israeli citizen for the last ten years.

Chaim Zarfati was born in the city of Fez in 1933. He immigrated to Israel in 1951, when he turned eighteen, following in the footsteps of his eldest brother. He joined the army, took a course to become a signal officer, and was posted to the air force. Later, during the Sinai Campaign, he served as a liaison officer with the French army units that landed near Port Said. Zarfati later joined the Mossad. He had heard rumors that this organization also dealt with rescuing Jews, and Zarfati very much wanted to be a part of saving the Jews of his homeland. This desire, as well as his professional skills, got him a position as a Mossad radio operator in the French port city of Marseilles. Afterward, he was sent into the lion's den and stationed in Morocco and Gibraltar, also operating on boats that ran the waters between them.

He kept his activities strictly secret. During the whole period when he worked in Morocco he didn't once visit his family, most of which was still living in Fez. The one and only time his longing overcame him, he went by his family home and took a picture from a distance of his mother, Pnina, sitting at the entrance to her house. He dared not do more than that.

In September 1960, the Mossad purchased a boat to transfer Jews secretly across the straits that separated Africa and Europe. The tiny boat, *Pisces*, was named *Egoz* in the Mossad documents. The name *Egoz* (Nut) hinted at the fact that the tiny boat was nothing but a nutshell, a toy of the mighty waves of the Mediterranean. It was clear that only Chaim Zarfati, of all the Mossad agents in the area, was suited to be the radio operator of this boat at sea.

Zarfati sailed on the *Egoz* twelve times, and twelve times he returned home safely. Each time he was extremely anxious. "I am afraid," he said to one of his senior colleagues, "that if a disaster occurs, I won't be able to report on our location in time, and then you won't be able to send help." He was less worried about his own welfare. Everyone knew he was an excellent swimmer, and that if anything should go wrong he would be able to manage.

Twelve times his fears and anxieties were dispelled, and there was no reason to think that anything would go wrong in the future. At the end of 1960 Chaim Zarfati was supposed to return home, to Israel. His girlfriend, who also worked for Intelligence, was looking forward to their wedding. All the arrangements had been made. In Zarfati's coat pocket, in a safe house in Gibraltar, was an El Al plane ticket from France to Israel. Along with it, in a brown envelope, was a letter to his eldest brother, Rachamim. The letter said the following: "My brother, I promise you that this is really my last trip. This time I am coming home. . . ."

But things were fated to be otherwise. The *Egoz* was supposed to make one more voyage with Moroccan immigrants, which was to be its thirteenth and last voyage. Chaim Zarfati's replacement was supposed to be the radio operator on this voyage, but he asked Chaim for a small favor. "You are going to be married," he said. "I got married a few days ago, and I'm on my honeymoon. Are you willing to go instead of me?" Chaim agreed without hesitation.

Of course he did not work alone; he was a central link in a chain that had begun its activities in Morocco during World War II. This group had expanded its efforts greatly in the mid 1950s. The first emissary of Aliya Bet, Ephraim Ben-Chaim, reached Morocco in 1943. A few other emissaries followed him. But the illegal immigration from this country began only in 1947. A few hundred Jews, who were inspired by the idea, were ready to risk their lives and suffer hardships to carry it out. They crossed the Algerian border on foot and reached three boats, moored in Algerian and French waters. Algeria was then French sovereign territory. The boats sailed one after the other. The first two, the *Yehuda Levi* and the *Shivat Zion* (Return to Zion) sailed from the coast of Algeria. They were intercepted by the British navy and driven away from the Palestinian coast to Cyprus. The third boat, *Haportzim* (Those Who Will Break Through), which sailed from France, managed to disembark its passengers in Tel Aviv. In the first eight years after the founding of the State, ninety-two thousand Jews immigrated from Morocco. Most of them came after Morocco had won its independence, when the Jews were afraid of what might happen in the future.

Their absorption problems, which won't be dealt with here, did not dampen their enthusiasm, especially since the situation in Africa was becoming much worse. The influence of the Egyptian tyrant Gamal Abd el-Nasser was increasing greatly, and in the shadow of the Suez Crisis of 1956, all possible escape routes were being blocked. On September 26 of that year King Mohammad V signed a revised formulation of clause 424 of the country's constitution. From then on, "Moroccan Jews were forbidden to settle in Palestine and those who had already left Morocco were forbidden to return." The Mossad was already prepared in advance to replace the Mossad le-Aliya Bet, the organization in charge of illegal immigration before the State was founded.

The head of the Mossad, Iser Harel, realized in 1954 that Nasser—who had just begun to work his way toward becoming the leader of the Arab world—was Israel's most dangerous enemy. He understood that Nasser wanted to get the French out of the Maghreb (North African) countries as soon as possible. The conclusion was clear—the Jewish community in these countries was in great danger. Therefore, he explained to his superiors, Prime Ministers Moshe Sharett and David Ben-Gurion, that it was necessary to form a self-defense organization in those communities. (Similar organizations had been established in other Arab countries, such as Iraq.) Shlomo Havilio, who was sent by Iser Harel to the Maghreb countries, confirmed the first conclusion on his return—the Jews of the Maghreb, he said, especially the Jews of Morocco, were very worried about what was going to happen to them when the French left. He found proud young Jews in Morocco and in the neighboring countries who were resolutely committed to Israel, and ready to take part in clandestine activities. They could be the core of self-defense groups. But he also warned that it would not be possible to set up efficient self-defense groups everywhere, certainly not in remote areas. Therefore, besides preparing a self-defense program it was also necessary to begin urgent preparations for bringing these Jews to Israel, even if it meant doing so illegally.

At the beginning of 1955 Harel authorized Havilio to set up an Israeli underground network in North Africa. The name of this network was Misgeret (Framework). Its core was made up of a few scores of Israeli agents, who went on to draft hundreds of local activists. All of these were divided up into five departments: Defense (Gonen), which was in charge of security; Intelligence; Home Front, which dealt with the relationship between the Moroccan authorities and the Jewish institutions; there was also the Choir, and the Dance Troupe, which dealt with immigration. The Dance Troupe was supposed to find candidates for immigration—both individuals and families—and make the initial contact with them. The Choir was in charge of developing the connection and making the arrangements for them to leave Morocco.

They knew that time was of the essence. The decrees were getting worse from day to day, and the exit routes were being closed off, one after another. For example, at one time it had been possible to get people out with relative ease through Tangiers, which had been an international zone since 1923. But in October 1956 it lost this special status, and the Moroccan police took control of the city. Until June 1957 it was still possible, nevertheless, to use various methods to smuggle people out through the port, but soon this exit was also closed. Despite the difficulties, the cruel treatment, and the arrests, the Misgeret never stopped functioning or trying to get people out.

In 1960 a new way was found. Israeli navy crews went secretly to check out the Moroccan coast and see if it might be possible for the Mossad to act independently, without having to

rely on the goodwill or whims of local smugglers. As a result of their investigations it was decided to send out ships between the port of el-Husseima and Gibraltar, over three hundred
kilometers of water, which was not always calm. Later the Mossad agents rented the boat *Pisces*,
which was known for its great speed, and had been used in the Second World War to rescue
British pilots who had parachuted into the sea. It became the *Egoz*, and was fitted to transport
passengers, under the watchful eyes of navy representatives.

In September 1960—under a Honduran flag, and with a Spanish captain and two Spanish crew members—the *Egoz* set sail, with the faithful and dedicated Chaim Zarfati in the communications cabin.

At the beginning of December 1960 a man posing as a British businessman came to
Casablanca, accompanied by his beautiful secretary, who also was his mistress. In actual fact
they were none other than Alex Gatmon, who had been appointed head of the Misgeret, and
his wife, Carmit. Gatmon, a Holocaust survivor, a partisan, and an air force reserve colonel,
had seen many an adventure and had a lot of experience. He began to carefully plan the last
voyages of the *Egoz*. Before every sailing of the *Egoz*, Gatmon's wife took it upon herself to
phone the meteorological service to find out whether conditions were suitable for her to sail
her yacht out of the el-Husseima port.

The twelfth voyage of the *Egoz* took place on January 7. The passengers were sixty children
between the ages of ten and twelve, from Casablanca. Some of them knew that their parents
would follow them on the *Egoz*'s thirteenth voyage two or three days later. The thirteenth voyage was to be made up mainly of immigrants "with experience"—those who had already set
out on the long trip between Casablanca and el-Husseima three or four times and been sent
back, either because of poor weather conditions or because of security problems in the area.
The Misgeret agents checked and rechecked all the details, repeating the instructions to the
passengers: "First, you've got to reach the city of Vezan. If anybody asks you, on the way, where
you are going, tell them that the purpose of your journey is to visit the grave of Rabbi Amram
Ben-Divan, in Vezan." After Vezan, at the second stage of their journey, the emigrants' cover
story would be that they were going to a big wedding in el-Husseima.

After a long and exhausting journey of eight hundred kilometers (five hundred miles), the
convoy finally reached its destination, a bridge near el-Husseima. Here they all got out of the
cars and made their way down to the rocky shore on foot. "The mothers walked hugging their
children, who were wrapped in blankets," said Meir Knafu, the commander of the operation.
"The old people walked in a separate group. One eighty-year-old woman was carried the whole
way on the shoulders of the men in the group."

The sea looked calm, but Chaim Zarfati whispered his fears to his friends. "I don't trust
the weather forecast," he told them. "Perhaps we should put off the voyage." The suggestion
was rejected. He accepted the decision and went to his cabin. The convoy escorts turned back
to Casablanca.

But when they reached Casablanca, Gatmon was waiting for them. His face showed his distress. "The boat sank. There are no survivors," he said, telling them briefly what he himself had learned a short time earlier.

A heavy storm had erupted suddenly at sea and swallowed up the light boat. It later was discovered that Chaim Zarfati had radioed calls for help over a long period of time. His friends believe that Chaim could have saved himself if he had left his transmitter and swum away from the sinking boat. But Zarfati did not leave his post even when water started coming into the hull of the ship. Various boats—including that of the radio operator in Gibraltar—received Zarfati's calls for help, but for various reasons were late in starting a search. After several hours the captain and his two assistants were pulled out of the water, and later twenty-two bodies were found floating on the surface. All the other passengers of the *Egoz* were lost at the bottom of the sea.

The bodies were buried hastily in the Jewish cemetery in el-Husseima and remained there until they were brought to Israel in December 1992. The Moroccan police began tracking down the Misgeret activists, and the relatives of those who had drowned. Some of them were subjected to awful torture. Among them was "Marlene," Rachel Giladi, who suffered terribly but did not reveal any secrets. This extraordinary woman aroused a lot of admiration in Morocco and in Israel. An old-time Palmach leader, Eliezer Shoshani, called her "the Hannah Senesh of the Moroccan immigrants." Shoshani had been appointed to investigate the incident.

On February 9, 1961, thirty days after the sinking of the *Egoz*, Gatmon put Operation Bazak into action. The members of the underground spread leaflets all over Morocco that said: "A two-thousand-year-old hope demands that we return to Zion and Jerusalem, by whatever means possible, in any way. . . . Do not despair. Be strong and courageous! The struggle for our rights and our freedom continues!"

And so it was. More than eighty thousand Jews emigrated from Morocco to Israel after the sinking of the *Egoz*.

Unfortunately, many questions surrounding the disaster still remain unanswered. But not one of them reflects on the heroism of Chaim Zarfati and his dedication to his mission.

David Levy, a member of the Knesset, is a former foreign minister of Israel.

THE EGYPTIAN ARMY BEGAN TO MOVE

THE SIX-DAY WAR

by Chaim Herzog

The Independence Day Parade of 5727 (1967) took place in Jerusalem according to the conditions of the cease-fire agreement between Israel and Jordan—without tanks, or even half-tracks, and without a display of aircraft (even light reconnaissance aircraft). The evening before, in a nighttime rally at the Hebrew University stadium, a passage was read from a Natan Alterman poem: "Arabia, Arabia, before the die is cast,/Before the sunlight turns to darkness for both of us/Draw back your hand from lifting/The latch of the gates of war!/And see the difference/Between a calamity that cannot be described or named/And the blessing of peace and an age of prosperity/The likes of which the sons of Shem have never known."

A short while later, in the middle of the Independence Day party in a private home in Jerusalem, Chief of Staff General Itzhak Rabin was called to the telephone. On the other end of the line was General Aharon Yariv, the head of IDF Intelligence. Yariv reported that the Egyptian army had unexpectedly begun to move into the Sinai Peninsula. The Sinai was a part of Egypt, and as a general rule, only small Egyptian units were stationed in the desert peninsula. The crossing of the Suez Canal by large, elite army units, which now were moving toward the Israeli border, was a sign of aggressive intentions.

This began the countdown toward the war that broke out on June 5; at the end of that war—only six days later—the Middle East had changed. On June 10 the IDF was deployed over the whole area from Mount Hermon in the Golan to Sharm el-Sheikh, at the tip of the Sinai peninsula; and from the Jordan River in the east down to the Suez Canal.

This war was fought, as opposed to all previous scenarios, on three fronts: first against Egypt and Jordan together, and later against Syria. During the war the air forces of the neighboring states were destroyed; tank defense lines and fortified, entrenched battle positions were broken through; battles were fought in built-up areas, and firm Israeli control was established over the Golan Heights. To carry this out the most modern weaponry and massive firepower were brought to bear. And as in all of Israel's wars, once again, the human factor proved to be of prime importance. Eight hundred and three fighters did not return home from the battlefield. Many of them fell while courageously exposing themselves to mortal danger; others survived against all odds. Twelve of the soldiers who took part in the Six-Day War were found worthy of the Medal of Valor—twelve again, as in the War of Independence, representing the twelve ancient tribes of Israel.

Four of them fought on the Sinai battlefields, from Rafiach to the Suez Canal, and one in the Gaza Strip; two of the heroes participated in the Battle of Jerusalem; one distinguished himself in northern Samaria, and four others on or near the Golan Heights. Scores of others were awarded the Distinguished Service Medal and the Gallantry Medal. The stories of those who won the Medal of Valor will be presented here, some in more detail, some in less, partly due to the limits of space and partly due to the dramatic nature of some of the stories. But as one who has seen these fighters at their best, I would like to make it clear that I do not intend in any way to rank them in terms of their courage.

In the spring of 1967, Benny Inbar, twenty-three, was making plans to study at Hebrew University the following fall. He had filled out the proper forms and mailed them in. When his acceptance letter arrived, during the second half of May, he was already serving as staff sergeant in his reserve unit, the Patton Battalion, somewhere near the Egyptian border. At dawn on June 5, his battalion got the long-awaited order to advance into the Sinai and destroy any Egyptian force in its way. Benny's battalion darted westward. The war had started.

All of a sudden, Benny saw from the turret that his tank, and that of his company commander, were facing eight Egyptian tanks. He hit five of them, and only after the other three had fled did he see that they were Soviet-made Stalin tanks. He then also realized that he had been wounded in the back of the neck, but decided that this was not reason enough to stop fighting. Only when he came close to the fortified compound of Sheikh Zuweid and saw that there was a short lull in the action, did he get out of his tank and ask to have his wound dressed.

The medical team that treated him noticed that he was very dizzy and suggested that he be evacuated to the rear because of both his dizziness and his wound. Benny Inbar refused vehemently. He continued moving toward the strong Jiradi fortifications, firing continuously. He managed to destroy another three Egyptian tanks and a few antitank guns. Suddenly his tank was hit by two shells and burst into flames. Benny didn't lose his head. First he moved his tank to the side of the road so it wouldn't block the way for those behind him. Then he told his gunner to take all the essential equipment out of the tank, including the firing pin of the gun and the radio transmitter. If the fire goes out, he said to himself, the Egyptians shouldn't be able to use this equipment. Only after all this did the two begin to crawl along the open road, looking for cover. While they were crawling, they were hit by enemy fire from the trenches at the side of the road, and both were killed.

During those very moments Ori Vaisler was attacking the Egyptian forces in Rafiach. Ori, born in Kibbutz Givat Brenner, was a platoon commander in a brigade commando company that assailed the southern part of the Rafiach defenses on the first day of the war. His half-track went over a mine and was damaged. Some of the soldiers in it were wounded, including Ori himself, who was blown out of the half-track. The enemy fire hit another half-track that was moving close to him. Ori didn't lose control. He hurried back to the damaged vehicle, found a medium-sized machine gun, and opened fire, from the side of the wrecked half-track, onto the post he had been instructed to destroy. At the same time he established contact with the rest of the forces, and also began to organize his soldiers. He got those who hadn't been hurt to evacuate the wounded from the two damaged half-tracks. Ori Vaisler's incessant machine-gun fire significantly helped the forces that reorganized, attacked the enemy position, and captured it. When the battle was over, Ori refused to be sent back for medical care and continued fighting with a commando company during the following days.

He didn't live to receive his Medal of Valor, though. Exactly a month after the battle of Rafiach, Ori Vaisler led his platoon in a battle against Egyptian forces on the eastern bank of the Suez Canal, where he was shot and killed.

On June 5, while Ori Vaisler was firing at the Rafiach entrenchments, Second Lieutenant Moshe Tal observed the Ali Muntar Hill overlooking Gaza. Moshe was a platoon commander in Paratroop Battalion 202, which was ordered to capture the strategic hill. Perhaps he didn't know that this hill had already seen many battles, from the days of Alexander the Great, through the military expeditions of Napoleon, to the campaign that cost the British several casualties in the First World War. Nevertheless, Moshe Tal had no doubt about the gravity of the situation he was faced with. The company commander and his deputy had been killed. An ambush of the four Egyptian Stalin tanks was mercilessly destroying the armored vehicles carrying his company. The paratroopers began retreating through a nearby grove to organize their defense, but many of them soon lay wounded or dead on the road.

The young platoon commander ran back from the grove to the road and started evacuating the wounded, moving them to cover. At the same time he kept up the morale of his company. He ran around from group to group, giving practical instructions and cheering his men with words of encouragement. More than once he pointed out to them that he was still standing, so there was nothing to worry about. In the end, in a run to the road, he was hit and seriously wounded. He asked that the others be evacuated before him. When he was brought to cover, he died from his wounds.

That same day, on that same front, the war began for Yossi Lafer, twenty, from Moshav Nir Israel. On June 5, he advanced with his unit to Kafr Shan, close to Sheikh Zuweid in the Rafiach opening. His tank was badly hit; he and his crew had to jump out. They grabbed their personal weapons and hand grenades and began mopping up the enemy positions in the area, under Yossi's command. By the following day he already had a new tank, but luck was not with him this time either. This tank hit a land mine on the main street of the town of Khan Yunis, in the Gaza Strip. Yossi lost consciousness for a short time from the shock. When he recovered, he realized that he was alone in the tank, and that there were no Israeli soldiers nearby. He was completely surrounded by large enemy forces.

Yossi looked around the area and realized that there was no escape route. When he inspected the tank, he found that most of its systems were working—enough to allow him to start his own "private war." For many hours, which seemed like eternity, using the tank's cannon and machine gun, Yossi fired at anyone trying to come near him. That included Egyptian vehicles and Egyptian positions that fired at him or at other Israeli soldiers in the area. From time to time he made radio contact, and in the end managed to guide another tank toward him. By the time he was evacuated he had already been wounded in his chest and hand by Egyptian fire. His "private war" had lasted more than eight hours, during which he had held at bay, and also destroyed, large Egyptian forces. Yossi's war became legendary in the army and won him the Medal of Valor.

Captain Daniel Vardon, born in Givat Brenner and a member of Kibbutz Beit Govrin, got his first citation as a corporal in the Golani Brigade in the early sixties. He and two of his friends had repelled a Syrian force that had tried to capture a hill overlooking Kibbutz Kfar Szold. He received his second citation more than a year later, when, as a second lieutenant, he was in charge of a commando platoon of the Golani Brigade. This was after he had been sent to mop up the northern trench of the Mukein stronghold during Operation Swallow. Three of his soldiers were dead; the sergeant major of the company escorting them was missing, and Daniel Vardon wouldn't give up looking for him. He even went back to the enemy position, but in vain. During the battle itself he had continued fighting for almost an hour and a half—breaking through in the advance force, exchanging his Uzi, when it ran out of ammunition, for a Soviet assault rifle, jumping out of the trench when a grenade exploded and back in again to avoid a grenade exploding outside.

The third time he demonstrated his courage was on June 7, 1967, at the end of the third day of the Six-Day War. Daniel fought in the Sinai. He was deputy commander of the brigade commando unit that first fought at Um Katef and then headed north toward the northern Sinai town of El Arish. There the brigade commander heard about a group of wounded soldiers that Egyptian soldiers had surrounded in a narrow alley, inside the city. Daniel Vardon was ordered to enter that alley in a jeep escorted by half-tracks and evacuate the wounded soldiers who had been trapped there from the start, as well as all those who had been wounded trying to rescue them. When they realized that the alley was too narrow to drive into, Daniel decided to enter on foot, along with the medic and the signal operator. The heavy fire that they met forced them to retreat. They made a second attempt, with grenade cover, in which the other two were wounded. But Daniel Vardon didn't give up. He entered the deadly alley again for the third time, and was mortally wounded by a burst of fire. The Medal of Valor was given to him for his bravery, and for his volunteering, "knowing full well that by this act he was endangering his life."

While the Israeli forces were storming through the Egyptian defenses in the Sinai, on their way to the Suez Canal, dramatic events were happening in Jerusalem as well. At two thirty, on Tuesday, June 6, 1967, Battalion 66 of Paratroop Reserve Brigade 55 began its assault on the formidable Ammunition Hill. This hill dominated the road leading to Mount Scopus, in northern Jerusalem. It was situated in the Jordanian-controlled part of the city. Since 1949, the Jordanians had continually improved the Hill's fortifications, and had turned it into a fearful, impregnable stronghold, surrounded by deep communication trenches with cement walls. A few internal trenches stretched across the width of the hill, and forty fortified, well-camouflaged positions were located on the surface, each one placed so that it could cover the other.

When the battle began most of the Jordanian soldiers stationed in the Police School nearby stormed into the trenches and positions on Ammunition Hill. This fact soon became clear to Company A of Battalion 66, which attacked Ammunition Hill and suffered many casualties. Company B moved past Company A, and the paratroopers began to advance through the eastern and central trenches. They also suffered heavy casualties. Company A was called back to help mop up the trenches. Its depleted forces were divided in half. One part fought in the central trench, and the other in the western trench, the most fortified trench on Ammunition Hill. The advance in this trench was slow because of heavy enemy fire coming from positions higher up and from bunkers on the sides.

"There were nine of us left," the commander of the force later said. "We stopped in the trench briefly to reorganize. Suddenly a grenade was thrown at us from the outside. It exploded beside us, but by some miracle none of us was hurt. I began to suspect that the Jordanians running around outside might begin bombarding our part of the trench with grenades. This would wipe out all of us. We had to prevent this no matter what. In order to do so one of us had to jump out of the trench and see what was going on out there. I sent Eitan. I knew I was sending him on a suicide mission, but I hoped he would come back alive. I didn't have time to ask for volunteers."

Eitan was Eitan Nava, who was twenty-three years and a few days old, born in Moshav Moledet. During his service in Kibbutz Almagor, it was always Eitan who was called in to dig out a stuck car or solve a serious problem in the field. Now he heard the order and did not hesitate for a moment. Armed with his automatic rifle, he jumped up to the edge of the trench and began to run forward along it, drawing enemy fire and responding with heavy fire of his own that kept any potential grenade throwers at bay. "I thought," said the commander who had sent him, "that a heavy machine gun was firing at my right. The amount of gunfire that Eitan produced was wild. What was also amazing was the speed with which he changed his magazines." He also shot at the entrances of the bunkers in the internal trench, and did not stop until he was hit in the head by a bullet and fell dead into the trench. His friends later counted more than thirty Jordanian soldiers in the trench, who had been killed by Eitan. "Only then did we realize," said his commander, "what a slaughter he had saved us from." He was posthumously awarded the Medal of Valor. His friends conquered Ammunition Hill, and took Jerusalem.

Eitan's comrades from the Fifty-fifth Paratroop Brigade fought the bloodiest battles for the liberation of Jerusalem. Mordechai "Mordi" Freedman, a twenty-nine-year-old mechanical engineer, was the deputy commander of Company A in the Twenty-eighth Battalion of the Paratroop Brigade. During the morning hours of June 6 he was at the head of the company driving up Nablus Road, into East Jerusalem. He was in charge of clearing the left side of the street. After he took control of the crossroads of Nablus Road and Salach a-Din Street, he continued moving forward at the head of the company, clearing a few more positions. At the same time, his old friend Leizerke, Sergeant Eliezer Regev from Moshav Lakhish, was advancing on the right side of the street. Leizerke suddenly noticed a narrow alleyway that led to the southwest. He tried to enter it, but was hit with flat-trajectory fire, and died almost instantaneously. Mordi ran across the street, and while he was pulling Leizerke's body out, heard a feeble cry: "Medic . . ."

At the entrance to the alley—which was later called the Alley of Death—another paratrooper lay wounded. Mordi put his friend's body in a safe place, came back, and stormed into the alley to save the wounded soldier. He then returned to the alley for the third time, a grenade clasped in his hand, to wipe out the position from which the two had been shot. While raising his hand to throw the grenade, he was shot in the head and killed.

While the battle for Jerusalem was being fought, other units of the Israeli army overran the West Bank, fighting the Jordanians all the way down to the Jordan River. In the Dotan Valley, in the heart of northern Samaria, Jacob's sons had sold their brother Joseph, the dreamer, to a caravan of Ishmaelites. In this same valley, on June 6, 1967, fierce battles raged between Israeli and Jordanian tanks. Gad Refen, twenty-two years old, commanded a platoon of Sherman tanks in the armored brigade that invaded the sun-scorched valley. He participated in the capture of the village of El-Amun, and later took part in the breakthrough toward the city of Jenin. In the battle that took place in the hills south of Jenin, the company commander was hurt, and Gad Refen took his place. He led the forces in a battle against the Jordanian Patton tanks, without even taking their technological superiority into consideration. His tank was hit, then three others. Gad organized the orderly retreat of the crews, all of which had been wounded, to a pump house where he found cover for them. There he distributed the men in defense positions and kept up their spirits until a rescue team arrived. He did all this despite his wounds. Besides badly spraining his hand, he had suffered painful burns earlier, while still standing exposed in the turret of his tank, leading the forces into battle.

As the sun set on June 8, 1967, most of the guns fell silent in the Sinai, the West Bank, and Jerusalem. The fighting there was over. The next morning, June 9, Israel attacked its third enemy, who dominated the north of Israel from the formidable plateau called the Golan Heights. It was a natural fortress, strewn with entrenchments, bunkers, artillery and machine-gun positions, tank formations, double and triple barbed-wire fences, and many thousands of land mines. The Israelis had to fight their way up the winding roads leading to the Heights, and take the deadly strongholds, one after another.

Tel Faher was a heavily fortified Syrian compound near the northern part of the Golan Heights, between Tel Azaziyat on the west and the pipeline road to the east, below Kafr Zaura. Those in the know considered it the strongest and best fortified enemy post in the whole northern front. Whoever held it controlled a large group of settlements in the Hula Valley, north of the Lake of Tiberias. On June 9, 1967, the Barak Battalion of the Golani Brigade, under the command of Lieutenant Colonel Moshe "Mussa" Klein, was ordered to capture this post. Klein, who had already received a citation for Operation Kadesh (he later was given the Gallantry Medal), deployed his forces in half-tracks and set out for Tel Faher behind some tanks. The convoy encountered heavy antitank fire, and several vehicles were hit. Moshe Drimer, twenty, one of the best sappers in the battalion, was now a deck gunner in a half-track. He had insisted on taking this position before they set out for the battle. The armored vehicles advanced under intense Syrian fire. Drimer opened heavy fire on the Syrian positions and covered the soldiers escaping the half-track in front of him, which had been hit. While doing so he was wounded badly in the legs and face. Yet he did not stop covering his comrades even though his eyes were awash with blood. Later, a shell hit the gas tank of the half-track, and the vehicle caught on fire. Moshe Drimer died with his finger still hooked around the trigger of his gun. He was given the Medal of Valor posthumously.

The battalion commander ordered all those who were still unwounded to launch an assault on foot on Tel Faher. A few dozen soldiers moved under constant fire toward the post's fences, which they tried to break through with field cutters. After it became clear that they couldn't continue under such heavy fire, and that the bangalore pipe bomb that had been placed in the last fence had not exploded, David Shirazi, on his own initiative, ran to the head of the line and lay down across the fence. One after the other the soldiers crossed over on his back, jumped into the trenches, and began to clear them from west to east. When the last soldier had crossed, Shirazi stood up, ran after his fellow soldiers, and began shooting his machine gun. "He fired continuously in the direction of the northern target," said his commander. "Even under fire he wasn't afraid to raise his head, identify various targets, and silence them with the help of his heavy machine gun. He managed to disable almost all of them." While trying to improve his position, he was shot by a Syrian sniper and killed on the spot. His courage and perseverance won him the second Medal of Valor awarded for the battle on Tel Faher.

The Eighth Brigade joined the battle toward the end, when victory on the Egyptian and Jordanian fronts had been assured. "The spirit of the armored corps," said brigade commander Colonel Albert Mandler to his men before the war, "is its strong fighting instinct, as well as its daring, its high level of performance, and its perseverance. The difference between the infantry and the armored corps is that the foot soldier has to use all his physical strength, while the armored soldier has to use all his own strength as well as the strength of his vehicle." The brigade was now being asked to translate these words into action, using Super-Sherman tanks, left over from the Second World War. From the beginning, the newer IDF tanks had been meant for use on the southern front.

On Friday, June 10, at 11:30 A.M., the Super-Shermans began to cross the Israeli-Syrian border and climb the Golan Heights. The commander of the attacking battalion was a former paratrooper, Lieutenant Colonel Arye Biro. In front of this battalion was a company under the command of first Lieutenant Natanel "Nati" Horowitz. The assignment of this battalion was to capture the Zaura fortified compound and to get onto the highway leading north in the direction of Masada. The first stages were carried out without any special problems. Nati's company easily passed by the posts of Gur el-Askar and Naamush.

"No problems. It's just like an exercise," Nati reported to the battalion commander. He asked for permission to continue his advance and capture the village of Naamush. Permission was granted. Immediately after that Nati was supposed to turn northward and get onto the pipeline road (along the pipeline of the Tapline Company), but he couldn't find the turnoff, so he decided to veer south and first capture the el-Uktcha stronghold, which had been concerning him. After that he moved along the patrol road, running close to the border, to the fortified village of Sirat a-Dib. At this point the battalion commander realized he actually wasn't advancing in the direction of Zaura. The field conditions would not allow him to back up the tanks or turn northward. Should he continue moving in the direction of Kala, which had not been his objective in the first place? He asked his senior officers for instructions. The question was relayed up the hierarchy and finally reached the command post of the OC Northern Command David Elazar.

Chief of Staff Itzhak Rabin was also present at the advanced headquarters. The response was positive, and Battalion Commander Biro told Nati to array his company in such a way as to reduce the chances of being hit. Immediately afterward Biro was hurt badly in the upper part of his body, including his lower jaw. He could no longer talk. He tried to direct the fighting by means of notes that he passed on to his signal operator. When he was wounded again, he gave orders in writing to transfer command to Nati. This order was never carried out, because in the meantime a shell had destroyed the transmitter in Nati's tank. As Nati didn't respond, the commander of the brigade commando unit, Rafi Mokadi, assumed command. Shortly after this, Rafi was killed. Now Nati realized what was happening, and he took command over the battalion. The brigade commander, Albert Mandler (who was killed six years later in the Yom Kippur War), quickly gathered some tanks and rushed to help him.

Nati took charge of twenty-one of the battalion tanks, in three companies, and began an assault on Kala. A fierce battle developed. Suddenly a bullet hit his helmet and wounded him. The blood that was streaming from his head dripped into the control box and put his transmitter out of commission. In the heat of the battle he was not aware of his wound. After his tank was hit again he moved on to another tank. He told his men, "Every tank in working order should break through and attack Kala. Tanks that can't move should cover the other tanks." Eleven tanks covered them. Ten broke through, one after another, under Nati's command. He had to shout out his orders since his transmitter had broken down. By the time the tanks reached Kala there were only three left. Then another one was hit, and Nati, with two tanks, found himself facing ten Syrian tanks coming up from the south as reinforcements.

Nati stopped the tanks at the outskirts of Kala, collected all the men from the tanks that had been hit, and turned them into foot soldiers whom he sent to comb the village. He contacted air force planes that arrived around sunset and coordinated their activities as well. He also directed the shooting from the two working tanks, which managed to destroy two Syrian tanks. He did all of this under the most difficult topographical conditions. As a result, this first lieutenant, who had become battalion commander in the middle of a bloody battle, carried out extensive operations that brought about the main breakthrough into the Syrian front lines in the Golan Heights. By nightfall Nati was able to report to Major General David Elazar: "Kala is in our hands." When the fighting was over he was awarded the Medal of Valor.

In Biro's battalion, which became the battalion of Nati Horowitz, there was also a tank under the command of Sergeant Shaul Vardi, from Kibbutz Naan. Vardi later reticently reconstructed his actions: "This is what my friends told me; I don't remember a lot of all of this." He had good reason to forget; during the action he was wounded and suffered a concussion. Nevertheless, he still kept on fighting.

> When we were stopped by an antitank roadblock at Sirat a-Dib, the first tank in the convoy got a direct hit. The tank in front of me tried to help out, but was unsuccessful. It was also hit. I moved forward to the first tank and got the tank commander out. . . . When I came back again I was wounded in my body and my head. I thought that I had gone blind. I asked for someone to replace me. But there was no one. . . . After a while I got an order to circle around and attack a Syrian tank from the side. I carried out the order and the tank was destroyed. But at the same time my tank was hit and caught fire. From here on I don't remember anything. From what they told me, the Syrians began to retreat and tried to pass through the Israeli forces. I ran to my commander and took all the grenades I could from him. While my crew was busy giving first aid to the wounded, I ran up to the small houses along the road and threw grenades into them in order to prevent the enemy from getting close to our tanks and disabling them.

Only afterward was Shaul Vardi taken to the hospital, where his memory returned two days later. He also received a Medal of Valor.

Itzhak Rabin, the chief of staff during the Six-Day War, summed up the acts of bravery of his soldiers in his world-famous speech on Mount Scopus, less than three weeks after the war: "In the Six-Day War there were acts of bravery far beyond the spontaneous, unique daring assaults by soldiers who attack the enemy without thinking twice. In several places there were protracted, desperate battles—in Rafiach, El Arish, Um Katef, Jerusalem, and the Golan

Heights. In these places and in many others, the Israeli soldier demonstrated great heroism, bravery, and perseverance. There is no man who would not stand in awe in the face of this spectacular, amazing human phenomenon."

The late Major General (res.) Chaim Herzog was a president of the State of Israel. He wrote this chapter shortly before his death.

INTO THE FIRE

ESTHER ARDITI

by Tamar Avidar

At the height of the bloody battle for Jerusalem, an unknown woman in white, slight and quick, appeared beside the Israeli soldiers. She carried a large first-aid kit. "The White Angel," the wounded paratroopers of the Fifty-fifth Brigade called her. An angel she was indeed, quick, sweet, compassionate, dressing their wounds under fire, soothing their pain, cheering their spirits. Much later they learned her name: Esther Arditi-Borenstein. For the veterans of that battle, Esther will remain the "White Angel of the Paratroopers" forever.

But almost twelve and a half years earlier, at the beginning of February 1955, as a regular soldier in the air force, she became famous for another deed. She showed extraordinary courage when she ran to rescue a pilot and navigator from the flames of their Mosquito plane. The plane had caught fire when its ammunition exploded, and threatening pieces of shrapnel were flying all around. Esther received a citation from Chief of Staff Lieutenant General Moshe Dayan for her act of bravery under those conditions, for "demonstrating exemplary courage." She later received a Distinguished Service Medal, making her the only woman in the history of the IDF to be awarded this decoration.

The two events mentioned above—the daring rescue from the plane that was about to explode, and the dedicated help she gave the paratroopers at the height of the gunfire and shelling—were of course significant events in Esther's life. But even without these events she lived a very dramatic life. It can even be said that Esther's acts of bravery were part of a life that is a fascinating reflection of Jewish history from the eve of World War II onward. Combined in this small woman are traces of the Holocaust and the renaissance of the Jewish people, devotion to the Zionist idea, love of her country, and self-sacrifice of the highest order.

Esther Arditi is a small, dark woman, with a turned-up nose and a gentle, broad accent, typical of a native of the city of Livorno in the Tuscany region of Italy. In 1943, when she was a child of six, the most terrible nightmare of her life began. The Nazis occupied northern Italy, including the region where the Arditi family lived. The eldest son of the family joined a partisan battalion that was active in the nearby forests. The parents, Esther, and the youngest son took shelter in a bakery in a remote village. One winter day the Gestapo, who had already purged the area of all Jews, discovered them. They broke into the small village bakery, found those hiding there, and acted quickly. The father was handcuffed and sent for interrogation in the nearby city. The Germans decided to kill the mother and small brother on the spot. One of the officers shot both of them in the presence of the terrified little girl. For some unknown reason he did not shoot Esther. The moment they left the bakery she ran for her life from this horrific place and managed to reach the forest. What happened next was completely mixed up in her mind, which is not surprising. This young child, whose whole world had been destroyed in a moment, wandered among the trees, instinctively struggling to survive. Is it any wonder that she doesn't know how long she spent there? All she remembers is that she lived off roots and the milk of a lost sheep she happened to come across. She also remembers that suddenly, one morning, two bearded young men appeared, and one of them—as unbelievable as it may seem—was her eldest brother.

Now, at least, there was someone to take care of her. Her brother took her to his partisan unit, and after a while he put her in a convent. What did she do there? How did they treat her? What was it like to live in the shadow of the cross and the black robes of the nuns? All this remains a closed book as well. She has not shared those experiences with anyone. When the war was over her brother took Esther out of the convent and brought her home, to Livorno. There, to their great joy, they found their father. He had been lucky. He had held out, despite the torture and imprisonment, and remained alive.

Three years later, when she was eleven, Esther heard about the establishment of the State of Israel. She felt immediately that Israel was where she belonged. She broke her savings bank, bought a ticket, and hopped on a train to Naples. She sneaked into the port and climbed onto a boat that looked to her as if it were sailing to Israel. After three hours she was found and sent back to her father's house. But she wouldn't give up on her dream to go to Israel. Five years later, at the age of sixteen, she joined a pioneer training group of the Hehalutz movement. No one could stop her now. The group reached Israel and was sent to Kibbutz Amir. Esther felt as if she was coming home. For some reason many of the other members of the group felt differently. Within a year and a half they decided to return to Italy.

Esther went to the recruiting station in Haifa and begged the clerks to draft her into the army. It wasn't an easy task. "I was perhaps the youngest conscript," she remembered years later, but her stubbornness paid off. At the age of sixteen and a half she was already in uniform. She was short—a mere meter and a half tall—and slim. In the early Fifties most of the girls in the army did secretarial work. But Esther knew that she had not joined the army for that. She took a course for combat medics, and was assigned to one of the air force bases.

The winter of 1955 was cold and stormy. One night, during a storm, lightning hit an air force Mosquito plane as it was landing at Esther's base. Unfortunately, it was a bad hit, so bad that the pilot lost control of critical control systems, and the body of the plane caught fire.

From the flames the ground crew could tell that the Mosquito had fallen in a field outside the base's outer fence. Judging from the voices coming from the plane, it was clear that something terrible was about to happen. It turned out that the plane was full of ammunition, and this ammunition was now beginning to explode, due to the enormous heat generated by the flames. Bullets were flying all over the place, endangering the lives of anyone in the immediate vicinity, especially the lives of the pilot and the navigator who were trapped in the plane. As if that weren't enough, the fire engines that had rushed over from the base toward the burning Mosquito got stuck in the deep mud of the field, as did the ambulance in which Esther, the medic, was riding.

To this very day Esther Arditi cannot explain how she functioned under such difficult conditions, with such terrible pressure and fear. She finds it even harder to explain what force drove her to overcome her fear and run straight into the flames. It was as if she were trying to commit suicide. She says:

> I was serving in the air force but I didn't know much about airplanes. I saw one huge bonfire, and tracer bullets shooting out of it in all directions. And suddenly, in the dark, I heard someone shout, "Mother!" I grabbed my first-aid kit, jumped out of the ambulance, and ran toward the plane. Someone behind me called out, "Are you crazy? Where are you running to?" It was hard to run in the mud, but I reached the plane. I saw a body hanging half out of the plane, and I began to pull him. He grabbed me and said, "Keep going." I kept at it. I began to roll him over and managed to pull him out of the plane and even move him away from it. I was sure that was the end of it. As I said before, I didn't know much about planes, and I couldn't imagine that there was more than one person in a plane. But then the man I had taken out murmured to me, "Get the pilot out." I later understood that a Mosquito plane has both a pilot and a navigator, and I had first rescued the navigator. His name was Shlomo Hardami. Ten days later he died from complications. He had been burned too badly.
>
> When I heard what the navigator said, I went back to the plane. I didn't see anything. It was dark everywhere, but in front of me there was a blinding flame. I found the pilot by the smell of burning from his legs. He was unconscious and still fastened into his seat. I didn't know how to release him. I pulled and pulled, and then he fell out of the plane along with his seat and parachute. I fell too, but I managed to stand up and pull him through the mud. No one besides me knew what had happened to the crew of the plane. No one knew that I had managed to drag the pilot and navigator to a safe distance. When the firefighters moved forward, I heard them saying, "Poor girl, she's gone too." From that moment on I started believing in God.

Later it turned out that the pilot Esther Arditi had rescued was the squadron commander, Yaacov Shalmon, a third-generation Israeli. He was a descendant of the famous Yoel Moshe Salomon, a leader of the Jewish community in Israel and the founder of the city of Petach Tikvah. Yaacov was the son of an Orthodox family from the religious Sanhedria neighborhood of Jerusalem. Naturally, it took him a while to recover, and so he only met Esther Arditi for the first time two months after she had saved his life. His parents knew about her act of heroism. They also knew that they owed their son's life to her. They invited her to their Passover Seder, to which Yaacov Shalmon arrived in bandages. When he saw her, he was in shock at her description of the details of this amazing rescue. He could not understand how tiny Esther had been able to drag him out of the fire. At the time of the accident he had weighed ninety kilograms, whereas this petite, young, female soldier weighed no more than thirty-nine kilograms.

Esther Arditi and Yaacov Shalmon met many times afterward. Yaacov's parents adopted Esther into the family, and when she turned eighteen, they made her the first birthday party she had had since she was a young child. Her relationship with the Shalmon family continues to this day.

Esther was released from the army, studied at the School of Nursing in Haifa, raised a family, and moved to Jerusalem, where she worked as a nurse at the Magen David Adom, the Israeli equivalent of the Red Cross. After a while she decided to change professions and began a course for tour guides. During the state of alert in May–June of 1967 she was in the middle of her course. She had also just gotten divorced. The course was stopped, so Esther found an outlet for her energies, as well for her desire to contribute to her people, by returning as a volunteer to the Magen David Adom. There was no question that this was what she had to do.

The Six-Day War broke out on the morning of June 5. The big battles were raging in the south, but after a few hours the Jordanian army began to shell Jerusalem. Esther rushed to the Magen David Adom station. There were a few wounded from the Jordanian shelling, but it was still not clear whether the actual fighting would reach the city. That evening Esther still didn't know that a paratroop brigade, under the command of Motta Gur, had reached her neighborhood of Beit Hakerem, arriving from the coastal plain in a roundabout fashion. Only after some time did Esther begin to notice the movement of forces from Beit Hakerem eastward. She was burning with curiosity. She asked one of the soldiers where they were going. His response left her in shock. "To liberate the Temple," said the soldier, perhaps seriously.

Those four words electrified Esther. She now felt that some mysterious, hidden higher power had brought her, of all people, a Holocaust survivor, to this place at this time. She knew that she could not make do with being a bystander.

She ran home and found someone to take care of her son and daughter. "Behave yourselves, and don't worry about me," she said to them. She took her first-aid kit and joined the advancing soldiers with her ambulance. She asked to go right onto the battlefield and so reached a collection point for the wounded near the Mandelbaum Gate. At a glance she saw that she would have plenty to do. The paratroopers had suffered heavy hits by Jordanian shells and bullets before even beginning their assault. As Motta Gur himself testified afterward, "We suffered our first casualties before we even came in contact with the enemy because the Jordanians knew the whole area well. There had been shooting since the morning. We already had many casualties from the first rounds of fire. . . . Even at our meeting areas we were shot at by artillery, some twenty-five pounds, some eighty-one millimeters, and, here and there, even a hundred twenty millimeters."

As a result, many soldiers were now lying wounded at the crossroads. They didn't yell out, but it wasn't difficult for Esther to understand that they were in need of immediate care. She began running around madly from one wounded soldier to the other. She gave shots of morphine, applied tourniquets, bandaged open wounds. She didn't pay the slightest attention to the shells exploding around her or to the bullets whistling through the air. She surely didn't have time to even think that this was exactly the same situation she had found herself in near the burning plane. She acted, actually, on her own initiative, without getting orders from anyone, but she knew that she wasn't alone in the field. She knew that if she needed to there was always someone she could consult with. A few yards from her was the medical officer of the brigade, Major Dr. Yaacov "Jackie" King (who has since died). She noticed him immediately, but he was completely absorbed in trying to save lives and did not become aware of her for a while.

"It was a dark night," she remembers, "and suddenly, after working for a long time, Dr. King noticed that someone was beside him. He said to me, 'Go away; this is not a place for women!' I answered him, 'I'm not leaving here while I am still needed!' He then agreed to let me stay in the area under one condition—that I wear a helmet. I accepted his condition. Someone also put a huge army shirt on me, which covered up the bloodstains that had already spread all over my white coat." The helmet, which she was given on the orders of Dr. King, she keeps as a memento of that day.

In the meantime, while Esther Arditi was assisting the brigade doctor in caring for the pre-battle wounded, the main battle broke out on Ammunition Hill, across from the Police School on the crossroads to Mount Scopus. The sounds of that stormy front reached Esther's ears, and an inner voice again told her that she was needed there. She climbed onto an armored car heading toward Ammunition Hill. When she got there she was confronted with a horrific sight—dozens of wounded were lying on the battlefield, with no doctor around, and the few medics who were there were finding it hard to manage. She quickly joined them and began to care for the wounded. Again she gave morphine shots, applied tourniquets and splints, and bandaged wounds. At first she counted the wounded that she was caring for, but when she got to 180 she stopped counting. And the fighting was not over yet.

At dawn Esther Arditi jumped into an armored car going south from Ammunition Hill to the Arab neighborhood of Sheikh Jarrah, where the battle was still raging. Esther figured she would find work there. Suddenly she saw a frightened Arab woman coming out of one of the houses with a one-year-old baby in her arms. The baby was bleeding profusely; the fact that

the woman had dared to go out into the street under heavy fire meant that the child's condition was very serious. Esther didn't hesitate for a moment. She jumped off the vehicle and told
the paratroopers to go on without her. She then looked at the child and saw he needed a blood
transfusion immediately. She grabbed him and ran to the monastery nearby. She handed him
over to two monks and ordered them to give the baby a blood transfusion right away. Did she
remember at that moment how her brother had handed her over to a convent in Italy more
than twenty years earlier?

When she went out into the street again an old Arab came up to her—apparently the
grandfather of the baby—and thrust a huge box of chocolates into her hands, almost as big as
she was. She continued walking on her own, without a weapon, down the empty lanes. She
noticed a wounded Arab woman. A minute after she dressed the woman's wounds, an Arab
boy appeared and spat on her. Esther Arditi became frightened and ran without stopping until,
exhausted, she reached the Rockefeller Museum, which overlooks the Stork Tower, at the
northeast corner of the walls of the Old City. The paratroopers, who had taken the museum
not long before, welcomed her with open arms. After she rested a little someone was found to
take her home to her children. Esther Arditi's part in the war for Jerusalem had come to an
end.

She later remarried and even became a grandmother. Most people around her are unaware
of her past. She spends her time taking Italian tourists around the country, and considers herself to be on the front lines of Zionist education. "It seems to me," she says, "that this is how
I contribute to the country. Both the Foreign Ministry and the IDF ask me to give lectures, vol-
untarily of course, to new immigrants and soldiers, and I do it a lot, with pleasure. In fact,
when I am asked to volunteer I usually do so with pleasure." Of course, she points out, "the
family of the pilot Yaacov Shalmon has remained my family."

She says little about the feelings her visits to Ammunition Hill stir in her heart. "The truth
is that today I find it difficult to go there. It's too sterile for my tastes. I remember how it was
then, on the day it was liberated. I remember the barbed-wire fences, the shelling, the gunfire,
and my wounded paratroopers."

Tamar Avidar is a writer and an editor for the newspaper Maariv.

BECAUSE MY LAND AWAITS ME

YECHEZKEL AVI SHABI MAOR (POLAREVITCH)

by Nechama Lifshitz

. . . As a legendary leader in prayer I stand here, deeply moved, by the title page of my last book, and I wrap myself in five symbolic, imaginary prayer shawls, tell my story and sing my final swan songs.

The first shawl is woven from the years of my stormy youth, bursting with love for my homeland, and crowned with the suffering of a Prisoner of Zion who spent seventeen years in Soviet "machseger"* and exile.

The second shawl is dipped in the blood of ghastly torture, when the Lithuanians, the murderers of Jews, arrived at my machseger at the end of the Second World War. I had to breathe the same air with them in the hut, in the dining hall and on the taiga, twenty-four hours a day.

The third shawl is soaked in the horrific shock I felt when I returned to Lithuania and stood before the pits where my murdered brothers lay. . . .

The fourth shawl is inlaid with the bones of the murdered Jews that my wife and I collected . . . and brought to Israel for Jewish burial. . . .

The fifth shawl is spun with the purity of the dreams of my only son, Dr. Shabi Yaacov Maor, a first lieutenant in the IDF and the doctor on the *Dakar* submarine. . . .

*A word made up by Yechezkel Polarevitch, which stands for the cruel prison-concentration camp that he survived.

So wrote Yechezkel Avi Shabi Maor "instead of an introduction" to his book *Two Dawns*, which was published in 1987.

"Yechezkel is a poet and a storyteller with a history. . . ." wrote Professor Yosef Nedava.

One cannot understand his poetry without tracing its background to the context of his life. However, it seems to me that, beyond his personal calling as a writer, he is a symbol of our tormented era, a typical example of the twentieth century and all its upheavals, its fears and the lights of hope that shine on its horizon. What is the source of the spiritual strength that has made it possible for him to withstand all these tests? It seems that this secret is found in the feeling of optimism that never leaves him for even a moment. . . . Perhaps the answer is . . . inherent in the Jewish way of life in which Yechezkel was steeped from childhood. . . . His existence in the Diaspora is but a temporary one, a way station. His spirit and dreams and desires are all focused on another landscape, the historical.

Yechezkel Avi Shabi Maor-Polarevitch was born in 1912 in Lithuania in the town of Joniskis, and got a Jewish and Zionist education in a Tarbut school in Sabile. The Jews of Lithuania had complete cultural autonomy. The kindergartens and schools, the youth movements, yeshivas, and gymnasiums used the school curriculum used in Eretz Israel. There was spiritual assimilation, but it was much less than what we see in Israel. A Jew there had deep roots in his ancient tradition.

From 1928 onward Yechezkel was active in the Betar youth organization. There he met Ella Eidelson, who became his girlfriend and life partner. The lives of this couple were closely linked to the life in Eretz Israel. In 1938 they heard of the hanging by the British of a proud Betar member, Shlomo Ben-Yosef, in the Acre prison. When their son was born on April 15, 1939, they devised a name for their child out of the initials of Shlomo Ben-Yosef. They named the child Shabi-Yaacov.

In 1940 Lithuania became a republic of the Soviet Union, and the whole world of the Jews changed—the Tarbut school network was closed down, the Zionist youth movements became illegal, Hebrew was declared an "anti-Soviet" language, people were persecuted and arrested for their opinions. . . .

Yechezkel was expelled from the university where he had been studying chemistry, and was arrested. After a while he was released, but he was under constant surveillance. On June 14, 1941, he was arrested again, for the "sin" of Zionist activity, and was sentenced to ten years' imprisonment and "exile for the rest of his life to Siberia." His wife, his son Shabi, who was two years old at the time, and his mother-in-law were also exiled to Siberia.

Yechezkel wrote in his story about Shabi:

> A mountain does not meet another mountain, [but] a prisoner's car meets another prisoner's car. Two windows face each other—a small window covered with iron bars. . . . By chance, in the opposite car, women, children, the families of prisoners. Now we are all prisoners, the men, the women and the children. A two-year-

old child looks out of the barred window, his mother holding him and saying: "There's your father. Say something to him."

"Shabi, Shabi," shouts a man from the other car through the bars, but the child is silent, his face is pale, and his broad chestnut eyes express terrible shock and pain, which he has not yet learned to hide with a smile.

Thirteen years passed until the family was reunited in a village in the taiga. For ten years Yechezkel "lived in machseger" as he called it. From Medvezjegorsk near Murmansk he was taken on foot and on open freight car platforms through the taiga and tundra to the freezing cold of Karaganda in northern Kazakhstan, hungry and in terrible pain, dressed in tatters with "Sorgat" shoes on his feet, made from rubber tires. . . .

Elinka, his wife, managed to find him from her place of exile in a Lithuanian village. In 1947 he managed to smuggle a message out to her from his "machseger" in Koand-Ozero:

> You—
> Ray of sunshine
> Soft
> And silent
> Caressing gently
> Warmly
> Humbly
> That set
> On the village
> This frozen morning.
>
> I—
> Guiltless
> Rotting
> In green hatred,
> In a satanic
> Paradise
> Choked
> At night
> Against my will
> On the gallows.
>
> I—
> In chains
> Beat out for you

A song of suffering
A crown
From my tunes
In your honor

You and I—
One faith
One torch of fire
When parting,
When meeting. . . .
In our looks—devotion,
In our kisses—love.
In our steps—the victory
of simple
human
purity.

Along with his fellow sufferers—Zvi Fergerzon, Meir Baazov, and Mordechai Shenker, the saintly one of the group—he "celebrated" the Jewish holidays, spoke Hebrew, sang in Hebrew, prayed.

From this came the song that became their anthem:

Despite your wishes I sing and will continue to sing
My tone is of faith in victory
I shall remove the veil of lies from your faces
From your fawning, deceitful words,
O, make way for me!
I will kindle lights in my night
Whatever may come,
I will sing my song in secret. . . .
Today my song is stifled and mute,
But it still remains alive!
And tomorrow it will bravely burst forth
From my brothers' burning lips. . . .

In 1957, long after the death of Stalin, the Polarevitch family returned to Lithuania. When they got there they went from town to town, from one mass grave to another—and were struck dumb. "Our" Jewish Lithuania was *judenrein*. The few survivors gathered together in the big cities.

I will never forget our first meeting on the shores of the Baltic Sea. Jews from all over the Soviet Union met in the holiday resorts, looking for a bit of *Yiddishkeit* (Jewishness).

I was sitting with a group of Prisoners of Zion, and one of them admired the Soviet song that I sang in Yiddish translation. I told him that the song was meant only to pay lip service to the censor; all the Jewish content was there, and that was what mattered. And then my eyes met Yechezkel's eager glance; his eyes smiled at me with his good-hearted and understanding smile. We were not a very large group with the children and the teenagers, but we would get together and sing. We would sing Hebrew songs from the old days, on the shore of the Baltic. I learned the song "Make Way," which became my anthem also.

In December 1964 our mutual friend Eliezer Gordonov made *aliya* and sparked a hope in us for a miracle. Eliezer met Menachem Begin, who had known Yechezkel in 1939, and managed to arrange an immigrant's visa for his family. On May 8, 1965, Victory Day, Elinka and Yechezkel came to say goodbye to me. They were going to Israel. He had one request. It was dangerous to take his poems from the "machsegerim" and from Siberia with him. The poems stayed with me, wrapped in newspaper. My daughter kept the precious package among her schoolbooks, and later we managed to pass it on to Yechezkel in Israel, through the Israeli consul, David Bar-Tov. His first book of poetry, *I Was Crucified on the Red Star*, was published in 1968.

The Polarevitch family felt a great sense of belonging to Israel. Absorption problems did not bother them at all. From childhood they had learnt to give of themselves and make sacrifices for the country. They never even thought of asking for anything in return. He was one of the founders of the Organization of Prisoners of Zion from the Soviet Union and served as its chairman for years. He was also active in the Herut movement.

But the sacrifice of Elinka and Yechezkel was not over yet. Their only son, Shabi, who had become a doctor, volunteered for service on navy submarines, replaced another doctor on the *Dakar* submarine, and was lost at sea.

Yechezkel, who had changed his name from Polarevitch to Maor, added to it the words Avi Shabi—Father of Shabi.

In *The Story of Shabi-Yaacov Maor* Yechezkel says:

> Shabi learned Hebrew very easily. In fact the first words that came out of his mouth as a child were in Hebrew. Of course his mother taught and sang Hebrew songs to him. And so, when he met with his father after twelve years of complete separation, he picked up Hebrew pretty quickly. (This meeting took place when he and his mother, his grandmother, and his mother's sister, were brought from their place of exile in Altai, accompanied by armed guards, to his father's place of exile-imprisonment in a sealed-off, remote Siberian village in the heart of the northern taiga.) His first lesson with his father was the biblical story of the sacrifice of Isaac from the prayerbook, the only Hebrew book that his grandmother happened to have. . . .

Yechezkel's house was open to everyone. He would go from school to school, from one army unit to the other, meet with Israeli children and tell them about the Diaspora, about resurrection and hope.

In 1969 his second book came out, *The Short Story of the Long Death*. In the dedication to me, he wrote: "Happy are we that after the long death I am sitting here in your house in Tel Aviv and presenting you with the fruits of my pen and my spirit."

We met again in March 1969. We stood on the terrace of the hotel facing the loud, billowy Mediterranean, and we were silent.

"What do you think?" said Yechezkel. "Does he hear us down there at the depths of the sea?"

In October 1970, an Armored Corps Day, I was invited to take part in the celebrations at the Mann Auditorium in Tel Aviv. The IDF orchestra, a choir of three hundred armored corps soldiers, and the choir of a school in Ramat Gan performed for the first time the song of Avi Shabi Maor, "Make Way": "I will kindle lights in my night. Whatever may come. . . ."

I could not see Yechezkel when he went up onto the stage, for the tears that filled my eyes. . . .

In his third book, *Two Dawns*, which came out in 1987, he wrote:

> But the song
> As a refuge
> Rhymes slowly for me
> Because my land
> Awaits me
> Motherly and soft
> To my steps
> Forever. . . .
> We will pray, my child,
> We will pray:
> God
> Dispose of
> The trenches of hate
> And bless
> Peace
> And understand:
> The day has come
> Let it be. . . .

Elinka died on the 1st of Av, 5755 (July 29, 1995), and Yechezkel died a few months later, on the 19th of Cheshvan, 5766 (November 12, 1995).

In the plot for bereaved parents in Kiryat Shaul, on the marble gravestone, between their names, is a white plaque, which reads: DR. SHABI-YAACOV MAOR. I stand at the gravestone, and in my ears echo Yechezkel's words: "No, my friends! No, my children! We are not immigrating to Israel—we are going *up* to Israel, making *aliya* to it!" Because if we are not, why have we sacrificed so much?

Nechama Lifshitz, a singer, is considered the national singer of the Russian Jews, and in many ways symbolizes their struggle for immigrating to Israel. She herself came on aliya *from the Soviet Union.*

HE RUSHED INTO THE HEART OF THE STORM

ZORIK LEV

by Ezer Weizmann

The announcement from the control tower was very short. Only three words in French: "Mamonta Alfa crashe." The small group of Israelis who were present at the French air force base near Paris, this night in 1955, were greatly alarmed. They knew that "Mamonta Alfa" was the code name for the Ouragan plane of Zorik Lev. They also knew that this plane was not in the best shape, that the weather conditions were bad, and that there were a lot of clouds. They knew too that "crashe" meant that it had crashed. A quick check showed that for the moment no one knew anything except that communications with the plane had broken down. Later it turned out that none of the other control towers in the area had managed to make contact with the Israeli pilot. A few helicopters were sent up to look for signs in the area; they didn't find anything. There could be no doubt; Zorik had crashed. He had come to France with some other Israeli pilots for an advanced training course on the Ouragan jet fighters. We had lost him.

And then the phone rang in the office where Zorik's deputy was sitting. On the other end a calm, familiar voice was heard. The lost pilot, whose radio transmitter had broken down, had managed to fly below the clouds, guide himself according to what he saw on road signs, find an army airport, and land at it—with his last drop of gas and without getting permission. He somehow explained, in simple French, that he had no evil intentions, and managed to get out of the situation without any problems. He was happy. For him, this further justified his battle with the Israeli air force to continue using the Ouragan jets.

He had fought many of these kinds of battles to promote the causes he believed in: to get his men to strictly follow safety regulations and keep proper order, to make sure they got the treatment they deserved, to remind everyone that the machine was very important in the air, but the man who was controlling it was much more important (as well as being the one who took care of it on the ground). He also fought many battles in the air, of course, literally to the last moment of his life.

He graduated among the first classes of fighter pilots in the Israeli air force. This was after the War of Independence, when all the foreign volunteers had left. Because of his unusual first name it was not difficult to guess when he was born and to which political camp he belonged. When he came into this world on Succot 5694 (October 1933), his parents, Leah and Nehemiah, named him Arlozor (which everyone shortened to Zorik) in memory of the Labor movement leader they so greatly admired, Chaim Arlozorov. Unknown assassins had murdered Arlozorov a few months earlier on the beach in Tel Aviv. Zorik's roots were firmly planted in the Labor movement, and were even stronger because he was the first son born in Moshav Kfar Bilu, outside Rehovot.

He grew up close to the orange grove and the beehives. He lived and breathed agriculture. But he also heard and saw planes from childhood. Not far from Kfar Bilu was the Ekron base of the Royal British air force, which is now known as Tel Nof. Across the road, among the orange groves of Kibbutz Naan, the pilots' platoon of the Palmach was based. These pilots might not have flown very often, but they were already a source of legends in the whole area. Later, in 1948, he watched air battles from the water tower of the moshav between the first Israeli air force planes and Egyptian planes.

Beside him on the water tower was his best friend, Ehud Dolinsky. Both of them began to dream vaguely about flying. In the meantime they both went to the Kadoori Agricultural School at the foot of Mount Tabor. A tall boy from Afula named Yak—Yaacov Nevo—studied in the class above them in Kadoori. One day, after he had graduated, Yak came to visit, wearing the uniform of an air force cadet and full of stories about flying. These stories did not come anywhere near those that would be told in the future about the amazing exploits Yak later performed in his career as an outstanding fighter pilot. But they were enough to spark Zorik's and Ehud's imaginations and to get them to take the flying tests before their conscription into the army.

They passed the tests successfully. Before he began the course, Zorik swore to his parents that they had no reason to worry; he would never give up agriculture, nor would he forget what he had learned in Kadoori. He soon added a pair of cushions to his flying gear. He was short. He needed one cushion to sit on and one for his back so that he could sit properly in a training plane, reach the gas pedal, and look out the window.

A year later Zorik and Ehud were among those who received their wings. Zorik became a Mosquito pilot. The Mosquito was an old wooden plane that the air force had purchased from the surplus of the Second World War. It wasn't exactly the Mustang or the Spitfire, which were considered the front-line planes in those days. One of the great advantages of the Mosquito was its ability to fly low. Because of this Zorik was able to become an expert at photographic sorties outside the country's borders. Because of this he almost stopped flying.

Fifty feet. The orders were clear. That was the minimum altitude. But Zorik and a few of his more daring friends did not always follow orders. Sometimes, when they were feeling mischievous, they would dive down over cars on the road, scaring the drivers half to death. Then they would swing up again at the last second before they actually touched these four-wheeled vehicles. One day, while making a dive over the Sodom road, they got too close and hit the antenna of a car in the convoy of Baron de Rothschild. A complaint soon arrived, and the commander of the base, who was sick and tired of the pilots' games, gave Zorik a prison sentence. While he was in military prison he was ordered to report to the chief of staff, Moshe Dayan. Dayan had also decided that it was time to put an end to these violations in the air force. "You're going home," Dayan said to Zorik. "The Army is releasing you to serve as an example to others."

As a senior officer in the air force, I thought that Dayan had done the right thing. The force greatly needed a real shake-up like this. But at the same time I also knew that we were losing an excellent pilot and a true friend. Zorik asked the chief of staff for a pardon. In a letter, which Dayan made sure was published in the army newspaper *Bamachane* so that everyone would learn the lesson, the young second lieutenant explained: "For a pilot this is indescribable suffering. . . . I am sure that I will return to the squadron as a pilot who is physically young but mentally mature. It was hard for me to decide to write to you. My pride would not allow me to ask for pity when I was in your office. A pilot, especially a fighter pilot, must be a man and take his punishment in silence. But, believe me, the punishment is too great to bear." He even dared to write to Dayan at the end of the letter that he sincerely wished that he would never make a mistake in the future.

The chief of staff did not respond to his heartfelt request, and Zorik returned to work in the alfalfa fields at Kfar Bilu. He worked on the family farm for a year and a half, never giving up his efforts to return to the air force, or even to fly again. He became ever more determined after his good friend Ehud Dolinsky was killed in a training accident. Now he felt that he must fly not only for his own sake but also to take the place of the dead pilot. In the end he got what he wanted. In 1955 the chief of staff decided that both the air force and Zorik had learned well that they could not run wild. He also decided that the air force couldn't give up on such a promising pilot, especially since there were signs that the Sinai Campaign was on the horizon. Zorik was back in uniform. He retrained to learn how to fly a jet plane, and was stationed at the Hatzor base, of which I was the commander.

He was now a night fighter pilot in a Meteor squadron. He was green with envy at the best pilots, who were retraining to fly French Ouragan planes. It was said that these pilots would later go on to even newer planes—Mystères. He solved the problem in his own way. As a night pilot he was free during the day, so he got permission to sit in on the course for the Ouragans. Later he got permission to be tested—and passed the tests. When the first position became available in an Ouragan squadron, he was the most natural candidate and got the job. After some time, when I had to send a few pilots to bring back the first Mystères from France, Zorik was, of course, one of them.

He took part in several sorties in the Sinai Campaign, often as the second-in-command to Yak, his old friend from Kadoori, who was now an expert at downing Egyptian Migs. But Zorik himself never got the chance to down a single plane. After the war he became an instructor at the flying school, and he demanded operational discipline from his students which he himself had learned the hard way after the Sodom road incident. Later he became Yak's deputy commander in a Mystère squadron. He became a first lieutenant and an outstanding pilot, and the life force of the squadron and the wing. His enormous energy, his dedication to his friends, and the optimism that radiated from him always raised morale wherever he was.

So it was when he was appointed the commander of an Ouragan squadron, and later when he commanded a squadron of Super-Mystères. It is important to note that he knew when to be cheerful and friendly and when to be tough. One Friday, for example, he confined a young pilot to the base because he hadn't followed the rules for order and cleanliness, and gave him all kinds of maintenance jobs. In the evening he invited him home for a family dinner—Zorik was already the father of three of his six children—and on Sunday he came down on him until he finished perfectly all the jobs that he hadn't managed to get done on Friday.

In the mid 1960s I was already the head of the air force. I put Zorik in charge of a Mirage squadron; we learned together how to fly this excellent plane. Then it became his turn to serve as a staff officer. From this position he was called on to fly a Mirage and to lead formations in the Six-Day War. He was part of the second wave that was sent to destroy the Egyptian air force. He was assigned to the distant el-Minia field, west of the Nile. It was there that he finally managed to down a Mig-17. On the morning of June 11, when he read the announcement of Motti Hod, the commander of the air force, that said: "All the missions assigned to us have been completed," he was sure that the blessing at the end of the message would be realized: "The people of Israel will live safely in their country."

Unfortunately, he was wrong. After the Six-Day War came the War of Attrition, with more sorties and more friends who fell in battle. And after that came the Yom Kippur War. In the meantime Zorik's family had grown; he now had six children. He also began university study (although not in the agriculture school, as he had wanted to do). He had reached the rank of colonel and was appointed head of the air force base at Ramat David. Zorik was a dedicated father to his base. He always made absolutely sure that everything was orderly and clean and polished, and was always ready to listen to any problems his soldiers had. But above all, he worried about the operational skills of every pilot and every plane under his command. He also made sure to keep up his own skills as a combat pilot.

Zorik was about to finish his job and become the head of the Personnel Branch of the air force with the rank of brigadier general. But on the eve of Yom Kippur 5734 (October 5, 1973) he was called to General Headquarters and heard what was going to happen. The base, under his command, went into high alert. The next day the families were evacuated, and the war began. Many of the planes that took off from Ramat David never returned; others came back damaged and scarred by missiles. Besides that the Syrians managed to launch Russian-made Frog missiles directly into Ramat David.

Zorik ran around organizing things, urging his men on and encouraging them, but he was very worried. Would these young pilots be strong enough to take off again to the fronts from which their friends had not returned? Would the heavy missile fire break their spirits?

He was especially worried about the Skyhawk squadron, which had suffered great losses. On Tuesday, October 9, he heard from its acting commander—the commander and his deputy had been wounded previously—that he was about to lead a formation of three planes southward. "I'll be your second-in-command," he stated forcefully, leaving no room for protest. He was convinced that if he, as wing commander, flew with them, it would greatly raise the morale of the soldiers. If they saw that he was not afraid of the missiles, that he was willing to enter the fray, despite the fact that a man of his rank was not required to do so, they would be encouraged. None of them would even think that an officer would send them to a destination he would not be willing to attack himself. Personal example—that was the essence of his approach between wars. How could he not follow that same path now? "We are much stronger than it seems," he announced, and entered the cockpit.

The formation attacked in the area of Port Said. Suddenly Zorik's plane dove, hit the water, and disappeared. Colonel Arlozor Lev had been hit, and couldn't even jump from his wrecked aircraft. Our friend Zorik was lost at the bottom of the Mediterranean. He was forty years old.

A year later David Ivri, the future commander of the air force, wrote about him: "There is surely some hidden airport,/Where old-time pilots land,/Slowly, slowly they glide onto the runway,/Their motors silenced/Onto the lane, without screeching of brakes, joining/The ranks of the few/To whom so many owe so much."

Major General (res.) Ezer Weizmann is the president of Israel.

BLOOD BROTHERS

ABD EL MAJID HADR EL-MAZARIB ("AMOS YARKONI")

by Binyamin "Fuad" Ben-Eliezer

Amos Yarkoni, otherwise known as Abd el Majid Hadr el-Mazarib, has been awarded the Medal of Valor, three citations (only the details of one of his citations were publicized), and the Alon Prize, for his exemplary pioneering work, which contributed to the security of Israel. Amos is the father of the IDF's scouts doctrine and one of the dominant supporters of its policy of preemptive action.

Amos Yarkoni was a central figure in the Shaked commando unit during the first twelve years of its existence, from 1955 to 1967. His last army position was as military governor of Sinai. After his release from the IDF, with the rank of lieutenant colonel, he was appointed by the Housing Ministry to be responsible for the minority population in the south of Israel. His close friend, General Rechavam "Gandhi" Ze'evi, who served with him for many years, said of Amos: "He was the initiator of the commando units of the army regional commands and in this respect one could describe him as the father of guerrilla warfare in the IDF."

Abd el Majid Hadr was born sometime between 1922 and 1924 in Kafr Naura. His parents, who belonged to the Mazarib Bedouin tribe, tried to settle in Naura but returned later to their previous encampment near Nahalal. Abd el Majid became friendly with the children of the moshav, one of whom was Moshe Dayan. In his youth he was a shepherd in the tribe. His brother Salah, who was also a scout in the Shaked unit, said he was "a bright boy. When a cow or sheep got lost he would be called in. He had an open mind and always helped out the weak. He helped the Jews because he thought they were the weak ones."

In the book *Spirit of the IDF*, in the chapter about the Shaked commando unit, it is written: "If you are passing through the desert, pick up a small pebble, spit on it and put it back in its place. If Abd el Majid Hadr passes by that spot a hundred years later, he will notice immediately that the stone is not in the place where Allah put it. He will pick up the stone, discover the signs of your spit, follow your footsteps to the entrance of your tent, and since he won't find you there—as you won't live a hundred years—he will knock on your tombstone and ask, 'You "ibn-kalb" [son of a dog], why did you spit on that stone?' "

When Amos Yarkoni was in an officers' training course he served one night as the gunner in an assault exercise in Maale Giva, during which a small part of his machine gun fell off. In the morning, when the platoon went out on exercises, he asked permission to look for the part. "How will you find a small part on a large hill?" the commander asked in amazement, but he let him go.

"The commander," said Amos Yarkoni, "stopped the lesson, and everyone watched what I was doing. Afterwards they called it 'a lesson in methodology.' I climbed the hill, found the part, and came back."

In 1936, during the Arab riots, Abd el Majid joined the Arab gangs and became an expert at blowing up the Haifa-Iraqi pipeline. There was a disagreement among the members of the gang, and some of them accused Abd el Majid and two of his friends of committing treason and of not being willing to destroy their opponents. The three of them were held prisoner in an empty water pit. There they awaited their sentence. They knew that the judge, a blind old sheikh, usually sentenced people to death. At night Abd el Majid climbed on to his friends' shoulders, got out of the pit, and helped them out. The three of them escaped the Mazarib encampment. Afraid of the vengeance of the gang, they ran off to the new moshav of Shimron near Nahalal. Moshe Dayan, at the time a young officer in the Hagana, allotted them a small area for pasture land, and assigned Jewish guards to protect them. He also supplied them with food and water. The Bedouins stayed for two weeks in Shimron until they were reconciled with the gang.

"After I ran away from the pit the Jews told us we should work with the British to find out where the gang had hidden us," said Abd el Majid. "At first I didn't want to, but later I agreed, and I found the pit. I went back to the Bedouin camp and worked as a shepherd. My friendship with the Jewish settlers grew."

In 1947 Abd el Majid worked in the oil refinery in Haifa. When Etzel men threw a bomb into the yard of the refinery and killed six Arab workers, he ran to the foreman and suggested he evacuate the Jewish workers from the factory immediately. But he was too late. That day thirty-nine Jews were murdered in an Arab attack. "That day was a warning sign for me," said Abd el Majid. "I decided to help the Jews."

An acquaintance of his, an old-time field guard called Oded Yanai, recommended him, and Abd el Majid carried out assignments that cannot be talked about to this day. On December 17, 1948, he joined the Minorities Unit of the IDF, served as a private for a while, and then took a squad commanders' training course. He became an instructor of a squad commanders' course in the Minorities Unit. At the time he was the only Bedouin squad commander in the IDF. When there were disagreements between the Bedouin and the Druze in the unit, he kept his identity from the Druze and was given the Hebrew alias "Amos Yarkoni" to protect him. In

1949 he was released from the army and returned to his tribe, but five days later he was asked to return. From then on he remained in uniform for twenty years, until 1969.

In Minority Unit 300 Yarkoni was the role model of his fighters. He and his men took part in ambushes and patrols, searched for hikers who had gotten lost in the desert, and drove out Bedouin tribes that entered the Negev from Sinai. Eventually a company of Druze camel riders was set up in the unit, and Amos Yarkoni was made its commander. On the roads in the south and in the Negev he would sometimes come across the men of Commando Unit 30, which had been set up by Major General Moshe Dayan, OC Southern Command, and the two units would occasionally work together.

In 1953 he took his officers' training course. "The course was difficult for me only because of the Hebrew and because of the subjects I had not been familiar with previously," he said, "but when they took me out into the field I was a lion." There were only two minority soldiers in this course. The other one was a Druze. When Yarkoni finished the course he asked to join the intelligence corps but was turned down. He returned to Unit 300 as a platoon commander.

In May 1955, when his platoon was stationed across from Khan Yunis, he got an order to report with a team of his men to the operation officer of the Central Command, Shmuel Glinka. Glinka assigned Yarkoni and his men, along with a paratroop squad under the command of Nadav Noiman, to look for Egyptian Intelligence men who had infiltrated into Israel. The scouts and the paratroopers found the Egyptians south of Ashkelon. Yarkoni was later attached to a special unit made up of scouts from the Minorities Unit and paratroopers. It included twelve soldiers and was later called the Shaked Commando Unit. (To this day it is not known if the name came from the initials for Shomrei Kav Hadarom [Guards of the Southern Line] or Sherut Commando Darom [Southern Commando Service]. In Yarkoni's opinion the name came from the Hebrew word *shaked*, which means "almond.") In the beginning the unit was semiclandestine. The soldiers wore civilian clothing, and most of their weapons were irregular. Their job was to keep out infiltrators from the southern border. The south of the country at the time was a paradise for infiltrators who hid in deserted villages and their orchards.

It has been forty-two years since the Shaked Unit was set up. It had a few commanders, including the author of this chapter, and most of them moved on to command large units during peace and wartime. Amos Yarkoni, the Bedouin from the Jezreel Valley, was and remains a hallmark of the unit, an indisputably respected officer. While he was still unknown to the Israeli public, this scout and Bedouin officer became a unique figure in the army and throughout the south. Aside from his natural modesty and charm, he was also known as one who could read the map of the Negev with his feet and who showed amazing sharpness of all the senses given to man.

The Shaked fighters under the command of Amos Yarkoni carried out hundreds of raids and other preemptive actions. One of the first raids was near Kibbutz Ruhama in February

1956. Those who took part in it were Amos Yarkoni, Nissim Alfandari, Farid Farras, and the late Muhammad Abu-Gans, otherwise known as Herzl.

Amos Yarkoni described the raid:

> It was raining that night. The area was all muddy and our vehicle got stuck. We went on foot, and at sunrise we reached several caves, where we discovered charred remains of campfires. We followed the footprints. The infiltrators saw us and ran off. The next day we found them near Shderot. In the gunfire that ensued we killed one of them on the spot, and one escaped to the wadi and was killed there. But there had been footprints of three men so I continued looking until we got to a narrow, deep pit. On one side of the pit there was fresh mud.
>
> "The man has fallen into the pit and can't escape," I said, and so it was. When we brought him up it turned out that he had been sent on an assignment by the head of Egyptian Intelligence in Gaza, Colonel Mustafa Hafez.

On December 1, 1959, a reconnaissance team went out north of Ashkelon under the command of Amos Yarkoni. "About half a kilometer before the end of the patrol," he said, "we discovered the footprints of three members of an Egyptian squad. They realized we were there, and hid. I walked step by step to the Chamama marsh, and the footprints stopped there. I moved into the reeds. I walked on with my men behind me. Suddenly I felt a strong blow and fell. A burst of fire had hit me. My right hand was left hanging, but I couldn't feel the pain. I shot my whole magazine into the reeds. I told my men to run, and I lay there. I said to myself, 'This is the end.'"

Twenty-five years after this raid Yarkoni said, "We couldn't avoid that encounter. There are times when either you are afraid and you don't act, or you're not afraid, and either you get them or they get you. We could have not gone into the reeds and said, 'They're there; bring in forces to surround them.' That's not how we were trained. If the enemy enters my area I attack him without thinking twice."

Despite his serious wounds—his right hand was hanging by tendons—Amos refused to let his friends carry him and left the field on his own power.

In 1960 Amos Yarkoni was appointed commander of the Shaked Unit in the place of Dov Strelitz. He said:

> When I was deputy commander I trained myself to take over the command. Every day I learned something new, in the hope of becoming the commander some day. I knew I had all of the necessary qualifications. I decided that if I became commander I would choose my men myself, and they would be men with potential, roots, and love of the country. Everything else they would learn during training and

afterward. I decided to give up on regular discipline and concentrate on battle discipline. This discipline would hold from the minute the soldier got into the command car until he got out. I would make sure that there were all the best things on
the base—food, equipment, entertainment.

Amos was the best day-to-day field fighter in the Shaked Unit and personally led almost
every raid in the area of the Southern Command. During his years of service in the unit he
spent a lot of time and energy developing the relations between the Jewish soldiers, most of
whom were from kibbutzim, and the Bedouin. The quality of these relations was what gave the
Shaked Unit its special spirit.

In 1964 Amos was seriously wounded again, this time in the leg. He came back to the unit
from the hospital with an artificial hand and a deformed leg. In December 1965, when the OC
Southern commander, Zamir, retired, he described some particularly exciting moments:

> Somewhere in the south a group of infiltrators was discovered. A chase ensued after
> another unit had encountered them and forced them to make a hurried escape.
> The assigned team from the Shaked Unit, under Amos's command, moved quickly.
> Suddenly their vehicle broke down and they couldn't continue the chase. The
> commander had been wounded in the leg a while before in an attack and had only
> returned to active duty a few days earlier. Would he be able to continue the chase
> on foot, quickly and under dangerous conditions, despite his wounded leg? It was
> a difficult area to move in. The weather was very hot. Of course, Amos could have
> given up, stayed in the vehicle, and handed command over to one of his deputies,
> but the chase was a challenge for him. He overcame his pain, the difficulty of walk-
> ing, and carried out the mission successfully. When he continued I felt great satis-
> faction, and not necessarily as a commander, but as a friend.

When he retired from the army, the OC Southern commander at the time, General
Yeshayahu Gavish, wrote to Amos Yarkoni, "Amos, my friend, I know to what extent your methods, your fighting techniques, and the performance level of your unit is a model for all of the
army. You personally sacrificed your health for the State of Israel. There are only a few people
who know about your deeds, but the IDF and the State of Israel will not forget what you have
done. Many owe their lives to you."

About his ties to the State and to Jewish society Amos had this to say: "An event like Independence Day is a special holiday for me. I am not a Zionist. But I love this country with all
my heart. Three principles have guided me in all my life—honor, justice, and loyalty."

During that time I was appointed his deputy. After the Six-Day War I became commander of the unit. Amos told the boys: "Good-bye, friends, I am leaving tomorrow morning. I have gone this far with you. From now on Fuad will take my place."

Brigadier General (res.) Binyamin "Fuad" Ben-Eliezer is a Knesset member and a former minister of housing.

Under Unprecedented Fire

The War of Attrition

by Shlomo "Chich" Lahat

The mission of the IDF forces in Sinai during the War of Attrition was to stop the Egyptian army from getting a foothold on the east bank of the Suez Canal, and make sure their forces did not infiltrate into the Sinai and capture any territory.

In order to do this we were positioned along the Canal at thirty-one huge strongholds, which were for the most part well fortified and protected against artillery fire. The strongholds were located at places considered particularly vulnerable to Egyptian attack.

The Egyptian army that faced us consisted of five infantry divisions, which included 100,000 soldiers, and two armored divisions, with 600 tanks and 750 artillery guns.

Eleven hundred soldiers were positioned in these strongholds. Sixty-five tanks guarded the open areas between them and supported the strongholds. There were also scores of artillery guns.

At the rear, in the Bir Gafgafa, another armored brigade and an artillery battalion were training. They were meant to serve as reinforcements at the Canal line if the fighting escalated.

The War of Attrition was one of the most difficult wars the IDF has ever fought, especially as far as the individual soldier was concerned. The strongholds were subjected to massive artillery fire. The shells were falling continuously, in unprecedented numbers, sometimes up to two thousand on each position. Those sitting in the bunkers under this barrage of bombs were usually well protected physically, but the emotional stress was enormous. Besides that, even during the shelling, lookouts were placed at exposed positions in the strongholds so that there would be no surprises. Being a lookout was not an easy task, and a lot of the casualties were soldiers who fulfilled this task, as well as field medics and other soldiers who ran out to take care of the wounded.

Entering and leaving the stronghold, in a vehicle and even on foot, was very complicated and risky as well. The same went for patrols along the dike at the Canal. The Egyptians often crossed the canal to our side and ambushed these patrols. We had difficulties catching the small enemy units. It is worth noting that on the northern front of the Canal the patrol road had been built between two bodies of water: the Canal on the west and a large swamp to the east, so that it was impossible to ever go off the road.

Of all the important experiences I had during the War of Attrition the most outstanding for me was to meet with the Tigers. These were experienced reserve officers, with professional training, of the rank of captain or major. These men volunteered to serve as commanding officers of the strongholds for a month or two. There were more than a hundred of them, and their contribution was extraordinary. It is also important to point out that almost no soldiers deserted or went AWOL. The fighters at the Canal demonstrated overall responsibility, loyalty, and dedication. In general, the forces carried out their assignments admirably. Seventeen Egyptian attempts to infiltrate and capture the strongholds were recorded during the war. Every one of them was repelled—thanks to the fighting skill, dedication, professional level, and determination of the soldiers.

In the end the cost in human lives was heavy. This ruthless war left three hundred Israeli soldiers killed and fifteen hundred wounded.

Major General (res.) Shlomo Lahat, the commander of the Sinai Division, later became a mayor of Tel Aviv.

The Dark Shadow of Green Island

Ami Ayalon

by Mike Eldar

"There were a few of us, short guys, in the training course and we decided to call ourselves the Knights of the Ground Floor—perhaps small in size, but the biggest in every other way. When they made us run, they put the same load of sand on everyone's back—they didn't put one gram less on ours. In other words, we went through a harder course, and as a result came out better fighters. That was how we turned a subjectively negative situation—our shortness—into a positive one. And this is actually the essence of the whole survival theory." This is what Amichai "Ami" Ayalon, from Kibbutz Maagan, had to say about his beginnings in a naval commando course. At the end of the course he joined a small group of fighters from the unit who took part in the Six-Day War. The fighters from the squadron participated in a few operations and failed in most of them. Now all of them felt like "knights of the ground floor"—and they looked for a way to turn this negative situation into a positive one.

The War of Attrition gave them new opportunities. During the war it was necessary to cross water barriers—the Suez Canal and the Suez Gulf—and that was definitely the field of expertise of the men in the squadron. Ami and his friends crossed over to the Egyptian side several times either to lay mines or to man boats for the Sayeret Matkal commando fighters, when they went out on ambushes, or on reconnaissance and intelligence-gathering operations. But these activities were not enough for the frogmen. They wanted to do something more daring. They found their opportunities later on in the war.

The line of strongholds along the Suez Canal was not yet fortified properly, and Egyptian shells caused a lot of casualties. The IDF responded with shelling of its own and with deep penetrations into Egyptian territory, in the Nile Valley. But this did not change the situation along the Canal. It was then decided to raid the Egyptian lines. On June 12, 1969, the squadron fighters attacked a guard station at Adabiya from the sea, killed thirty-two enemy soldiers, blew up the facilities, and returned home without a scratch. Their success made the General Command decide to attack another objective.

Green Island, about a quarter of an acre in size, was a fortified structure at the southern entrance to the Suez Canal. According to intelligence information, about seventy soldiers were stationed there. It was defended by six antiaircraft guns, controlled by radar, and machine guns in concrete-fortified positions. On a tower at the northern part of the island was an antiaircraft fire control radar installation, and below that a concrete pier.

On July 9 the Egyptians attacked an Israeli post on the eastern bank of the Suez Canal. They killed seven tank fighters. It was clear to the IDF commanders that they would have to take action once more against the Egyptians and strike them hard. It was decided to destroy the radar and artillery on the island and prove to the Egyptians that the Israeli fighters could beat them in hand-to-hand combat. Forty fighters from the Thirteenth Squadron (also known as Flotilla 13) and from the Sayeret Matkal commando unit were chosen for the mission. They trained for three weeks. The more they learned about the objective, the more they realized that they would have to do things that no one before them had ever done. A company would have to swim and dive with all its battle equipment and then fight in an area that was built up and complicated. To top it all off, the chief of staff informed them on the night of the attack that the success of the mission would be measured by the number of losses they incurred. They knew that they had nowhere to retreat from the island and that the Egyptians were also trapped there. That meant that both sides would have to fight to the bitter end. Their commander, Zeev Almog, reminded them of the lesson the squadron had learned from the Six-Day War—don't come back until you've completed the mission!

They set out on July 19, 1969, the night the *Apollo* spacecraft landed on the moon.

The striking force, which included twenty naval commandos under the command of Dov Bar, sailed in dinghies under the command of Major Shaul Ziv. The force included an attack squad commanded by First Lieutenant Ilan Egozi. First Lieutenant Gadi Krol was in charge of destroying the radar, First Lieutenant Ami Ayalon was supposed to capture the roof of the structure, and First Lieutenant Gil Lavi commanded the guard squad that was supposed to follow and occupy the roof. The second wave, General Staff commandos and reserve fighters of the squadron, were being brought in in boats under the command of First Lieutenant Danny Avinon.

The striking force reached the spot where it was to enter the water at 11:00 P.M. The men began to swim toward the objective. The sea was calm, and there was a gentle breeze. The heavy equipment made things difficult for them, and after an hour Dov realized that because of the currents, the force was not progressing as it should have been. He decided that his men should proceed under water. Half an hour after they dived, they emerged on the surface and discovered that they had been pulled too far south.

Dov reported later:

This was a kind of diving that we had never experienced before, and the currents didn't help either. The orders I gave in sign language under the water did not get to everyone in time, and not everyone understood them. Time was running out, and I was afraid they were going to tell me to turn back, so I didn't let the base know what was happening. Despite the fact that there was a full moon I decided to go back to swimming for the last part until we got close to the objective, and then—dive again. The men were afraid they would be discovered and were opposed to the idea. I shouted at them; I even swore. I said that they had to make the effort. I knew I couldn't bear the shame of not carrying out the mission.

Uzi Livnat and Yossi Zamir were at the head of the line, swimming on their backs and holding the rope that tied all the divers together. Dov swam in front of them with the compass. After half an hour they got to within 150 yards of the island. They dived, Dov in the lead, and everyone else behind him, all connected by two ropes. After about a hundred yards the water became shallow. Dov kept sticking his head out of the water to see what was happening. The last time he did so he found himself beside the tower, and he identified two guards. The attacking squad came to the surface. Dov ordered Ilan to break through the fence that surrounded the island. They reached the rocks and crawled, trying to remain in the shadow of the building. A soldier knocked into an empty tin can, someone giggled, and someone else tried to shut him up. Yossi and Israel Assaf began to cut the fence. Suddenly a light went on, and a guard approached the fence with a flashlight in his hand. Ilan opened fire on him. He covered the rest of the men as they ran inside.

The battle had begun. Ilan received shrapnel wounds in both legs. The Egyptians started shooting flares that illuminated the scene. Three Egyptians were killed, and the squad that was supposed to destroy the radar set out. Israel threw two grenades at the tower, and Gadi wiped out two machine-gunners. Israel shot an RPG (rocket-propelled grenade) at one of the artillery positions. At the same time the rest of the force was preparing to storm the roof of the structure. Yaacov Pundik leaned against the wall. Zalman "Zali" Roth and Ami Ayalon, both of whom were in excellent physical condition, scrambled in turn onto his shoulders and climbed up first. They knew that two antiaircraft positions and a heavy machine gun were located in the section of the roof above them. Ami recalled later:

When I looked up I was hit in the forehead. I threw a smoke grenade to give me some cover, but it didn't go off. I threw an explosive grenade at the position that had fired on me—it didn't go off either. Zali threw an explosive grenade at the next position on the left. I shot off a long burst of gunfire and attacked the position. I was fired upon from another position, and both of us returned the fire. An Egyptian soldier who had been shooting at us with an automatic rifle was hit, and his position caught on fire. Behind us Dov and other soldiers were climbing up to take control of the artillery position. We ran ahead to the roof, and Zali yelled out that his fingers had been cut off. Amos and Didi bandaged his wound, and he continued fighting. I threw a grenade into another position, but it didn't explode either. Then the men who had just mopped the radar position joined us. I thought that together we could destroy the position. We fired continuously, and almost finished the ammunition we had brought with us.

They took the corner of the roof that controlled the pier, and Dov called in the second wave of soldiers. No one answered, so he fired a green flare. Another flare signaled to the holding force to stop shooting. This force, under the command of Captain Paulin, reached a concrete float on a "pig" (a miniature submarine). Their diversionary fire, from two machine guns and a bazooka, was countered with an effective response from the Egyptians. They hid behind the float. Later they returned to the position and continued firing.

The second wave of soldiers was waiting fifteen hundred meters from the objective. A few boats were tied to the float, and other boats were tied to them. When the firing on the island began they were detached and moved to the deployment point. On the way the soldiers saw the flare and picked up speed.

The second wave was delayed, and Dov knew that he shouldn't wait for them in one place. He sent a few soldiers forward. An Egyptian soldier jumped out of a position that had been cleared and threw a grenade. Chaim Shturman and Yoav Shachar were killed on the spot. Yossi killed the soldier and silenced the position with five grenades.

At this point the boats of the second wave had reached the island. In one of them was Brigadier General Rafael "Raful" Eitan, the chief paratroop and infantry officer. They brought with them the empty boats of the first wave. Sayeret Matkal commandos darted to their objectives and Danny Avinon sent Mark, Herz, and Kvashni to the roof, with extra ammunition.

Six commandos reached the positions on the roof that had already been cleared, and were briefed on the situation. At that very moment their commander, Captain Ehud Ram, was hit by a bullet in the forehead, and died on the spot.

Ami Ayalon recalls: "I heard them coming closer, and I told them to get into position. Suddenly a grenade was thrown, there was a huge explosion, and I lost feeling in my right side. A burning object entered my neck, and I thought I was going to choke. I remembered the death rattle of the Egyptians I had heard before. It is something unbearable. Suddenly the same sounds were coming out of my throat. I said to myself, 'They got you too.' This made me very angry. All I felt was anger. Since I was out of ammunition, I retreated to the dinghies, leaning on one of my friends."

At the same time more soldiers advanced toward the source of fire. Israel described the situation: "Dov told us to attack. It was a difficult decision because when we ran to the roof we were like sitting ducks on the horizon. We ran past the first artillery position, then the second, and at the third we were stopped. I tried to shoot an RPG bomb, but it didn't go off. I threw it into the water and tried to put another one in. Then a grenade exploded beside me."

Israel was wounded and lost consciousness for a while. Later he heard the voice of Menachem Digli, the commander of the Sayeret Matkal commandos, booming over a megaphone, calling to the Egyptians to surrender. Another burst of fire hit the ammunition dump, causing a series of explosions. Below in the courtyard the commando fighters continued clearing out the rooms of the buildings. During this action Yuval Miron was killed.

At this stage Almog's boat, which had been held up due to some mechanical problem, reached the island. He went up onto the roof, and Dov explained to him what was happening. After a few minutes he realized that the Egyptian resistance was weakening, and at 2:15 A.M. he reported to the command post on the situation. At 2:25 A.M. it was decided to evacuate the objective even though not all of it had been captured. Shaul Ziv collected all the explosives in the northern hall.

During the evacuation Amnon Sofer and Staff Sergeant Ori Matityahu, Ram's deputy, attacked one more position. The position caught fire, and Almog called them back. Gadi Krol stood at the northwest corner of the roof to cover the evacuation and killed two Egyptians who came around the corner of the building. During the evacuation they realized that two soldiers were missing. The bodies of Danny Vaza and Danny Levi were found, one on the pavement and the other at the water's edge. They must have fallen off the roof after being shot.

Around 3:00 A.M. the island was evacuated, and the boats left for the Israeli base at Ras Sudar in the Sinai, under heavy Egyptian fire. One of the boats was hit while it was still at the pier. Fifteen minutes later the demolition charges exploded on the island. The doctor, Shimon Slavin, hopped from boat to boat, taking care of the wounded. Some of them were evacuated to the shore, and others were put on helicopters. The damaged boat was left behind, and the soldiers who had been in it swam away from the island. They were picked up at dawn, under fire, by two helicopters.

The operation was over. Almost half of the soldiers had been hit, and the senior commanders, who had said that success would be measured by the number of casualties, were in shock. In the debriefing the next morning it was reported that at least thirty-six enemy soldiers had been killed. It was also reported that there had been no radar at the objective, and that the artillery was rusty dummy guns. The Egyptians claimed that the Israelis had fallen into a trap and had been forced to withdraw after suffering heavy losses. An Egyptian military historian claimed later that whatever the results of the operation were, it could not alter a major fact: the raid on Green Island had constituted a turning point in the war. From then on the military initiative in the War of Attrition was in the hands of the Israelis.

The minister of defense, Moshe Dayan, eulogized the soldiers:

> Yesterday at dawn we stood on the shore of the Gulf of Suez. Soldiers came toward
> us, young men who had completed their mission. They had won the battle, and

on their shoulders they bore the price—six dead and eleven wounded. These boys, who live their lives this way, fight this way, and so die, are the most wonderful thing we have in our lives—as parents and as friends—and in the life of Israel as a nation as well. There are simple events that in time turn into legend. Ehud and his friends are a legend that has become a reality. They are the dream of a nation in exile, sorrowful and humiliated, a dream that has become a reality—a reality of independence, of a homeland, of Jerusalem, of the settlement of the mountain and the desert, of planting trees and flowers. But they are also a reality of blood and battles, of bodies carried home on stretchers at dawn. All that is left for us is to embrace them with a love that cannot be expressed in words. Now they lie before us, their blood gone dry, watching us with silent eyes.

That was the end of the story of Green Island—six soldiers died, and six were given citations. After the Yom Kippur War, when the law establishing the awarding of medals was passed, Ami Ayalon was given the Medal of Valor. The Gallantry Medal was awarded to First Lieutenant Gil Lavi. Distinguished Service Medals were given to First Lieutenant Ilan Egozi, Captain Dov Bar, First Lieutenant Gadi Krol, and Staff Sergeant Zalman Roth.

Ami Ayalon escaped from the convalescent home where he had been sent after the battle. He took part in the Escort Campaign, in which two enemy torpedo boats and their crews were blown up. The Israeli force suffered three casualties, another three of Ami's friends. In the Yom Kippur War he fought as the commander of a force of Dabur fast boats, which destroyed an Egyptian guard boat and scores of fishing boats used for transporting commando forces. Eventually, after Ami had become commander of the Thirteenth Squadron, the whole unit received a citation from the chief of staff for its antiterrorist operations, without having suffered any casualties of their own.

"I am more proud," Ami said, "of the citation given to me together with this wonderful group of people for all our work, than I am of the Medal of Valor I received for a personal act, during a short operation that cost so many lives."

Ami recalled the Green Island battle:

During my service in the squadron I have taken part in many campaigns, and I maintain that this action was a landmark as far as proper preparation and execution are concerned. It was clear to us as soldiers that there was no retreating until the island was taken. It was just as clear that the Egyptians had no escape routes. Therefore, we understood that we were going into an action that was, in our terms—"at all costs!" . . . During the action we were in a "do or die" situation, but we went ahead. It is true that we had problems and many casualties. Today we would have done things differently, especially after the lessons we learned on Green

Island. In my opinion, and in the opinion of many who took part in the attack on
Green Island, this operation was our test of manhood as a fighting unit.

Passing this test cost a lot of lives but led to some important achievements. The latter citation from the chief of staff—for the activities of the squadron carried out without casualties and with all wisdom (not "at all costs" . . .) proved that Ami and his friends, who had considered themselves on the "ground floor" after the Six-Day War, had learned their lessons well.

Ami Ayalon later became the commander of the Israeli navy, with the rank of major general. After coming out of uniform at the end of his service, he was once again called to the colors. At the beginning of 1996 he was appointed head of the Shabak, the Israeli Secret Service, and took upon himself the main responsibility for the fight against terrorism.

Colonel (res.) Mike Eldar is a writer.

THE ISRAELI FIGHTER TIPPED THE SCALES

THE YOM KIPPUR WAR

by Ehud Barak

"War will break out today," was the message that arrived around 4:00 a.m. on Yom Kippur 5734 (October 6, 1973). Urgent phone calls woke up Israel's leaders and senior officers, informing them that today, in a few hours, the State of Israel would face a massive attack from the south by Egypt and from the north by Syria; today, before the signal was given for a general call-up of the reserves, the main fighting force of the IDF; today, while the public was relatively complacent, untroubled by the very real possibility that cannons would thunder on the various fronts, that tanks would storm past military positions, and that planes would sow terror from the air; today, without any real time for diplomatic or preventive action; today, by complete surprise, and apparently at a high price.

The price, indeed, was terrible. In the bitter war that ensued, 2,569 Israeli soldiers were killed, more than 7,500 wounded, and over 300 captured. Our deterrent power suffered great damage. Our national morale was broken and undermined. We lost valuable military equipment, and our economy suffered a heavy blow. This price could have been even higher, if the huge waves of attack had not been shattered by the true strength of Israel, if it hadn't become apparent, during the desperate fighting, that the real human factor could muster up the courage and tip the scales even when the starting point had been so critical. This price could have been even higher, if the Israeli fighter hadn't stepped forward to defend his nation and his home, overcome the short-sightedness and poor judgment of the national leadership, prevail over electronic military innovations, and come out of the bloody battle, the frustration, and pain at a distance of 101 kilometers (63 miles) from Cairo and 35 kilometers (22 miles) from Damascus. This Israeli fighter was one of tens of thousands of soldiers sent to the front. He was every citizen that obeyed orders faithfully and took the initiative. He was best represented in the select group of soldiers and officers of all branches of an army that outdid itself, performing valiantly under the most difficult conditions, with courage, wisdom, and self-control.

After the fighting was over and the dead were laid to rest, there was time to examine and consider. In the Yom Kippur War, 269 fighters were found worthy of medals; 167 were awarded the Distinguished Service Medal, 87 Gallantry Medals, and eight the highest decoration of all, the Medal of Valor. Five of those who won the Medal of Valor fought in the Sinai, two took part in the battles on the Golan Heights, and one was from the navy.

The following chapter is devoted to the actions of the eight recipients of the Medal of Valor, two of whom—tank fighters in the Golan—will be described in more detail. The choice of these two was influenced by the geographical location of the battlefield. When they confronted the enemy they did not have the open spaces of the Sinai Desert behind them. They were part of the force that held back the breakthrough of the Syrians right into the Galilee. Their courage was, therefore, different, without diminishing that of their fellow heroes.

On October 6, in the early afternoon, Egypt and Syria attacked Israel simultaneously. Syria's armor swiftly advanced across the Golan, aiming to break through the Israeli defenses and reach the exposed, vulnerable Jordan Valley. From there the road to Haifa and Tel Aviv was open. The Syrian forces included three infantry divisions with 230 tanks each, followed by two armored divisions with 300 tanks each.

According to the plans of the Israeli army, two armored divisions with all their weapons and equipment were supposed to confront these forces, if prior warning had been given in time. But as things turned out, when the war broke out, there was one division only on the Golan Heights. That division was under the command of Brigadier General Rafael "Raful" Eitan. It included two regular armored brigades (with 177 tanks), two infantry battalions, eleven artillery batteries, two engineering companies, and two antiaircraft companies. The armored brigades were the Barak Brigade (under the command of Colonel Yitzhak Ben-Shoham), an organic part of Eitan's division, and the Seventh Brigade (commanded by Colonel Avigdor Ben-Gal), which had been moved up north a few days earlier and was given tanks from another brigade.

When it became clear that the war was starting and that most of the units allocated to the Golan were still far away, the order of OC Northern Command, General Itzhak Hofi, to General Eitan was quite short: Hold back the Syrian advance as long as you can! Eitan, whose headquarters in the Nafach Camp were soon exposed to direct Syrian attack, obeyed the orders to the letter. He retreated from the camp only after several hours, after fierce fighting, and after the Syrians were already inside the fences, or, as he said, "when retreat would no longer have been a shameful act." Before that he had ordered the Barak Brigade to confront the Syrian assault at the outskirts of Rafid, at the southern end of the Golan Heights. The Seventh Brigade was to hold the assault from outside Kuneitra, at the northern end.

The military history of Israel is full of stories of forces that were formed while fighting was in progress, according to the needs of the moment. These forces have usually been given the names of those who commanded them. The division commander was now informed over the transmitter that such a force had been formed in the Barak Brigade. The Zvika Force was named after First Lieutenant (later Colonel) Zvi Greengold, a young native-born Israeli and a member of Kibbutz Lohamei Hagetaot. He acquired his own force because he had had no definite assignment. He had just gone out on a two-week leave before beginning a course for company commanders. On Yom Kippur morning, when he heard about the general call-up all over the country, he hurried to the battalion that he had belonged to before his vacation, willing to take on any available task. At battalion headquarters, which was also in the area of Camp Nafach, Zvika met Lieutenant Colonel David Israeli, the deputy commander of the brigade, heard briefly about the terrible situation that had developed, and was assigned his own personal force. He was given three tanks that were quickly taken out of the repair workshop and was ordered to lead them in a holding action on the pipeline road, a wide dirt road that ran parallel to the oil pipeline of the Tapline Company.

It was one of the longer roads that pass through the center of the Golan Heights. According to the information that Lieutenant Colonel Israeli had received there were already Syrian tanks on the southern part of this road, and they were heading in the direction of Nafach. Zvika was supposed to wait in ambush for those tanks and use various stratagems to block them. The "balance of power"—three tanks in not very good condition as opposed to a large armored force—did not leave room for any other option.

The ambush was set up south of Nafach in the late evening. After a short time Zvika saw the first of the line of Syrian tanks. He fired a shell from close range, and the tank caught on fire. But it was at such close range that the force of the explosion put out the communications system in Zvika's own tank. From his position on the turret Zvika signaled with his hand to the commander of one of the other two tanks to move closer to him. The two of them exchanged tanks, and Zvika ordered the commander of the second tank to follow him and do exactly what he did. Immediately afterward Zvika started moving southward, but after he had gone a few hundred meters he discovered to his surprise and dismay that his force had been reduced to one tank. The two other tanks had remained behind for some reason, and his calls to them over the radio went unanswered. Zvika decided to go off the road and climb a nearby hill. When he got to the top, he saw three Syrian tanks, advancing with full lights on, and he quickly destroyed them, one after the other, before they found out he was on his own.

He then rushed to a different position to one side of the pipeline road and got ready for another attack, assuming that it was soon to come. Within half an hour a long convoy of Syrian tanks suddenly appeared. He counted close to thirty vehicles, tanks and trucks. He noted that they were traveling "as if in a parade," and waited until they were well within range. In his situation, he thought, there was no room for error. He destroyed the first tank in the line from a distance of twenty meters. Immediately after shooting Zvika changed his position, moved forward, and shot at another tank in the line, and he continued like this. After he had destroyed ten more tanks in this way, the Syrians assumed that they had encountered a large Israeli force, and they quickly retreated. In the meantime, reserve units as well as tank transporters began to arrive at Nafach. The first seven tanks were put under the command of First Lieutenant Uzi Mor, who went south; and Zvika, who had managed to renew contact with his two other tanks, was ordered to join that force. After they met the ten tanks turned south—Mor on the pipeline road, and Zvika, in parallel, along the pipeline itself. Suddenly all ten tanks fell into a Syrian ambush. They were subjected to heavy fire from both east and west, in a narrow area in which it was hard to maneuver.

The crews fought valiantly. They managed to hold the Syrians on the pipeline road for a few more hours. But in the early hours of the morning all of Uzi Mor's tanks had been hit, and in his turret he himself had been struck by a bazooka, which resulted in his going blind and losing his left hand. Zvika's three tanks at first managed to pull back, but after a few minutes they also entered the range of Syrian artillery and went up in flames. At the last minute Zvika and his crew jumped out of their tank and rolled into a ditch at the side of the road, while putting out the flames on their clothes.

While rolling into the ditch and fighting the fire, Zvika noticed three Israeli tanks that had somehow reached the area and were undamaged. He jumped onto the turret of the closest tank and saw that its commander was of a lower rank than he. He sent him to evacuate the wounded from the forces of Uzi Mor, and he himself took command of the tank. He quickly announced on the brigade communications network that the Zvika Force was still in action. The calm voice of the brigade commander, Colonel Ben-Shoham, congratulated him on his announcement. His voice was like a shot of adrenaline for Zvika. The burns he had suffered not long before, despite his efforts to smother the flames, had suddenly made him feel weak, and he had fainted for a minute. He probably wouldn't have pulled himself out of it if it hadn't been for the commander's words.

He woke up just in time, for in front of him stood two menacing Syrian tanks. He shot at the first, ordered the driver to move aside, and immediately shot at the second. He then managed to find the tank of the deputy brigade commander, Lieutenant Colonel David Israeli, and continued fighting at his side. Part of the time he was busy covering for the commander's tank, and served as a relay station between the commander and the other tanks in the brigade. Between giving orders to his men, Ben-Shoham himself had managed to destroy five Syrian tanks and a few armored personnel carriers. When communication broke down between him and his deputy, he hoped that it was only a technical problem. He didn't know that David Israeli had run out of shells and that all he had left against the Syrian tanks was a machine gun. In the end his tank was hit, and he was killed. Ben-Shoham was also killed a few hours later by a burst of machine-gun fire aimed at him from a damaged Syrian tank.

When Zvika discovered that David Israeli had been killed and his tank totally destroyed, he decided not to continue on the pipeline road but return to Nafach. He turned back and cut across toward the camp, without knowing that the war had already reached him. But he soon became aware of the fact. He saw more and more Syrian vehicles in the area, and shot at them as best he could. Near Nafach he saw a lone Israeli tank that didn't belong to the Barak Brigade. He didn't have time for niceties. The two tanks became a coordinated combat team that shot in all directions and soon joined the efforts to save Nafach. Zvika's tank driver had gone into shock and was unable to respond to his commands. But that new calamity did not delay him long. As if out of nowhere a new driver appeared, took the wheel, and drove Zvika wherever necessary.

On Sunday afternoon, October 7, a small group of Israeli soldiers was left at the back of the Nafach camp. With only bazookas left, they confronted the Syrian tanks trying to break through what was left of the fences. Suddenly an Israeli tank rushed forward, opened heavy fire on the last Syrian tank, and silenced it. That was Zvika's tank. The other tanks that followed after him put an end to the Syrian assault on the camp. Zvika then told his new driver to stop. Somehow he got out of his tank, collapsed into the arms of the brigade intelligence officer (the only soldier left from the command post of the Barak Brigade), and was taken to the hospital. After a week, he left—or more correctly, escaped from—the hospital and returned to the fighting on the Golan Heights.

"By standing firm," said the scroll that came with his medal, "by showing supreme bravery, he delayed and prevented the Syrian advance toward the Jordan River."

Battalion 77 was the first battalion of the Seventh Brigade to be sent up to the Golan Heights. Its commander was Lieutenant Colonel (later Brigadier General) Avigdor Kahalani, who had won the Distinguished Service Medal for his feats in the Six-Day War. On Sunday morning, October 7, the brigade commander, Colonel Avigdor Ben-Gal, stationed this battalion in the center of the brigade's designated sector, facing a valley, north of Kuneitra, that was later to be called the "valley of tears." Throughout the previous night this valley had been full of burning bodies and smoke from Syrian tanks, trucks, and armored trucks. It seemed blocked. But now, under heavy artillery fire, the Syrians managed to open up a new way through it and get into very close range of the Israeli tanks. All the forces of the Seventh Brigade, after the first day of fighting, consisted of forty-five Centurion tanks (out of 102 tanks that were in the brigade when the battles started). They were continually maneuvering around the five hundred Syrian tanks. What was even worse, the Syrians had Soviet infrared sights, which gave them a distinct advantage at night.

The tank battle that began on Sunday morning continued until 1:00 the next morning. In this battle 130 Syrian tanks and scores of armored carriers were destroyed, whereas the Seventh Brigade succeeded in holding on to forty functioning tanks. A lot of credit for this goes to the great resourcefulness of the ordnance unit. The fighting was renewed on the morning of October 8 and continued full force throughout the whole day. Besides the heavy fire there was also the problem of physical exhaustion. The tank operators, involved in intense and dangerous combat for sixty hours, had barely had a chance to eat or sleep. They were clearly becoming less and less effective. On the evening of October 8 heavy Syrian artillery fire was added to all this, which hit many of the Israeli tank commanders who as always, rode into battle exposed in their turrets.

Under these circumstances brigade commander Ben-Gal had no choice but to order most of the tanks to retreat beyond the range of the Syrian artillery. At the same time he instructed Kahalani to be on the alert with the six tanks he had left. When the cloud of smoke from the Israeli retreat had lifted, Kahalani's force rushed into the former Israeli positions. They found Syrian tanks there, and destroyed four of them in ninety seconds. The rest of the Syrian tanks retreated. Ben-Gal took full advantage of the momentum that Kahalani's force created. The Seventh Brigade moved in after the six tanks and took a high spot above the "valley of tears." Kahalani himself held the upper part of the slope of Tel Hermonit, higher than any other force in the field. Ben-Gal then learned that one of his three battalions had lost a lot of men, including its commander. He put what was left of this battalion under Kahalani's command. Immediately afterward, he told him: "Assad's force is facing you." Kahalani knew that Assad's force was the Syrian elite armored unit commanded by Rifaat Assad, the brother of the Syrian president. This didn't seem to faze him. "I am a black panther," he answered the brigade commander, referring to his Yemenite origin. "They won't get past me."

Actually, Kahalani was addressing those words to his soldiers, who were listening to the battalion radio communications. He was afraid that their spirits had fallen after all they had been through and after seeing more Syrian tanks moving around the area. He decided that he had to use psychological tactics. Later he said that at first "they didn't hear me, or understand me." But he couldn't give up, and continued his passionate rhetoric: "Look how bravely the enemy has moved up to the positions facing us," he shouted. "I don't understand what's happening to us. After all, we're stronger than they are! Start moving forward and keep in line with me."

By the time Kahalani's weary soldiers absorbed what he was saying, he had managed to urge the brigade commander to send reinforcements. He was told that the state of the brigade was the same as that of Battalion 77. There were no reinforcements available, but the brigade commander said he would pass his request on to the division. At division headquarters the request was received by Brigadier General Eitan, who understood the seriousness of the situation but kept his head. "Tell Kahalani," he answered Ben-Gal, "that he should hold on for a few more minutes. Things will be OK." He didn't want to say over the radio that in the meantime he had managed to organize a force of eleven tanks and send it onto the battlefield. Kahalani, who didn't know about the reinforcements, kept encouraging his soldiers, while maneuvering his tank around and shooting at the Syrians. The six tanks he had left held off all the Syrian attempts to take control of the foot of Tel Hermonit below them. They held on for a few minutes, a few minutes more, and a few minutes more, and then the reinforcements did arrive.

Considering their superior topographical position Kahalani felt that they, along with the reinforcements, could now fire heavily on the Syrian tanks crowded below them. Finally, they could turn this valley into a "valley of tears" for the enemy. A few hours later the tanks of the Seventh Brigade—now only thirty-two in number—could move forward and take the positions that controlled the former 1967 cease-fire line. When dawn broke on October 10, the brigade held the same positions that had been deserted in the middle of the night of October 7 after a Syrian night attack. The division commander soon explained to Ben-Gal, Kahalani, and all the other officers that were still on their feet: "In situations that are considered difficult and serious after the fact, there is one simple rule: The difficulties you're facing are the same as those facing the enemy. The important question is: Who can cause more difficulties to the other, and who can overcome more difficulties?"

In this case the answer to this important question was given in the scroll that came with the Medal of Valor awarded to Kahalani, on which was written:

> Lieutenant Colonel Kahalani, with his leadership ability and personality, served as a personal example to his soldiers, who were close to the breaking point. He attacked the Syrian enemy first, along with one of his subordinate officers. The rest of the force followed after him and managed to recapture the positions under Syrian control, which were key positions for the whole area. After recapturing these positions, they destroyed the Syrian force—which included dozens of tanks—and the last assault on the Golan Heights was halted. He thus prevented the Syrians from breaking through the front in the northern theater of the Golan Heights. Lieutenant Colonel Kahalani displayed admirable leadership qualities and personal courage in this difficult and complicated battle, the results of which changed the face of the campaign on the Golan Heights.

At the very same time, acts of heroism were also being carried out in the far south, on the way to the Suez Canal.

On October 6, huge units of the Egyptian army, which had been deployed along the western bank of the Suez Canal, purportedly for "maneuvers," suddenly attacked the few hundred Israelis who held the line of strongholds, known as the Bar-Lev Line. With the support of heavy artillery fire, tanks, and aircraft, the Egyptians crossed the canal on boats and launches, and rapidly built pontoon bridges. In a few hours they had succeeded in crossing the Canal at many points, bypassing or surrounding most of the strongholds, and pushing forward, toward the vast sand plains of the Sinai Peninsula, the buffer between Egypt and the unprotected territory of Israel.

Staff Sergeant Shlomo Arman was at the Oracle stronghold when the Egyptian attack began on three strongholds in a row at the northern end of the Bar-Lev Line. He was a sergeant in a tank platoon stationed in these positions. The force included three tanks and half-tracks. As soon as the bombardment of the Oracle area began the platoon commander was killed, and Shlomo Arman took command. The next day the Egyptians, who had crossed the Canal, managed to conquer Oracle C and to take some of its soldiers prisoner. Until then, as well as afterward, Shlomo Arman operated his tanks both inside the position and out, trying to hold back the Egyptian attack from even the closest range. At 5:00 P.M. on October 7 the soldiers in the position had decided to retreat. Shlomo Arman's tank stood at the head of the retreating force. From his position in the turret he effectively prevented the Egyptian soldiers from blocking his soldiers' way. He fired at them with his own weapon, threw grenades, and shot the tank's gun at close range. The assault was successful, and the force, under Arman's command, continued to move with its two tanks and a half-track toward the Israeli lines. They encountered two ambushes on the way, which they overpowered. But a third ambush was awaiting them, and Arman's tank was hit. Many were killed in this ambush, and a few were taken prisoner. Shlomo Arman managed to organize his crew and lead them out on foot to a safe place. They walked through marshes for fifteen kilometers. Arman continued, encouraging them all along the way, serving as an exemplary model of courage and perseverance. He was carrying on his shoulders a wounded soldier he had picked up along the way. But his luck did not hold. At dawn on October 8, close to an Israeli position, an Israeli force failed to identify this short line of men approaching from the Egyptian lines, and opened fire on them. Arman, the brave, resourceful soldier, was killed just as he was about to complete his mission.

"By these deeds," said his Medal of Valor scroll, "he demonstrated military comradeship, courage, resourcefulness, and heroism at great risk to himself."

While Arman was leading his men through the marshes, another hero was fighting his private war not very far from him. On the first day of the war Yuval Neria was the deputy commander of a tank company that fought on the northern front of the Suez Canal, near Kantara. He, therefore, had to face the first wave of the Egyptian attack. Yuval soon discovered that most of the tanks in his company had been hit, but he didn't lose heart. He continued to fight in his tank, until it was hit. He made great efforts to rescue the wounded and tanks from the field. The next day, after he was left without a tank or a crew, he gathered together three officers from his company who were in a similar situation, and the four of them manned a tank under his command. A day later a fifth member joined the crew—the operations officer of the battalion. Yuval Neria gave over command of the tank to him. This tank immediately afterward joined a brigade from the division of General Avraham Adan. They took part in the counterattack in the area of Firdan, thirty kilometers south of Kantara. During the attack, which failed in the end, Yuval Neria noticed a tank whose commander had been wounded. He moved over to that tank and commanded it until the end of the attack.

After a few hours at the rear Yuval Neria organized a kind of private force—three tanks that had been separated from their original units—and at the head of this force he joined the battle of another unit. During the fighting four more tanks joined him, and he became the commander of a company in a new unit. Neria fought with this company for the next few days until October 14, when he found himself part of a counterattack on an Egyptian division. During the battle he managed to destroy several tanks. The following night he led his company in the area of the Chinese Farm, a former experimental farm on the eastern bank of the Suez Canal, that became the theater of one of the bloodiest battles in the Yom Kippur War. When Neria's tank was hit, he joined another tank as a crew member, and then another tank as a commander, and continued fighting. On October 18 he appropriated a tank for himself so he could take part in the brigade attack north of the Chinese Farm. During that battle he was seriously wounded, and was taken to the rear.

The medal was awarded to him for his "courage, leadership ability, and limitless fighting spirit during twelve days of continuous fighting."

Moshe Levi also fought on the bank of the Suez Canal. A sergeant in an armored infantry platoon, he was the commander of a half-track in a battle against an Egyptian ambush on the Sea Road that led to the Budapest stronghold. In the heat of the battle his vehicle was hit, and an antitank shell cut off his right arm at the elbow. He realized the seriousness of the situation and ordered his soldiers to get out of the half-track. He got out with them, and, despite his serious wound, grabbed a grenade in his left hand, pulled out the pin with his teeth, and threw it at the position that had fired on them. The position was silenced. Moshe Levi himself was wounded by shrapnel from the grenade because he had been very close to the position. Nevertheless, he asked the evacuation team to first take care of the other wounded soldiers. "By these deeds," said the scroll that accompanied his medal, "he demonstrated supreme courage at the risk of his life, self-control, and perseverance."

Captain Gideon Giladi began his army service as a paratrooper, but moved over to the armored corps, hoping to take the place of his brother Amnon, who had been killed commanding a tank company in the Six-Day War. After a few days of strenuous containment battles against the Egyptians, the IDF regained control. On the night of October 15, Giladi participated in an operation that was to open a road to the Suez Canal for Israel forces, amidst large Egyptian units. Gideon's company was ordered to break through the Tirtur Road, between the north part of Great Bitter Lake and the large military base of Refidim, from a westerly direction. During the action the force suffered many losses, including some of Giladi's tank crew. Giladi went on to command another tank. In the end there were only two tanks left in working order with which Giladi broke through the enemy resistance and cleared the road in the area assigned to him. These tanks were also hit, and Gideon Giladi was killed. But the road was open, and a paratroop force passed through, crossed the Suez canal in dinghies, and established the Israeli bridgehead on Egyptian territory. That was to be the turning point in the battle with Egypt.

"By these deeds," Gideon Giladi's scroll read, "he showed perseverance, exemplary leadership ability, courage, and supreme heroism."

The paratroopers who set up the bridgehead immediately encountered fierce Egyptian resistance. On October 17 Captain Asa Kadmoni commanded a detail of reserve paratroopers which had been separated from their battalion headquarters. They had been trapped in Serapeum, west of the Suez Canal, inside the fortified compound of an Egyptian battalion. One of his soldiers was killed and another wounded. Kadmoni fought a lone battle that went on for four hours straight against a large Egyptian force. He even managed to destroy two trucks full of Egyptian soldiers. His superiors found that his "courage, perseverance, and supreme heroism at the risk of his life" made him worthy of the Medal of Valor.

Among the heroes of the Yom Kippur War there was also the man of silence, whose name and deeds could not be publicized for a long time. Captain Oded Amir, says the scroll that came with his medal, commanded "a force of divers who entered Port Said and destroyed three enemy warships, even though the port was well protected, including a patrol force and depth charges in the waters of the port." He completed his entire mission, according to the scroll, "demonstrating perseverance and supreme courage at the risk of his life."

Captain Oded Amir did not return from this mission.

The end of the Yom Kippur War, which Israel won against all odds, was also the beginning of the process of negotiations that led toward peace with Egypt. The heroes of the Yom Kippur War, the living and the dead, saved their country and laid the foundations to a new reality of peace with Egypt, the strongest nation in the Arab world.

Lieutenant General (res.) Ehud Barak, Knesset member and head of the Labor Party, is a former foreign minister of Israel.

PART VII

THE WAR AGAINST TERRORISM AND THE FIRST STIRRINGS OF PEACE

1973–1998

In the aftermath of the Yom Kippur War, bitter public opinion forced Golda Meir to resign. With her, most of the senior ministers left the government. Moshe Dayan, Abba Eban, and Pinchas Sapir were no longer part of the new cabinet formed by Itzhak Rabin, recently back from a tour of duty as Israel's ambassador to Washington. Shimon Peres became the minister of defense.

The two men were rivals and disliked each other. They cooperated, though, in rebuilding Israel's strength after the war and carrying out the disengagement agreements with Egypt and Syria, by which Israel accepted to retreat partially on the Golan and Sinai in exchange for security arrangements with her enemies. The war against terrorism became the main concern of Israel now. Israel had to face hijackings, hostage-taking, cruel massacres of civilians, and bombings. The war against the terrorists culminated with the Entebbe operation, a daring coup by which Israeli commandos liberated more than a hundred hostages, captured in an Air France hijacked plane by Arab and German terrorists, and taken to the distant capital of Uganda.

In 1977 another dramatic change occurred, which was an aftershock of the Yom Kippur War, combined with widespread criticism of corruption in the top echelons of the ruling Labor Party. The Likud block, led by Menachem Begin, defeated the Labor Party and won the elections for the first time since Israel was created. It was a political earthquake of unprecedented magnitude.

Begin made Ezer Weizmann minister of defense, and surprised everybody by making Moshe Dayan, now a Labor Party Member of Knesset, minister of foreign affairs. Although known as a hardliner, Begin was ready to talk peace. A few months after his inauguration, he welcomed to Israel President Sadat of Egypt, who addressed the Knesset and offered to make peace with Israel. The peace treaty was signed in 1979, under the auspices of U.S. president Jimmy Carter. Israel gave back to Egypt the entire Sinai Peninsula in exchange for peace.

In 1981, in a much-acclaimed operation, Israeli jets attacked and destroyed an Iraqi reactor at Osiraq, to prevent the Baghdad government from achieving nuclear capability. The following year, after winning another election, Begin's government launched the controversial War of Lebanon, known as Operation Peace for Galilee. It was presented at first as an operation against the PLO terrorists in South Lebanon, limited in scope and in time. It became the longest war in Israel's history, causing more than six hundred Israeli casualties, and raising questions about its necessity. In August of 1982 it seemed that Israel had won after all, when the Syrian army and Yassir Arafat were forced to leave Beirut. But soon after, Christian militias massacred hundreds of Palestinians in the refugee camps of Sabra and Shatila in Beirut. An Israeli board of inquiry ruled that Defense Minister Ariel Sharon should resign his position. Menachem Begin, apparently broken by the number of Israeli casualties in Lebanon, resigned the following year. Itzhak Shamir was the new prime minister.

The results of the 1984 elections were inconclusive. A National Unity government was established, with Shamir and Peres alternating as prime minister. When Peres was prime minister he ended the Lebanon War and brought the army back home, except for a security zone Israel kept in South Lebanon.

In 1992 Itzhak Rabin, who succeeded Peres as the head of the Labor Party, won the elections and became prime minister. Peres and Rabin initiated peace talks with the leaders of the PLO, in Oslo, the capital of Norway. The consequent peace agreement was signed in September 1993, at the White House. The following year a peace treaty was reached with a longtime secret friend—King Hussein of Jordan.

The peace process was marred, though, by a cruel terrorist campaign, waged by the Islamic fundamentalist groups Hamas and the Islamic Jihad. Fanatical suicide bombers blew themselves up in buses and crowded streets in Tel Aviv and Jerusalem, and the casualties were heavy. Several Israeli soldiers were kidnapped and murdered. The failure of the Israeli authorities to halt the bombings stirred unrest and skepticism toward the peace process.

In November 1995, Itzhak Rabin himself was assassinated by a right-wing fanatic. The murder stunned the Israeli society and the supporters of the peace process throughout the world. But at the general election that followed, six months later, Rabin's successor, Shimon Peres, was defeated by Benjamin Netanyahu, the new leader of the Likud Party. Netanyahu declared he would stick to the peace process, and strive to achieve peace with all of Israel's neighbors.

In September 1997, Israel published its annual statistical report. Its dry figures indicated that during the last few years, a huge wave of immigration had arrived in Eretz Israel. Out of 4.6 million Jews (in a total population of 5.7 million), 850,000—almost twenty percent—came from the former Soviet Union. The Jewish communities of Ethiopia, Yemen, and Syria had been rescued and brought to Israel. For the first time in history, all the Jews throughout the world were free to depart from the countries where they lived, and immigrate to Israel.

The Jewish State was now strong and secure. It was said to possess a secret nuclear striking force. That ruled out most of the plans of its neighbors to destroy it, and accounted for their choosing to make peace with Israel.

In its fifty years of existence Israel had become a safe haven for all the oppressed and persecuted Jews in the world, fulfilling Herzl's dream of a hundred years before; of that night when, writing the words "The Jewish State," he had felt the wings of history flap above his head.

THE BEARER OF THE SHEAVES

YONI NETANYAHU

by Shimon Peres

In the dead of night, a week before the operation, I met Yoni at a military camp near Lod Airport (today Ben-Gurion Airport). I was the minister of defense, and this was at the end of June 1976, immediately after the first news had arrived about the hijacking of an Air France plane by terrorists. The airliner had been on its way from Israel to France and had been hijacked after a stopover in Athens. The first reports said that the hijacked aircraft had turned eastward toward our area. We immediately called out a special unit, which would storm the plane if it landed in Lod, and free the hostages.

Yoni was the head of this unit. I watched Yoni and his men while they were training for the attack. There was a special atmosphere among this group of soldiers. The officers briefed their men, weighing every word that came out of their mouths. On the wall were diagrams of different planes, since it was not yet clear which kind of plane had been hijacked. On the side stood models of ladders. Everything looked well thought out, organized, disciplined, so military. Except maybe for the boys themselves. With their rebellious kibbutz-style curly hair, they looked so young, so serious, men who knew what awaited them and who were prepared, bravely knowing full well what might happen. In the darkness one couldn't see the insignia on their shoulders. But that wasn't necessary. One could easily distinguish the natural leaders, each man in his place, each man with his degree of responsibility.

Yoni was the coordinator of the camp. He was a young man, who stood erect, and didn't talk much. He had a curly head of hair, a pleasant face, and a personality that inspired trust and radiated charm. All questions and comments were directed toward him, and it was to him that messengers brought news, suggestions, new maps, information about the possible behavior of the terrorists. I asked him what he thought was preferable—to attack the plane the moment it arrived or to let it land, start negotiations with the terrorists, and only afterward decide on a plan of action.

Yoni thought for a moment. "It is better to attack immediately," he finally answered. "There is the same risk in an immediate or delayed attack, but if we attack immediately we have the advantage of the element of surprise. This way we have more of a chance of saving lives."

While we were talking the news arrived that the plane was flying in an easterly direction but had turned south toward Africa. Now that the tension had let up a bit, I couldn't help asking Yoni if he was familiar with the poetry of Natan Alterman (considered the Israeli national poet). Alterman and Edgar Allan Poe were his two favorite poets, he answered immediately. His favorite book was *The City of the Dove* by Alterman.

Yoni had been appointed head of the unit a year earlier. This appointment requires serious deliberation, both on the part of the General Staff and of the soldiers and their officers. The commander chosen is responsible for very daring acts, which are sometimes dangerous. The morale and the skill of such a unit are to a large extent dependent on the commander. His character, his courage, his resourcefulness, and his leadership ability are constantly being tested. Thus, before making such an appointment, the general staff not only asks the opinion of the candidate's senior officers, but also of his future soldiers. Yoni was a natural choice, an appointment undisputed both by those above him and by those below him. He had already proved himself in actual battles to be a man of rare courage, resourcefulness, and unusual wisdom.

There are two kinds of reports given on soldiers and officers, one through the hierarchic channels of the army, and one an unofficial report that circulates among the men. The official report determines the rank of the man; the unofficial one determines his status. In unofficial circles the Netanyahu family had already become a kind of legend—three brothers, who fought like lions, and had accomplished a lot both in their army service and in their civilian life. Their fame had spread even before the reports on them. And Yoni was the oldest, a fearless officer. (His brother Benjamin was to become prime minister of Israel.)

His path in the IDF had been that of a fighter and officer in the paratroopers and the elite units. He had been wounded in the Six-Day War, participated in secret operations, and had been awarded the Medal of Valor in the Yom Kippur War for his bravery in fighting the Syrians. He had been out of the army for a while, and he studied at Harvard University in the United States and at Hebrew University in Jerusalem. It seemed that the highest ranks of command were open to him. His character was imbued not only with the magic of heroism but also with the charm of poetry and philosophy.

The first task of a commander of an elite unit in the IDF—at times a crucial one—is to choose his men. The real heart of such a unit is its men, each one individually and all of them together. If a commander chooses good men he begins well. Since the unit is a very prestigious one it attracts the best soldiers. A commander must choose the one in ten or twenty volunteers who is the best of all.

The unit is based on humility, which has to do with the nature of its activity, and on modesty, which reflects the character of its men. Woe to the one who speaks an unnecessary word or displays even a hint of bravado. Yoni insisted on this. He used to say to his men, "I believe that the danger in the life of the unit is to allow ourselves to become smug. I would like the men in the battalion to always feel a bit worried that there is something else we could have done, that we could have improved on."

"During the period of over a year that I have been in charge of the battalion," said Yoni to his men, "I have seen you grow and mature, I have gladly seen the formation of a healthy framework of regular soldiers in the battalion, both NCOs and officers. I have seen the battalion progress from week to week and not stagnate. I have seen you, soldiers and officers, achieve good results, but always wanting to do better . . ."

The operations his unit carried out demanded both secret and broad knowledge. About this Yoni said, "I believe that we must pay special attention to detail. Whoever does not do this and tries to save himself work, in the end will miss the main objective—preparing the unit for war."

The officers in Yoni's battalion studied their maps as their forefathers had studied Gemara. Every contour of land, every hidden channel was checked with great care, clarified, explained, and debated, to discover any concealed wrinkle, any unfamiliar aspect, any possibility that might be unmarked.

Daytime was for the self-indulgent. For these fighters their field of vision and activity was at night. Pleasant weather was not a trustworthy ally. The battalion knew how to function on a rainy day, on a stormy sea, during a windstorm. Its fighting power came to a large extent from the great demands the men made on themselves: exhausting training, spare use of water and food, long patrols, and marches under difficult weather conditions with heavy equipment on one's back—and each time the effort to achieve better results.

"I believe," said Yoni to his men, "that one can't compromise when it comes to results. In the battalion, don't ever make do with a result that is not the best one possible—and even that must be improved upon, perfected."

When all the details of the plan have been well worked out, and it is ready to be carried out, when the soldiers are already properly trained, it is still up to the heads of the unit, and first and foremost its commander, to convince their superiors that it is worth doing and has a chance to succeed.

Yoni could always be trusted in this respect. By nature he was a man of truth, meticulous about the truth, but at the same time he was inventive and had the ability to surprise. He knew how to explain things clearly without exaggerating or oversimplifying. He had a well-thought-out, realistic approach, but a lot of imagination as well. Yoni had the full trust of both his soldiers and his officers.

Yoni was asked to lead his men in one of the IDF's most crucial and dangerous missions—Operation Entebbe.

Entebbe was a name that few people in the country had heard of before that mad day when terrorists hijacked the Air France plane, but it soon was to become a symbol in Israel and in the whole world. Entebbe was the capital of Uganda, the country of Idi Amin, one of the cruelest dictators in Africa. In the past he had been a friend of Israel and had even trained here. But in the last few years he had turned into a fanatic; he ruled his nation with an iron fist, and had become the ally of Libya and the terrorists. The group that hijacked the passenger plane found safe refuge in his country. The hijacked Air France plane flew deep into the African continent and landed at the Entebbe airport. The hostages were held under the guard of the terrorists and soldiers from Idi Amin's army. They were held hostage while the terrorist leaders tried to extort large concessions from the State of Israel in exchange for their lives.

In theory, we had no choice. Entebbe was four thousand kilometers (2,500 miles) away from Israel. In theory, there was no military option of saving the hostages. In theory, the terrorists could walk around the airport safely and complacently. Israel could not reach them there under the protection of Amin.

But only in theory. The Israeli government decided to do the impossible, and initiated a daring operation to free the hostages. It was decided to send an airborne task force to Entebbe that would land at the airport, break into the building where the hostages were being held, release them, and bring them back to Israel. The operation was entrusted to Yoni.

The boys trained day and night in the short time given them under Yoni's guidance. A model of the Entebbe airport was built, and every detail of it was learned by heart. Every square mile of the map of Africa on the route to Entebbe was examined diligently. The weather all along the route was checked, as were the range of the radar screens and the most efficient flight plans. The seats in the planes were assigned, the weapons and vehicles were chosen, and the order of the attack was decided upon—which vehicle would go first, which officer would be first in line, who would bring up the rear. An excellent medical team was organized, and stopovers were chosen in case there were problems. An escape route for the hostages was outlined. The whole operation was worked out down to the minute, from landing to takeoff. Close cooperation was established with the air force. The daring and resourcefulness of the pilots could determine the fate of the mission.

On Friday, a day before the operation, we learned that Idi Amin, who had been outside the country, was about to return on Saturday night, perhaps at the same time that the operation was to begin. The boys decided to create their own Idi Amin.

"Our" Idi Amin, it was decided, would travel in a Mercedes, which was to be brought from home. The Ugandan leader liked to travel in the newest, most expensive Mercedes limos. A check on the computer revealed which Mercedes cars could be found in Israel. A vehicle was found that was similar to that of the Ugandan president, but it was light-colored, whereas Idi Amin had a penchant for dark cars. Yoni and his men got hold of the car, and on the last day before the operation they managed to paint it black and dry it. Everything was planned down to the last detail, including unloading the black Mercedes at the airport. Inside the Mercedes there would be an Israeli soldier posing as Idi Amin. This was meant to increase the element of surprise and confusion among the Ugandans and the terrorists. The idea and its implementation were typical of the unit and of its commander. One of their standing rules was that their skill should not be less than their daring, so they wouldn't have to rely so much on luck.

Saturday, July 3, 1976. The government met in the morning. The decision was made within a short time, considering the general state of mind of the ministers throughout the week. During the many discussions held on how to free the hostages, it seemed that there was a willingness to exchange the hostages for PLO prisoners held in Israel. The members of the general staff and I worked hard that week to find a way to free the hostages ourselves. We knew that the right decisions had to be made, but more than that we knew that we needed the right men, men on whom the fate of the operation would depend.

The meeting ended with the decision to approve the daring operation, which would be assigned to Yoni and his men.

We went to the base from which the forces would leave for the operation. I was very tense, but at the same time I was excited, and confident that this wonderful group of men would succeed in carrying out their mission. The chief of staff and his officers and I, as minister of defense, stood on the runway. We took our leave of the unit that was taking off toward an objective thousands of miles away to face the unknown. The boys, armed from head to foot, began to climb the ramps of the enormous Hercules planes, whose motors were already roaring. They were in good spirits, and you could see that they were aware of the significance of the mission and the difficulties of the tests that awaited them. We shook hands with the officers. "Don't worry," they kept telling us, and they walked vigorously toward the plane. When they reached the ladder they turned back, waved good-bye, and were swallowed up into the belly of the giant bird. The planes took off, one after the other.

The tension was at its height. During the day there was no radio contact. It was decided that the silence would be broken only if there was a problem, or, heaven forbid, a catastrophe. So we were happy for every minute of silence. Time crawled by. At seven in the evening, two minutes after the designated time, the radios came on. In his familiar, matter-of-fact-tone Major General Dan Shomron, head of the operation, announced laconically: "We have landed. Don't worry. If anything goes wrong, I'll let you know."

When the mission was completed—one of the most daring missions in military history—another message came: "We have a casualty."

There was absolute silence in the room. For reasons of security, and perhaps because of the terror in our hearts, no one dared to ask who had been hit and what his condition was. There were also two major generals in the room whose sons were taking part in this terribly dangerous mission. The expressions on their faces did not change. At a time like this they were all our sons, and we were all their fathers. At three in the morning Motta Gur entered the chief of staff's rooms and said, "It's Yoni!"

We had not talked about or guessed who had been hurt when we heard the news over the radio, but our hearts told us that beneath the hidden tremor in the voice that spoke was concealed a very precious name.

Motta's throat tightened, as did mine. There was nothing to add. The name "Yoni" said it all. "Yoni—a constant battle against sleep, fatigue, self-indulgence, forgetfulness, inefficiency, helplessness, lying," was how one of his friends described him. "Yoni turns the impossible into the possible."

Later we found out the details of the operation. It had begun two minutes late and finished four minutes early. The surprise was total. Our boys broke into the buildings where the hostages were being kept. The passengers and crew were saved. The terrorists, Arab and German, were killed. Within a few minutes the hostages were put on our planes which took off on their way to freedom. Idi Amin, who wanted to perform a grandiose show before world public opinion, lost the game this time and came out looking ridiculous and pathetic. And Yoni? He had been at the head of the attack force at Entebbe, his friends told us. While leading his men at the airport he was hit by a bullet in the heart.

At four in the morning on July 4 the planes landed in Israel, one after the other, bringing the hostages back from Entebbe. In the United States there was great rejoicing at the success of the mission on American Independence Day. The world was flabbergasted at the description of this unimaginable mission.

We went to the military airport in the south to welcome the soldiers and the released hostages. The first person to get off was Yoni's second-in-command, who had taken charge as soon as his commander fell. He immediately gave a short command: First—Yoni, and after him the paratrooper who had been seriously wounded.

When he was asked how it happened, he answered, "He went first, and fell first." Engraved in my mind that night was the thought that he had trained at the head of his soldiers for the rescue mission. But Yoni's memory is not connected to one operation, not even to one generation. His name has gone beyond the chronicles of the battlefield, to a chapter in the history books.

During his lifetime he was a fighter with a great reputation. His name was a synonym for courage, leadership ability, love of our country, knowledge of our country; a synonym too for human curiosity that went beyond the moment, and for reaching beyond the known.

After his death his name became a concept, a concept that describes how geographic distance can be overcome by human intelligence, how reason can be combined with determination, how foresight can be translated into the willingness of an officer to expose his chest to the bullets flying around him. It is a concept that gives way to wonder—part of the reality of our lives.

Yoni symbolized in his life and battles the preparedness of the army and its high standard. He excelled at both, in the overall war and in the war against terror. He proved that even in the accepted military front of lines, and rules and ranks—numbers are not everything. He showed that in the civilian front, where cruelty takes the place of heroism, and the lack of human norms is the norm—even in such a war the battle is not lost.

Operation Entebbe, with Yoni at its heart, was the first sign to the world at large that one must not give in to terror, that it is possible to overcome it. Until then many had tried to appease terrorists, to give in to their blackmail, to politically capitulate instead of facing them with military might. Operation Entebbe turned out to be a persuasive force for millions of people, proving that the confrontation with trigger-happy terrorists is not a lost battle. In any case, it was a turning point that caused the world to relate differently to the scourge of terrorism and to the criminal mind of its perpetrators.

The world learned that it has the means to win this battle as well—if it is willing to use them and use them properly. Yoni proved that the strategy of terror would fail, and even the Palestinians, who believed that terror is a result of their tragedy, are now understanding that their tragedy is a result of their reliance on terrorism.

Yoni once wrote, "I must feel, that not only at the moment of my death can I give an account for the time I have lived—but that I will be ready at every moment of my life to face myself and say, 'This is what I have done.'" This is a moving account, an account that continues even after his life is over and his image continues to live and grow.

Perhaps it is possible to add to it a few lines from a poem in *The City of the Dove*, which he loved so much:

> The times are like the field
> On which love and hate and war are plowed,
> And the earth will burn until
> The bearer of its sheaves arrives.

Shimon Peres, a Knesset member, was defense minister during the Entebbe Operation, and later prime minister of Israel.

A FORTRESS OF FIRE
AND STONE

THE LEBANON WAR

by Ori Or

The war that broke out on June 6, 1982, in Lebanon, was the most controversial war in the history of the State of Israel, but in its first stages it enjoyed almost total national support. Its declared aims at the time were to ensure that all the Galilee settlements were out of firing range of the terrorists, and to establish a security belt forty to forty-five kilometers wide from the Israeli border northward. At the beginning of the war the government promised that in this whole area there would no longer be any PLO terrorist bases acting against Israeli civilian targets. The entire infrastructure set up by the PLO to carry out terrorist attacks would be destroyed. All the terrorists would be driven out. Local residents who wanted to live in peace with Israel, those who had supported the Christian militia led by Major Saad Hadad, would be strengthened and would see that Israel would take care of its allies.

During the first days of the war it looked as if the efforts to achieve the declared goals were being carried out in full force. On the fourth day of the war, June 9, the air force even had an opportunity to demonstrate its superior ability. Its planes destroyed seventeen of the nineteen menacing missile batteries the Syrians had set up in the Lebanese Bekaa Valley and also brought down twenty-nine Syrian planes. All this was done without losing a single Israeli aircraft. Besides that, the Israeli-made Merkava tanks—the product of Israeli know-how, experience, and resourcefulness developed over the years—passed their first trial by fire with great success and turned out to be truly superior tanks.

However, all of this was later followed by a lot of complications and disillusionment. It turned out that beyond the declared objectives there were also others, not all of which were considered absolutely necessary. The internal friction in Lebanon led to problematic military moves on the part of Israel. There were also problems concerning the government's supervisory role over the military. And later came the massacre of Christians by Moslems in the refugee camps of Sabra and Shatila, which intensified the gloomy mood in the country. Altogether the campaign, which was first known as Operation Peace for Galilee, got bogged down in a deep morass of blood and bitterness.

But these unfortunate developments, which gave rise to many demonstrations and rallies, and to even a few conscientious objectors, could not diminish the efforts made by IDF soldiers in the battlefield. The ground, air, and sea forces, trained in their duty to obey the legal orders of an elected government, did their best to overcome the enemy under the given field conditions. They tried as much as possible to limit the dangers to the settlements in the Galilee from the areas occupied by the terrorists in Lebanon. During this intensive activity there were a number of heroic acts performed by individual men and women that became part of the IDF's glorious heritage. When the fighting was over, and the political powers were still agonizing over efforts to translate the blood and sweat into formulas for compromise and agreements, many IDF soldiers were found worthy of recognition for what they had done during this terrible war. The deeds of two of these soldiers, which earned them the Gallantry Medal, will be described below.

In 1982 First Lieutenant Mordechai "Motti" Goldman was a commander in the Golani Commando unit, a unit with a very distinguished reputation. Among their other achievements they had taken part in the battles at Tel Faher in the Six-Day War and on Mount Hermon during the Yom Kippur War. When the war approached, they heard that the main mission planned for their unit would be to capture the Beaufort Fortress (Kalat a-Shakif). As someone who had previously done a lot of his military service on the northern front, Goldman knew well the contours of this enormous fortress. The Beaufort towers over Ramat Arnon to a height of seven hundred meters (about 2,100 feet) above sea level. From the time of the Crusades in the eleventh century it has commanded a view of the bend in the Litani River and of its lower channel, which runs toward the city of Tyre. "The Beaufort," Goldman said years later in a newspaper interview, "was not only a military objective. For us, and for the enemy as well, the Beaufort was a symbol of power. During our training before the war, we would always look up at this gigantic Beaufort, waiting for the day we would be able to climb and conquer it. That was our challenge."

Their time to face this challenge arrived on the second day of the war. The day before, the Golani soldiers had been part of the force that crossed the Akiya Bridge over the Litani River, southwest of the Beaufort. They advanced to the area of Nabatiya and reached an observation point overlooking the fortress from the north. From there they could see how ineffectual the aircraft and artillery fire directed on the Beaufort really was. This ancient fortress, whose large stones had seen so many upheavals in the Middle East, looked to the men with the brown berets as if it were laughing at all the fuss around it.

Major Goni Harnik looked over the soldiers that got off the personnel carriers at the point of departure. The week before he had finished his term as commander of the unit and was beginning to plan his civilian life. The war had brought him back into service, and when he heard that his replacement, Moshe, had been wounded in the first confrontation at Ramat Arnon, he quickly took over the job he was so familiar with. He saw before him twenty-one commandos, led by Motti Goldman, and a demolition force, led by Zvika. According to the battle plan he had received Goldman and his men would capture the northern part of the fortress, and the sappers would take the southern part. But first they had to capture the hill on which the fortress was standing. This was the hardest part of the mission.

"There were 150 meters of open ground in front of us," said Goldman, "exposed to the fort above. The only thing we could do was to run this distance, under fire, and that was what we did. When I reached the end, I looked back and saw that I was left with only ten soldiers." Should he continue to carry out his mission considering he was left with only half his soldiers? If he decided to stop, he would have very good reasons for doing so. Already during the early 1950s the chief of staff, Moshe Dayan, had determined that a rate of casualties reaching over 50 percent was the only reason for a unit to return home without completing its mission. But Motti Goldman didn't remember this norm, and if he did, he chose to ignore it.

"I began to run toward my objective with the soldiers," he said.

> About fifty meters before the trench, I suddenly saw someone running toward me. I shot at him, and he stopped. I reached the first trench. I threw a grenade into the first sheltered position and sent a team into the trench. At the first bend in the trench a terrorist was waiting for them. He shot a round and killed Avi Sharf and Razi Gitterman. I ordered Ami to rescue them. He dragged them back while I ran to the next position and threw a grenade inside. Suddenly I saw another terrorist facing me at a distance of half a meter, but I was faster than he was, and I shot him.

Now a problem of size arose. Motti explained, "The trenches were narrow and I am quite broad. Besides that I had my flak jacket and all my equipment. I couldn't move forward inside the trench. I got out and then, when I looked back inside, I realized that I was left with only two soldiers, the others were busy evacuating the wounded."

Only a seventh of the original force left was left to fight the battle. Goldman contacted the company commander, who promised to send reinforcements, so he decided to wait. "At that moment," he remembered, "I wanted to lie down and never move again. Suddenly I understood how important and precious life is." But this understandable thought was replaced by another thought, "a terrible one," according to Goldman.

> The reinforcements that would arrive would not be made up of Golani commando fighters but of other soldiers. The thought that some stranger was going to come to rescue us was shameful to me. This made me get up and continue fighting from outside the trenches. I ran to the position across from me, threw a grenade and jumped in. As soon as I got inside I saw a wounded terrorist who still had a gun

in his hand. I beat him to the draw and killed him. Because I was the only one firing I had already gone through three magazines. I took the terrorist's rifle and his
magazines and continued onward, running like a madman that only a burst of gunfire could stop. I ran above the trench, while my men, Scott and Eitan, threw me
grenades from time to time which I rolled into the trench.

Later, after he had cleared out the ramified trench by himself, Goldman encountered a
camouflaged machine-gun position. He threw a grenade inside it and thought he had solved
the problem, but he soon discovered that was not the case. This position stood on a two-room
bunker, and the terrorist who was holding it moved quickly from room to room dodging
Motti's fire. While the terrorist was running back and forth he shot Goni Harnik, who passed
by a camouflaged opening in the bunker's wall. Motti, shocked by the death of his commander, kept on fighting at that bunker for the next two hours. "The moment this terrorist was
killed," he concluded, "we knew that the fortress was in our hands, because the real job was,
as I said, to capture the hill under the fortress. In the morning we brought in the reserve and
tank units. We continued in the direction of the fortress, constantly firing and throwing
grenades. But there was no longer any resistance and we finished the job without any problems." The scroll that came with his medal read: "By these deeds he demonstrated courage,
self-restraint, resourcefulness, and leadership ability."

Captain Moshe Kravitz, who had wanted to be a pilot but ended up in an armored corps
unit, began the war as a deputy company commander of the Barak Armored Brigade, leading
Yeshivat Hesder soldiers. (These are religious soldiers who, during their military service, study
in a yeshiva part of the time and serve in the army for a continuous period, often in combat
units considered among the best in the IDF.) He moved with his soldiers along the western
axis of the war, and on June 10 his company got caught in a missile ambush of a Syrian antitank battalion near the town of Chalda.

> The fire that hit us damaged two tanks, including the tank of the platoon com-
> mander that was hit by three missiles one after the other. The company com-
> mander began to direct our fire and took care of the evacuation of the wounded.
> He moved his tank forward toward a front battery and was hit by a missile. I took
> over command of the company. I saw that the company commander's tank was
> going up in flames and that only three soldiers were lying beside the battery. I un-
> derstood that someone was still inside the burning tank. I jumped out of my tank
> and ran toward the wounded. I entered the tank and identified the gunner's body.
> I tried to get it out of the tank but I couldn't do it. I was beginning to choke from
> the smoke. I got out of the tank, but not before I put out the fire with a fire extin-
> guisher.

We continued fighting until there were only four tanks left. We were being fired on from two fronts. One soldier asked if he could say the Battle Prayer over the transmitter. This prayer helped us a lot. It raised morale and gave the men faith in what they were doing. The Battle Prayer was like a life-giving drug for many of the Hesder soldiers. We were fired on immediately afterward, and my tank was hit by a missile. It was a frightening sight. I saw a round, burning "sun" rapidly coming toward us. I gave the order to escape to the rear, and then we were hit by another missile. This time the tank caught on fire. I ordered the crew to evacuate, while we got out the loader who had been wounded. At the same time my sergeant's tank was hit ten meters from me. At the casualties collection point I saw that my driver was missing. I ran back to the tank; I was sure that he had been wounded. I opened the hatches and saw that the compartment was completely empty. I went back to the collection point, but he wasn't there either. I thought I had missed him and returned to the tank. Again I opened the hatches, but the compartment was empty. Suddenly I recognized him, by the dike. He had been taken forward to another collection point. I called out to him, but he was afraid of being hit by Israeli fire. I got to him, and we ran back together to the collection point. When we got back, they told me that the second tank was also missing someone. I ran to the tank and found the loader sprawled on the floor. He died in my arms.

Immediately afterward Moshe Kravitz decided to start evacuating the tanks. After he moved some of them to a protected spot, he said, "suddenly a missile hit the tank I was standing on. I was thrown backward. I got up and went back to my tank. Kobi, who had been helping me with the evacuation, was lying there, dying. He still managed to say the *Shma Israel* prayer."

Like Mordechai Goldman's scroll, Moshe Kravitz's also said, "By these deeds he demonstrated courage, self-restraint, resourcefulness, and leadership ability."

After receiving the medal, he said, "I must tell about the performances of the whole company. They were a Hesder company that fought like lions. They were a very close group. This closeness and their faith helped them to overcome great difficulties." He added, "The battle was fought by everyone. One individual alone cannot do anything, not when it comes to tanks."

Major General (res.) Ori Or, a Knesset member, is a former deputy defense minister.

IN ALL THE COMMANDOS, IN ALL THE BATTLES

MUKI BETZER

by Menachem Digli

On the morning of March 21, 1968, Muki Betzer was climbing a steep slope to link up with his commander, Matan Vilnai. He had been hit by a bullet in the jaw and was breathing through a hole in his neck. Another bullet was lodged in his leg. He was bleeding all over. He felt that he was fading fast, but still he climbed, crawled, and reached the top.

Operation Karame, during which this took place, was one of the most controversial events in the history of the IDF. It was an attack of the Israeli army on the village of Karame, in Jordan, which had become a base and headquarters of the PLO. Yassir Arafat himself was said to be based in this village. The operation misfired, and resulted in many Israeli casualties. But the exemplary behavior that Muki Betzer demonstrated during the operation was beyond all doubt. He was in mortal danger. He had to draw on all his battle experience, his resourcefulness, his training, and his character to move forward. He had good reason to do the exact opposite—to turn back and flee the danger. He rejected this option for one reason: the same combination of military camaraderie and perseverance that he had shown since he put on a uniform. Who can say where such a combination comes from, that gives such enormous strength to fighters like Muki Betzer? Who can explain how it is that one man has the determination, the skill, the physical fitness, the self-restraint, and all the other elements that make him into a hero? Who can say, watching the youth who runs into enemy fire, that he is of the same breed of the daring heroes whose deeds have been recorded in books and whose personalities have been immortalized by history?

There is not one answer to these questions, but when it comes to Muki Betzer it is clear that it has something to do with his roots. He was born in Moshav Nahalal on October 13, 1945, the grandson of two founders of that moshav who had taken part in some of the most significant events of the Second Aliya (1904–14). Israel Betzer and his wife, Shifra (who was born into the legendary Shturman family), were among the first settlers of Kibbutz Degania and Kibbutz Merhavia. Before that they had managed to make their mark in the settlements in Judea and in the Galilee. Their son Nachman, Muki's father, had been active in his youth in the Hagana. He was a graduate of the Hagana third commanders' training course, a member of Wingate's night squads, and a commander in Commando Battalion 89 in the War of Independence. Moshe, Nachman's brother, volunteered for the British army at the beginning of the Second World War, served in Transport Company 462, and was killed on his way to the Italian battlefields.

Muki was called Moshe after his uncle, who had given his life in the war effort. From his youth he was surrounded by the atmosphere of the verse from prophet Nehemiah: "With one hand he did the work and with the other he held the weapon" (Nehemiah 4:11). The stories of the Hashomer watchmen and the Palmach, the riots of 1936–39, the battles of 1948, the reprisal raids, and the Sinai Campaign—all these were not just historic events in Nahalal. They were first and foremost events connected to live people—relatives, friends, neighbors—who came and went in the house, who could be seen in the street and in the fields, who took part in family celebrations. They were workers on the land that he knew well, who knew the battlefield well and bore arms whenever they were called upon to do so. When it was his turn to join the army, at the end of 1964, he saw no option other than to follow the family tradition and become a leader. His older brother, who had served before him, was in the paratroops, a member of its elite commando unit. Muki aspired to do the same. He had been groomed for this and was eager to achieve his aim. He was in perfect physical shape and ready for the challenge.

The atmosphere in the IDF at the time was relatively quiet. The Sinai Campaign already belonged to history; the Six-Day War was yet to come. Many believed that the Arabs had completely lost hope of ever destroying Israel, because there had been no more wars. But Muki was not deluded. He wasn't planning on a long military career, but it was clear to him that he had to train himself to be an outstanding soldier.

He joined the paratroop commandos, and soon emerged as an excellent soldier and NCO. His superiors sent him to an officers' training course. He began to make a name for himself. Very tall, somewhat ungainly, he was nevertheless quite agile. He didn't talk much, but knew how to stand up for his opinions. As an officer he joined the Shaked Commandos. After the course was over, he was told that if he wanted to return to the Paratroop Commando Unit, he would have to sign up for long-term service in the regular army. This was not what he had been promised beforehand—and Muki did not like being deceived, even in a matter like this. He therefore chose Shaked.

In the Shaked unit he became the protégé of the legendary Amos Yarkoni (see "Blood Brothers"), who passed on to him some of his amazing skills in field orientation. In this unit he also participated in his first war, the Six-Day War, as the commander of a patrol unit on the central front in Sinai. Later, despite his plans to leave the army, he accepted the offer of Matan

Vilnai, commander of the Paratroop Commandos, to become his deputy. Perhaps the big wars were over, Muki thought at the time, but Israel would now have to face a prolonged war against terrorism, and in this war mainly small elite units would be needed. Their operations would need daring planning and would have to be carried out perfectly. They would have to confront the enemy at close range, on a one-to-one basis. This challenge attracted Muki, and so he put off his civilian life and stayed in the army.

Muki had to spend a few months at home after suffering serious wounds in Operation Karame. When he recovered and began to consider going back to the commandos, he was of-fered a new option. El Al, the Israeli airline, which had been subjected to terrorist attacks, set up a unit of security officers, which Muki joined for a year and a half. This period was too quiet for his tastes. He never had to draw his gun or prevent a terrorist attack on any flight. A bit bored, he left El Al and joined a new commando unit, Egoz, which had been set up in the Northern Command and was intended to fight the war against the terrorists in the area. He was assigned to train the soldiers of the unit after he had been given a definite promise that he would take part in all operational activities. That was his way, as he said later, to test whether Operation Karame had affected his psychological makeup and whether he was still motivated enough to go into battle.

The "test" took place at the beginning of 1971 in the town of al-Hiam, which was theo-retically under Lebanese sovereignty, but in fact was located in the so-called Fatahland, a vast area in South Lebanon, totally controlled by the Fatah (PLO) terrorists. An Egoz force attacked the Fatah regional headquarters located in al-Hiam. Five officers were to carry out the last stage of the attack—blowing up the building. One of the five officers was killed, and three were wounded. Muki attacked the building alone, killed the terrorists who were guarding the place, and placed the explosive charges. On his way back toward Israeli territory, his mission ac-complished, he knew for certain: Karame had not beaten him.

At the end of his service in Egoz, Muki was sent with his family to Uganda by the IDF to train Idi Amin's paratroopers and to enjoy the enchanting African scenery. Four months later Amin decided to break off relations with Israel, and Muki was expelled from the country along with all the other Israelis. The army received him back with open arms. Matan Vilnai wanted to draft him back into the paratroopers, and Ehud Barak, who was now the commander of Say-eret Matkal, the number one commando unit of the IDF, wanted him at his side. Muki left the decision up to them. He landed in the Sayeret—after the decision had gone as far as the chief of staff, David Elazar. He settled into this elite unit immediately as a senior officer (even though he had come from another unit), and took part in the kidnapping of senior Syrian officers who were to be exchanged for Israeli prisoners in Damascus.

A few months later he participated in the Spring of Youth Campaign as part of the efforts to kill senior members of the Black September terrorist organization. This organization had been responsible for the murder of Israeli sportsmen during the Olympic games in Munich. An IDF elite force reached Beirut by sea, including commando fighters dressed as tourists. The tall Muki Betzer was one of these "tourists," along with his "wife," Ehud Barak, who was wearing a woman's clothes and a blond wig. They broke into the apartment of three arch terrorists, killed them in their beds, and managed to retreat to the coast, where they were picked up by missile boats—all within half an hour. It was again proven that the strength and resourcefulness of the commandos allowed them to set new limits of fighting ability. And once more Muki's fellow soldiers witnessed his special talents in this area.

He continued to play a central role in the day-to-day activities of the unit, but was planning to leave the army and return to civilian life. But then the Yom Kippur War suddenly broke out. The commando unit, which was designed to carry out operations under special conditions, had no specific assignment. Muki, who commanded part of the force, went looking for assignments. He found them, and carried them out to perfection, first in the Golan Heights, and later on the western side of the Suez Canal. Along with his friend Yonatan "Yoni" Netanyahu he managed, among other actions, to wipe out the Syrian commando force that had been flown into the Golan by helicopter. He also penetrated through the Leja plain to Tel Shams, and rescued the unit of his friend Yossi Ben-Hanan, which had been trapped there. From there he and his soldiers joined Ariel Sharon's division at the approaches to Ismailiya, by the Suez Canal, and soon afterward took control of Jebel Ataka, a strategic mountaintop in Egypt.

After the war, during which some of his close friends had been killed, Muki came to the conclusion that he must develop a new doctrine for the activities of the special units. They had to be prepared for their own operations in time of war. To achieve these plans he took an extended vacation from the unit, not before taking care of his personal interests: he was promised on a handshake that he would be called in to take part in any action to rescue hostages.

He was indeed called in again and again all over the country to deal with terrorist attacks and suicide bombers. In his car, besides his fighting kit, he kept a street map of all the cities in Israel, so that he wouldn't waste time if he had to go directly to the spot. He was in the heart of the action when terrorists infiltrated into Kiryat Shemona, Maalot, and Beit Shean, always leading the assault team, which was willing to take risks. They always kept their eyes and ears open to everything that was going on, ready to learn and improve their methods in the future.

A while after his leave was over, Muki Betzer returned to Africa, in a very unconventional manner, which of course had not been planned for in advance. On June 27, 1976, Air France flight 139 was hijacked on its way from Tel Aviv to Paris, and landed in the end at the Entebbe airport in Uganda. Idi Amin cooperated with the PLO hijackers. They made enormous demands on the Israeli government, accompanied by threats on the lives of the more than one hundred hostages. They had set a new precedent in international terror by holding hostages in a hostile environment, and it seemed that they could get anything they wanted. Muki was called in soon after the report on the hijacking came in. He was supposed to lead the operation that would storm the plane if it landed in Israel. He was called in for a first consultation at General Headquarters, when it was discovered that the plane would be landing in Entebbe.

Muki took a very active part in working out the plans for one of the most celebrated operations in the history of the IDF. His battle experience, his intimate knowledge of the abilities of the Sayeret Matkal, and other elite units, as well as his knowledge of Uganda, contributed greatly to the preparations.

He also helped convince his superiors that this was a realistic option. It was obvious that he would lead the first force that entered the airport and rescued the hostages from their kidnappers. It was also not surprising that later, during the attack, Muki would deal with any sudden problems that arose along the way that threatened the success of the operation in Entebbe itself. His quick instincts, his resourcefulness, and his daring helped him to deal with any situation that arose. Operation Yonatan (named after the fact, in honor of Yoni Netanyahu, who was killed during the operation) was in no small way Muki Betzer's operation.

After Entebbe, Muki realized his dream and set up the kind of elite unit he had envisioned. It is still too early to talk about the Shaldag Unit in detail. One can only say that it too gives expression to his unique qualities as a farmer and a fighter. He plows and plants patiently and thoroughly, knowing that if he doesn't, there won't be an actual harvest; and he runs ahead into the battle, knowing that this is the mission of utmost importance, that he must carry out to perfection.

Colonel (res.) Menachem Digli was the commander of the Sayeret Matkal Commando Unit.

SOMEWHERE THERE WILL BE A SOLID MONUMENT

AVIDA SHOR

by Yaacov Hisdai

In the winter of 5733 (1972), Avida Shor, a soldier in a paratroop commando unit, was about to complete an officers' training course. In a letter to his girlfriend he wrote that he hoped he would have a "solid monument in some secluded place . . . that would express silently all that has happened to me till now—and so much has happened—so that I can visit it from time to time (preferably at sunset), look at it, think and remember, look and think. . . . Everything will be on the monument, but its form and size will be without measure; otherwise it would have to be limitless, infinite. I could fill endless lines and pages . . . but it's impossible to write it all down, so perhaps only the monument that will stand somewhere will contain everything and I will come from time to time. . . ."

Avida was a son of the Shor family from Kibbutz Shoval, and belonged to the first generation of Israelis born after the establishment of the State. His personality and his views were formed by this background. Like all the children in the kibbutz he grew up with a group of his own age, first in a "children's house," then in other common frameworks. Avida and his friends studied together, played together, and worked together throughout their childhood and teenage years. Shibolim, the youngsters' group in which he grew up, was a very close-knit team. Avida was a focus of warmth and joy in this group. "His handshake was so warm, it gave everyone the feeling that Avida liked him in particular," say his friends from Shibolim. When he grew up he turned out to be optimistic by nature. He gave you the feeling that "the whole world was good and that everyone was good to you," said his girlfriend, describing his character. "What made him so special was his constant smile, his good spirits, his stoic calm. . . . Life around him was always fun. . . ." The kibbutz was his home, and when he grew up he began to work in the wheat fields. The old-timers looked with affection upon this boy who was the last to come back from work in the evening. When he enlisted they kept saying, "Things in the fields are difficult, but when Avida comes back it will be easier."

He intended to come back. When he was asked to sign on with the regular army he brought the decision before a kibbutz meeting and told the members that the kibbutz was where he wanted to "drop anchor."

When he joined the army—the paratroop commandos—he took on the values of warfare, loyalty, and perseverance of the unit. His sense of duty and his desire to prove himself are re-flected in one of his first letters from basic training. After describing the difficult, exhausting training he was going through, he added, "It's nice to write, that in spite all of the above, we are still standing straight and tall and continuing to bear up." In the spirit of the unit's tradi-tion he was proud to go out on missions and eager to go into battle. But he did not forget the values he had been taught at home and on the kibbutz. His kibbutz "house mother," the woman who took care of him and the children of his age group, remembered him as "the child with the laughing eyes." She saw his eyes sad only once when he grew up, and that was when he came back from the raid on Tripoli.

When he was a child his innate sense of respect for others' rights already made him set limits to the power and authority of the group and the majority. If there were four boys living in a room and one of them wanted to sleep, said Avida, the others must respect his wishes.

When his age group in Shibolim reached bar mitzva age, there was a disagreement over the way the money they received should be used. Avida insisted that each one had the right to de-cide for himself what to do with his share.

This was how Avida's character was formed and how he prepared himself for the direction he chose. He had learned to think for himself and even stand alone against all the others, if the matter was important to him.

Avida's independent ways and unique character were also noted when he joined the army. Although he was considered a disciplined and responsible soldier, his officers noticed there was something different about him. They said, "Whenever we officers gave orders and explained them to him, he always had something to say. He never accepted anything as self-evident." When he became an officer his officer friends said of him, "Whatever Avida did was special. He never did what everyone else did, but what he thought and believed was right and should be done."

In 1971 Avida arrived at the Officers' School in Mitzpe Ramon, and that was where I met him, as his commander in the officers' training course. Over the months I got to know him as a good cadet, talented and diligent, one of the guys. As a kibbutznik in a company made up mostly of kibbutzniks, he didn't seem different from them in his opinions and actions—until the educational seminar.

One day the whole company was sitting together, listening to a talk on the image of the officer in the army. There was a visiting lecturer, a reserve officer, whose opinions and outlook were close to those of the kibbutz movement. Throughout the lecture I heard murmurs of agreement behind me, and by the end of it I felt that the whole company identified with the lecturer. But suddenly Avida made a surprising statement. Actually, he expressed an opinion that was different from that of the speaker, and even contradicted the part of the lecture that had been most well received by the cadets. In essence, Avida's position was completely different from what I could expect of him, considering his education and his origins. On that day I learned that Avida had his own way of looking at things, and that he would express his opinion, even if it was different from everybody else's.

At the end of the series of lectures I asked the cadets to write an essay on what they considered the image of a good officer to be. Avida developed his arguments from the discussion after the lecture with great skill. A few months later he was made an officer in the commando unit. I heard about him often. People said that he had become a tough and demanding officer, that he kept aloof from his soldiers and was very strict. I remembered the talk and his essay, and this description made sense.

On April 10, 1973, First Lieutenant Avida Shor was killed in Operation Spring of Youth, in a battle with terrorists during a daring IDF raid in the heart of Beirut.

At the beginning of that year Israel had been faced with a serious problem: the murderous arm of terror was striking again and again in the country and abroad. The massacre of the Israeli athletes at the Olympic games in Munich was one of the more painful demonstrations of this problem. This massacre demanded far-reaching conclusions concerning the security of the Israeli civilian population. One of the conclusions was the need for a direct attack on the planning and control centers of the terrorist organizations, in their Beirut headquarters. Several of the most cruel and powerful terrorist organizations, including the infamous Black September group, were operating with full impunity from their headquarters in Beirut. The Lebanese government and army felt too weak to act against them. The Palestinian terrorists, during these years, were the real masters of Lebanon.

The operation against them would be daring, precise, and dangerous. In order for it to succeed, the best IDF fighters had to carry it out. One of its main goals was to blow up the headquarters of the Democratic Front for the Liberation of Palestine, under the command of Naif Hawatmeh. This building was guarded and well protected; it was situated in an area swarming with terrorists. The assignment was given to a small force that was supposed to carry it out in secret. The advance team of this force was made up of two soldiers whose job it was to lead the force, wipe out any resistance at the entrance to the building, and allow the rest of the soldiers to get into its lobby and set off the explosion. First Lieutenant Avida Shor, the deputy commander of the commando unit, was chosen to lead this advance team.

He was not chosen by chance. First and foremost it was a sign of recognition of Avida's high qualifications, his talent as a fighter and of the faith his officers had in him. But in the planning of the operation there were two events that showed distinct sides of Avida's character and personality: First, even though the brigade commander had chosen every one of those who were to participate in the raid, Avida insisted on choosing his own partner. When the commander agreed, Avida ignored considerations of rank and status and chose the man he thought best for the job, a veteran experienced sergeant, Hagai Maayan.

Later, the demolition plan was presented to the commando. That included facts and figures. One of the officers mentioned the weight and magnitude of the explosive charges, which were to be placed under the pillars of the building. Most of those present at the briefing were senior officers, but Avida did not hesitate to ask why such a large amount of explosives were needed. The officer answered that this was the amount needed to assure that the whole building would collapse. Avida remembered that one of the outer walls of the terrorists' building was adjacent to that of a house inhabited by civilians. He suggested that a smaller amount of explosives be used. The officers present disagreed with the idea, but Avida stuck to his guns and explained himself. "I don't care if the whole building doesn't collapse completely," he said, "and that maybe fewer terrorists will get killed, but what I do care about is that the civilians living in the house next door don't get hurt."

When the argument continued, Avida added, "I take it on my conscience to lead the force and to kill the terrorists' guards, but I am not prepared to kill women and children."

The chief of staff, David Elazar, who was present at the briefing, accepted Avida's opinion. The values that Avida had learned at home and on the kibbutz guided him when he chose Hagai as his partner in the advance team of the raid, and when he decided to act, in order to spare the lives of the civilians in a house next to the terrorist headquarters.

The operation began according to plan. The soldiers landed by sea, and the force that was supposed to blow up the headquarters of the Democratic Front made its way toward its objective by car. Some distance from the building the force continued on foot, led by Avida and Hagai.

When they approached the building, the two of them encountered the guards and shot them at close range. But at that moment some other terrorist guards, positioned in a nearby car, opened fire, and both of them were shot. A battle ensued at close range between the Israeli soldiers and the terrorists inside the building and around it. Coolly, courageously, and with perseverance, the soldiers carried out the mission assigned to them. The building blew up and collapsed like a house of cards. The other houses in the vicinity were not damaged, and no civilian was hurt. They then evacuated the wounded and returned by sea to Israel.

From where did Avida get the strength to be different; how did he choose his own unique way?

In the stories Avida's friends told about him, a trunk played a special role. It turns out that he always had a trunk. On the kibbutz it was a trunk of work tools; in the army it was his trunk of personal equipment. His friends on the kibbutz and those he knew in the army always talk about his special attitude toward his trunks. He used to keep them in perfect order and had an emotional attachment to every personal object in them, as if they were part of him. This trunk was an external expression of an important part of Avida's soul, the part that was closed up tight to outsiders, which no one could share. This was where he defined and marked the area of his independence and responsibility, from the water hose he used in the kibbutz field to the demolition bomb in the heart of Beirut.

Among his letters there is one that points at that "trunk" in Avida's soul, at that closed, hidden part of him. This is what he wrote in a moment of frankness about the other part of his personality: "From childhood I never got close enough to anyone so that I could express my inner feelings . . . I never told anyone my troubles or things that it would be logical to share with someone else . . . and that was because I kept close guard on my inner self."

Avida's trunk, and his soul, were closed and sealed from outsiders. One held his tools; the other—his character and his decisions. He was a loner, closed and independent, whom many knew as a close friend, cheerful and well liked. He was a part of the group but in his own way, a way of daring, courage, and integrity.

Colonel (res.) Yaacov Hisdai was Avida Shor's commander in the officers' training course.

DEEP IN ENEMY TERRITORY

THE RESCUE AND EVACUATION UNITS

by Moshe Zonder

On Thursday, December 8, 1988, at four o'clock in the morning, an IDF force left by sea for the industrial district of Nueima, near the town of Damur in Lebanon, only eight kilometers south of Beirut. The declared aim of the operation was: "to carry out a night raid with a designated sea force that would land on the Damur coast, move on foot towards its objectives, kill terrorists, destroy equipment and weapons, and return to our territory." The objective was a bunker housing the central headquarters of the Sabra and Shatila Battalion, one of the main units in the terrorist organization of Ahmed Jibril. The code name chosen for the operation was Blue and Brown, to emphasize the cooperation between the air forces, the "blues," and the ground forces, mainly soldiers from the Golani Brigade, the "browns." The person who chose the name could not have imagined how crucial the cooperation between the two forces would be. This was the scenario:

At 9:43, after an exhausting seventeen-hour trip, the forces land on the Lebanese coast. They divide into three main groups. At the head of the first one is Major Erez, the commander of the Golani commando unit. Behind him is Amir's Force, under the command of Lieutenant Colonel Amir Meital, the head of a Golani battalion. The third force is led by G, the deputy commander of the Thirteenth Sea Squadron (Flotilla 13). The march toward the targets turns out to be harder than expected, and their timetable is thrown off. Lieutenant Colonel M, the commander of a Cobra air squadron, is waiting at the base for the signal to take off in his helicopter to the area where he is to carry out his previously defined task. M still does not know that he will endanger his life much more than planned.

Erez and the Golani commando soldiers reach their objective at the bunker of the headquarters at 2:25. Amir's Force is still far from its target—six man-made caves in the side of the mountain where the terrorists lived. Erez thinks that one of the terrorists stationed at the window has noticed him, so he opens fire on him. This is the signal to begin the operation. The commandos get the terrorists, but the element of surprise, of which Amir's Force was supposed to take advantage, is lost.

Meital and his men run to their objective instead of sneaking up on it. Not only that, but according to foreign reports, Amir's Force was meant to use dogs carrying explosives and gas balloons that would be sent into the terrorists' caves and activated by remote control. The explosives were supposed to cause the roof to collapse. The gas was meant to force the terrorists outside into the gunfire of our forces. If such a plan existed it too was disrupted. A few seconds before Amir's soldiers arrive at their shooting position, they are shot at. Meital is killed on the spot. His radio operator and one of the other soldiers are wounded. The doctor, Dr. Zvi Steinberg, hears the cries of the wounded and runs down from the next hill to help them. A well-aimed burst of fire hits him in the knee and causes him to lose a great deal of blood.

At 3:16 Lieutenant Colonel M arrives at his Cobra helicopter, accompanied by a second helicopter. Their job is to help Amir's Force regroup and retreat. Two helicopters shoot at the terrorists' caves and cover Amir's soldiers. While they are doing this they sustain heavy fire. At 4:14, while leaving the runway, Lieutenant Colonel M's helicopter gets hit by antiaircraft fire. He is wounded in the leg and is bleeding profusely. This does not bother M. He flies the Cobra to Israeli territory and lands safely at 4:42.

In the meantime a new problem arises on land. Eli's Force, a subunit of four soldiers from Amir's Force, commanded by First Lieutenant Eli Shalom, is waiting at the objective assigned to it, thirty meters east of the caves. But his radio transmitter is disconnected. Eli is not disturbed by the silence from his wireless. He is convinced that Amir Meital, a respected battalion commander, will pick him up as planned when they withdraw. He, of course, has no idea that Meital has been killed.

Lieutenant Colonel M returns to the field with another Cobra plane. Two main forces—Amir's, which also includes Golani commando soldiers, and the smaller unit of the sea force, which has completed its assignment—are ready to leave. Sunrise, at 5:32, is getting closer and closer, and Eli's Force is not there. Four soldiers are missing.

The officers at the advanced tactical headquarters are faced with a difficult dilemma. Should they continue to look for the missing soldiers, and make the whole force stay deep in enemy territory during daylight, or should they order them to leave? Chief of Staff Dan Shomron makes the hardest decision of his long military career by himself. At 4:51 he orders the withdrawal. Two Yassur helicopters take off to evacuate the soldiers, oblivious to the dangers they face. The pilots of these huge helicopters risk their lives and land without being able to see the ground below them.

At first light, Eli Shalom and his three soldiers see the huge helicopters taking off and moving away. They understand that they have been left behind in the field. Eli stays calm and gives instructions to his soldiers. Under no circumstances, he says to them, will we be taken prisoner. The four of them take cover among the thick bushes.

The main problem, Eli says to himself, is that I don't have a clue how to use the special communications device for identification in an air rescue, their only means of contact with the outside world. Along with his soldiers he reads the instructions in English that are glued to the device. He tries to follow them. More than two hours pass. Only at 7:35 does the pilot of a Yassur helicopter patrolling the area first hear the call from Eli's force. At 8:35 the first two-way wireless contact is established between the air force pilots and Eli's force. From that moment on, the air force prepares for a rescue as best it can.

At 9:10 two F-16 planes attack the source of the antiaircraft fire. Skyhawk planes drop smoke bombs in order to create a smokescreen and make the rescue easier. Two formations of Cobra helicopters are rushed to the area. Each formation consists of two helicopters. Lieutenant Colonel M leads one of the formations, returning for the third time within a few hours to Nucima. The other pilot behind him is First Lieutenant D. The pilot of the second plane is Captain A, and the pilot behind him is Captain M. The leader of the second formation is Lieutenant Colonel H. (The full names of the pilots are withheld by Israeli censorship.)

Lieutenant Colonel M has a very bad feeling. He is afraid, convinced that things do not bode well for the Cobra helicopters that are making their way to an area filled with antiaircraft fire during daytime. They are like sitting ducks. It is clear to Lieutenant Colonel M that he may be killed, or at least taken prisoner by the terrorists. They are all going to be shot down. But he does not leave the area. The four helicopters cross the coastline. The terrorists shoot at them, and they return fire and hit the terrorists' vehicle. Radio contact is made with Eli, who hears the helicopters but can't see them. The two helicopters under the command of Lieutenant Colonel H run out of gas and have to turn back. The two helicopters of Lieutenant Colonel M are left alone in the field, but M can't see the four soldiers. The first rescue operation fails.

There is a very heavy atmosphere in the control post of the air force. Phantom planes go out on additional bombing and sniper sorties to cut down the antitank fire and to get the terrorists away from the Golani soldiers. At 10:08, twenty minutes later, the bombing is stopped, and the second rescue operation begins. At the same time Lieutenant Colonel M, who is left on his own in the field, asks that two more Cobra helicopters be sent out.

He himself goes back into the field with the second Cobra. The terrorists shoot at them but they still can't find the Golani soldiers. Besides that, the Doppler system in Lieutenant Colonel M's helicopter breaks down. He doesn't know where he is and is afraid that an unseen terrorist will hit his helicopter. On the other hand, the pilot of the second plane in the formation, Captain A, is convinced that he is seeing the area clearly and that he also knows where the four soldiers are. He guides Lieutenant Colonel M, and the two aircraft continue flying and find themselves facing a smokescreen. They renew contact with Eli. Lieutenant Colonel M finds the approximate location of the four soldiers. The helicopters advance toward them, but then the lead helicopter is hit by RPG grenades. The situation looks desperate.

At this moment Captain Y, the commander of a pair of Cobras left hovering at sea, enters the picture. Due to his initiative the exact location of the four Golani soldiers is finally determined, not before Captain Y identifies them incorrectly as a terrorist cell. He fires a missile at them and almost kills them. Fortunately, the missile barely misses them. Eli shouts at Lieutenant Colonel M that he is shooting at him. Lieutenant Colonel M sees the mushroom cloud of smoke from the missile and realizes, at last, where the four are hiding.

The second pilot, Captain A, suggests that Lieutenant Colonel M go down and collect the four of them on the runners of the helicopter while he covers him. Lieutenant Colonel M tells Eli that he is coming to rescue him.

The nightmare is about to end, but Lieutenant Colonel M's helicopter is hit again with nine bullets. The weapons and outside communication system of the helicopter stop working. At that moment the two pairs of Cobra helicopters that Lieutenant Colonel M requested half an hour ago enter the picture. When they arrive, Captain Y takes charge. He instructs one pair of helicopters to join them and cover them, and the other pair to cover them from farther back. Captain A makes contact with Eli Shalom and tells him to be ready with his soldiers for the third rescue attempt. The soldiers are supposed to climb onto the runners of the helicopters, open the ammunition doors, and sit on them as they learned to do in the exercise before the operation.

The two helicopters covering them are spitting fire. The Cobras of Lieutenant Colonel M and Captain A glide into the narrow wadi. The four soldiers cross the dirt path two at a time and run to the helicopters. The four of them sit down on the runners of the helicopter. Yechezkel Berkovitz, who isn't able to open the ammunition door, holds on to the runner of Captain Y's helicopter and is in danger of sliding off. At 10:29 Captain D, the pilot behind Lieutenant Colonel M, reports to the air force flight controller that the helicopters are carrying out the rescue and that all four of them are safe and sound. He asks to be directed to the closest navy ship. Within a minute, which seemed an eternity to the four soldiers, the helicopters pass the firing zone and the coastline. Less than two minutes later the four soldiers jump into the Mediterranean and are picked up in rubber boats let down from missile boats sailing in the area. The soldiers on the missile boats let out a roar and cheer.

The crew of the Yassur that had saved the main part of the force—the pilot, Major N, his deputy, Captain A, and the crew, First Lieutenant A and Staff Sergeant R—were given citations by the air force commander, Major General Avihu Ben-Nun. "The evacuation by the Yassur helicopters was done under impossible conditions," said Ben-Nun, "in an unplanned-for location, amid electrical wires, in complicated field conditions and with inadequate coordination. I think this was one of the best evacuation operations I know of, as far as perseverance, performance level, professionalism, and the performance of individuals are concerned."

The chief of staff, Dan Shomron, awarded a citation to Lieutenant Colonel M, the commander of the formation of Cobra helicopters, and to Captain A, commander of the second helicopter in the same formation. First Lieutenants D and M, the second pilots in the two Cobras, received citations from the commander of the air force, Major General Avihu Ben-Nun. About the actions of the Cobra pilots, Major General Ben-Nun said, "We have here an extraordinary example, but if I were to plan it, I would never have allowed them to do this. Because if you look at where they were and consider the dangers of leaving behind two or three Cobras under those conditions, you can see that it was an enormous risk." In the section that relates to this operation in the so-called "Air Force Book"—a volume narrating the most glorious actions of the air force—Ben-Nun wrote: "I believe that by these deeds the air force saved the nation and the army from a very nasty business, and proved again that there is someone who can be relied on."

Moshe Zonder is a journalist for the newspaper Maariv.

"I KNEW YOU WOULD COME"

by Efraim Sneh

The evacuation of four Golani soldiers in Operation Blue and Brown is a fascinating story of daring and perseverance.

I had the honor of setting up the Rescue and Evacuation Unit of the air force in its present format in 1978 and of being its commander for two years. It was then that we combined the Rescue Unit and the Evacuation Unit into one operational unit.

The rescue fighters of the air force go through difficult and varied training. The purpose of the training is to maintain a helicopter rescue arm capable of rescuing air crew and soldiers from every possible area under all weather conditions.

Halfway through the course the soldiers receive the unit pin, after a long and rigorous "stretcher march," which ends on Mount Sanson, overlooking the site of the last battle of the thirty-five Palmach fighters who were on their way to the eternal Etzion Bloc during the War of Independence. A plaque there says, "He who saves one living soul, it is as if he saved the whole world."

This motto is the code of values that is the basis for all rescue operations in the IDF, in which many have endangered their lives to save and bring home even one person.

The fate of the navigator Ron Arad, who, after parachuting in enemy territory has been wasting away in prison for more than ten years, is a terrible illustration of how important it is to make the effort to save our soldiers from being taken prisoner, from torture and from death. The knowledge that in every IDF operation, in every action, a whole force of pilots, soldiers, doctors, medics, planes, and helicopters stands ready to rescue our men provides those who go out on a mission with a feeling of security. "I knew you would come," said an air force pilot who had abandoned his plane in Egyptian territory during the War of Attrition to the helicopter crew that came to rescue him.

"I knew you would come"—there is no greater compliment than that. The sanctity of life, the concern for the fighting man meet in the values of the IDF and in the values of Judaism and receive their expression in the operations and feats of the Rescue and Evacuation Unit.

Brigadier General Efraim Sneh, a Knesset member, is a former minister of health.

FACING A DEADLY SWORD EMPTY-HANDED

ABD EL-KARIM ABD EL-RANI

by Ali Yehia

Purim 5752 began on March 19, 1992. This was in the middle of the month of Ramadan in the year 1370, according to the Muslim calendar. Because of this Abd el-Karim Abd el-Rani, an Arab citizen of Jaffa, changed his regular daily habits. He would usually begin the morning with a cup of black coffee, while sitting comfortably in his living room and looking out his high windows at the large grapevine that spread throughout his garden. Actually, in the past he hadn't kept the Ramadan fast and would have been sipping coffee this morning as well. But no longer. Now, at the age of forty-six, he had realized that man cannot live from pleasures alone and that the tradition of one's forefathers should not be taken lightly. For the first time in many years he had decided to fast during the holy month. And so he did not stay around the house after waking from his night's sleep. Instead he hurried out and reached his garage within a few minutes. The garage was located at the corner of Eilat and Oliphant Streets, at the very point where the newer city of Tel Aviv merges with ancient, biblical Jaffa. Ramadan or no Ramadan, he remembered, Purim or no Purim, a lot of work was awaiting him there, and no one would do it for him.

On Nitza Street in the Amidar housing project of Bat Yam, further south from the house of Abd el-Rani on 3062 Street in Jaffa, Ilanit Ohana was also getting up. Ilanit was a beautiful nineteen-year-old with smooth black hair. She quietly finished getting ready to go out to the office where she had started working at the beginning of the month. She was careful not to wake the rest of the family that lived with her in the small apartment. One of them, her sister, had also woken up early. They had arranged to go together, before work, for dental treatment. If there weren't any problems during the treatment (and why should there be, Ilanit probably said to herself), she would not be very late to the office on Eilat Street in Jaffa, not far from the corner with Oliphant.

Abd el-Karim swung up the metal shutters of the garage. While doing so, he probably cast a look on the sign GARAGE OF LEON AND OVADIA, which was displayed on the central shutter. The letters of Leon's name were half erased since he had retired, and the garage belonged solely to Ovadia. Ovadia was the Jewish name by which Abd el-Karim was known to his customers and the old-time residents of Jaffa. He didn't find anything wrong with this. Abd el-Karim, in Arabic, meant "servant of Allah, the Merciful and Compassionate One." And what was the difference between Abd el-Karim of the Arabs and Ovadia of the Jews? Ovadia also meant "servant of God," in Hebrew. Abd-Ovadia worked seven days a week in his garage. That was how he earned enough money so that his family would lack nothing. In this way, with the help of the salary of his beautiful wife, Salva, he had built a comfortable home and could give his four children whatever they wanted. He could raise them well, and save them from being drawn to the temptations of the city.

Other garage owners in the neighborhood did not complain about Abd el-Karim; nor did they hold it against him that he was supposedly breaking the rules and competing with them unfairly. This was partly because he was a good-hearted man who loved people, smiled at everyone, was happy with his lot, and always was willing to help others. It also had to do with the fact Abd el-Karim and his ways seemed an inseparable part of the special, real Jaffa—Jaffa of the ancient port and the rock to which Andromeda had been chained, according to the legend, Jaffa of the blend of churches and mosques and ancient Jewish cemeteries, of the tiny cups of black coffee and the shesh-besh (backgammon) cubes used by all the real sons of the city, no matter what their religion was.

Abd el-Karim glanced casually at the Fiat Uno car that he had finished repairing at midnight the night before and that was now awaiting its owner. Across from it stood a large American car, which still had to be repaired. If he hadn't started working now, if he had decided, for example, that Ramadan is not only for fasting but also for soul-searching and for taking account of his life till now, what would he have said to himself at this moment?

He had lived almost all his life as part of a minority group among Jews, unlike his father, Mohammed Abd el-Rani. His father had also been born in a Jaffa neighborhood, but he had spent his childhood and adolescence in Egypt. There he found his wife, Zeina, and returned to the bustling Jaffa of the days of the British Mandate to open a butcher shop, set up a home, and raise a family of five boys and four girls. Abd el-Karim, the fifth child, was born in 1946. Two years later the war broke out, and many people ran away from the town, even before the Jewish soldiers arrived there. Many more left afterward. But the Abd el-Rani family chose to stay, and so did not end up in one of the refugee camps. Mohammed, who ran his butcher shop in partnership with Jews, was not afraid of these people, definitely not enough to leave his home and go off into the unknown. When the fighting stopped and things returned to normal, Jewish immigrants began to take over almost every deserted house. The butcher shop was reopened, serving mainly Jewish customers. In time some of his family members began to work there as well.

But Abd el-Karim chose a different direction. After completing his basic education in the Moslem school near the Hassan Bek mosque, he decided he wanted to become a mechanic. According to the usual practice he studied while working as an apprentice. Later he became a hired worker in a number of garages, most of them owned by Jews. Most of his friends, the men he worked with and spent time with, were Jews. And so were his women friends. The good-looking boy who loved life so much was undoubtedly a good friend to have and was loved by all, Jews and Arabs alike.

When it came time to marry and raise a family, he chose Salva. Salva was seventeen years old. Her family, originally from the Sidni Ali village near Herzliya, had settled in Jaffa in 1948. When they got married he was still a salaried worker, but Salva urged him to open his own business, and that was how the Garage of Leon and Ovadia came into being, the same garage where Abd was working that morning.

Ilanit Ohana discovered, unfortunately, that her dentist had decided to celebrate Purim, so there was no reason for her not to go on to work. What was she thinking at that moment? About her army service, the date of which had not yet been set but would no doubt be soon? About Yoki, her boyfriend, who had visited her last night and had begun to talk about marriage? About whether she should get married and not go into the army? No one will ever know what thoughts were in her mind, and there will never be anyone to hear about them.

At ten minutes after nine a shiny red Leyland truck stopped at the gas station on Eilat Street. There was nothing extraordinary about the sight, and it did not arouse any suspicion. Those with sharp eyes noticed the license plates that showed the truck had come from the Gaza Strip. A huge bearded man got out of the truck. His eyes were hidden by large sunglasses. He wore a white *keffiyeh* on his head and held a newspaper in his hand. His general appearance was impressive. Some of the passersby eyed him with a half smile, imagining that he was a young Jew, dressed up in an original Purim costume. But Raid Mohammed Rifi was actually a twenty-two-year-old resident of Khan Yunis, in the Gaza Strip, and had no connection to the Jewish holiday. As a fervent activist in the Islamic Jihad terrorist group, he had gone out to commit murder. For this purpose he carried with him two weapons—a well-sharpened kitchen knife and a sword with a heavy wooden handle and a blade sixty centimeters (two feet) long.

The moment he felt the time was ripe, he drew his sword. He first stabbed a young boy who passed by him. The boy fell at his feet, bleeding, his screams filling the street. The huge murderer then ran around madly waving his sword. He noticed a dark young girl who had been walking innocently in the street. Ilanit Ohana felt the first stab of the sword and began to run for her life. She noticed the entrance of the garage, and ran in that direction. Ovadia, Abd el-Karim el-Rani, heard Ilanit's screams, saw the giant running after her, and understood immediately what was happening. He ran to the entrance of the garage and shouted to Ilanit, "Run!" He tried to get in between her and her assailant. At first he was unsuccessful. The terrorist, waving his sword with all his strength, stabbed Ilanit again. Abd el-Karim tried once more. He stood between the two and shouted in Arabic: "Ramadan, Ramadan," and then "I'm fasting"—in a vain hope that the huge man would understand that he was sinning not only in matters between him and his fellow man, but in his relations with God as well. Abd el-Karim also tried to grab the handle of the sword and stop this murderous weapon. And again, he was unsuccessful. The terrorist brutally hit him over the head, knocked him down, and again stabbed Ilanit. Both of them, Ilanit Ohana and Abd el-Karim el-Rani, collapsed on the dirty concrete, and lay bleeding to death next to each other. She died on the floor of the garage, and he on the way to the hospital.

The people outside gazed at the murderer coming out of the garage, their horrified eyes staring as mesmerized at the scene of carnage. No one showed the courage that Abd el-Karim el-Rani had shown a few minutes earlier. No one tried to block the assassin's way. He ran down the street, hit a taxi driver, and burst into a group of schoolchildren who had gathered at the entrance to the Real Time Club for a Purim party. Only there, after he had wounded some of the children, was his deadly, mad race brought to an end. A soldier from the border police happened to be there, and he shot and killed him.

The mourners and the many friends of Abd el-Karim el-Rani gathered in the *dar al-aza* (mourning tent) that the family set up near the house on 3062 Street. There were friends from all walks of life in Jaffa, his faithful customers who appreciated his workmanship and honesty, public figures, and also delegations of people from different parts of the country, Jews and Arabs, who came to pay their respects. Abd el-Karim's wife and her four children received those who came to comfort her. Through their tears they said that his actions had not surprised them. The circumstances were unexpected, they said. Who could imagine that a mad murderer like that would show up in Jaffa in broad daylight? But since that was what had happened, since the Islamic Jihad had chosen to strike such a blow on Eilat Street and of all places near Abd el-Karim's garage, it was only natural that this garage should serve as a shelter for someone being pursued, and it was only natural that the owner would come to her rescue without caring about his own life, without finding out who was asking for his protection and help.

Ilanit Ohana had probably walked past the Garage of Leon and Ovadia more than once in the last two weeks of her life. They had probably looked at one another. But the first time they exchanged words was when Abd el-Karim called out to her "Run!" and rushed in to protect her from her murderer. The man who was happy with his lot, loved life, this diligent worker that avoided all confrontations, who never used his muscles except for work, found himself facing a sword being brandished at his fellow men, and acted without hesitation, with true bravery.

In the middle of the month of Ramadan, a sacred time for the Moslems, Abd el-Karim el-Rani ran to protect a Jewish girl being chased by a Moslem fanatic who was trying to kill her. He had no connection to the war between the two religions, to any fanaticism. Abd's God was merciful and compassionate, He sanctified the life of everyone created in His image. Abd el-Karim's courage did not prevent blood from being shed, but his example was a small compensation to all those who believed in goodness and longed for peace. Moreover, the bravery that this man displayed on his last day proved to many that the poet spoke the truth when he said, "I still believe in man and in his spirit, the spirit of courage."

Ali Yehia, an eminent figure in the Israeli Arab community, is Israel's ambassador to Finland.

A Green Beret and a White Headdress

Ismail Kabalan

by Rafik Halabi

It is not by chance that Ismail Kabalan lives in the village of Usafiya on Mount Carmel.

Ismail Kabalan was the moving spirit of the fighters from the Jebel Druz, the Druze Mountain, who in 1948 dramatically transferred their allegiance from the Rescue Army of Kaukji, who had set out to destroy the State of Israel, to the Jewish fighting forces in Palestine. It is not surprising, therefore, that he decided to settle in the place where this military cooperation between the Druze and the Jews began back in 1928.

In those distant days Itzhak Ben-Zvi, who was later to become the second president of the State of Israel, approached Sheikh Hassan Abu-Rukun, a resident of the village, and asked him to do something about the Arab resistance to the Zionist movement and the Jewish community. The Sheikh wholeheartedly agreed to help. He realized that it was in the interests of the Druze to develop friendly relations with the Jews in Palestine. He began to work toward this goal through the connections he had built up with Jewish public figures and with the upper echelons of the Hagana in Haifa. Some of them even went with him to visit the Druze Mountain in Syria, which was in ferment at that time.

During the events of 1936–39, or the Great Arab Revolt, as they were also called, Sheikh Abu-Rukun could clearly see how right his basic assumptions had been. The Arab gangs that roamed the countryside attacked not only the centers of the Jewish population but also Druze villages. In he end the Sheikh himself was murdered by the gangs, and at his graveside our uncle Sheikh Labib Abu-Rukun swore to follow in his footsteps and side with the Jews.

At the time, apparently, Ismail Kabalan knew nothing about these developments, and it was not only because he was a young boy on Druze Mountain. He had been born there in a mountain cave, near the village of Hawiah. The year was 1925. The Druze, led by Sultan al-Atrash, had rebelled against the French forces that occupied Syria and Lebanon. French planes that circled over the mountain strafed and bombed the village, driving the residents from their homes. Ismail's mother trudged to a cave in the mountain and there gave birth to him. His father, who followed after her, called the newborn child Abu Jihad to commemorate the fact that he had been born during a *jihad*—a holy war.

At the age of sixteen Ismail Kabalan decided to become a soldier. The year was 1941, and his native land had become a battlefield between the French Vichy forces and the British army. Ismail joined the Syrian army, which was under the command of the British headquarters in the Middle East. He did his basic training in the Jauneh camp near Rosh Pina. For his officers' training course he was sent to Trans-Jordan (the future Kingdom of Jordan). Later he served in different military installations in Palestine and Syria. But in 1946, a few months after the end of the Second World War, his unit was disbanded, and Ismail Kabalan had no choice but to return to civilian life. But not for long.

At the end of 1947 the entire area was on fire. War was about to break out in Palestine, and an appeal went out to the Druze villages from the government in Damascus: "The Rescue Army will soon go to war in aid of our Arab brothers, including our Druze brothers living on the Carmel and in the Galilee. The lives, honor, and property of these brothers are in terrible danger," said the emissaries of Syrian Intelligence. Hundreds of young Druze felt they couldn't just ignore this appeal and stay idle at home. Ismail Kabalan was one of them, and thanks to his military past he was also one of the best. Together they all went to Damascus and were given arms. They came to the attention of Shahib Wahab, the commander of the Druze battalion of the Rescue Army. They were told that Fawzi al-Kaukji would be the supreme commander of the army. The Druze fighters then went to Kuneitra and waited for their assignment.

Kaukji decided that since the Jews were concentrating most of their forces on the battle for Jerusalem it would be easier for him to operate in the north of the country. He sent the Druze battalion to Shefaram, from where they would spread out over the area between Kibbutz Yagur and Kibbutz Ramat Yochanan. The Druze were not thrown into action right away. But on April 11, 1948, Kaukji—who had suffered a terrible defeat at Mishmar Haemek—urged them to take action. The next day Wahab ordered his men to attack the villages of Usha and Kseir, which were already in the hands of the Hagana. During the next four days, until April 16, bloody battles raged in that area.

"We had many casualties and so did the Jews," Ismail Kabalan would recall later. "And then, on the third day, a messenger arrived. His name was Khalil Kuntar, and he lived in the Druze village of Usafiya. He brought a letter from the leaders of the Jewish army and the Druze sheikhs on the Carmel. I was asked to meet with the sheikhs at Ramat Yochanan." Kabalan agreed out of respect for the sheikhs, but on his arrival, to his surprise, he was met by two Jews—Amnon Yanai and Mordechai Shackevitz. "I was embarrassed," he said, "and I made an aggressive speech: 'I have come to fight the Jews, not to talk to them.' I tried to evade them. I felt that they were trying to trap me. I didn't believe the Jews were being sincere when they talked about an alliance with the Druze and explained to me that there was no reason to continue fighting each other."

Besides the embarrassment, he began to feel fear that the war might be already lost. In the words of Ismail Kabalan, "At the gate of the camp, in the guard's post, a female soldier greeted me with a Sten gun in her hand. I said to my escorts that if a woman were guarding the camp, the Jewish army would never be defeated. This showed their determination. A nation that has a clear goal will not lose." Nevertheless, Kabalan still found it hard to go over to the other side—until he met Moshe Dayan. Giora Zeid, the son of the famous Hashomer watchman Alexander Zeid, made sure to take Kabalan and a few other Druze officers to Kiryat Amal, where Moshe Dayan was waiting for them. Dayan was the officer in charge of Arab affairs in the Hagana headquarters. Kabalan started off with the same speech he had made at Ramat Yochanan, but Dayan cut him short. "The ones who are suffering in the Middle East," he said, "are the Jews and the Druze. Your behavior is not appropriate for a people fighting for its survival in the face of the dangers in the Middle East. We ask for your help and you must help us."

Kabalan wanted to gain time so that he could understand what was going on. He therefore tried to use his rhetorical skills in a different direction. "Two of my cousins," he said, "have been killed. There is bad blood between us. I will not forgive you. First let us agree to a ceasefire so that we can get the bodies out of the wadi, and take care of the wounded. Only then will we talk about what comes next."

But Dayan's answer took the wind out of the sails of the Druze fighter. "My beloved brother," Dayan said, "was killed yesterday in a battle against you, and today I am talking to you like a brother, and I feel like you are a brother, without any differences of blood, and still you continue to make excuses."

The impact of these words was profound. At that moment Kabalan decided to stop fighting the Jews and move over to their side. He brought with him most of his friends. His influence was demonstrated in another meeting, which took place in the home of the Druze Sheikh Salah Hanifas in Shefaram. Hanifas, whose father had been killed by Arab gangs in 1936, had been an ally of the Jewish leaders for years. Since the outbreak of the war he had tried to decrease the participation of the Druze in the Rescue Army. He now called a meeting between the battalion commander Shahib Wahab and some of his senior officers, and Giora Zeid, Amnon Yanai, and Yehoshua Palmon from the Hagana. He demanded that they come to an agreement. Wahab insisted that they allow him to capture Kibbutz Yechiam so he could go back to Syria a hero. The Hagana officers rejected that demand immediately. Hanifas, with the help of Kabalan, cooked up a sophisticated performance. The Druze leaders quietly decided that from then on, their force would not carry out any real attacks, leaving the Hagana—and later the IDF—to easily take control of the areas they controlled. That was exactly what happened. Kabalan's wisdom saved the shedding of a lot of blood of both the Jews and the Druze.

But this obviously did not serve him well when he returned to Syria. There were those who slandered him and stated publicly that he was a traitor and a collaborator with the enemy. Things became so bad that Ismail Kabalan had to make a painful decision. He could no longer stay on Druze Mountain, and he escaped to Israel. But in Israel as well terrible difficulties awaited him. "I had to prove my loyalty all over again," he said. "The tough interrogators of the Hagana Intelligence handcuffed me and beat and degraded me." Fortunately, after three days Giora Zeid arrived. He arranged for Kabalan's immediate release, restored his honor to him, and drafted him into the Minorities Unit that was being organized in the IDF. Most of the soldiers in this unit were Druze from Syria and Lebanon, and Kabalan soon became a central figure among them. "The Israeli Druze," he said, "called us 'the village boys' because we were so tough."

Within a short time Kabalan began to visit the Druze villages in the Carmel and the Galilee dressed in an IDF officer's uniform. He convinced young Druze to follow in his footsteps. After great efforts two hundred men answered his call. "We divided them up into two companies," said Kabalan.

> One was sent to the Lebanese border and the second one, under the command of Chaim Levakov, was sent to the Negev. At the same time we continued drafting Druze into these companies. I joined Chaim Levakov. We were stationed in Beersheva, which was then almost at the end of the world. We took up command positions on the Jordan border, near Yatta and Samua, at the south of Mount Hebron, and were put in charge of guarding the area. Jordanians shot at us daily. We fought many battles. Gradually a camaraderie developed among the soldiers in the Druze unit. Quite a while later I was made a company commander and sent to Sodom. After three months I was ordered to move on to Ein Gedi. There was no road between Sodom and Ein Gedi at the time. We went out in motor boats through the Dead Sea and set ourselves up at the positions that were assigned to us. It was a deserted area. There was not a soul around.

The deeds of Kabalan became well known among the Druze of Israel. There was not a child that hadn't heard of him and that didn't consider him a hero. He was transferred to the border police in 1954, where in time he reached the rank of deputy police superintendent. The transfer took place after Kabalan had gone out on an intelligence mission to Lebanon, and it became clear that the Syrian intelligence had him in their sights. As a Green Beret, so thought his superiors, he would be safer.

The change in berets did not prevent him from continuing to risk his life. As a border policeman he took part in the Sinai Campaign, in the battles to capture Gaza and Dir el-Balah. Later he went back to the eastern border of the country and was responsible for security in the area south of Hartuv. One of his operations in this area involved the killing of the murderer Samueli. (His brother was also a murderer whose house had been blown up in Nebi Samuel by a group of soldiers in 1953, an action that had later led to the formation of Unit 101.) After Samueli killed a Jew in Moshav Nahum, near Hartuv, Kabalan set up ambushes in the area, and one of them trapped Samueli and killed him. In addition to this, Kabalan had to often intervene in fights between Jews in his area. More than one family feud between angry settlers was ended before it led to bloodshed, thanks to his forceful, wise mediation. Once, after a disagreement between a ritual butcher and a synagogue cantor in one of the settlements, Kabalan was unfortunately wounded in both legs by gunfire of one of the men, who had run amok. It was somewhat ironical that this old warhorse, who had come unscathed out of so many bloody battles, had been wounded in a local dispute between Jews, in which he even didn't have a part.

In 1969 Kabalan retired from the army, but not before he had managed to "put things in order"—as he said—after the Six-Day War, in Jenin and Nablus on the West Bank, and also in the towns of Kuneitra, Bukata, and Masaada in the Golan Heights.

But once a soldier, always a soldier. In 1982, after the war in Lebanon, Kabalan was asked to become military governor of the Lebanese village of Hatzbaya. Four years later he decided to return to practicing the religion of his fathers. Instead of a beret and helmet he started wearing a white Druze headdress. The fighter Ismail Kabalan began to study the Druze religion, whose secret contents are passed from one generation to the next.

Today, when he looks around him, he can easily distinguish his successors—soldiers and officers (for the most part very high-ranking officers) from the Druze community, who serve in the paratroops, in the armored corps, in intelligence, in military engineering, and soon also in the air force. His courage serves as an example to them, both directly and indirectly. Deep in his heart he hopes that soon there will in fact be a new Middle East, and that he will be able to go back and visit the village on Druze Mountain, where he was born. The day this happens he will feel that he has come full circle.

Rafik Halabi, a Druze, is a journalist and the head of the news division of Channel One of Israel Television.

THE MERCY IN HEROISM—
THE HEROISM IN MERCY

DAVID DELAROSA

by Avigdor Kahalani

During the seven weeks between Passover and Shavuot it is a Jewish custom to "count the Omer." The Omer was an offering of barley brought to the Temple at the end of Passover (16th of Nissan) in biblical times. The counting of the Omer is the injunction to count the forty-nine days from the 16th of Nissan to Shavuot (Pentecost). This period is considered a period of semimourning during which it is forbidden to marry or cut one's hair.

Our sages associate seven virtues with this custom which represent different days of the counting. Two of the virtues are mercy and heroism. The second day of the counting is known as the day of heroism in mercy, while the eighth day represents the mercy in heroism. David Delarosa, a handsome, good-hearted young man, is an exemplary model of the human embodiment of the rare combination of these two noble virtues. In his wonderful act of heroism he revealed the greatness of mercy, and by his display of amazing mercy in risking his life for his fellow man, he revealed the magnificence of heroism.

David Delarosa, known to his family and friends as Dudu, was born in Jerusalem. He was the fifth of the six children of Shlomo and Geula Delarosa, both descendants of longtime Jerusalem families. He began his studies in Jerusalem and later went to a yeshiva high school, Kol Mevaser, in Mevasseret Zion. He was a slim boy with black hair and brown, luminous eyes. His friends knew him as a pleasant, modest, sensible boy, who was very sensitive to the needs of others. His powerful simplicity and the warmth he radiated toward all his friends and acquaintances revealed a rare sensitivity that charmed many. He demonstrated these characteristics in whatever he did. Thus, for example, when Dudu reached bar mitzva age he chose to end his sermon with blessings for a full recovery to the wounded IDF soldiers, a blessing and prayer that were not to be fulfilled for him seven years later. On the front page of his prayer book he wrote in big letters: "I take it upon myself to fulfill the active commandment of 'Love thy brother like thyself.' It was as if he foresaw exactly what was going to happen to him in the not-too-distant future. A naive, powerful faith and rare piety, undying friendship, along with gentleness and nobleness—all these were part of the character of this wonderful boy, a source of pride to his family and an example to those around him.

After finishing his high school studies Dudu began to study in a *yeshivat hesder* in Kiryat Arba, a framework in which he could continue his religious studies while serving in the army. Later he joined a group of religious boys that were going to Kibbutz Alumim and did his army service in the Nahal Brigade. The characteristics he displayed earlier now became even more apparent. From the moment he put on a uniform he revealed his great love for his fellow man and an extraordinary willingness to give of himself and volunteer for any mission. He was the ideal soldier, and, as such, the dream of every commander. For a while he served as a battalion communications operator. He later discovered that he could not take part in a paratroop course with the rest of his fellow soldiers because his poor health exempted him from active service. But a determined boy like Dudu would not give in, and he consulted doctors to improve his health. When he was told that this would mean having an operation on his nose, which was blamed for his breathing difficulties, he responded, "Fine, I'll have the operation." Little did he know what would happen to him on the way to this operation.

On the evening of Sunday, October 30, 1988, Dudu left his unit, which was serving in Lebanon, and set out for Jerusalem so that he could go into hospital for the operation that would raise his profile. He got on Egged bus 961, which goes from Tiberias to Jerusalem, sat down on the second seat from the back, and fell asleep. The intensive military activity he had participated in during the days before this trip had made him very tired. The bus made its way down the Jordan Valley, past Jericho, where it was supposed to turn westward and climb on the winding road to Jerusalem.

A piercing scream woke Dudu. He opened his eyes and saw a terrible sight—the bus had turned into a ball of fire. He did not know that when they had passed through Jericho someone had thrown three Molotov cocktails into the bus from a thicket at the right side of the road. That was one of the deadliest methods of terrorist attacks in these years: The terrorists lay in ambush in the groves and bushes beside the main West Bank roads and hurled bottles full of a burning mixture through the open windows of Israeli vehicles, turning them into death traps.

The bus caught on fire in three different places, and the flames spread with deadly speed. The passengers tried to escape however they could. The army arrived within a few minutes and watched the burning bus in despair. To those who stood outside it was clear that they could not do much for those trapped in the bus. Perhaps there was nothing they could do.

Inside the bus, Dudu soon realized how desperate the situation was. He understood that these were Molotov cocktails, and he looked for a way out, like most of the passengers. But as he was looking he suddenly saw a woman sitting on the floor and screaming. Her name was Rachel Weiss. Her husband had already gotten off the bus. Dudu crouched beside her, despite his feelings of urgency, and tried to convince her to get up and leave with him. "Do you need help?" he asked. "Please, let me help you." But Rachel Weiss did not seem to hear him. She shook her head showing her refusal to leave and let out a scream: "My children, my children!" Her three small children, who had gotten on the bus with her, were hopelessly trapped by the fire at the back of the bus and were possibly already dead. She couldn't help them, but she also couldn't leave the bus. Dudu pulled at her again and again, but to no avail. In the heavy smoke, which was closing in on him, he had no way of determining the fate of the children. In those few seconds the fire kept advancing and enveloping Dudu and Rachel. The flames were all around them now. He realized that the bus door through which he had planned to escape and take Rachel Weiss with him was going up in flames too.

He managed to open one of the windows, and he stuck his head out to take a breath of air. He then pulled Rachel's hand and called out to her, trying to be as convincing as he could, "Come with me; there's a small opening over here." But Rachel refused to move. The whole bus was in flames. The smoke that enveloped the bus was filling Dudu's lungs. But the young man would not give up, and he continued to do what he could.

He tried again and again to convince Rachel, holding her hand and attempting with all his strength to get her out of this inferno. But Rachel wouldn't move. She would not be separated from her children. Dudu did not despair. He tried to break another window, but was unsuccessful. The fire was coming closer; his clothes began to catch on fire, but Dudu kept at it.

Rachel was deaf to his pleading. He pulled her arm again, but felt as if she was stuck to the chair. His hands and face began to burn, and his lungs were full of the thick, poisonous smoke. Still, Dudu would not give in. Then he heard Rachel's voice rising over the hoarse roar of the fire. She was shouting the Shma Israel prayer. As an observant Jew he knew what this meant: Rachel realized she was about to die; she said her last prayer.

Now there was nothing more he could do for her, and he tried to get out of the bus as fast as possible. He jumped through the flames and fell on the ground like a burning torch. Two people outside the bus ran to put out the flames that had taken hold of his body. They couldn't erase, however, the tragic knowledge that haunted him even at that moment, when he was on the verge of fainting: back in the bus, Rachel Weiss and her three children had burned to death.

But Dudu's contribution to his fellow passengers was not yet over. While jumping out of the bus he shouted, "Help! Help!" and these shouts drew the attention of the rescuers to a wounded young woman soldier, her whole body burned, lying beside him. Nobody had noticed her before. Hila Luger, from Beit Hashita, owes her life to Dudu's shouts.

After the charred bus was towed away, the rescuers found in the pile of ashes left on the road a bag of *tefillin* (phylacteries) that had remained untouched by the flames. On the bag was written: DUDU.

Dudu was taken to the Hadassah Hospital in Ein Kerem in Jerusalem. His condition was very critical. He was suffering from burns on his face and hands and from serious breathing problems. The enormous amount of smoke that had entered his lungs had destroyed them. The amazing story of his heroism spread throughout the country. Many hearts shuddered at the story of the young boy who could easily have been saved from the flames but risked his life for a woman and three children with whom he had never exchanged a word, whom he had never even met.

For seven weeks, Dudu fought for his life. Despite the terrible pain and physical suffering that never let up, he amazed his whole family, his friends, and the medical staff with his calm and the exemplary self-control that he demonstrated. He didn't complain. He smiled the whole time, giving courage to those who came to visit him. Where did he get such strength? Perhaps from those endless resources of faith and love for humankind that prevented him from escaping the burning bus while there was still a chance to save Rachel Weiss and her children. It seems that heroism and mercy joined together in Dudu's soul, raising it to almost superhuman heights. In the hospital, out of modesty, he didn't even want to tell what had happened to him in the burning bus. When his relatives urged him to reveal why he had remained in that firetrap while all the other passengers had escaped, he answered, "Because I could hear the screams of the children from the bus. How could I not try to help them?" It was so obvious, so simple. When they told Dudu that he was a hero, he answered, "I am not a hero. I didn't manage to save them."

After seven excruciating weeks, he still had not recovered. In the end the doctors decided that there was no choice but to send him to a hospital in London for a heart-and-lung transplant. This was a grim decision that did not augur well. Everyone knew that Dudu's heart and lungs had been irreparably damaged. Everyone knew that the chances for success of a combined transplant were very slight. Nevertheless, Dudu and his parents reached London full of hope and faith. And there, even before he was put on the operating table, Dudu's heart stopped beating. That heart so full of love and faith, heroism and mercy, stopped beating. But the story of Dudu's self-sacrifice still remains as a model and symbol for us all.

Avigdor Kahalani, a recipient of the Medal of Valor, is the Israeli minister of internal security.

To Give Without Asking Anything in Return

Nir Poraz

by Benjamin Netanyahu

His soldiers called him Father Nir. After his death they wrote, "Sometimes you seemed like a big brother, reacting to everything we did and showing your approval when it was needed, but the strongest feeling of all that filled our hearts was that we were like your sons. . . . Father Nir, in every mission and task that arose, you volunteered to take part. You would immediately gather us together—your children—and tell us about it with shining eyes and with a naughty smile that spread over your face. You swept us along with you, with complete faith."

But Nir Poraz himself had barely managed to call his real father by that name. He was orphaned at the age of two, and from then on he grew up in the shadow of the figure of that fallen hero—until he too fell as a hero, at the young age of twenty-four.

Maoz Poraz, Nir's father, was born in 1933 in Kfar Sirkin to one of the founding families of the moshav. From his youth he heard the buzz of the planes in the airport that the British had set up nearby. When the State was founded, he soon learned that a flying school of the air force had opened up at this airport. The next step was almost inevitable. In the atmosphere in which Maoz Poraz was raised it was clear that every good man must give his maximum for the defense of the country. This tradition was connected to the sights and sounds from the other side of the fence. He joined the air force and finished the flying course successfully.

In the Sinai Campaign, which started on October 29, 1956, he flew several air sorties, carrying out various missions. A few years later he left the army and decided to become a professional civilian pilot. He went to work for El Al but continued to do his reserve duty in the air force. When the crisis that led to the Six-Day War broke out, Maoz Poraz was on vacation in Spain. Upon hearing about the situation at home, he cut his vacation short. He hurried back to report to his squadron and took part in the Moked air strikes that wiped out the air forces of the neighboring nations. In one of the operations his plane was hit above the Sinai Desert.

He was forced to abandon the plane, parachuted, and managed to come out of the incident unharmed.

When he came out of uniform and went back to work for El Al, it turned out that the war was chasing him. Terrorist organizations had begun to carry out widespread attacks against Israeli targets and decided to also strike planes traveling to and from Israel. The first of these attacks took place on July 23, 1968, against an El Al plane that had taken off from Rome Airport on its way to Lod Airport. Shortly after takeoff three armed terrorists stormed from the passenger cabin into the cockpit of the plane and announced that they would start shooting—even if they caused the plane to crash—if the captain did not obey their instructions. Maoz Poraz, who was the copilot, tried to wrestle with them and was wounded in the struggle. But he and the rest of the crew did not manage to thwart the attack. The plane was forced to turn in the direction of Algeria and land there. The passengers and the crew were taken hostage. They would only be handed over to the Algerian authorities, announced the terrorists, on condition that Palestinian terrorists were released from Israeli prisons.

In Israel everyone was in an uproar. Many people understood that this was a dangerous precedent. Giving in to the terrorists' blackmail would only bring about more hijackings, more attacks like this one. But in the end the concern for the safety of the passengers took precedence. The exhausting negotiations that continued over a period of five weeks resulted in a bitter deal. The hostages were exchanged for terrorists who had received prison sentences for their actions. Maoz Poraz was not very happy with this agreement. His family and friends said he was very angry. When he came back to the country he claimed that the Israeli government had made a mistake by accepting the demands of the terrorists. Even if some of the hostages—of which he was one—had been killed, he stated, it would have been wrong to give in to terror.

In the Yom Kippur War, Poraz was assigned to a Skyhawk squadron and carried out a number of combat and bombing sorties during the first twelve days of the war. He was by then one of the oldest pilots, almost forty, but this chronological fact did not have any effect on him. He was never tired or afraid, like the younger pilots. In fact he even outdid them in this respect, thanks to his rich experience. On October 18 his luck ran out. His plane received a direct hit from an Egyptian missile above the Suez Canal. Maoz Poraz was killed. He left behind him his widow, Mattya, two daughters, Tamar and Amit, and a two-year-old son, Nir.

Mattya Poraz brought up her son on the valiant heritage of his father. He was raised in the spirit that had made Maoz wrestle with the terrorists and not hesitate to confront the enemy head on. Even in his youth he showed qualities of volunteering and giving. When he studied at the Rotberg Gymnasium in Ramat Hasharon he spent hours taking care of the school library. He was also a brilliant student and completed his studies in electronics and computers with honors. When the time came for him to go into the army, he decided that he must be as prepared as possible. He took a preparatory course for the army in which he acquired knowledge, fitness, and skills that would help him in his army service; but most important, he acquired the friendship of his instructor, Yuval Eilam. Despite the difference in age between them, they became fast friends, strengthening in each other the spirit of giving and doing. After the preparatory course Nir took the tests for the air force and passed them successfully. For him this was the most natural thing in the world. If his father's plane had been brought down in war, then he would have to replace him and "plow" the skies. But as the son of a bereaved family it was not only up to him. He needed his mother's signature, and Mattya refused to sign.

She suggested that he contribute to the army in the disciplines he had studied in school, electronics and computers. But Nir would not give in. He put pressure on his mother through friends and relatives, and in the end a compromise was reached. The loving mother agreed to sign for any kind of service, except flying. Nir then had to decide on which unit he wanted to join. It was clear to him that it would be the Sayeret Matkal, the best commando unit of the IDF. And that was what he did. Armed with a lot of goodwill and determination, he took a series of tests for the unit and passed them well. And again his choice and his success in the tests were not enough. The unit commanders tried to convince him not to carry out his decision, because he was the son of a bereaved family, but he insisted, and in the end he won. This was the beginning of five years of active service, at first as a commando fighter, and later as a team commander.

The commando fighters have a very special character. In their daring activities they are continually testing the blurred boundary between the possible and the impossible. To put it more succinctly, they are always pushing this boundary farther and widening the area of the possible, even if others have tried to do so before them. Nir described the unique character of the commandos in one of his letters: "[It is] our ability to carry out missions that seem impossible." This ability he himself tried to achieve as a fighter and to pass it on to his soldiers as a team commander. The words his unit commander wrote to Nir's family will bear witness to his success: "In the activities of the unit we always need to make a distinction between the limits of our ability and what is absolutely impossible. Officers and soldiers like Nir allow us to coolly and courageously go to the end of our limits, in areas that are dangerous and not mapped out in advance, but essential for the security of the country." From where did he get the almost superhuman strength to go to the limit and try to reach beyond it? From where did those who carried out these missions get their motivation? Is it just the desire to excel, to stand out, to be the best?

Nir gave a decisive answer to all these questions. At the heart of the matter is the desire to give of oneself and make a contribution. Nir's soldiers say that he would always tell them, "Give without asking for anything in return and not out of habit—but like the sun that shines, like a shadow that falls." This was what he said, and that was how he acted as a soldier and a commander. And this giving, it is worth remembering, was always anonymous and hidden. One cannot read about most of the commando operations in the newspaper or see them on television. It is even impossible to tell friends and brag to one's family and relatives. Everything is done in absolute secrecy, without the media and public relations, without photographers on the spot. Everything is done with the deep belief in true giving for one's people and one's country.

Nir had unique qualities as a commander that few manage to achieve—a rare combination of a tough commander who demanded the highest level of performance, and a man dedicated to professionalism, which he also demanded of himself. At the same time he was a good friend, who worried about his soldiers and had a warm human connection with them.

Because of this special connection he was called Father Nir. Because of this he succeeded in inspiring his soldiers to take part in every mission and every challenge. As the members of the team who served under him said, "Again and again we gathered our strength and followed you, inspired by your determination and daring, and at the same time from your self-restraint and your cool."

On Friday, the 9th of Heshvan 5755 (October 14, 1994), Nir and his soldiers needed all the physical strength and spiritual courage that they had acquired in the unit. Five days earlier a Palestinian terrorist cell had kidnapped an IDF soldier, Nachshon Waxman. The whole country held its breath when a picture of Nachshon in the hands of his cruel captors was shown on television. After intensive searches and widespread intelligence work of all branches of the army, the house where Nachshon was being held was discovered on the outskirts of the village of Bir-Naballa, north of Jerusalem, not far from the neighborhood of Ramot where he lived. Once again the terrorist organizations tried their hand at blackmail, taking advantage of the deep Israeli feelings for the sanctity of human life. Nachshon's life, the terrorists announced, is at stake, unless particular demands are met within a certain period. Despite the enormous difficulties involved in breaking into a house in which there were three armed fanatics, the government decided not to give in to the terrorists and to try and release Nachshon. All the Zionist parties in the Knesset united behind this ethical stand of the State of Israel. This was the stand that Maoz Poraz, Nir's father, had taken after terrorists hijacked the El Al plane. In the name of this principle IDF soldiers were sent, with the commandos at their head, to rescue hostages in Entebbe at a distance of thousands of kilometers from Israel. This is what Nir Poraz was taught and what he had taught his soldiers from the moment that he joined the commandos.

It was natural that this complicated mission would be entrusted to the Sayeret Matkal. It was also natural that in the framework of the Sayeret this mission should be assigned to Nir's team. Nir himself was already on leave, pending his release from the army. It was only natural that he should be called in and that he should report in immediately—without asking any questions, without any hesitation. There is no more faithful testimony of Nir's part in the operation than that of the unit commander: "On Friday, October 14, 1994, a force of the unit broke into the house in which Nachshon Waxman was being held in order to free him. Nir was at the head of the force, and the rest of the soldiers in his team came right after him. Nir quickly reached the door of the room in which the hostage was being held. He tried to break in to save Nachshon's life. During this attempt he was shot and killed, and ten of his soldiers were wounded. Throughout this operation he displayed courage and extraordinary determination. . . . I was not surprised; neither was the rest of the unit. Throughout his service Nir proved himself to be an exemplary soldier and officer. . . ."

During the Sayeret attack, the kidnappers murdered Nachshon Waxman.

For his leadership and determination in the battle in which he fell, Nir was awarded a citation from the chief of staff. The citation stated: "Captain Nir Poraz led the attacking force . . . with daring, determination, perseverance, and extraordinary courage, for which he paid with his life. In his role Nir inspired confidence in the attacking force and set a personal example."

Nir's grandparents had come to the country from Russia and settled the land. His father fought in the air and stood up to terrorists. Nir Poraz was an impressive link in this chain. We remember his exemplary life and his heroism in the light of his wonderful words to his soldiers: "To give without asking for anything in return and not out of habit—but like the sun that shines, like a shadow that falls." That was how he gave himself, spontaneously and naturally, as a daring volunteer, as a real son to his family and to his reborn people.

Benjamin Netanyahu, a former Sayeret Matkal fighter, is the prime minister of Israel.